Australia and Latin America

Challenges and Opportunities in the New Millennium

Australia and Latin America

Challenges and Opportunities in the New Millennium

Edited by

Barry Carr & John Minns

Australian
National
University

PRESS

ANU PRESS

Published by ANU Press
The Australian National University
Canberra ACT 0200, Australia
Email: anupress@anu.edu.au
This title is also available online at http://press.anu.edu.au

National Library of Australia Cataloguing-in-Publication entry

Author: Minns, John, 1956- author.

Title: Australia and Latin America : challenges and opportunities
                 in the new millennium / John Minns,
                 Barry Carr.

ISBN: 9781925021233 (paperback) 9781925021240 (ebook)

Subjects: Intercultural communication.
                 Australia--Politics and government.
                 Latin America--Politics and government.
                 Australia--Foreign relations--Latin America.
                 Latin America--Foreign relations--Australia.

Other Authors/Contributors:
                 Carr, Barry, author.

Dewey Number: 382.099408

Cover design by Nic Welbourn and layout by ANU Press

Contents

Acknowledgements

The Council on Australia Latin America Relations (COALAR) is tasked with enhancing Australia's economic, political and social relations with Latin America and provides funding to support projects that will enhance Australian engagement with Latin America. Without the financial backing of COALAR it would not have been possible to undertake this project.

The authors of chapter four, James Levy and Peter Ross, would like to acknowledge the effort of Dr Ruth Adler who kindly organised a seminar under Chatham House Rules concerning the marine environment. Also Professor Rosemary Rayfuse of the Faculty of Law, UNSW, who provided useful points on the law of the sea.

Pierre van der Eng and Don Kenyon are very grateful for comments received from Marcelo Alves, John Minns and two anonymous referees on previous versions of chapters five and six. They would also like to thank Carolyn Irving (DFAT) for clarifying Australia's current engagement in multilateral partnerships in relation to chapter six.

In addition to the personal communications cited in the references, John Sinclair wishes to thank the following individuals for their information and advice in gathering the material for chapter eight: Angel Calderón, Antonio Castillo, Victor Del Río, Danny Kaufman, Jesús Meza Morales and Ralph Newmark.

Contributors

Sean W. Burges is currently Lecturer in International Relations with the School of Politics and International Relations and Senior Associate with the Australian National Centre for Latin American Studies, The Australian National University.

Barry Carr is Adjunct Professor attached to the Australian National Centre for Latin American Studies at The Australian National University. He was formerly the Director of the Institute of Latin American Studies (ILAS) at La Trobe University, Melbourne.

Victor Del Río is a World Bank Consultant in the area of education, member of the Ethics Research Committee at Latrobe University and an active member of the Latino community in Australia since 1986. He is a founder of Competency Based Training Systems (CBTS) Latin America.

Bob Hodge is a Member of the Institute for Culture and Society at the University of Western Sydney. He is involved in many fields of social and cultural research, including Latin American and Australian cultures.

Don Kenyon (AM) is currently a Distinguished Visiting Fellow at The Australian National University Centre for European Studies. He was made a Member of the Order of Australia in 2002 for services to public administration, particularly the promotion of Australian trade and commercial interests.

James R. Levy is Senior Lecturer (Conjoint) in the School of Humanities and Languages, University of New South Wales.

John Minns is the Director of the Australian National Centre for Latin American Studies and Associate Professor in Politics and International Relations at The Australian National University.

Ralph Newmark is the Director of the Institute of Latin American Studies (ILAS) in the Faculty of Humanities and Social Sciences, School of Humanities, La Trobe University.

Peter Ross is Senior Lecturer, School of Humanities and Languages, University of New South Wales. His research interests include human development in Argentina since independence.

John Sinclair is an Honorary Professorial Fellow in the School of Historical and Philosophical Studies at the University of Melbourne.

Pierre van der Eng is Reader and Senior Fellow at the Research School of Management at The Australian National University College of Business and Economics.

Abbreviations

AAA	Accra Agenda for Action
ABS	Australian Bureau of Statistics
ACTU	Australian Council of Trade Unions
ADSL	asymmetric digital subscriber line
AEI	Australia Education International
AFP	Australian Federal Police
ALAF	Australian Leadership Award Fellowships
ALAS	Australian Leadership Award Scholarships
ALBA	Bolivarian Alternative for the Americas
ANCLAS	Australian National Centre for Latin American Studies (The Australian National University)
AOL	America On Line
APEC	Asia-Pacific Economic Cooperation
AQF	Australian Qualifications Framework
ASEAN	Association of South East Asian Nations
ASIO	Australian Security Intelligence Organisation
AILASA	Association of Iberian and Latin American Studies of Australasia
AusAID	Australian Agency for International Development
Austrade	Australian Trade Commission
ACI-FTA	Australia–Chile Free Trade Agreement
BBC	British Broadcasting Corporation
BNDES	Brazilian Economic and Social Development Bank
BRIC nations	Brazil, Russia, India and China
BSM	Benefit Sharing Mechanisms
CACM	Central American Common Market
CAFTA	Central American Free Trade Agreement
CELAC	Community of Latin American and Caribbean States
CELAS	Spanish Latin American Welfare Centre (Melbourne)
CER	Closer Economic Relations (Australia–New Zealand trade agreement)
CG	Cairns Group (Argentina, Brazil, Chile, Colombia and Uruguay)
CIA	Central Intelligence Agency (US)
CIDA	Canadian International Development Agency

CDM	Clean Development Mechanism
CNN	Cable News Network (US-based)
COALAR	Council on Australia Latin America Relations
COALAR-EAG	COALAR Education Action Group
COHA	Council on Hemispheric Affairs
Comisione Obreras	workers' commissions
CONAIE	Ecuadorian Confederation of Indigenous Nations
COP	13th Conference of Parties (for the 2007 Bali Action Plan)
COPEI	Partido Social Cristiano de Venezuela (Social Christian Party of Venezuela)
CPA	Communist Party of Australia
DBS	direct broadcast satellite
DDA	Doha Development Agenda—see 'Doha'
DEEWR	Department of Education, Employment and Workplace Relations
despachantes	trouble shooters
DEST	Department of Education, Science and Training
DFAT	Department of Foreign Affairs and Trade, Australia
Doha	Doha Development Agenda (DDA)
DORS	Australian Determination of Refugee Status Committee
DRR	disaster risk reduction
EC	European Community
ELICOS	English Language Intensive Course for Overseas Students
EZLN	Zapatista Army of National Liberation
FDI	foreign direct investment
FIPs	Five Interested Parties (US, EU, Brazil, India and Australia—Doha Negotiations)
FMLN	*Farabundo Martí* National Liberation Front, El Salvador
FSLN	Sandinista National Liberation Front (Nicaragua)
FTA	free trade area
FTAA	Free Trade Area of the Americas
FTAAP	Free Trade Area of the Asia-Pacific
G6	FIPs plus Japan
GATT	General Agreement on Tariffs and Trade
GDP	gross domestic product (of a given nation)

GFC	global financial crisis
GIZ	*Deutsche Gesellschaft für Internationale Zusammenarbeit GmbH* (The German International Cooperation Agency)
GNI	gross national income (of a given nation)
HDI	Human Development Index (United Nations)
HIV AIDS	Human Immunodeficiency Virus/Acquired Immune Deficiency Syndrome
ILAS	Institute of Latin American Studies (La Trobe University, Victoria)
ISI	import substitution industrialisation
ISPs	internet service providers
LA	Latin America
LAC	USAID's Bureau for Latin America and the Caribbean
LADP	Latin America Development Programme (New Zealand)
LAIA	Latin American Integration Association
LAN	*Línea Aérea Nacional*, Chile's national airline
MAS	Movement to Socialism (Venezuela and Bolivia)
MDGs	Millennium Development Goals
Mercosur	*Mercado Común del Sur* (Southern Common Market)
MLN	*Movimiento de Liberación Nacional Uruguayo* (Tupamaros) (National Liberation Movement)
MSO	Melbourne Symphony Orchestra
NAFTA	North American Free Trade Agreement
NAMAs	Nationally Appropriate Mitigation Actions (2007 Bali Action Plan)
NESB	non-English speaking background
NGO	non-governmental organisation
OAS	Organization of American States
ODA	official development assistance
OECD	Organisation for Economic Cooperation and Development
PAN	Partido Acción Nacional (Party of National Action), Mexico (conservative)
PES	Payments for Environmental Services
PRD	Party of the Democratic Revolution (Mexico's main centre-left party)
PSLP	Public Sector Linkages Program (Australian)

PT	Workers Party (Brazil)
REDD	reducing emissions from deforestation and forest degradation in developing countries
REDD-plus	REDD with additional afforestation planning
RTP	Rádio e Televisão de Portugal
RTVE	Radio Televisión Española,
SBS	Special Broadcasting Service (Australia)
SHP	(Australian) Special Humanitarian Program
SITC	standard international trade classification
Telmex	Mexican internet service provider
TPP	Trans-Pacific Partnership Agreement
TPP-FTA	Trans-Pacific Partnership Free Trade Agreement
TUMWC	Trade Union Migrant Workers Centre (Melbourne)
UBI	United Broadcasting International
UNASUR	Union of South American Nations
UNCTAD	United Nations Conference for Trade and Development
UNESCO	United Nations Educational, Scientific and Cultural Organization
UNFCCC	United Nations Framework Convention on Climate Change
Universo Online	Brazilian-based internet service provider
UNHCR	United Nations High Commissioner for Refugees
USAID	United States Agency for International Development
VET	vocational educational training
WTO	World Trade Organization
Zonas Especiales de Manejo	Special Management Zones Ecuador

Figures

Introduction

Barry Carr and John Minns

Introduction

It is almost as if Latin America has been rediscovered by Australia nearly 200 years after most of the region's countries declared independence from Spain. The resilience of the Latin American economies in the face of the Global Financial Crisis has spawned a cottage industry of books explaining how regional countries have gone from the disaster of the 1980s and 1990s to repeated successes in the early 21st century.[1] This triumphalist tone extends to individual country studies, particularly Brazil,[2] as well as through media accounts of the economic successes of such varied countries as Argentina, Bolivia, Chile, Colombia, Ecuador and Mexico. Investment flows to and from the region are booming. Exports are surging, not only in minerals and foodstuffs to China, but also in such widely differentiated value-added products as aircraft, consumer durables and high fashion. The Americas remain a destination for adventure and tourism, as captured in a number of best-selling travel books that have pointed the way for tourists looking to leave the beaten trail.[3] Rumours of El Dorado are again circulating, only this time the jackpot is the opportunity in these fiscally stable emerging markets, not dreams of endless rivers of gold.

The relationship between one country of 23 million and a region of well over 500 million is, inevitably, complex and multidimensional. It is best seen against the backdrop of very broad changes in international relations and international political economy over the last two to three decades. The first is the development of what has become known as the 'emerging economies'. The membership of this group has changed from time to time. Brazil, as a member of the BRIC group (Brazil, Russia, India, China), has consistently been dealt

---

1 Hal Weitzman, *Latin Lessons: How South America Stopped Listening to the United States and Started Prospering*, London: Wiley, 2012; Michael Reid, *Forgotten Continent: The Battle for Latin America's Soul*, New Haven, CT: Yale University Press, 2009; Javier Santiso, *Latin America's Political Economy of the Possible: Beyond Good Revolutionaries and Free-Marketeers*, Boston: MIT Press, 2007.

2 Larry Rohter, *Brazil on the Rise: The Story of a Country Transformed*, New York: Palgrave Macmillan, 2010; Riordan Roett, *The New Brazil*, Washington, DC: Brookings, 2010; Lael Brainard and Leonardo Martínez-Díaz, eds, *Brazil As An Economic Superpower? Understanding Brazil's Changing Role in the Global Economy*, Washington, DC: Brookings, 2009; Ricardo Lagos, *The Southern Tiger: Chile's Fight for A Democratic and Prosperous Future*, New York: Palgrave Macmillan, 2011.

3 For example, see John Gimlette, At the Tomb of the Inflatable Pig: Travels through Paraguay, London: Hutchison, 2003; Mark Adams, Turn Right at Machu Picchu: Rediscovering the Lost City One Step at a Time, New York: Dutton, 2011.

with as one of these since the term was coined. More recently, some have begun to speak of the BRICSAM (BRIC plus South Africa and Mexico). Thus at least the two largest countries of Latin America are now widely considered to be moving towards positions of greater economic and political potential in world affairs. Whether it is possible to extrapolate the growth rates of these two and other fast-growing Latin American economies to the point where they reach the status of the established and developed economies of the West and Japan is more difficult to tell. However, the progress that has already been made is itself significant, especially when one considers that in Latin America most of the 20th century—and especially its last three decades—was, broadly, a period of economic stagnation, political instability, and even ruthless dictatorship. The implications of this for Australia are considerable. The importance of the developing economies of Asia for Australia's future has been well understood for some time. But the tectonic plates of global economic and political power are not only shifting in Asia; there is a Latin American dimension as well. Indeed, there appears to have been some recognition amongst Australian government policy-makers that Australia might form a 'connecting rod' between some of the more open economies of Latin America, such as Chile, Peru, Colombia and Mexico, and the markets of Asia.[4]

A second factor, which has had an impact on relations, has been the breakdown of the bipolar world of the Cold War. In that period, trade, investment, strategic influence and intellectual ascendancy tended to move from the periphery of each of the major blocks to the core—in the case of Latin America, to the United States. While to some extent this has continued, the new shape of the world is one where connections between countries and regions are often more diverse. To use an ugly term, the system has become multidirectional. Just as the United States now accounts for only about one-eighth of Brazil's trade, other dimensions of its development have also become diversified. A significant number of its students under its huge *Science without Borders* Program—itself a major attempt to internationalise and modernise—will now go to institutions other than in the United States, some to Australia. Of course, the differences within Latin America in this regard remain extremely important. Mexico in particular has continued to hitch its economy and much of its future to its powerful neighbour. But the broad trend for most of Latin America is unmistakable. Australia, because of its relatively small size, will not constitute the most important direction in which Latin American money, goods and students head. But even a comparatively minor shift in this direction by half a billion people—amongst which is a rapidly increasing middle class—will have a significant impact on Australia.

---

4   Australian Government, *Australia in the Asian Century: White Paper 2010*, Canberra: Commonwealth of Australia, 2010, pp. 208–9.

The breakdown of the bipolar world has been paralleled by the declining fortunes of the United States. This must not be overstated—it is only a *relative* decline in influence and it is extremely uneven—but it has nonetheless meant that connections in economy, education and international politics, which were rare in the past, have now become more likely. The opening up of new Australian diplomatic and trade commission posts in Latin America reflects this recognition. In the past, Australia might well have developed official policy on events in Latin America and attitudes towards governments there by following the lead of the United States. While it often continues to do so, there is today a more self-reliant series of direct connections between Australia and Latin America.

A final broad trend against which the Australia–Latin America relationship must be seen is the much-celebrated notion of globalisation. Globalisation—at least in the pure form often put forward in the 1990s—had at least two important weaknesses. It undoubtedly described important changes taking place—greater connectivity in trade, greater cross-border investment, the technological changes that made communication, travel and trade faster and easier—cheaper airfares, the internet, containerisation of cargo, etc. It emphasised the globalisation of consumer tastes. In many of its theoretical variations it also posited a changed relationship between the state and the market—one in which the state played a massively reduced role while global markets increasingly determined how the world worked. To use Thomas Friedman's words, it became a 'golden straightjacket,' amassing wealth for those who plunged into globalisation, but also reducing the policy alternatives open to governments and therefore the range of political choice to the equivalent of one between Coke and Pepsi.[5]

The term globalisation did indeed describe aspects of the way the world was changing. However, as several sceptics pointed out at the time, there were serious exaggerations in the intensity of the process, and secondly around the role of the state. After around 20 years' experience we can say that all of these processes, while real, were extremely uneven. There was a significant measure of exaggeration in the picture painted by the globalisation enthusiasts. The world was not flat—rather it remained lumpy: the gap in wealth between poorer countries and the rich ones did not close dramatically.

But perhaps the most profound mistake made by those who rushed into the globalisation scenario with unbridled enthusiasm was to suggest that the role of the state was in historic and irreversible decline. Some even suggested that the great task of modern history—the construction of the modern nation-state over the last 500 years—was at an end. Moreover, they thought that whereas its rise occurred over centuries, its decline would be much more rapid—a matter of decades at most. Some argued that what would be left would be states

---

5 Thomas Friedman, *The Lexus and the Olive Tree*, London: Harper Collins, 2000, pp. 101–111.

that performed minimal functions of system maintenance, setting a legal and juridical framework within which the forces of the world economy would carve out their channels independently. Indeed, it is true that in many dimensions of the relationship between Australia and Latin America, the self-interest of business has led the way in creating links between the continents where they did not exist before.

But in fact, although the state retreated from various aspects of economic and social life, it has entered others with renewed vigour. The opening up of these new global markets drew states into the international arenas in ways not seen before. The connections in trade, investment, education and culture which have been developing for some time between non-government actors are now being developed further—or, as some of the chapters in this volume suggest, retarded—by the actions of the Australian state and its Latin American counterparts. The trade agreements that have been negotiated, the Australian aid program in Latin America, and the vigorous work by the Australian government to participate in the expansion of the Latin American global education market in ruthless competition with other major education providers have all illustrated the importance of state policy to the future of the relationship.

The fundamental error of the more extreme versions of globalisation theory was to assume that state intervention and the spread of global markets were at opposite ends of a conceptual seesaw. If one rose in importance, the other must decline. The simultaneous maximisation of both of these variables was precluded. But this was not correct—in the case of the Australia–Latin America relationship we have seen both greater interconnectedness and greater state-to-state involvement. That is why the decisions of policy-makers in Australia concerning the development of the relationship are crucial.

For decades Australia has had what might best be described as a policy of benign neglect towards Latin America. Government officials were aware of the region's existence, but short of occasionally coordinating positions at multilateral meetings little attention was given to the neighbours across the Pacific Ocean. Attitudes in the bulk of the business and civil society community were little different. The depth of official ambivalence was captured in the preamble to the 1992 report on Australia–Latin America relations released by the Senate Standing Committee on Foreign Affairs, Defence and Trade. While the Committee recorded its pleasure at the assistance provided by the Latin American diplomatic missions in Canberra as well as the large Australian mining and agricultural combines operating in the region, it also noted somewhat disparagingly that 'the Committee gained the strong impression that several government departments and agencies are now so preoccupied with Asia that little thought is given to the far-away countries of Latin America. In the Committee's view this is short sighted'.[6]

One of the key points that the Standing Committee raised after its analysis of over one hundred separate submissions was that Australia needed to take a professional approach to foreign relations. Thus while the Committee fully agreed that a greater emphasis on relations with Asia should be the main preoccupation for Australia, this should not translate into a neglect of Latin America. As the Committee noted, 'Even in the midst of pursuing opportunities in Asia, Australians must not lose sight of the fact that strategic planning and positioning regarding Latin America needs to be carried out *now*, not in the next century when the continent is expected to be a significant economic force'.[7] For its part, Austrade appeared to have already taken some of this message on board, advising the Committee that it was moving its senior trade commissioner from Miami to Buenos Aires and placing an additional trade commissioner specialising in mining and energy in the Australian Embassy in Santiago.

The broader vision of the Committee and Austrade's forward positioning set the stage for important elements in today's Australia–Latin America relationship. Indeed, much of the Australian engagement with the region is currently channelled through Santiago and the most substantive investment flows take place in the mining and energy industries. However, trade relations have stagnated due to the failure to follow through with over 60 specific recommendations made by the Committee and to commit resources and personnel to building the bilateral relationships. Although then foreign minister Gareth Evans gave a rousing speech in response to the Senate Committee's report, praising it for its vision and highlighting the potential that Latin America held for Australia,[8] Asia remained the indelible focus in Canberra. The Australian government followed the mining industry's lead and invested most heavily in building relationships in Chile, deferring attention to those countries with a more challenging bilateral relationship, such as Brazil and Mexico.

Concentration on one country—Chile—was hardly a surprising decision for the Australian government: resources are always scarce in foreign ministries and results are constantly demanded. This was particularly the case in the early 1990s when Chile appeared to be a beacon of economic hope in an otherwise financially dubious continent. Without a pressing domestic demand for deeper

---

6 Senate of Australia, *Standing Committee on Foreign Affairs, Defence and Trade, Australia and Latin America*, Canberra: Commonwealth of Australia, 1992: p. 4. http://www.aph.gov.au/Parliamentary_Business/Committees/Senate_Committees?url=fadt_ctte/completed_inquiries/pre1996/aust_latin_america/index.htm.
7 *Ibid.*,p. 5. Emphasis in original text.
8 Gareth Evans, 'Australia's Rediscovery of Latin America', Address by Senator Gareth Evans to the Columbus Quincentenary Conference, La Trobe University, Melbourne, 27 June 1992. http://www.gevans.org/speeches/old/1992/270692_fm_rediscoveryofla.pdf.

engagement with other countries in the region it is questionable whether it would have made sense for DFAT to build links that business and civil society would not then exploit. One subset of the recommendations in the 1992 Senate Committee report was devoted to supporting groups and activities that would build mutual understanding, particularly through cultural exchange and the support of Australian studies of Latin America. Eventually an agglomeration of these points was recycled in 2000 through a House of Representatives subcommittee examining what could be done to strengthen trade and investment relations with the region.

The 2000 House of Representatives investigation into trade and investment relations with South America was succinct: it was clear that the advice of the 1992 Senate Committee had not been followed and that 'Australian firms have *missed the boat* on a range of opportunities in South America especially in Brazil as that country sought to modernise its economy and develop its infrastructure'.[9] In particular the Committee was frustrated that little progress had been made in deepening bilateral economic relations despite repeated Australian government studies highlighting the growing importance of the Chilean and Mercosur markets. Taking up the question of why engagement was shallow, the Committee's final report returned to a central theme of the 1992 Senate report with a direct statement:

> In Australia there is a significant lack of awareness and knowledge about South America.... On its visit to South America, the Trade Sub-Committee found that the single biggest issue was the awareness factor. Awareness is a two way street. Many of the officials in the countries that the Trade Sub-Committee visited had not thought of Australia as a possible contender in their markets, especially as a source of expertise in the area of service exports including the areas of infrastructure and agricultural development.[10]

Matters were compounded during the Committee's visit to the region when the members inevitably found that South Americans had a better knowledge of Australia than vice versa.[11] Building on this experience, the Committee was clear that there is a role for government in fostering improved inter-society relations and that the Australian government must take steps to build mutual understanding if national firms were to have any hope of penetrating South American markets. Recommendations five and six of the report called for

---

9   Joint Standing Committee on Foreign Affairs, Defence and Trade, *Building Australia's Trade and Investment Relationship with South America*, Canberra: Commonwealth of Australia, 2000: p. 2. http://www.aph.gov.au/ Parliamentary_Business/Committees/House_of_Representatives_Committees?url=jfadt/samer/samindex.htm. Emphasis added.
10   *Ibid.*
11   *Ibid*, p. 48.

the creation of a government-run South America foundation. The principle was accepted, but with a semantic twist that resulted in the formation of a coordinating body that could help to build links: the DFAT-run Council on Australia Latin America Relations (COALAR).

Formed by the Australian government in 2001, COALAR is tasked with enhancing Australia's economic, political and social relations with Latin America. It is specifically charged with enhancing and strengthening links in the priority areas of business, education, sustainability, tourism and culture. Perhaps more significantly for groups seeking to increase mutual awareness and build trans-Pacific links, COALAR also provides funding to support projects that will enhance Australian engagement with Latin America. As acknowledged earlier, the book presented here is one example of COALAR-funding at work. Without the financial backing of COALAR it would not have been possible to undertake this project, which examines the nature of key elements of the inter-regional relationship and provides a series of broad recommendations that help to continue building Australia–Latin America relations.

This book has certainly been a long time coming and aligns neatly with COALAR's mandate. In 2006, Bernard Wheelahan, then the COALAR Chairman, noted in a conversation with one of this book's editors, Barry Carr, that there was no substantial book-length discussion of the Australia–Latin America relationship and that the time had come to produce such a treatment. As conversations with prospective chapter authors moved ahead during a series of meetings, topics were allocated to authors and consensus achieved on the structure and purposes of the volume. Authors would examine the current state of play in their respective fields and also forecast as much as possible in order to identify likely short-term outcomes and where possible make suggestions that could be incorporated into future actions by stake-holders.

Bernard Wheelahan made a particularly important suggestion when he urged the editors to avoid the trap of merely looking into the past—often a rather unhappy practice that results in wishful thinking, clichéd celebrations of goodwill and tearful laments of un-seized opportunities. His idea was that something more should be provided and that the contributing scholars venture into the realm of policy to provide concrete observations regarding what is working and what is not, leading to solid proposals that business, government and civil society might use to build stronger intercontinental relations. The editors have taken Bernard Wheelahan's suggestions very seriously. Chapter authors were tasked with providing a clearly researched background and analysis of their topic and then with using this background to provide workable ideas for practitioners. The resulting book is a major contribution to understanding the recent course of Australia's relationship with Latin America that not only identifies ongoing trends and opportunities, but also gives clear ideas of how to strengthen existing relationships and build new ones.

The book is particularly timely because this is shaping up to be a Latin American decade. After a shaky 2009, which saw GDP growth rates in Latin America retract by two per cent during the height of the Global Financial Crisis, 2010 marked a return to solid growth with an average regional rate of 5.9 per cent. This is in line with the medium-term growth trend of between four per cent and 5.8 per cent per annum GDP since 2004.[12] This growth rate has also been seen in the pattern of regional exports, rising 29.5 per cent and 23 per cent in 2010 and 2011,[13] largely due to high global commodity prices but also in response to increased manufacturing exports to North American and European markets. Economic growth has been accompanied by marked improvements in poverty levels, with the regional poverty rate dropping from 43.8 per cent in 1999 to 31.4 per cent in 2010,[14] which has translated into the emergence of a new middle class. All of this has a positive impact on Australian trade with the region, most particularly the major Latin American economies grouped together in the Asociación Latinoamericana de Integración: the Latin American Integration Association (ALADI). From 2004 to 2010, Australian exports to ALADI doubled from US$1,267 billion to US$2,576 billion. Australia's imports from the region experienced a similar rise, increasing from US$819 million in 2004 to US$1.766 billion in 2010.[15]

The story would thus seem to be optimistic for Australia and intercontinental relations, except that there has been little increase in the Australian market share in the Americas during the last half-decade. Latin American exports to Australia have barely risen proportionally since 2004, and still comprise only a tiny share of the overall trade picture. This points back to the very issues raised in the 1992 Senate report, the 2000 House of Deputies study, and the more recent comments by Bernard Wheelahan to the editors of this book. The pattern of benign neglect identified in 1992 continues in large part because mutual understanding remains thin. This book directly tackles this problem by setting out the nature and extent of Australia–Latin America linkages in a number of areas significant to the intercontinental relationship.

The over-riding message from the 1992 Senate report and the 2000 House of Representatives study was that successful Australian engagement with Latin

12   United Nations Economic Commission for Latin America and the Caribbean, *Statistical Year Book for Latin America and the Caribbean, 2011*, Santiago: United Nations, 2012: p. 77, Table 2.1.1.1.
13   United Nations Economic Commission for Latin America and the Caribbean, *Latin America and the Caribbean in the World Economy, 2010–2011*, New York: United Nations, 2011, p. 10, Table 2.
14   United Nations Economic Commission for Latin America and the Caribbean, *Statistical Year Book for Latin America and the Caribbean, 2011*, Santiago: United Nations, 2012: p. 65, Table 1.6.1.
15   Dataweb Intal. http://www.iadb.org/dataintal/.

America would require more than a simple focus on trade. A deeper appreciation of the nature of linkages and relationships was necessary, with efforts being devoted to strengthening all types of connections. This is the point at which this book enters the picture.

The first section looks at the main purview of Australian government policy-making: national and state relations. As the two parliamentary reports made clear, the point of departure for any serious grappling with Latin America is an appreciation of the underlying political realities and trends in the regions. The initial chapter by Barry Carr, 'Latin America: Changing Political Realities and Trends, 2000–2014', is consequently devoted to painting a picture of what has been taking place in the region and what developments we might expect. As Carr points out, such an exploration is particularly important at this juncture because democratic consolidation processes throughout the region can appear messy and unstable to the extent that an untutored eye might expect serious authoritarian retrogression. The reality is somewhat different, with democracy firmly entrenched throughout the region and subject to vigorous debate about how it will operate and what forms it will take. This extends to the region's bilateral relations, particularly with new loci of power such as China and Russia, and perhaps Australia.

An open secret in Australia's foreign economic policy is the centrality of educational services as the country's fourth largest export sector. Indeed, many Latin Americans have come to know Australia through educational exchanges, whether it is a period spent in the country to learn English, the opportunity to pursue a university degree, or training in a trade or profession. Sean Burges maps out the nature of Australia–Latin America education relations in the second chapter, pointing to this sector as a ripe area for growth and the expansion of mutual understanding. The challenge that he identifies would be familiar to the authors of the 1992 and 2000 reports, namely the need for Australian providers to approach Latin America as a site for partnership, not a market that can be exploited to maintain overseas enrolment numbers. In a book whose chapter authors hale mostly from the academy it would be remiss if we did not flag one of the most serious negative developments of the last decade: a serious decline in the numbers of Latin American specialists in the social sciences, whose contribution to sourcing information, analysis and advice is fundamental. In other countries—the United States, Canada, France, and the United Kingdom—the strengthening and sometimes the revival of relations with Latin America has proceeded alongside substantial investment in the development of studies of Latin America.

One of the central activities we find if we turn our attention to US, Canadian or European engagement with Latin America is the provision of foreign aid. The incredible reality that John Minns points out in chapter three is that Australia has virtually no history of providing official development assistance to Latin America. More to the point, Minns sets the recent decision by AusAID to initiate programming in the region within the context of Australia's successful 2012 bid for elevation to the United Nations Security Council. Again, the theme from the parliamentary reports comes through in Minns' analysis, with a shortage of understanding and experience in the region emerging as a central challenge to this expansion of AusAID activities. The flip-side to this challenge is that engaging in the necessary learning process becomes an ideal opportunity for the Australian government to learn about the region, but only if it expands development programming in a cohesive and targeted manner.

James R. Levy and Peter Ross take up one of the higher profile sites for bilateral engagement in their chapter four discussion of the environment. Two major lessons come from their study that can be replicated in most areas of the bilateral relationship. The first is that we are not dealing with a single bilateral relationship, but rather with a set of 20 bilateral relationships between Australia and the various Latin American countries. This introduces enormous complications into the coordination of international positions and requires the very expertise that official Australian reports have consistently found lacking. Despite this challenge, Levy and Ross are clear that there is enormous space for cooperation and collaboration because many environmental challenges are shared by Australia and Latin America. Perhaps more significantly the authors also point to existing, but scantily used multilateral mechanisms that might be leveraged fruitfully to boost intercontinental relations in this policy area.

Two chapters, both authored by Pierre van der Eng and Don Kenyon, focus on the core concern of the two parliamentary reports, namely bilateral economic relations. Their story is not particularly surprising. Bilateral trade and investment flows are increasing, but not at a dizzying rate. The substance of the economic relationship remains in the mining and energy sectors, although there is a rising tide of Latin American investment in Australia. The conclusions van der Eng and Kenyon offer would be familiar to the drafters of the parliamentary reports, focusing on the great potential for trade with Latin America as well as the rewards that could be reaped through deliberately coordinated approaches to a wide range of international issues. The message is not lost on Australian government policy-makers, but the abiding problem remains the lack of career-enhancing rewards for officials who elect to specialise on Latin America.

A common theme in the Senate and House of Representatives documents is that culture and diaspora can provide the impetus to build and sustain intercontinental relations. The four chapters in the book's second section take up this idea.

As Victor Del Río points out in the seventh chapter, the Latin American diaspora in Australia has not been a great deal of help with the cultural education of other Australians. While there have been a series of waves of Latin American immigrants to Australia, they have not formed the sort of vibrant and high visibility diaspora communities found in and around Greek and Italian descendants. Media coverage of Latin America has not helped matters. The picture painted by John Sinclair is one of scanty coverage despite efforts through government-launched networks such as SBS. Sinclair also points to the similarities in media industry structure, but highlights that this does not appear to have had much impact on the intercontinental relationship. In the ninth chapter Ralph Newmark engages in a detailed survey of the penetration of Latin American culture in Australia. The commercial importance of culture highlighted by Newmark stands as a useful reminder of how significant the unspoken and uncodified rules of social relations can be in successfully navigating intercultural experiences. Indeed, this is the central theme of Bob Hodge's chapter, which critically examines Australian myths about the difficulties and challenges of doing business in Latin America. The key, Hodge argues in this final chapter, is getting the conceptual translation right. At a fundamental level there is a great deal of similarity between Latin American and Australian attitudes to doing business if you take the time to understand the reasons for the seemingly bizarre response in each country to their national bureaucratic and administrative contexts.

The heartening theme that emerges from the individual papers collected here is that there is a foundation for building Australia–Latin America relations, but one that needs a great deal of further development. This is reflected in the sorts of research strategies that the contributors have had to undertake to fulfil their individual briefs. Existing material on Australia–Latin America relations is thin, particularly if we turn our attention to the contemporary context. The data and analysis collected here thus constitute an important initial step to a greater and more engaged understanding of intercontinental relations, providing one of the only considered assessments of material on the subject.

The major implications from the studies printed here are twofold. First, the Australian government needs to take a far more sustained and deliberate approach to engagement with Latin America. There are signs that this has begun with the opening of Australian diplomatic missions such as the embassy in Peru, and a Consulate General in Bogotá, as well as a growing list of ministerial and even prime ministerial visits. But the proof is at the working level within the bureaucracy, where it remains difficult for officials to build a successful career around a Latin American specialisation.

The second major implication is for business sectors in Australia, including the education sector. An attitude that focuses on the region simply as a market is not likely to reap many rewards. Simply put, Australian attempts to penetrate

Latin markets are always going to have to compete with existing relationships that regional actors have with their North American and European counterparts. A long-term investment in relationship building is the key, particularly in the major export sectors to the region, such as education. The early signs are that this idea is being taken seriously, with a series of high-level trips being organised by groups such as the Global Foundation and the G8 Group of Universities. Likewise, organisations in Australia are working to bring Latin Americans across the Pacific to events such as the annual Diggers Conference; the annual Australian National Centre for Latin American Studies 'Latin America and the Shifting Sands of Global Power' conference at The Australian National University; and the Melbourne–Latin America dialogue at the University of Melbourne.

Positive developments and outcomes over the last few years have to be recognised and celebrated. But this book is not simply a list of cheerful developments. It also attempts to identify serious gaps and policy failures or weaknesses. The editors and authors hope that in this way it has made a contribution to a relationship of enormous potential in the future.

Many people have contributed to the production of this book. However, we would like to thank, above all, the Council on Australia Latin America Relations and, especially, its inaugural Chairman, Bernard Wheelahan. Without his support and that of the Council this book would not have been possible. Its weaknesses are, of course, the responsibility of the authors.

References

Adams, Mark, *Turn Right at Machu Picchu: Rediscovering the Lost City One Step at a Time*, New York: Dutton, 2011.

Australian Government, *Australia in the Asian Century: White Paper 2010*, Canberra: Commonwealth of Australia, 2010.

Brainard, Lael and Leonardo Martínez-Díaz, eds, *Brazil As An Economic Superpower? Understanding Brazil's Changing Role in the Global Economy*, Washington, DC: Brookings, 2009.

Dataweb Intal, http://www.iadb.org/dataintal/.

Evans, Gareth, 'Australia's Rediscovery of Latin America', Address by Senator Gareth Evans to the Columbus Quincentenary Conference, La Trobe University, Melbourne, 27 June 1992. http://www.gevans.org/ speeches/ old/1992/270692_fm_rediscoveryofla.pdf.

Friedman, Thomas, *The Lexus and the Olive Tree*, London: Harper Collins, 2000.

Gimlette, John, *At the Tomb of the Inflatable Pig: Travels Through Paraguay*, London: Hutchison, 2003.

Joint Standing Committee on Foreign Affairs, Defence and Trade, *Building Australia's Trade and Investment Relationship with South America*, Canberra: Commonwealth of Australia, 2000. http://www.aph.gov.au/Parliamentary_Business/Committees/House_of_Representatives_Committees?url=jfadt/samer/samindex.htm.

Lagos, Ricardo, *The Southern Tiger: Chile's Fight for a Democratic and Prosperous Future*, New York: Palgrave Macmillan, 2011.

Reid, Michael, *Forgotten Continent: The Battle for Latin America's Soul*, New Haven, CT: Yale University Press, 2009.

Roett, Riordan, *The New Brazil*, Washington, DC: Brookings, 2010.

Rohter, Larry, *Brazil on the Rise: The Story of a Country Transformed*, New York: Palgrave Macmillan, 2010.

Santiso, Javier, *Latin America's Political Economy of the Possible: Beyond Good Revolutionaries and Free-Marketeers*, Boston: MIT Press, 2007.

Senate of Australia. Standing Committee on Foreign Affairs, Defence and Trade, *Australia and Latin America*, Canberra: Commonwealth of Australia, 1992. http://www.aph.gov.au/Parliamentary_Business/Committees/Senate_Committees?url=fadt_ctte/completed_inquiries/pre1996/aust_latin_america/index.htm.

United Nations Economic Commission for Latin America and the Caribbean. *Statistical Year Book for Latin America and the Caribbean, 2011*, Santiago: United Nations, 2012.

United Nations Economic Commission for Latin America and the Caribbean. *Latin America and the Caribbean in the World Economy, 2010–2011*, New York: United Nations, 2011.

Weitzman, Hal, *Latin Lessons: How South America Stopped Listening to the United States and Started Prospering*, London: Wiley, 2012.

1. Latin America: Changing political realities and trends 2000–2014

Barry Carr

Introduction and cautions

> The United States took longer to realize that a weak State does not generate a strong market. They needed the brutal financial crisis of 2008 to wake up.[1]

With this striking headline Luiz Carlos Bresser Pereira began his opinion editorial published in mid-June 2011 in the solidly respectable and centrist Brazilian newspaper *O Folha de São Paulo*. Bresser Pereira was commenting on a news story supplied by the newspaper's Washington correspondent, suggesting that President Barack Obama intended to 'create a bank similar to the BNDES [Brazilian Economic and Social Development Bank]' in order to finance transportation, energy and sanitation projects in the United States. Bresser Pereira continued:

> [Would the United States] be turning to the infamous developmentalism, after having flown for many years the flag for neoliberalism, after having preached privatization, liberalization and general deregulation, in the name of an allegedly higher rationality justified by mathematical economic models?[2]

Bresser Pereira then cites economic data showing a lagging US economy. Even though it is natural for an advanced country like the United States to have a lower growth rate than developing countries, he goes on to argue that the United States 'is finally acknowledging the high price it is currently paying for having adopted the neoliberal credo'.[3]

Whatever the status of the US government's thinking on the proposal for a new development bank, the opinion editorial's reference to the severe economic and financial crisis in the United States, the pricking of illusions about the natural superiority of US-set models for economic management, and its triumphant display of data—comparing low levels of GDP growth and other indicators in

---

1 Luiz Carlos Bresser-Pereira, 'A Developmentalist United States', *Folha de São Paulo*, 19 June 2011.
2 *Ibid.*
3 *Ibid.*

the United States with India, China and Brazil—deserve some careful reflection. Was the article simply an example of Brazilian triumphalism at a time when the Latin American giant's political, diplomatic and—above all—economic importance was finally being accepted internationally? Or was Bresser Pereira expressing an understandable satisfaction with the growing acknowledgment, even among orthodox analysts, that, as the Council on Hemispheric Affairs (COHA) suggested in a recent memorandum:[4]

> For the most part Latin America has managed to fend off the brunt of the world economic downturn by avoiding the West's prescriptions—featuring canned formulas and impositions by international financial institutions and the developed world that were so popular during the nineties. By all accounts, Latin American countries, even before the global crisis set in, took a realist, home-grown perspective about how to maintain sustainable growth and avoid the financial contagion which later spread to other regions of the developed world.

Were there lessons to be learned from the recent experience of not only Brazil but also other Latin American countries; lessons that might have relevance not just for other developing countries, but also for the advanced world, including Australia?[5]

This introductory chapter sets out to do two things: to identify the major shifts in the politics and political economy of the Latin American region in the last 15 years by examining the changed political landscape; and secondly, to sketch possible future scenarios and landscapes over the next decade. In conclusion, the chapter will briefly identify opportunities and challenges for Australian actors—government and non-government—arising from these scenarios.

Some familiar cautions concerning Latin America are necessary. The Latin American region is complex and multifaceted, with a number of key blocs that have been traditionally identified in the following way: Mexico and Central America; the Caribbean (an Anglophone and Spanish-speaking area with several French-speaking island states as well); the Andean region (Venezuela, Ecuador, Colombia, Bolivia and Peru); Southern Cone (Chile, Argentina, Uruguay, Paraguay); and Brazil, the unique linguistic and historical development and sheer size of which deserves a category of its own. But these familiar subunits are not homogeneous themselves: in recent years, Colombia and Peru have

---

4   Council on Hemispheric Affairs (COHA) Research Memorandum, 'Strauss-Kahn's Visit to Latin America: A New Economic Policy?' 22 March 2011.
5   On Brazilian developments over the past decade, see Riordan Roett, *The New Brazil*, Washington DC: Brookings Institution Press, 2010; Larry Rohter, *Brazil On the Rise: The Story of a Country Transformed*, London: Palgrave Macmillan, 2010; Zuleika Arashiro, *Negotiating the Free Trade Area of the Americas*, London: Palgrave Macmillan, 2011; Sean Burges, *Brazilian Foreign Policy After the Cold War*, Gainesville: University Press of Florida, 2009.

clearly followed a different political and economic pathway from those of its Andean neighbours Ecuador, Bolivia and Venezuela, although the election of the Ollanta Humala government in Peru in early June 2011 did modify some aspects of that country's trajectory. Further south, in the Southern Cone bloc, the experience and interests of the two smaller nations, Paraguay and Uruguay, are often in sharp conflict with the larger and richer Chile and Argentina, and especially Brazil. And so on. In spite of the ever-more-frequent celebrations and endorsements of growing Latin American unity, the region remains an extraordinarily complex area about which generalisations are unwise.

It is also the case that, especially in the political and international relations arenas, the element of novelty and surprise has become steadily more pronounced in the Americas. The rules of the political and economic game have been redefined in many areas, and there is little doubt that this will continue over the rest of the new decade. Old certainties and traditions have been challenged; new kinds of socio-political actors and forces have emerged—an increasingly assertive Indian population is one—and the ways in which Latin American states interact with each other, with the United States—the traditional hegemon in the Americas— and with the rest of the world, have also undergone significant changes. When it comes to governments making choices and developing policies and strategies, we are increasingly seeing unexpected outcomes. While continuities in the sphere of economic policy are much clearer, the political game is changing rapidly and outcomes are increasingly unpredictable. All of this makes Latin America a fascinating laboratory for observers interested in tracking political, economic and social change, albeit a laboratory that defies simplistic assessments and projections based on crude ideological assumptions of the political Right and Left.

Latin America has long been the originator of novel political, economic and socio-cultural projects and frameworks; one thinks here of the rise of the structuralist economic analysis pioneered by the teams led by Raúl Prebisch at the Economic Commission for Latin America, or ECLA in the late 1940s and early 1950s, and the subsequent development of dependency theory among Latin American social scientists; the military developmentalism associated with authoritarian military regimes in Chile, Argentina, Brazil and Peru in the 1960s, 1970s and 1980s, and the role played by Latin America, most especially Brazil, in incubating the development of the World Social Forum over the past decade, a movement that has spread from the Americas to influence social and political action more widely in Africa and Asia.[6]

---

6   Edgar J. Dosman, *The Life and Times of Raúl Prebisch 1901–1986*, Montreal: McGill-Queen's University Press, 2008; Joseph Love, 'Raúl Prebisch and the Origins of the Doctrine of Unequal Exchange', *Latin American Research Review*, Vol. 15, 1980: pp. 45–72. Prebisch was appointed Director of the Economic Commission for Latin America in 1948. Between 1964 and 1969 he was the founding general secretary of the United Nations Conference on Trade and Development (UNCTAD). While Prebisch's work on historical trends in international

If history has anything to teach us we should expect the Latin American region to continue this innovative role over the next decade, and to continue to surprise even the best-informed observers and stakeholders. Taking bets on the future is always a dangerous project, especially for this author, who was trained as a historian, albeit a historian very much concerned with modern and contemporary history. But it may very well be that the momentous political, economic and cultural shifts that have occurred within the past 15 years in Latin America could once again generate momentum for a new model of development, or at least a new set of imaginaries and sensitivities that blend competing ways of practising politics and economics inherited from the past to forge a new synthesis that comes close to the developmentalism spoken of by Luiz Carlos Bresser Pereira in the opening paragraphs of this chapter.

Finally, the rapid increase in the pace of Latin America's insertion into global political, economic and diplomatic circuits must direct our attention to the international arena where uncertainty and surprises have also accelerated in the last five years. The obvious development here is the enormously destabilising impact of the Global Financial Crisis (GFC) of 2008–10; the sovereign debt crises in Europe of 2010–13; and the emergence of several Asian nations—China in particular but India and Vietnam are also important players—as major economic and political stakeholders.

Making predictions about the future direction of politics and economics in Latin America is, therefore, all the more dangerous these days. Nevertheless, despite the often substantial national and regional differences visible in developments unfolding in political and economic spheres of the last decade, one of the arguments of this chapter is that it is possible to detect some clear trends and to identify ways in which these may develop over the next decade.

One of the most striking trends is the emergence throughout the region of a flexible and non-ideological commitment to economic management. After several decades of rigid adherence to the tenets of neoliberal economics throughout the late 1970s, 1980s and 1990s, most Latin American countries have abandoned religious devotion to the market—most particularly the market dogmatism so common in the 1980s and 1990s—and embraced policies that stress the importance of state intervention in infrastructure, e.g., technology, energy, transport; education, finance, labour-management relations; and the general relationships between public and private spheres, in a way that orthodox neoliberal theory could not grasp. Whatever the radical flourishes of official discourse—such as the Venezuelan references

---

terms of trade and his espousal of import substitution industrialisation (ISI) warrant substantial modification in light of the mixed experiences with ISI and the striking improvement in terms of trade for many third-world countries in recent years, his work has once again attracted attention from scholars and practitioners in regard to the failures of doctrinaire neoliberalism and the discrediting of much orthodox prescription as a consequence of the global financial crisis of 2007–10.

to 'a new socialism' and a 'socialism of the 21st century'—the governments of the so-called Pink Tide, now the largest bloc in Latin America, have certainly not broken with many key elements of the neoliberal package. Nonetheless, they have increasingly insisted on the importance of granting a bigger role for state engineering. The neo-structuralists, who have dominated economic policy-making in these countries in recent years, argue that states must fashion institutions that promote policy stability, adaptability, and coherence and coordination of markets. The institutions must be of high quality and embody 'public regardedness' rather than personalistic clientelism.[7]

Another important trend visible in the last decade is what the US-based Brookings Institute has termed 'a common desire for Latin America's autonomy from its northern neighbors, manifested in the sudden proliferation of regional organisations such as the Union of South American Nations (UNASUR) which emerged in mid-2008, and the Latin American and Caribbean Community of States'.[8] As the Brookings Institute argued further, 'the Organization of American States (OAS), which for decades has been the main guarantor of choice of the Inter-American Democratic Charter, is facing a challenge to its legitimacy and continuation as the premier diplomatic forum of the western hemisphere'.[9]

Similarly, the Uruguayan Foreign Minister, Luis Amagro recently described UNASUR as 'the most important political convergence instrument at the continental level', a reference to the organisation's efforts in promoting peace, stability and democratic governance in Latin America.[10]

The newest regional forum to emerge in the Americas is the Community of Latin American and Caribbean States (CELAC), founded in December 2011 and made up of the 33 Latin American and Caribbean states. CELAC has created a parallel organisation to the traditional and until recently US-dominated Organization of American States and neither the United States nor Canada is a member of the new body. Although CELAC was founded with the active and enthusiastic support of the late Venezuelan president, Hugo Chávez, the organisation has now become the main regional mechanism for political dialogue among Latin American

---

7   The literature on the Pink Tide phenomenon in Latin America is large and growing rapidly. A representative selection of texts would include the following: Nikolas Kozloff, *Revolution! South America and the Rise of the New Left*, London: Palgrave-Macmillan, 2008; Jeffrey Webber and Barry Carr (eds), The New Latin American Left: Cracks in the Empire, Lanham: Rowman and Littlefield, 2013; William I. Robinson, *Latin America and Global Capitalism: A Critical Globalization Perspective*, Baltimore: John Hopkins University Press, 2008; Kurt Gerhard Weyland, Raúl L. Madrid, Wendy Hunter (eds), *Leftist Governments in Latin America: Successes and Shortcomings*, Cambridge: CUP, 2010; James Petras, Henry Veltmeyer, *What's Left in Latin America? Regime Change in New Times*, Ashgate Publishing Co., 2009; Sebastian Edwards, *Left Behind: Latin America and the False Promise of Populism*, Chicago: University of Chicago Press, 2010.
8   Brookings Institute: 'Latin America's New Political Landscape and OAS' (summary). http://www. brookings.edu/events/2010/03/15-latin-america, accessed 5 October 2013.
9   *Ibid.*
10   MercoPress, 'UNASUR Secretary General officially takes office May 9 in Guyana', 30 April 2011.

nations and marks a clear break with Washington's Latin American stance. This was made particularly clear by CELAC's strong criticism of US policy towards Cuba. In January 2014 CELAC held its summit meeting in Havana, Cuba with the meeting coinciding, perhaps intentionally, with the 50th anniversary of the breaking of diplomatic relations with Cuba by most Latin American states.

How far and how quickly these new regional forums and continental organisations develop, and whether hard results emerge from the often overblown rhetoric that has surrounded the launching of some of these initiatives—such as the Bank of the South and other ideas launched by the late President Hugo Chávez—is something that we cannot yet assess.[11] However, tracking and assessing these new initiatives and learning to work with them is one of the major challenges facing many of the non-Latin American states— Australia is one—that have been accustomed to the more predictable outcomes and behaviours associated with older and more familiar multilateral forums and organisations. The simplistic judgments that developments excluding the United States are unhelpful and anti-American will not be productive and run the risk of seriously underestimating the real and symbolic content of the new order emerging in Latin America.

The changing contours of Latin America 1998–2013

The broad outline of trends in politics and economics is fairly clear. The 1980s saw the end of the right-wing military dictatorships in Chile, Argentina, Uruguay and Brazil, and the re-emergence of pluralist, more inclusive and more democratic politics. However, such democratic pluralism is tainted by what analysts have termed a significant 'democratic deficit' associated with incomplete removal of some institutional practices and structures created during the dictatorial past, and a less-than-ideal grappling with continuing high levels of poverty and social exclusion. While politics became unquestionably more inclusive in the 1980s and early 1990s, there was substantial continuity in the broad economic strategies followed by civilian governments of all stripes. The era of neoliberalism continued and the so-called Washington Consensus that underpinned the neoliberal vision was not fundamentally disturbed; almost everywhere, the same policy mix prevailed—an emphasis on outward trade-

---

11   The Bank of the South (Banco del Sur) was launched under Venezuelan sponsorship in 2009 as an explicit challenge to the dominance of traditional bodies such as the World Bank, the International Monetary Fund and the Inter-American Development Bank, and the beginnings of what its proponents have termed 'the New Regional Financial Architecture' in Latin America. Its founding members were Ecuador, Bolivia, Paraguay, Uruguay, Venezuela, Argentina, and Brazil. The Bank initiated operations in 2013 with an initial capital of seven billion US dollars.

led growth; the liberalisation of trading barriers; privatisation; macroeconomic equilibrium privileged over everything else—although the weighting of individual prescriptions was altered. The only significant shift in the socio-economic sphere in these two decades was a modest, but regionally uneven shift towards the adoption of policies promoting social and educational investment and welfare.[12]

In the latter phase of this period there were important developments in regional economic integration—most spectacularly with the launching of Mercosur (founded in 1991 by Argentina, Brazil, Uruguay and Paraguay and with Bolivia, Peru, Ecuador, Chile, Colombia and Venezuela having associated member status), and of NAFTA (launched in January 1994 by the United States, Canada and Mexico). While NAFTA is an example of a classic Free Trade Area (FTA), Mercosur has been launched as a Customs Union and, especially in its pre-foundational phase, the organisation had an explicit goal of consolidating pluralist and democratic governance and minimising threats of the return of military regimes. Its ambitious goals have also included commitments to the development of inclusive national and regional governance and, with less success so far, to the promotion of a deep regional culture of belonging, sometimes referred to as *conciencia mercosureña*. These regional economic integration projects have not displaced bilateral free trade agreements such as the one between Chile and the United States. However, there has been a distinct shift from favouring regional agreements over US-driven initiatives—such as the Free Trade Area of the Americas (FTAA), which never saw the light of day—to criticism within important Latin American circles, weak support within the US Congress and, above all, opposition by Brazil. The spectacular failure of the FTAA by the end of 2003 was an indication of the real limits to US hegemony in Latin America.

Political outcomes during the 1980s and 1990s were modestly positive—with no significant challenge to the democratising and pluralising effect—although there were problems: for example, brief, and fortunately unsuccessful, military challenges to the new civilian government in Argentina in the 1980s, while the transition to civilian rule in Chile took longer than anywhere else. But, in the economic sphere the result was the famous 'Lost Decade' of the 1980s, lasting in some areas until the early 1990s: an outcome that has led some analysts to talk of the 'Long Lost Decade.' For the 20 years between 1980 and 2000, the economies of Latin America grew by only 11 per cent in per capita terms. This was the worst 20-year growth performance in over a century. As a point of comparison, Latin America experienced a per capita GDP growth of 80 per cent during the two decades between 1960 and 1980. The most basic measure of human wellbeing,

---

12   A balanced discussion of recent economic and political developments in Latin America is Peter Kingstone, *The Political Economy of Latin America: Reflections on Neoliberalism and Development*, London: Routledge, 2011.

income per person, fell dramatically, by 3.1 per cent in the peak phase of the lost 'long decade' (1980–90).[13] The era of import substitution industrialisation (ISI) between 1950 and 1970 may have produced some unwelcome outcomes, but its record on growth rates was without question more impressive than the record of fundamentalist neoliberalism during the following 25 years.

A reaction against the politics and economics of ideologically rigid neoliberalism set in all over the region from the mid-1990s onwards. The depth of this reaction and the nature of the political outcomes it elicited were regionally very uneven, but some of the main trends can be identified. Between 1995 and 2014, in country after country, new political constellations emerged—most noticeably at the level of national government, but of course with different timetables and different flavours. A series of centrist, centre-left and left wing governments emerged in virtually all the countries of the region. Prominent exceptions included Mexico, where the conservative Party of National Action (PAN) ruled until 2013 under presidents Vicente Fox and Felipe Calderón following the historic defeat in 2000 of the centrist Institutional Revolutionary Party (PRI), which had governed Mexico in various guises since 1929. But even here volatility and unpredictability have been striking; Mexico's centre-left PRD party emerged in second place in the 2006 elections—although it has been wracked by division ever since—and it has won and maintained power over Mexico City since 1999, ever since the capital city regained its political independence. The return to power of the PRI after the July 2012 elections marked a return to the political centre, although many of the initial policies introduced by the new PRI, led by President Enrique Peña Nieto, are close to traditional platforms of the nominally more conservative PAN.

The other exceptions are Colombia, although at the regional level—especially in Bogotá, the capital city—left-of-centre coalitions have won power on several occasions, most recently in October 2011; and, to a lesser degree, Peru, although even here the centre-left was growing in strength in the years after 2007, leading to the victory of Ollanta Humala in June 2011. By the middle of 2011 around 70 per cent of the population of Latin America lived under governments that either want to modify elements of the Washington Consensus substantially or—and this is the case for only a few of these new governments, namely Venezuela, Bolivia and Ecuador—make a sharp break with this set of prescriptions.

In reality, the Pink Tide phenomenon embraced an immense variety of strategies and styles. There was no single model being propounded. However, some common features can be identified. The Pink Tide governments were all,

---

13 Mark Weisbrot and David Rosnick, *Another Lost Decade? Latin America's Growth Failure Continues into the 21st Century*, Washington DC: CEPR, 13 November 2003. Recent developments have not supported the overall pessimism about future growth prospects in Latin America expressed in this important paper. However, its analysis of past policies and their outcomes is impressive and difficult to refute.

without exception, the result of electoral politics. This is an obvious point but one that warrants some reflection. The fact that, with no exception, the Pink Tide governments have come into office through the ballot box—and in some cases have reaffirmed their legitimacy in numerous electoral and referendum events—means that the shift we have been witnessing has enjoyed much more legitimacy than many left of centre governments in the past. It also means that the leftward shifts have been able to mount political and economic policies that mostly involve occasional breaks with US preferences without bringing about significant and permanent ruptures with Washington, even in the cases of the more radical transitions such as those that have occurred in Venezuela, Bolivia and Ecuador.

The electoral path has also raised a series of challenges for parties and coalitions committed to transformational or emancipatory politics. The coin has two sides. Legitimacy conferred through elections has its advantages; it certainly has involved a radical break with the Latin American Left's traditional suspicions of electoral politics. But, necessarily, it also means that the emancipatory politics that come to prominence in a well-institutionalised capitalist state have had to cope with the resistance of sectors within existing state structures that 'act to constrain, dilute, institutionalize and co-opt mass struggles, to reproduce the old order.'[14] Most importantly, it is crucial to understand that electoral victories can be overturned in future contests. Thus in Chile—ruled by a series of centre-left coalitions of the Concertación since the end of the Pinochet dictatorship—the Conservative candidate Sebastián Piñera won the presidential election in January 2010, defeating the Concertación's Eduardo Frei (however, the centre-left returned to power in early 2014 under Michelle Bachelet). Further to the north, in Peru, the domination of politics by parties and candidates of the right and centre-right came to an end with the victory in the middle of 2011 of Ollanta Humala. In Venezuela, the era of massive electoral victories by *chavista* parties has come to an end, judging by the surprisingly slim majority achieved by the governing party and its presidential candidate, Nicolás Maduro, in the April 2013 elections.

In most cases the political forces and leading personalities who have been successful in recent Latin American politics have come from non-traditional political backgrounds. Hugo Chávez in Venezuela came from outside the traditionally alternating COPEI and *Acción Democrática* parties and had no links of any kind to the large array of Venezuelan parties of the left. The political party Movement to Socialism (MAS), founded by Evo Morales in Bolivia and which helped propel him to power in December 2005, was created less than a year before the electoral victory. Rafael Correa in Ecuador, an economist and Christian radical, ran in the 2006 elections on the ticket of the National Alliance,

---

14   William I. Robinson, *Transformative Possibilities in Latin America*, p. 11.

an ad-hoc grouping of small left-wing parties, disaffected members of traditional centrist organisations and some social movement representatives. The two main Ecuadorian indigenous movements, CONAIE (Ecuadorian Confederation of Indigenous Nations) and *Pachakutik*, refused to join Correa's winning ticket. Correa was re-elected in 2013. Fernando Lugo, elected president of Paraguay in 2008 and removed from power in 2012, was a former Catholic bishop with a history of activism on behalf of the rural poor but with almost no history of involvement in institutional politics. In Brazil, Luiz Ignacio da Silva, or Lula, was elected president twice on the platform of the Workers Party (PT). While the PT was not a recent creation—it was founded in 1980—its style and modus operandi marked a sharp break with the traditions of the older political parties formed before and during the lengthy period of military rule in that country. This growing tendency for political leadership and political actors to emerge from unexpected quarters makes careful tracking and observation of the Latin American region, free from the policy and partisan constraints that limit much official analysis, a particularly important task in the years to come: a task that requires support for the establishment of what Latin American universities, NGOs and analysts call an *observatorio*.

In other cases where the new politicians at the national level in Latin America have come from older traditions of radical politics, their institutional underpinnings have all undergone major transformations in the last decade and a half. This is the case with Argentina's Peronist party, the base of the two Kirchner presidents of Argentina—where Cristina Kirchner won re-election in late 2011—and of the Sandinista National Liberation Front (FSLN) in Nicaragua, whose candidate Daniel Ortega was successful in the presidential elections of late 2006 and November 2011. In El Salvador a brutal civil war had been waged in the 1980s, pitting the FMLN (Farabundo Martí National Liberation Front) against a series of military and military-dominated governments of the right and centre right. After the armed conflict concluded in 1991, the FMLN suffered a number of major splits and moved to adjust its style and moderate its program to gain greater electoral support. The former guerrilla fighters and activists and their political allies who won power in 2009 with Mauricio Funes as the presidential candidate of the FMLN had moved a considerable distance from the positions the FMLN had articulated two decades earlier. The emergence of Ollanta Humala, a former Peruvian army officer, as an electorally successful standard bearer for the Left, is one more example of a figure whose mass support and commitments to social policies favouring the poor were forged almost entirely outside the action of traditional radical and left-wing political parties.

But outside the sphere of struggles over control of the national government, important changes were also being registered in other political spaces, including the growing prominence of municipal and regional political arenas as locales for non-traditional forces. One thinks here of the emergence of Bogotá and Mexico City in the last few decades as centres of oppositional politics—with the Party of the Democratic Revolution (PRD) maintaining its control over Mexico City over the past 17 years, while various leftist figures, most recently Gustavo Petro, have won power in Bogotá. Another trend has been the virtual disappearance of the option of armed struggle in Latin America, with the exception of Colombia and an increasingly more isolated and marginalised Zapatista (EZLN) movement in southern Mexico.

In the economic sphere continuities still prevailed over ruptures. Neoliberalism certainly entered into a major crisis after the lost decade. As an intellectual discourse with an almost religious dimension, neoliberalism became increasingly discredited as a set of inflexible policy recipes with disappointing outcomes. But, certainly at a national level, the Pink Tide did not bring a major overall shift in economic policy. Statism has been widely discredited, although public sector expansion has been noticeable in certain sectors, for example, in petroleum and gas. The emphasis on export-led development remains dominant. Even in countries with left-wing governments—Venezuela and Bolivia—in spite of sometimes overblown rhetoric by national leaders, capitalist social and economic relations have not been fundamentally challenged.

There have, however, been some extremely important changes registered in the politico-economic arena that are easily masked by an excessive concentration on national electoral politics and the role of traditional parties; an overly narrow focus on the politics of nation states; and a neglect of international political economy.

One particularly remarkable development has been the growing importance in Latin America of involvement by non-traditional state actors—China and Russia in particular, and to a lesser extent India. This is, of course, a regional manifestation of the rise of the BRIC nations (Brazil, Russia, India and China). A push for diversification of their international trade and investment partners by Latin American countries has coincided with a thirst in Asia for raw materials—not just petroleum as is often argued, but also for iron ore, soybeans and other commodities.

The increased importance of these new actors can be seen in both the trade and investment sectors. In 2010, for example, China became Brazil's main export destination displacing the United States to second position. The scale of the transformation in what is admittedly a particularly dramatic case, given the size and potential of Latin America's largest economy, is breathtaking. Brazil's imports from China in 2012 reached $75 billion, an increase from $1.2 billion in 2000. Brazilian exports to China grew from $1 billion to $41.2 billion in 2012.

Elsewhere in Latin America, China has also emerged as a major market and source of investment. The interest in diversifying foreign trade by developing closer links with the People's Republic of China straddles governments of all political colours. In Colombia, for example, one of the countries closely tied politically and militarily to the United States, the country's current president, Juan Manuel Santos, expressed in an interview with the UK *Financial Times* the range of motivations behind his country's interest in promoting closer relations with China by referring to Asia as 'the new engine of growth for the world economy': a familiar refrain. But as the respected Washington analyst Larry Birns noted in commenting on Santos' declarations:

> close ties with the Asian giant are encouraged, in Colombia's case not only by Colombia's status as a rising world power, but also by China's use of soft power…a foreign policy formulation based upon the creation of sustainable trade markets rather than direct physical control of nations…a form of relief for countries that have grown tired of the United States' continual use of hard power in which Washington projects its military strength in order for it to control outcomes in the Western Hemisphere.[15]

Birns concluded with an assessment that might be applied equally to other Latin American states regardless of their political colouring: 'Although Santos assured interviewers that Colombia still regards the United States as a strategic partner despite its new relationship with China it is clear that the exclusive one up, one down relationship America [*sic*] once had, almost by right with Latin America, is steadily unravelling.'[16]

This development should not, as some analysts have argued, necessarily be seen as signifying the emergence of an adversarial political relationship between recipient countries, BRIC nations, and the United States. The driving force here is mostly an increased level of trade and investment competition, although such competition can, and often in the past has created fears of loss of US dominance. A flavour of this concern can be gained from a report by the normally balanced and cautious US consultancy firm Price Waterhouse Coopers, which predicted that:

> in 2020, the G7 (the United States, Japan, France, Germany, the UK, Italy, and Canada) will have an economic weight equal to that of the emerging nations, recently christened the E7: China, India, Brazil, Russia, Mexico, Indonesia, and Turkey. In 2010, the difference in favor of the G7 is about 35% (in 2000 it was 70%). This margin of advantage will have

---

15 Larry Birns, 'Clinton Plays Hostess in a Failed Attempt to Mend US–Latin American Relations', COHA News Release, Washington DC, 28 May 2011.
16 *Ibid.*

evaporated in less than a decade. By 2030, China will have overtaken the United States and be first place in terms of economic power. The United States will be closely followed by India, Japan, and Brazil.[17]

The changing constellation of international political and economic power as it affects Latin America can also be viewed in other arenas. In the last decade the importance of south-south regional diplomacy—involving Latin American states and the BRIC nations plus South Africa—has grown considerably. Some analysts have argued that the development of horizontal ties binding Latin American states to other nations in the Global South is a further manifestation, along with the growing influence and self-confidence of the BRIC nations in Latin America, of the enhanced bargaining capacity of the Latin American bloc in a global system in which old certainties, the dominance of US, and to a lesser degree European hegemony politically and economically, were no longer obvious and rock solid. Put very simply, over the past decade there has been more room for manoeuvre for Latin American states, especially the larger countries, e.g., Brazil, Mexico, Argentina, all the more so given the desperate search by developed and developing nations to secure reliable energy supplies.

During the same period some Latin American states and regional forums have exhibited greater boldness and self-confidence in the international arena. Latin American states are no longer—if they ever were—predictable and automatic supporters of the stances taken by successive US administrations. This growing independence or flexing of muscles has been exhibited in a series of events over the last decade. The Brazil–Turkey initiative on Iran—known as the 'swap deal'—in May 2010 is one example, although here Brazilian domestic criticism of Lula's initiative, the extremely negative response of the United States, and subsequent UN Security Council actions taken against Iran exposed the limits of Brazilian power.[18] Other conjunctures in which Latin American states adopted policies that in some way challenged traditional US policies would include the role played by Brazil in the Copenhagen climate talks in 2009; the almost unanimous refusal by Latin American nations to support Washington's position on the Honduran coup in the summer of 2009; and the Obama administration's attempts to reinsert Honduras into the Inter-American system after the elections of November of that year, which brought to power a government whose legitimacy was challenged by many nations in Latin America.

Other manifestations of this increasingly unpredictable and dynamic international relations landscape include the growing tendency for Latin American states to operate outside traditional forums such as the Organization

---

17   Raul Zibechi, 'Brazil as a Key Player', *CIP Americas Program Report*, 17 February 2010.

18   For a summary of an interesting discussion of the Brazil–Turkey Nuclear Initiative held at the Wilson Center (Washington DC) in February 2011 involving Brazilian, Turkish and US academics, see http://www.wilsoncenter.org/index.cfm?fuseaction=events.event_summary&event_id=650768.

of American States (OAS), an organisation that for most of its history they have been reluctant to challenge. And the OAS itself has in recent years increasingly refused to play by the old rules, as was shown in its role during a serious border dispute between Ecuador and Colombia in 2008. Following a Colombian raid into Ecuador a regional war seemed to be a possible outcome. Although the Bush administration resolutely supported the Uribe government's stance, in this case the support for the Correa government's protests shown by the Rio Group of Latin American countries and later ratified by the 18 March meeting of the OAS summit in Washington against strong opposition of the United States, revealed once more the very real limits to US power in the new Latin America.

Mention has already been made of the emergence of new forums and networks of cooperation in Latin America, which do not include the United States; examples already discussed include UNASUR, CELAC and the Bank of the South. There have been many other forums designed to promote Latin American hemispheric cooperation and development including the nations of Venezuela, Nicaragua, Bolivia, Ecuador and Cuba, which are members of the Bolivarian Alliance, or ALBA (*Alianza Bolivariana para los Pueblos de Nuestra América*). The South American Defense Council is another new project, holding its first meeting in 2009; although Colombia initially refused to participate in the project because of its close military ties with the United States, it did in the end agree to join the Council.

It should be noted that many of these new initiatives were initially very fragile. They had difficulties in securing financial support from governments and, as one observer noted, 'they have remained to a large extent as meetings and gatherings of heads of state and ministers of foreign affairs. So the only institution with enough capacity, not only to convene the entire region but also to implement and execute, is the OAS'.[19] Nevertheless, by early 2014 UNASUR and CELAC, at least, had consolidated their position and influence.

Latin America's performance in the Global Financial Crisis of 2008–10 and in the boom of rising commodity prices visible up to early 2012 has also contributed to the growing self-confidence of many Latin American states. Latin America certainly did not escape completely unscathed. This is particularly the case with Mexico, with its high dependence on the US economy. But in global terms the impact of the crisis on Latin America was less than might have been expected. Once again, the Brazilian experience is worth noting here. Brazil's GDP growth was 5.1 per cent in 2008, with only a small decline in 2009. By early 2010 the growth rate was once again impressive: two per cent in January 2010.

---

19   Mauricio Cárdenas, Latin American Initiative, Brookings Institute. Transcript of meeting in 2010.

Even though growth rates fell in 2012 and 2013, Brazil's fiscal and monetary discipline—much praised by orthodox observers—plus newly discovered oil reserves have certainly contributed to this favourable outcome.

Some of the most ambitious future economic projects involve continental economic and political cooperation. One much-touted project would involve the building of a South American multi-modal container handling system that would enable goods to be transported from the Pacific coast of South America via railways and highways over or through the Andes and into the Amazon Basin, and down to Manaus in Brazil.

This discussion of recent trends in Latin America has thus far concentrated almost entirely on national, state-level politics and national and international political economy. However, the rapid and often dramatic changes in landscapes in Latin America are also the product of developments in other spheres: in civil society; in the battle of ideas; and in struggles over the definition of national, regional and hemispheric identities. The transformations in Latin America, then, are much wider and deeper than electoral events suggest. Not everything that is important unfolds in presidential palaces or legislatures; the different social actors at the heart of social change in the region, and their often novel ways of conducting politics and economics and envisioning alternative ways of transforming everyday life have shifted debate, undermined old certainties and wounded, sometimes fatally, conventional narratives and prescriptions. Space limitations make a discussion of these topics very difficult, but a couple of developments warrant attention here because they may offer opportunities for a deeper and more productive engagement by Australians on a variety of levels with Latin American actors.

One important development, the significance of which has not been registered sufficiently outside the academy, is the emergence and acknowledgement of what one might call 'Indianism' and questions of indigenous identity in countries with a significant indigenous population. This has been especially visible in the Andean area comprising Peru, Ecuador, and Bolivia in particular, although its echoes have also been heard in parts of Mexico, Guatemala and Chile. Given the historic exclusion of the Indian masses from the benefits of economic growth and political power, the emergence of indigenous issues at the centre of political, social and cultural debate is an enormously significant development. The Indianist upsurge is closely linked to the emergence of new social movements and actors all over the Americas, especially notable in the aftermath of the 1992 Columbus Quincentenary celebrations and protests. These new actors have almost without exception—even in the case of the Chiapas-based Zapatista Army of National Liberation (EZLN) in southern Mexico—practised a politics which has eschewed armed struggle even while it often emphasises innovative forms of direct action and mass mobilisation. The strongest manifestations of this new Indianism, in contrast with much writing and expectation, have been urban and working-class rather than rural and peasant, although both rural and urban movements have been important. The most powerful insurrections in recent Bolivian history with an Indianist but also class content were rooted in El Alto, an informal proletarian and indigenous city on the outskirts of the capital La Paz. Most Mapuches in Chile today, for example, are urban, and large groups of both permanent and transitory indigenous people from Mexico and Central America now live in major urban centres throughout the south-eastern and western United States, as well as in scattered towns and cities in the Midwest and Carolinas in the United States.

In several countries, most particularly Bolivia and Ecuador, the Indianist resurgence has also detonated another fascinating and crucially important political phenomenon: the attempt to refashion the constitutional basis of state legitimacy is no less than an attempt to create a new foundational narrative for nation states. One dimension of this process has been the efforts to write new constitutions that would guarantee indigenous representation in congress and recognise rights to communal property and a degree of autonomy for indigenous peoples. The new social movements that make claims on behalf of indigenous peoples have become important players in Ecuador and Bolivia, sometimes supporting the programs of the so-called Pink Tide governments, but in other cases maintaining a firm independence from political parties and formal legislative processes that has made life enormously complicated for national and regional governments in these countries. In Ecuador, for example, the powerful Confederation of Indigenous Nationalities of Ecuador (CONAIE) has been a thorn in the side of President Rafael Correa, accusing his nominally pro-Indian government of betraying the cause.[20]

Australian observers would not be surprised to learn that an important element in the programs of the new Indianist organisations has been the demand for greater Indian control over decisions on how the environment is to be handled, especially in regions where national and transnational capital have been engaged in exploiting rich mineral and forestry resources. The battle of ideas and political-economic practices around land rights, autonomy, mining, forestry, and other forms of development spurred by an ever-greater demand for resources, has led to bitter struggles and often bloody outcomes in many regions. None of

---

20   Marc Becker, 'Correa, Indigenous Movements, and the Writing of a New Constitution in Ecuador', *Latin American Perspectives*, Vol. 38, 2011: 1, pp. 47–62; Leon Zamosc, 'The Indian Movement in Ecuador: from Politics of Influence to Politics of Power', pp. 131–57 in Nancy Grey Postero and Leon Zamosc (eds), *The Struggle for Indigenous Rights in Latin America*, Brighton, England: Sussex Academic Press, 2004; Bonaventura de Sousa Santos, 'Las paradojas de nuestro tiempo y la Plurinacionalidad', pp. 21–62 in Alberto Acosta and Esperanza Martínez (eds), *Plurinacionalidad: Democracia en la diversidad*, Quito: Abya Yala, 2009; Kenneth J. Mijeski and Scott H. Beck, 'The Electoral Fortunes of Ecuador's Pachakutik Party: The Fracaso of the 2006 Presidential Elections', *The Latin Americanist* 52, June 2008: pp. 41–59.

these concerns are foreign to Australia's experience, and there could be fruitful opportunities for the exchange of ideas, histories and experiences between NGOs, governments and academics from the two regions.

Looking to the future

The Pink Tide may weaken in the immediate future, at least in terms of national political rule. There was an electoral shift to the right in Chile, although the centre-left Concertación's Michelle Bachelet returned to power in early 2014. In Venezuela, while the 2012 presidential elections returned the Chávez government with a substantial majority, the death of Hugo Chávez and the slim majority won by his anointed successor Nicolás Maduro in presidential elections in April 2013 are signs of a weakening of popular support for key parts of the Bolivarian project. On the other hand, the shock emergence of a serious Green presidential candidate in Colombia in 2010 and the sharp break with the hardline stance of President Uribe visible in the government of the successful candidate Juan Manuel Santos; the defeat of the conservative PAN in Mexico's presidential elections in mid-2012; as well as the continuing electoral successes in 2010 of the PT in Brazil, where the party won office again under Dilma Rousseff, are all evidence of the ongoing volatility and unpredictability of politics in the new Latin America.

In any case, the shift towards greater economic, political and diplomatic autonomy, and the challenges to inherited orthodoxies in Latin America are independent of the ideological make-up of national governments. The tendencies outlined in the first part of this chapter are likely to continue over the next decade. The United States will continue to be by far the most important external economic and political player in the region, but the trends, which have seen a growing European and especially Asian involvement, will continue. The obsessive focus on the United States as a player, common among both left- and right-wing analysts, will increasingly be seen to obscure rather than clarify Latin American developments and our understanding of them. The ideologically driven use of terms such as 'populism' to excoriate policies in Latin America will also be unhelpful.

If commodity prices remain steady—and the upward trend began to reverse in 2012 and 2013—then Latin America's economic growth will continue to be modestly satisfactory. After a slow down in 2009, Latin America's economic growth in 2010 reached 5.9 per cent and while growth fell to three per cent in 2011, rebounding a little to 3.5 per cent in 2012, the region's overall performance is still impressive compared to the performance of the European and US economies. The price of petroleum is especially significant here—most obviously for Mexico, Venezuela and Ecuador. However, a double dip in the global economy would have a serious dampening impact given that recent economic growth has been overly dependent on international trade. Still, current projections by orthodox analysts have Latin America following the Asian region in terms of economic growth over the US economy and that of its even more troubled EU partners.

The significance of Brazil's emerging profile on the world stage cannot be underestimated: it is the single most important geopolitical and economic development in Latin America. Australia should be monitoring this development very closely, as it may have implications for increasing the weight of our diplomatic presence in Brazil, and accelerating plans for improving the currently woeful level of air communications with Brazil.

Over the next ten years we are unlikely to see a return to overt military intervention in politics of the kind that we witnessed in the 1960s, 1970s and early 1980s. Civilian rule and electorally legitimated regime transitions are likely to continue. However, there are some warning signs and a number of possible flash points. The military intervention in the ousting of the Honduran Zelaya government in 2009 was deeply worrying, and the decision by the United States to revive its Fourth Fleet in the Caribbean is not a welcome sign. The Colombian–Venezuelan and Colombian–Ecuadorian borders may still be the sites of inter-state conflicts and these may exacerbate conflict throughout the entire region. The sheer scale of petroleum reserves now claimed by Venezuela and Brazil necessarily will force oil and energy-rich states to step up their capacity to defend their resource-rich territories, and this could be the source of inter-state tensions.

What opportunities might the trends discussed in this chapter offer Australian actors who are engaged or interested in engaging with Latin America?

We need to put much more energy into observing, tracking and analysing ongoing developments in Latin America. Government ministries and agencies, including Austrade, DFAT, the Australian Federal Police, and a variety of intelligence agencies, currently shoulder the burden here. The Council on Australia–Latin America Relations (COALAR) has promoted and supported important research on the Australia–Latin America relationship, and this has increased the gathering of data and analysis, most notably on the export of Australian education resources in vocational and technical education, the teaching of English as a second language, and the provision of university education.

University-based scholars have also made an important contribution. But while there have been some positive developments on the university front—the growth of interest in Latin America in Sydney-based universities; the emergence of the

Australian National Centre for Latin American Studies (ANCLAS) at ANU; and the impressive growth of Spanish language teaching throughout the university sector—teaching and research on Latin America outside the language, literature and cultural studies arenas has stagnated and even moved backwards in recent years. Social science specialists committed to Latin America have retired and not been replaced; Latin American Studies programs in several universities have disappeared or been drastically reduced at Flinders University and at La Trobe University; and there are very few dedicated Latin American specialists working in key disciplines such as Politics and International Relations—the ANU is an exception here—while there is not a single university economist whose full-time teaching and research commitments are focused on Latin America. Latin America-focused Sociology, Anthropology and History are also barely represented in the academy, a sad reversal of earlier strengths.

The thinness of the dedicated Latin Americanist social science presence in Australian universities seriously reduces Australia's capacity to engage with Latin American reality, to track ongoing developments and identify and pursue opportunities for fruitful cooperation. As if this was not serious enough, the commitment to Portuguese in the 1970s has reverted to the almost total absence of Portuguese language training in Australian universities at a time when Brazil's political, economic and diplomatic importance has increased; this is a serious anomaly and a major handicap in Australia's ability to study and profit from the Brazilian juggernaut's emergence as a world actor. One modest but potentially effective way of addressing this deficit in universities would be the establishment of what Latin Americans call an 'observatory', the role of which would be to gather data, undertake analyses of unfolding conjunctures, and disseminate this information via printed and electronic/web-based means. Observatories that monitor and analyse developments in their respective areas have emerged, especially since the second half of the 1990s, in a variety of national and multinational institutions such as Mercosur, the European Union, UNESCO, government departments, unions, NGOs, municipal and regional governments. Observatories have focused on both narrowly defined topics—developments in mass media and human rights—and broader issues such as the development of public policy and the tracking of economic, trade and immigration data on a regional scale.[21] An Australia-based and university-supported Latin American observatory would be able to assemble a group of scholars involved in monitoring developments, collecting data and providing evaluation on ongoing issues. The results of this work would be disseminated online as well as through the holding of regular regional and topical updates

---

21   Luis Albornoz and Micael Herschmann, 'La experiencia de los observatorios ibroamericanos en información, comunicación y cultura—balance de una breve trayectoria', *UNIrevista*, Vol. 1: No 3, July 2006.

that might inform and hopefully help shape policy in public and private sectors. Some of the developments mentioned in this chapter warrant particularly close attention from any social science observatory.

The 'Latinisation' of the United States is one of the most dramatic events of the post-WWII period. The Spanish-speaking community has now eclipsed African-Americans as the largest ethnic minority. In 2010, the Hispanic population of the United States reached 50.5 million, 16.3 per cent of the total population, of which the largest component by far comprised Mexican-Americans (31 million). And it is increasingly the case that the growth of Spanish-speakers is now being fuelled more by births than by immigration, both legal and undocumented. There are enormous implications flowing from this for the US economy; such domestic political pressures partly shape and constrain foreign policy choices, and these should be of interest to governments, investors and traders in Australia. But this phenomenon also has the potential to transfer the global character of US society and identity as well as reshape the relationship between the US and Latin America.[22] Today, more than ever, a focus on Latin America that excludes an examination of the spectacular growth of the Latin American population of the US would seriously handicap the work of policy analysis and decision-making.

Another topic of great significance is the emergence of indigenous issues and an enhanced sense of indigenous identity as well as greater indigenous activism and claims-making in Latin America. This is likely to continue growing and should provide a bridge to actors and stakeholders in Australia whose experiences and concerns—relating to development and to community involvement in environmental policy-making—parallel those of Latin American indigenous actors.

Other chapters in this book address some of the more familiar items that have long been on the agenda of those advocating closer relations between Australia and Latin America. In the education area, exports are likely to increase, although at a slow rate due to exchange rate problems caused by the rise of the Australian dollar (a tendency that was reversed in late 2013), and growing competition from countries such as the United States and the United Kingdom, which are experiencing cuts to government budget expenditure on higher education.

The challenges posed by the state of Australia's communications with Latin America have been an ever-present concern in discussions of Australia–Latin America relations since the 1980s. While air links with Chile and Argentina have

---

22   Pew Hispanic Center report, 14 July 2011, pewhispanic.org: 'The Mexican-American Boom: Births Overtake Immigration'; Paul Taylor and Mark Hugo López, 'Six Take-Aways from the Census Bureau's Voting Report', Pew Research Center, 8 May 2013.

improved substantially in the last decade, there are still no direct air services to Brazil and the termination of Qantas flights to Argentina in 2012 and Aerolíneas Argentinas flights in mid 2014 were deeply disappointing.

The scale of Australia's diplomatic representation in Latin America is also still modest. Although the re-establishment of an embassy in Peru was a welcome move, the number of embassies in Latin America remains the same as it did 30 years ago. This is a growing embarrassment when one takes into account the impressive growth in Latin American diplomatic representation in Australia at ambassadorial level. Most urgently, since Australia is a middle-level power, its relationship with Latin America necessarily involves it in dealing with at least three other middle-level powers—Mexico, Brazil and Argentina—and our diplomatic presence in, and overall engagement with these countries should be greatly strengthened. This is particularly urgent in the case of Brazil; as this chapter has argued in several places, there is a disturbing lack of fit between Brazil's current and likely future political, economic and diplomatic strength and Australia's insufficiently robust engagement with the Latin American giant.

References

Arashiro, Zuleika, *Negotiating the Free Trade Area of the Americas,* London: Palgrave Macmillan, 2011.

Becker, Marc, 'Correa, Indigenous Movements, and the Writing of a New Constitution in Ecuador', *Latin American Perspectives*, Vol. 38, 2011: 1, pp. 47–62.

Birns, Larry, 'Clinton Plays Hostess in a Failed Attempt to Mend US-Latin American Relations', *COHA News Release*, Washington DC, 28 May 2011.

Brazil–Turkey Nuclear Initiative (conference), Wilson Center (Washington DC), February 2011. http://www.wilsoncenter.org/index.cfm?fuseaction=events. event_summary&event_id=650768.

Bresser-Pereira, Luiz Carlos 'A Developmentalist United States', *Folha de São Paulo*, June 19, 2011.

Brookings Institute, 'Latin America's New Political Landscape and OAS' (summary) http://www.brookings.edu/events/2010/03/15-latin-america, accessed 5 October 2013.

Burges, Sean, *Brazilian Foreign Policy after the Cold War*, Gainesville: University Press of Florida, 2009.

Cárdenas, Mauricio, 'Transcript of meeting in 2010', *Latin American Initiative, Brookings Institute*, http://www.brookings.edu/~/media/Files/events/2010/0315_latin_america/20100315_latin_america.pdf, accessed 13 October 2013.

Council on Hemispheric Affairs (COHA) Research Memorandum, 'Strauss-Kahn's Visit to Latin America: A New Economic Policy?', 22 March 2011.

de Sousa Santos, Bonaventura, 'Las paradojas de nuestro tiempo y la Plurinacionalidad', pp. 21–62, in Alberto Acosta and Esperanza Martínez (eds), *Plurinacionalidad: Democracia en la diversidad*, Abya Yala: Quito, 2009.

Dosman, Edgar J., *The Life and Times of Raúl Prebisch, 1901–1986*, Montreal: McGill-Queen's University Press, 2008.

Edwards, Sebastian, *Left Behind: Latin America and the False Promise of Populism*, Chicago: University of Chicago Press, 2010.

Kingstone, Peter, *The Political Economy of Latin America: Reflections on Neoliberalism and Development*, London: Routledge, 2011.

Kozloff, Nikolas, *Revolution! South America and the Rise of the New Left*, London: Palgrave-Macmillan, 2008.

Love, Joseph, 'Raúl Prebisch and the Origins of the Doctrine of Unequal Exchange', *Latin American Research Review*, Vol. 15, 1980: pp. 45–72.

MercoPress, 'UNASUR Secretary General officially takes office May 9 in Guyana', *MercoPress: South Atlantic News Agency*, Montevideo, 30 April 2011. http://en.mercopress.com/2011/04/30/unasur-secretary-general-officially-takes-office-may-9-in-guyana, accessed 5 October 2013.

Mijeski, Kenneth J., and Scott H. Beck, 'The Electoral Fortunes of Ecuador's Pachakutik Party: The Fracaso of the 2006 Presidential Elections', *The Latin Americanist*, 52, June 2008: pp. 41–59.

Petras, James, and Henry Veltmeyer, *What's Left in Latin America? Regime Change in New Times*, Burlington, VT: Ashgate Publishing Co., 2009.

Pew Hispanic Center report, 'The Mexican-American Boom: Births Overtake Immigration', 14 July 2011, *pewhispanic.org*.

Robinson, William I., *Latin America and Global Capitalism: A Critical Globalization Perspective*, Baltimore: John Hopkins University Press, 2008.

————, *Transformative Possibilities in Latin America*, Global and International Studies: UC Santa Barbara, 2007.

Roett, Riordan, *The New Brazil*, Washington, DC: Brookings Institution Press, 2010.

Rohter, Larry, *Brazil On the Rise: The Story of a Country Transformed*, London: Palgrave Macmillan, 2010.

Taylor, Paul and Mark Hugo López, 'Six Take-Aways from the Census Bureau's Voting Report', Pew Research Center, 8 May 2013.

Weisbrot, Mark and David Rosnick, 'Another Lost Decade? Latin America's Growth Failure Continues into the 21st Century', Washington DC: CEPR, 13 November 2003.

Weyland, Kurt Gerhard, Raúl L. Madrid; Wendy Hunter (eds), *Leftist Governments in Latin America: Successes and Shortcomings*, Cambridge: Cambridge University Press, 2010.

Zamosc, Leon, 'The Indian Movement in Ecuador: from Politics of Influence to Politics of Power', pp. 131–57 in Nancy Grey Postero and Leon Zamosc (eds), *The Struggle for Indigenous Rights in Latin America*, Brighton, England: Sussex Academic Press, 2004.

Zibechi, Raul, 'Brazil as a Key Player', *CIP Americas Program Report*, 17 February 2010.

2. Australia–Latin America Education Relations

Sean W. Burges

One of the main challenges in building a solid relationship between Australia and Latin America is finding an area of convergence. The distances between the two areas are vast, the linguistic barriers significant, and the level of mutual knowledge and understanding small. At first blush matters are further complicated when attention is turned to economic questions, with Latin America and Australia appearing more as competitors than complementary actors in international natural resource and agricultural commodity markets. Bilateral flows of trade in goods are correspondingly small, further hampered by the logistical difficulties of travelling between the geographic areas by air or sea. The one sector that stands out as a potential champion of bilateral exchange is education, with Australia serving as an important destination for Latin Americans seeking formal qualifications and English language training.

The export of educational services is big business,[1] and particularly so for Australia.[2] In 2011–12 education was the country's third largest export sector, with over 515,000 students in 2012 bringing in $14.768 billion in revenue, down from $17.35 billion in 2009–10, and supporting over 125,000 jobs. Moreover, the government of Australia is clear that foreign students studying in Australia provide additional boons in the form of enriching the cultural context of Australian educational institutions and providing a pool of casual labour for the service industry.[3] Australia's decidedly commercial approach to the educational sector consequently holds mixed blessings for the deepening of inter-continental relations with Latin America. There is a demand in Latin America for access to higher education, vocational educational training (VET) and English language training (ELICOS), and Australia is viewed as an amenable destination or source for such activities. The issue is that educational relations

---

1   Simon Marginson, 'Dynamics of National and Global Competition in Higher Education', *Higher Education* 52, 2006: pp. 1–39; Philip G. Altbach and Jane Knight, 'The Internationalization of Higher Education: Motivations and Realities', *Journal of Studies in International Education* 11, 2007, (3/4): pp. 290–305; Rajani Naidoo, 'Repositioning Higher Education as a Global Commodity: Opportunities and Challenges for Future Sociology of Education Work', *British Journal of Sociology of Education* 24, 2003, (2): pp. 249–59.

2   Simon Marginson and Erlenawati Sawir, 'University Leaders' Strategies in the Global Environment: A Comparative Study of Universities Indonesia and The Australian National University', *Higher Education* 52, 2006: pp. 343–73.

3   Brendan Nelson, *Engaging the World through Education: Ministerial Statement on the Internationalisation of Australian Education and Training* (Canberra: Department of Education, Science and Training, Australian Government, 2003); Council of Australian Governments, *International Student Strategy for Australia, 2010-2014* (2010), http://www.coag.gov.au/reports/docs/aus_international_students_strategy.pdf: p. 5.

are currently framed and largely pursued as an implicit service provision arrangement, not as a partnership that sees a sustained and substantive flow of Australians heading to Latin America for educational training and collaborative research. As a consequence, education in its current form is a relatively shallow device for raising mutual awareness. If this form of educational relations persists, the existing Australian beachhead in Latin America might easily be lost should other OECD countries emerge as cost-effective, quality alternatives. Indeed, this is a concern that preoccupies the government of Australia and has resulted in a series of reviews and strategies, most recently with the release of the *International Student Strategy for Australia, 2010–2014* that has sought to improve quality assurance and boost international marketing strategies. Such initiatives are necessary, particularly when attention is turned to the explicit efforts by countries such as the UK to use foreign student fees as an anchor to maintain national university systems that are being heavily impacted by post-Global Financial Crisis budget cuts.[4] Moreover, recent declines in education export earnings from 2009–13 suggest that the Australian government should be concerned about declining global market share and the core attractiveness of the Australian brand.

This chapter will focus on the nature of Australia–Latin America educational relations. Attention will first be turned to the factors underpinning trade in educational services as well as academic exchange, pointing to two different sets of motivations. For Australia, the driving factors are a combination of explicit attempts to boost national export income from services and attempts to develop some measure of soft power connection with Latin America. The corresponding push from Latin America is more focused on development priorities, concentrating on the acquisition of the skills and knowledge necessary to grow national economies sustainably and exploit international opportunities. Overarching these different motivations are transnational economic pressures, particularly from the resource extraction industries that dominate both regions. The second section of the chapter will map out the results, tracing the changing levels of Australian educational exports. Finally, the third section will explore the challenges and opportunities in the Australia-Latin America educational relationship.

---

4   Daniel Boffey, 'British bid to attract 10,000 Brazilian students', *The Observer*, 10 July 2011.

Latin American recruitment

As noted above, trade in educational services is big business and Latin America is a growing market for Australia.[5] The export of Australian educational services to the region has surged over the last decade, rising from $155 million in 2002–03 to a high of $824 million in 2009–10, and then down to a post-GFC level of $755 million in 2011–2012. As Table 2.1 sets out, growth in Australia's Latin American income far outpaces the global rate, which rose from $6.6 billion in 2002–3 to $18.5 billion in 2009–10, before fading to $14.7 billion in 2011–12. While the Latin American share in the overall Australian educational export totals remains comparatively small, it has grown from 2.3 per cent at the beginning of the period to 5.1 per cent at the end. This growth is not accidental, reflecting a conscious push by private firms, universities and the Australian government to recruit more students from the region.

Over the last quarter-century the Australian government has become increasingly aware that educational services are an important part of the country's export picture, and one that could be grown with judicious policy assistance. In his October 2003 policy statement 'Engaging the World through Education', then Minister for Education, Science and Training Brendan Nelson mapped out an internationally engaged vision for the Australian education sector.[6] In what was to become the model for future policies, Nelson emphasised two crucial priorities within the government's larger plans. First, a great deal of emphasis was placed on ensuring the quality of Australian education, strengthening the regulatory and oversight frameworks necessary to ensure that the Australian Qualifications Framework (AQF) would be internationally respected as a benchmark for quality academic and vocational training.[7] Second, resources were channelled into the international arm of the Department of Education, Employment and Workplace Relations (DEEWR), Australia Education International (AEI), to work with Austrade not only to promote greater student numbers, but also to encourage market diversification. Of particular relevance for this chapter was the 2003–04 Commonwealth Budget funding provision for Latin American offices—first in Chile (2004) and then in Brazil (2005) after a visit by Minister Nelson—managed by an Australian-based diplomat.[8]

---

5   In this paper the Reserve Bank of Australia's definition of educational services is used: 'Exports of education services can be delivered either offshore (by the internet, correspondence or Australian professionals travelling overseas) or onshore (by foreign students entering Australia for the purpose of study).' http://www.rba.gov.au/publications/bulletin/2008/jun/pdf/bu-0608-2.pdf.

6   Brendan Nelson, *Engaging the World through Education*, op. cit., note 3.

7   Ann Doolette, 'Australian Qualifications Framework', Powerpoint Presentation to the 2010 COALAR–EAG Roundtable, Canberra, 10 September 2010.

8   Wendy Katherine Jarvie, 'Latin America: Opportunities and Risks in Education', *Global Education News, Australia*, 13 April 2011: www.austrade.gov.au/export_markets/industries/education/enewsletter.

Table 2.1: Australian educational services exports ($ millions)

Countries	2002–03	2003–04	2004–05	2005–06	2006–07	2007–08	2008–09	2009–10	2010–11	2011–12
Argentina	5	4	4	4	5	6	6	8	8	8
Bolivia	1	-	1	-	-	-	1	1	1	1
Brazil	74	81	111	175	234	311	414	401	331	318
Chile	3	5	6	10	18	25	38	51	52	60
Colombia	48	43	40	55	100	168	242	277	227	232
Cuba	-	-	-	-	-	-	1	-	-	-
Ecuador	1	2	2	2	3	3	4	5	5	6
El Salvador	-	-	1	1	1	1	2	3	3	3
Guatemala	-	-	-	-	-	-	1	1	1	1
Mexico	15	20	25	26	33	38	39	42	41	42
Panama	-	-	1	-	-	1	1	1	1	1
Paraguay	-	1	-	1	1	1	1	1	-	-
Peru	3	4	6	11	22	40	60	71	59	50
Uruguay	-	1	1	1	1	1	1	1	1	1
Venezuela	5	4	4	4	5	8	13	20	28	32
Latin Am total ($m)	155	165	202	290	423	603	824	883	758	755
Global total ($m)	6,638	7,767	8,743	9,745	11,109	13,536	16,735	18,507	15,510	14,768
Latin Am % of world	2.3	2.1	2.3	3.0	3.8	4.5	4.9	4.8	4.9	5.1

Source: Australian Bureau of Statistics, *International Trade in Services, by Country, by State and by Detailed Services Category, Financial Year, 2011–12* (ABS Catalogue no. 5368.0.55.003): Table 9.4.

The work being undertaken by the Department of Eduation, Science and Training (DEST) and AEI was paralleled by a more general sense that the Americas should probably be receiving more attention from policy-makers. A central coordinating mechanism for Australia's push to increase engagement with Latin America is the Department of Foreign Affairs and Trade's Council on Australia Latin America Relations (COALAR), which was formed in 2001. One of the outcomes of a March 2003 COALAR-funded education symposium was the decision to launch the Council's Education Action Group (COALAR-EAG) and provide seed funding for a research project by Australia Education International that sought to identify opportunities for the export of educational services to Latin America.[9] This reflected the general pattern of cooperation that would emerge between DEST and its successor ministry, the Department of Education, Employment and Workplace Relations. The marketing of Australian educational opportunities would be chiefly driven by a blend of AEI, DEST/DEEWR and Austrade, while the COALAR-EAG would focus its efforts on facilitating and funding fact-finding missions and exchanges to strengthen inter-institutional links. A succession of visits built upon this institutional framework, with senior delegations from Australia travelling to Mexico and Chile to highlight Australian expertise and gain an understanding of the requirements of those two countries. A reciprocal visit from Mexican Minister of Education Dr Reyes S. Tamez Guerra resulted in Australia being listed as a priority destination for Mexican study abroad schemes.[10]

One of the benefits that COALAR brought to the education file was its ability to arrange crosswalks between different areas. Of particular note were the efforts in 2004–05 to start exploring opportunities for the provision of vocational and professional training in the mining and mineral industry by promoting the possibilities inherent in the Australian Qualifications Framework. These efforts were further supported by a series of governmental and educational peak body delegations from Brazil, Chile and Colombia seeking a better understanding of how the Australian training system and qualification certification scheme worked and what sort of synergies might be available. The impact was noticed by Chilean and Colombian officials, with both countries regularly referring to the AQF program as a model for the sorts of systems they were seeking to construct in their respective countries.[11] The COALAR-EAG contributed to this process through an analysis of higher education enrolment numbers, which were declining, and the decision to formulate a strategy to reinvigorate the flow of Latin American students to Australia.[12]

---

9 Council on Australia Latin America Relations, *Annual Report 1 July 2000–30 June 2004*, Canberra: Department of Foreign Affairs and Trade: p. 10.

10 Council on Australia Latin America Relations, *Annual Report, 2004–2005*, Canberra: Department of Foreign Affairs and Trade, p. 19.

11 Jarvie, 'Latin America', *op. cit.*, note 7.

12 Council on Australia Latin America Relations, *Annual Report, 2005–2006*, Canberra: Department of Foreign Affairs and Trade, pp. 8–10.

By 2008 some of the strategic sheen had come off the COALAR–EAG's programming, with activities shifting more to the encouragement of direct bilateral links through the funding of a series of study trips and visiting fellowship schemes designed to bring Latin American scholars and officials to Australia. In part this amounted to recognising that the mission had been accomplished. Education-related official Australian government representation in Latin America had received a boost by the 2008–09 fiscal year, with the full operation of DEEWR's AEI offices in Chile, and Mexico, which were overseen by a DEEWR officer located in Santiago, Chile.[13] Conceptions of the type of soft power seen in the British Chevening and US Fulbright scholarship scheme also began to appear in the Australian framework.[14] An initial scholarship program designed to bring foreigners to Australia was launched through DEEWR and then combined with AusAID programming in 2010 to create the 'Australia Awards'. Over $200 million was committed annually to bring 5,000 students and professionals to Australia for additional training as well as help Australians travel to other parts of the world for education.[15]

The re-launch of Australia's overseas scholarship programs under the unified banner of the Australia Awards dove-tailed nicely with a growing awareness in the more advanced Latin American economies that the region was facing a desperate need for technical skills and scientific capacity.[16] Indeed, the situation facing major resource extraction companies was sufficiently severe that Brazilian multinational energy corporation Petrobras set up its own university in Rio de Janeiro, and firms such as Eletrobras—a substantial Brazilian power utility—began unilaterally offering training programs to technical officials in Bolivian and Paraguayan utility companies.[17] For its part, Australia focused on being named as a preferred destination for such scholarship programs as Chile's Becas Chile, Colombia's COLFUTURO and Mexico's Becas SEP–Australia. Targeting of these scholarship programs combined with a flurry of memoranda of understanding and the presence of Australian educational trade representatives in Lima, Mexico City, Santiago and São Paulo to create the rapid rise in educational exports to Peru, Mexico, Chile and Brazil seen in Table 2.1.

To this point the focus has been almost exclusively on the idea of market penetration, of capturing Latin American training opportunities for Australian

---

13   Council on Australia Latin America Relations, *Annual Report, 2008–2009*, Canberra: Department of Foreign Affairs and Trade, p. 10.

14   Joseph S. Nye Jr., *The Paradox of American Power*, Oxford: Oxford University Press, 2002: pp. 71–4.

15   http://www.australiaawards.gov.au/about.html, accessed 30 May 2011.

16   Stela Meneghel, Debora Mello, Erasmo Gomes and Sandra Brisolla, 'The University–Industry Relationship in Brazil: Trends and Implications for University Management', *International Journal of Technology Management & Sustainable Development* 2 (3), 2004: pp. 173–90.

17   Glauber Gonçalves, 'Pré-sal provoca boom de cursos de petróleo', 2010; *O Estado de São Paulo*, 20 June 2010; Nicola Pamplona, 'Um 'Vale do Sílico' para o pré-sal', *O Estado de São Paulo*, 7 March 2010; 'Estatal investe para renovar quadro', *O Estado de São Paulo*, 1 November 2010.

educational service providers. While this aspect certainly dominates in the annual reports from COALAR and the communications issued by the COALAR-EAG, there were parallel efforts to encourage collaborative research and exchange of students, which in part explains the flurry of memoranda of understanding. Between 2004 and 2009 the number of inter-university MOUs linking Australia and Latin America grew from 80 to 230.[18] Unfortunately, the reality has been that while government-to-government agreements make for nice press conferences and MOUs are a good line for university annual reports, they have a poorer history of translating into concrete scholarly collaboration and student exchange. Although there has been a rise in Australian students travelling to Latin America for study, this is largely accounted for by the popularity boom that Spanish is experiencing as a second language in Australian schools and universities. The innovative International Studies program at the University of Technology Sydney,[19] which sends students in a wide range of disciplines overseas and to Latin America for an extended period of study, remains very much the exception rather than the norm. In part the issue is that even institution-to-institution agreements provide only a weak basis for concrete collaborative projects. Effective collaboration almost always requires active engagement and involvement from individual researchers, which in turn requires mutual awareness and outreach that perforce would require a rise in the number of Australian-based researchers seeking out knowledge and collaboration opportunities in the Americas. While this latter aspect is improving, partly due to Australian government encouragement, progress is slow and will take some time as general awareness of the possibilities of cooperation grows beyond the small group of scholars currently engaged in collaboration with Latin American colleagues due to regional specialisations or because they happen to have personal links to the region.

Recruitment results

As it stands, the trade in educational services is very much a one-way flow. The figures in Table 2.2 point to a massive Australian educational trade surplus with Latin America, with little going on in the way of study-abroad programs that operate outside of the area of language instruction. The challenge is thus to get individual researchers collaborating with their counterparts, something that the Australia Awards program is intended to address. Increased Australian interest in the Americas, captured most notably through the 2012 launch of a Bachelor in Latin American Studies at The Australian National University, is slowly creating the grounds for something other than a commercial relationship. As the trade figures highlight, this evolution will be a slow process, but one that will be supported by the surge in enrolment numbers and student visits to Australia.

---

18   Jarvie, 'Latin America', *op. cit.*, note 7.
19   UTS, 'International Studies', http://www.internationalstudies.uts.edu.au/, accessed 23 October 2013.

Table 2.2: Australian educational service imports ($ millions)

Countries	2002–03	2003–04	2004–05	2005–06	2006–07	2007–08	2008–09	2009–10	2010–11	2011–12
Argentina	-	2	-	2	2	2	4	2	3	2
Bolivia	-	1	-	-	-	-	-	-	-	-
Brazil	2	2	1	1	-	1	1	1	-	-
Chile	1	-	1	1	2	1	1	2	2	-
Colombia	-	-	-	-	-	2	-	1	-	1
Costa Rica	-	-	1	1	1	-	-	1	1	1
Cuba	1	1	-	-	1	-	-	-	-	-
Dominican Republic	-	-	-	-	-	-	1	-	-	-
Ecuador	-	-	-	1	-	-	-	-	0	1
El Salvador	-	-	-	-	-	-	-	-	-	-
Guatemala	-	-	-	-	-	-	-	-	-	-
Honduras	1	1	-	-	-	-	1	-	-	1
Mexico	2	1	3	2	4	3	2	2	2	2
Nicaragua	-	-	-	-	-	-	-	-	-	-
Panama	1	-	1	-	-	-	-	-	-	-
Paraguay	-	-	-	-	-	-	1	-	-	-
Peru	2	1	-	1	1	-	1	1	1	3
Puerto Rico	-	-	-	-	1	-	-	-	-	-
Uruguay	1	-	-	-	-	1	-	-	-	-
Venezuela	-	-	-	-	-	-	-	-	1	-
Latin American total	11	8	7	9	11	10	12	10	10	11
World	**654**	**698**	**702**	**741**	**780**	**846**	**829**	**878**	**914**	**977**

Source: Australian Bureau of Statistics, *International Trade in Services, by Country, by State and by Detailed Services Category, Financial Year, 2009–10* (ABS Catalogue no. 5368.0.55.003): Table 10.4.

Table 2.3: Total educational visa grants, 2005–2012

	2005–2006	2006–2007	2007–2008	2008–2009	2009–2010	2010–2011	2011–2012
Argentina	102	129	112	141	216	201	226
Bolivia	11	14	10	22	21	16	17
Brazil	6,679	8,219	11,096	12,609	11,444	9,780	9,697
Chile	401	624	768	1,300	1,294	1,356	1,373
Colombia	1,663	3,294	4,951	5,954	6,312	5,055	5,716
Costa Rica	0	17	10	13	24	9	20
Cuba	0	3	7	2	6	14	9
Dom. Rep.	2	3	11	98	4	5	9
Ecuador	50	61	75	45	110	100	176
El Salvador	15	11	23	45	71	50	50
Guatemala	6	10	10	17	12	11	26
Honduras	5	5	7	2	5	4	6
Mexico	835	1,037	1,104	1,115	1,146	1,063	1,094
Nicaragua	3	0	3	4	3	3	8
Panama	10	7	13	19	6	12	12
Paraguay	18	18	16	9	11	9	20
Peru	350	590	1,009	1,326	1,166	916	851
Uruguay	21	19	20	24	20	18	25
Venezuela	97	134	278	352	578	721	573
Lat Am. totals	10,268	14,195	19,523	23,097	22,449	19,126	19,665
World totals	**186,099**	**223,988**	**273,663**	**316,287**	**265,647**	**250,438**	**253,046**
Latin America as % of total	5.5%	6.3%	7.1%	7.3%	8.5%	7.6%	7.8%

Source: Department of Immigration and Citizenship, Student Visa Grants by Sector and Country: http://www.immi.gov.au/media/statistics/study/.

The most accurate way to get a sense of how many foreign students are coming to Australia and what sort of educational path they are following is to track a mix of visa grant data from the Department of Immigration and Citizenship and enrolment and actual commencement data from Australia Education International. Similar data for Australians travelling to Latin America is not available. As Table 2.3 highlights, the absolute numbers of Latin Americans seeking Australian visas for educational pursuits has increased over the five years 2005–11 and the Latin American proportion of the total has risen as well. From a starting point of 10,268 visa grants in 2005–06, the number rose to a high of 22,449 in 2009–10, representing a shift from 5.5 per cent to 8.5 per cent of the total number of visas issued, before dropping to 19,655 in 2011–12 and 7.8 per cent of the total issued. Of particular importance for validation of the export promotion strategies outlined above is the pattern of where these students came from. Recruitment efforts in Brazil, Chile, Colombia and Peru paid particularly handsome dividends, contributing a substantial proportion of the more than doubling of student flows over the time period (Table 2.5a and 2.5b). Careful work in Colombia stands out in particular, prompting a near four-fold rise, followed by the near tripling of numbers from Chile and Peru. While some of the rise can be attributed to the surging economic growth these four countries experienced as a result of the global commodities boom, the underlying reality is that Australia is not the automatic focus of attention in Latin America, suggesting that the recruitment strategies were beneficial.

Table 2.4a: Latin American enrolments by educational sector (2002–2008)

	2002		2004		2006		2008	
	Number	% of total	Number	% of total	Number	% of total	Number	% of total
Higher education	1,510	19.1%	1,949	23.8%	1,964	12.3%	2,460	8.6%
ELICOS	3,472	43.9%	3,199	39.0%	8,454	53.1%	16,592	57.9%
VET	2,196	27.7%	2,179	26.6%	4,442	27.9%	8,668	30.2%
Other	738	9.3%	867	10.6%	1,072	6.7%	942	3.3%
Total	7,916	100.0%	8,194	100.0%	15,932	100.0%	28,662	100.0%

Source: https://aei.gov.au/research/International-Student-Data/Documents/INTERNATIONAL%20 STUDENT%20DATA/2010/2010_basic_pivot_all.zip.

Table 2.4b: Latin American enrolments by educational sector (2009–2012)

	2009		2010		2011		2012	
	Number	% of total	Number	% of total	Number	% of total	Number	% of total
Higher education	3,030	8.9%	3,609	10.8%	3,883	12.3%	4,044	12.5%
ELICOS	19,867	58.5%	18,351	55.2%	16,987	53.9%	18,156	56.2%
VET	9,998	29.4%	10,403	31.3%	9,785	31.1%	9,049	28.0%
Other	1,057	3.1%	901	2.7%	858	2.7%	1,049	3.2%
Total	33,952	100.0%	33,264	100.0%	31,513	100.0%	32,298	100.0%

Source: https://aei.gov.au/research/International-Student-Data/Documents/INTERNATIONAL%20 STUDENT%20DATA/2010/2010_basic_pivot_all.zip.

Table 2.5a: Total Education program enrolment and commencement (2002–2008)

	2002		2004		2006		2008	
	Enrolled	Started	Enrolled	Started	Enrolled	Started	Enrolled	Started
Argentina	202	120	144	65	138	84	174	105
Bolivia	22	12	7	3	16	11	14	8
Brazil	4,214	3,169	4,702	3,473	10,080	7,612	15,925	11,888
Chile	144	105	256	187	539	416	1,017	787
Colombia	2,296	1,354	1,570	781	2,995	2,168	7,680	5,530
Costa Rica	15	10	10	2	5	0	13	8
Cuba					2	1	7	5
Dom. Rep.	4	2	8	4	5	5	9	5
Ecuador	57	30	70	35	81	54	128	84
El Salvador	11	8	17	9	25	12	36	24
Guatemala	5	2	9	6	9	5	16	11
Honduras	5	3	3	1	6	3	8	2
Mexico	572	419	1,015	657	1,240	866	1,466	982
Nicaragua	3	2	3	0	3	2	6	5
Panama	14	11	9	5	11	4	23	12
Paraguay	8	5	13	9	19	13	22	19
Peru	118	61	168	108	570	412	1,705	1,180
Uruguay	9	5	28	17	20	11	21	13
Venezuela	217	113	162	77	168	104	392	275
Latin Am. total	7,916	5,431	8,194	5,439	15,932	11,783	28,662	20,943
World total	**273,702**	**160,332**	**323,979**	**175,391**	**379,939**	**207,137**	**541,587**	**323,321**
Latin Am. as % of World total	2.9%	3.4%	2.5%	3.1%	4.2%	5.7%	5.3%	6.5%
Latin Am. start as % of enrolled		68.6%		66.4%		74.0%		59.7%
World start as % of enrolled		58.6%		54.1%		54.5%		59.7%

Source: https://aei.gov.au/research/International-Student-Data/Documents/INTERNATIONAL%20 STUDENT%20DATA/2010/2010_basic_pivot_all.zip.

Table 2.5b: Total Education program enrolment and commencement (2009–2012)

	2009		2010		2011		2012	
	Enrolled	Started	Enrolled	Started	Enrolled	Started	Enrolled	Started
Argentina	207	139	267	184	279	188	280	188
Bolivia	23	15	29	20	26	15	25	15
Brazil	17,558	12,598	16,072	11,826	15,266	11,306	15,092	11,207
Chile	1,608	1,229	1,715	1,182	1,972	1,399	2,005	1,324
Colombia	9,861	6,944	10,034	6,846	8,917	6,284	10,148	7,477
Costa Rica	11	5	28	22	22	9	31	20
Cuba	14	9	4	0	12	8	11	6
Dom. Rep.	6	1	6	4	8	7	7	3
Ecuador	169	115	192	113	171	105	274	206
El Salvador	76	55	106	73	98	59	77	55
Guatemala	26	19	28	15	21	14	13	5
Honduras	7	3	5	2	10	6	9	8
Mexico	1,534	1,079	1,576	1,124	1,586	1,070	1,568	1,047
Nicaragua	7	4	6	3	3	1	0	0
Panama	25	17	24	18	18	7	15	9
Paraguay	9	4	13	7	11	7	12	6
Peru	2,248	1,510	2,270	1,471	1,985	1,258	1,773	1,159
Uruguay	26	16	26	21	32	20	26	17
Venezuela	537	383	867	634	1,076	736	931	535
Latin Am total	33,952	24,145	33,268	23,565	31,513	22,499	32,297	23,287
World total	630,630	364,087	619,119	329,352	554359	295,928	515,853	279,335
Latin Am as % of World total	5.4%	6.6%	5.4%	7.2%	5.7%	7.6%	6.3%	8.3%
Latin Am start as % of enrolled		71.1%		70.8%		71.4%		72.1%
World start as % of enrolled		57.7%		53.2%		53.4%		54.2%

Source: https://aei.gov.au/research/International-Student-Data/Documents/INTERNATIONAL%20 STUDENT%20DATA/2010/2010_basic_pivot_all.zip.

As has been noted above, one of the overarching characteristics of Australian educational engagement with Latin America is its commercial nature. This does not necessarily fit well with the rhetoric of collaboration, exchange and mutual learning that forms the soft power core of official Australian government rhetoric on inter-continental educational relations, which is generally framed around conceptions of post-secondary education in pursuit of undergraduate and graduate university degrees. Similarly, the public and repeated promises of collaboration from a number of leading Australian research university heads have yet to be backed with the resources to kick-start necessary researcher-to-researcher links. The rationale for the disjuncture between the rhetoric and reality is made clear in Table 2.4a and 2.4b.[20] Although Australia is home to a number of world-class universities, university education has declined in relative significance in terms of Latin American enrolments despite rising in absolute terms. While higher education enrolment numbers have risen from 1,510 in 2002 to 4,044 in 2012, the relative share of university students as a proportion of the Latin American student body in Australia has fallen from 19.1 per cent to 12.5 per cent. During this same period enrolments in ELICOS programs have soared from 3,472 to 18,156, moving from a 43.9 per cent to 56.2 per cent share of the total number of Latin American students in Australia. Vocational training has seen similarly impressive gross number gains, going from 2,196 enrolled students in 2002 to a high of 10,403 in 2010, before receding to 9,049 in 2012, marking a steady proportion of about 28 per cent of students.

While all three of the major educational visa categories have seen huge gains, reflecting a 408 per cent increase in enrolments, by far the largest gains have come in the ELICOS sector. This is partially a reflection of three factors motivating Latin American educational travel. The first is a desire to acquire English language skills. Second is distaste for the cultural marginalisation that occurs in parts of Europe and the United States, where Latin Americans can be pejoratively dismissed as 'Latinos'. More important in this context is the relatively greater difficulty of getting away from Spanish and Spanish-speaking communities in significant portions of the United States. The smaller Latin American and Iberian community in Australia means that there is little in the way of cultural and class-based preconceptions and even less pressure to continue using Spanish or Portuguese. These factors are reinforced by the third, namely the widespread availability of well-paid part-time work in Australia and the provisions in Australian visa regulations that allow for a considerable amount of part-time employment, which is partially offset by the

---

20   While all data presented here is from the Australian government's Australia Education International database, there are several critical weaknesses that must be highlighted. First, data for the 2010 academic year was only available through to September, and thus has not been included in the discussion because it would not provide an accurate portrait of trends and developments. Second, AEI releases enrolment and commencement data in a complex 'pivot' table for Microsoft Excel. Unfortunately, an error appears to have been made in the construction of the table's underlying formula. When 'all months' is selected, the total presented is the sum of the cumulative total for each month, which means that January is counted twelve times, February eleven times, March ten times, and so on. To avoid grossly inflated and inaccurate numbers, this chapter makes use of the data for December of each year as representative of the entire academic year in question.

higher cost of living. Employment possibilities are an important consideration for individuals who may not have sufficient funds saved to cover the entire cost of their educational program.

Two items are critical to attendance at overseas universities: cost and access to visas. As Table 2.6a and 2.6b highlights, it is in precisely those Latin American countries possessing either rapid economic growth rates or strong scholarship schemes that Australian universities have most successfully recruited students. Expressed as a percentage of total foreign higher education students actively studying in Australia, Latin America remains small at two per cent in 2012, marginally up in proportional terms from 1.5 per cent in 2002. In absolute terms the change has been a more substantial doubling in numbers, going from 865 to 1,795 students. The most rapid substantive growth has occurred in those countries where DEST/DEEWR has educational trade missions and where the Australian government has directed its assistance for international education fairs.[21] Chile, Colombia and Mexico have been the drivers of the growth in numbers. Colombia has emerged as a particularly significant source of students thanks to a mixture of aggressive recruiting and the growth of the COLFUTURO scholarship program. Chile's rapid growth reflects increased efforts by the Chilean government to have its students spend a period of time overseas, which was reiterated in 2011 through a memorandum of understanding between the Australia Group of Eight Universities and the University of Chile to promote collaborative research, commercialisation of research and consulting, and mutual recognition of qualifications.[22] Increases in Mexican numbers stem from sustained efforts to strengthen inter-governmental and inter-institutional linkages around 2004–05. While Brazilian numbers have grown, the rate has been less than might be expected given the economic growth the country has experienced. In large part this is explained by the bureaucratic difficulties of getting Brazilian accreditation bodies to recognise foreign degrees, including those from major Australian, UK and US universities.

21   'Primera Feria Educativa Latino Australia Education', *El Tiempo* (Colombia), 2 September 2010; 'Estudar no exterior é tema de três eventos', *Folha de São Paulo*, 30 August 2009.

22   Group of Eight, *Memorandum of Understanding between the Council of Rectors of Chilean Universities and the Group of Eight, Australia*, Canberra, 2011: http://www.go8.edu.au/__documents/university-staff/international-collaboration/go8-chile_mou.pdf, accessed 30 May 2011.

Table 2.6a: Higher education (2002–2008)

	2002		2004		2006		2008	
	Enrolled	Started	Enrolled	Started	Enrolled	Started	Enrolled	Started
Argentina	90	49	98	35	63	24	63	22
Bolivia	12	7	4	1	5	1	3	0
Brazil	393	225	426	173	461	217	583	299
Chile	42	26	90	46	135	72	180	105
Colombia	614	363	677	249	575	238	732	383
Costa Rica	8	4	6	1	2	0	8	4
Cuba					2	1	4	2
Dom. Rep.	1	0	2	1	4	4	5	2
Ecuador	22	14	37	16	30	16	48	24
El Salvador	5	4	6	0	8	2	7	4
Guatemala	2	0	4	3	7	3	5	3
Honduras	2	2	2	0	4	2	5	1
Mexico	212	121	399	187	384	178	413	192
Nicaragua	2	1	3	0	0	0	0	0
Panama	1	1	5	4	7	2	7	1
Paraguay	1	1	2	1	4	0	3	1
Peru	37	17	83	51	206	116	304	127
Uruguay	5	2	9	7	6	1	5	3
Venezuela	61	28	96	47	61	22	85	48
Latin Am. total	1,510	865	1,949	822	1,964	899	2,460	1,221
World total	115,405	56,680	150,748	65,136	169,599	66,345	181,412	77,427
Latin Am. as % of world total	1.3%	1.5%	1.3%	1.3%	1.2%	1.4%	1.4%	1.6%
Latin Am. start as % of enrolled		57.3%		42.2%		45.8%		42.7%
World start as % of enrolled		49.1%		43.2%		39.1%		42.7%

Source: https://aei.gov.au/research/International-Student-Data/Documents/INTERNATIONAL%20 STUDENT%20DATA/2010/2010_basic_pivot_all.zip.

Table 2.6b: Higher education (2009-2012)

	2009		2010		2011		2012	
	Enrolled	Started	Enrolled	Started	Enrolled	Started	Enrolled	Started
Argentina	74	35	75	31	79	34	91	42
Bolivia	3	1	8	6	11	5	12	6
Brazil	690	343	762	361	762	320	755	318
Chile	335	252	440	213	506	233	508	217
Colombia	899	495	1,116	605	1,234	611	1,312	595
Costa Rica	6	2	15	11	14	3	15	6
Cuba	4	1	0	0	4	2	5	1
Dom. Rep.	3	0	1	0	3	3	5	2
Ecuador	49	23	84	44	79	33	134	90
El Salvador	7	1	6	1	9	5	17	13
Guatemala	13	11	13	3	8	3	7	2
Honduras	4	2	2	0	4	1	3	2
Mexico	470	239	539	260	563	252	584	243
Nicaragua	0	0	1	0	0	0	0	0
Panama	6	1	3	2	3	1	5	3
Paraguay	4	2	4	1	4	2	5	2
Peru	334	162	327	132	300	114	274	129
Uruguay	8	5	10	7	8	2	5	1
Venezuela	121	69	203	120	292	164	307	123
Latin Am. total	3,030	1,644	3,609	1,797	3,883	1,788	4,044	1,795
World total	**202,314**	**88,454**	**243,591**	**102,538**	**241,181**	**95,406**	**230,923**	**89,326**
Latin Am. as % of world total	1.5%	1.9%	1.5%	1.8%	1.6%	1.9%	1.8%	2.0%
Latin Am. start as % of enrolled		54.3%		49.8%		46.0%		44.4%
World start as % of enrolled		43.7%		42.1%		39.6%		38.7%

Source: https://aei.gov.au/research/International-Student-Data/Documents/INTERNATIONAL%20 STUDENT%20DATA/2010/2010_basic_pivot_all.zip.

An interesting aspect of Table 2.6a and 2.6b is the extent to which Latin American uptake of Australian higher education visas continued throughout the global financial crisis, a period marked by a decline in numbers from other parts of the world. In part this represents value for money. Despite the higher international fees and the cost of living in Australia, the sum total still remains less than that of an equivalent university education in a leading US or British university. Moreover, the second critical aspect—visas—is also an important factor. Indeed, the visa question is a policy research area in its own right, with Australian immigration and visa procedures being nearly universally held up by Latin Americans as burdensome, expensive, demeaning and insulting. To put it in context, Australia's list of electronic travel authority eligible countries does not include a single Latin American nation. The saving grace for Australia on the visa front is that competing education providers such as Britain, Canada and the United States have similarly exclusionary immigration procedures in place. When combined with the cost factor this has helped push students towards Australia. Climatic considerations also matter, with the range of temperatures and lifestyle in Australia's major cities paralleling those found in cities such as Bogotá, Santiago and São Paulo.

The pattern of student recruitment being concentrated in the small group of countries with an Australian trade mission is repeated in the pattern of granted ELICOS visas. As Table 2.7a and 2.7b highlight, Latin Americans as a percentage of total ELICOS participants jumped five-fold from 2002 to 2012, going from 2,741 to 14,551. This compares to numbers for global ELICOS participation that grew two-fold through 2012. Global numbers grew from 42,118 in 2002 to 105,877 in 2009, dropping to 75,377 in 2012 after the global financial crisis. Again, Latin American students were predominantly drawn from the wealthier countries of Brazil, Chile, Colombia and Mexico. The increase in the number of Peruvians during the period surveyed in the table highlights the linkage to the importance of growing disposable income in the source country. In all cases the growth in numbers corresponds with consolidated economic stabilisation and the trickle-through of the commodity boom. As a number of observers in Brasília reiterated, Australia may be far, but it is still relatively cost-effective compared to Britain and the climate in Queensland is very similar to that along Brazil's coast. The potential for comparatively well-paid part-time work as well as the proximity to Asia also emerge as positive factors for students who wish to extend their study into work-visit periods.[23]

---

23 Fred Hilmer, 'The Dumb Blonde of International Education', *The Australian*, 1 November 2010, p. 14.

Table 2.7a: ELICOS (2002–2008)

	2002		2004		2006		2008	
	Enrolled	Started	Enrolled	Started	Enrolled	Started	Enrolled	Started
Argentina	53	39	21	14	41	33	56	43
Bolivia	8	4	2	1	4	3	7	6
Brazil	2,222	1,876	2,301	1,936	5,668	4,615	9,673	7,929
Chile	54	43	105	90	296	253	563	471
Colombia	846	575	459	332	1,736	1,441	4,622	3,591
Costa Rica	1	1	0	0	1	0	1	1
Cuba					0	0	2	2
Dom. Rep.	1	0	4	3	1	1	1	0
Ecuador	18	10	20	14	32	27	46	36
El Salvador	4	2	2	2	5	3	16	14
Guatemala	1	0	1	1	1	1	3	2
Honduras	1	1	0	0	0	0	0	0
Mexico	153	123	191	151	337	267	441	325
Nicaragua	0	0	0	0	2	1	5	4
Panama	6	4	0	0	1	1	14	10
Paraguay	4	3	7	6	12	11	11	10
Peru	27	15	44	37	239	195	904	723
Uruguay	1	1	9	4	7	6	7	5
Venezuela	72	44	33	18	71	59	220	158
Latin Am. total	3,472	2,741	3,199	2,609	8,454	6,917	16,592	13,330
World total	**57,452**	**42,118**	**61,743**	**45,371**	**76,905**	**59,127**	**127,206**	**100,737**
Latin Am. as % of world total	6.0%	6.5%	5.2%	5.8%	11.0%	11.7%	13.0%	13.2%
Latin Am. start as % of enrolled		78.9%		81.6%		81.8%		79.2%
World start as % of enrolled		73.3%		73.5%		76.9%		79.2%

Source: https://aei.gov.au/research/International-Student-Data/Documents/INTERNATIONAL%20 STUDENT%20DATA/2010/2010_basic_pivot_all.zip.

Table 2.7b: ELICOS (2009–2012)

	2009		2010		2011		2012	
	Enrolled	Started	Enrolled	Started	Enrolled	Started	Enrolled	Started
Argentina	70	59	90	77	91	76	84	82
Bolivia	13	10	13	8	9	6	7	5
Brazil	10,502	8,197	9,081	7,329	8,627	6,946	8,556	6,831
Chile	907	732	860	677	984	809	974	753
Colombia	6,380	5,056	6,206	4,592	5,449	4,345	6,921	5,662
Costa Rica	1	0	5	5	6	4	10	9
Cuba	7	6	3	0	7	5	6	5
Dom. Rep.	0	0	1	1	3	2	1	0
Ecuador	75	59	64	41	48	36	90	76
El Salvador	45	36	54	38	42	30	23	18
Guatemala	3	2	6	5	5	3	4	2
Honduras	0	0	2	2	2	2	2	2
Mexico	401	312	436	359	377	283	370	293
Nicaragua	4	2	2	1	0	0	0	0
Panama	11	9	12	10	5	1	2	2
Paraguay	1	0	3	3	3	2	2	1
Peru	1,132	867	1,011	779	773	585	708	555
Uruguay	9	7	10	10	11	7	12	9
Venezuela	306	236	492	397	545	389	374	246
Latin Am. total	19,867	15,590	18,351	14,334	16,987	13,531	18,146	14,551
World total	**137,477**	**105,877**	**113,477**	**83,604**	**95,005**	**72,341**	**95,224**	**75,377**
Latin Am. as % of world total	14.5%	14.7%	16.2%	17.1%	17.9%	18.7%	19.1%	19.3%
Latin Am. start as % of enrolled		78.5%		78.1%		79.7%		80.2%
World start as % of enrolled		77.0%		73.7%		76.1%		79.2%

Source: https://aei.gov.au/research/International-Student-Data/Documents/INTERNATIONAL%20 STUDENT%20DATA/2010/2010_basic_pivot_all.zip.

Australian ELICOS providers do face several serious challenges in the expansion of their Latin American market share. The first is the perception of Australia as a safe and welcoming place to study. As one São Paulo-based observer noted in an informal discussion, the May 2009 attacks on Indian students in Melbourne were noted with some concern by Latin Americans trying to decide between Australia and a US culture where Spanish has become an unofficial second language.[24] The 18 March 2012 killing of Brazilian Roberto Laudisio Curti by Tazer-wielding Sydney policy did not help calm these concerns.[25] Compounding these perceptions was a rising sense that the Australian ELICOS sector was poorly regulated and far from concerned with the welfare of visiting students or their educational outcomes; as *The Sunday Age* noted with an attention-grabbing headline: 'Students from abroad treated like cash cows'.[26] Australian governments at the national and state level did respond to these concerns, reforming standards in the sector, increasing insurance funds to ensure that students received an education even in circumstances where a particular ELICOS school became insolvent, and instituting a series of student crisis lines and police response units. All of these steps appear to have helped maintain the growth rate in this sector.

When attention is turned to educational linkages, thoughts generally go first to university exchanges and language training. The reality in the Australian case is that vocational educational training (VET) is a more important part of the services export picture, encompassing not only the provision of educational programming in Australia, but also training programs conducted in Latin America. In terms of enrolments, VET visa class programs represented 28.0 per cent of the total Latin American student body in 2012, marginally up from 27.7 per cent in 2002 (Table 2.4a and 2.4b). Areas covered by VET programs are broad, encompassing everything from hairdressing to the operation of heavy mining equipment. The importance of resource-related skills, information technology and tourism training shows in the concentration of VET visa grants to nationals from Brazil, Chile, Colombia and Peru (Table 2.8a and 2.8b), four countries seeking rapid expansion of technical skills in these industries. Surges in the number of students coming to Australia from Latin America and the rest of the world for VET programs speak to the concentrated effort that this sector has made in building the industry in Australia.

---

24   Phil Mercer, 'Indian Students Claim Epidemic of Racist Violence in Australia', *Voice of America Online*, 4 June 2009; Andrew Harrison, 'Indian Students Grow Wary of Australia Following Attacks', *Wall Street Journal*, 3 June 2009.

25   Jared Owens, 'Coroner Condemns "Thuggish" Police Over Tazer Death of Brazilian Student Roberto Laudisio Curti', *The Australian*, 14 November, 2012.

26   Natalie Craig, 'Students From Abroad Treated Like Cash Cows', *Sunday Age*, 23 May 2010, p. 13.

Table 2.8a: VET (2002–2008)

	2002		2004		2006		2008	
	Enrolled	Started	Enrolled	Started	Enrolled	Started	Enrolled	Started
Argentina	43	17	17	9	27	21	43	28
Bolivia	2	1	1	1	5	5	3	2
Brazil	1,226	732	1,594	1,036	3,486	2,360	5,334	3,344
Chile	18	10	15	8	37	25	185	126
Colombia	712	330	375	159	610	427	2,271	1,510
Costa Rica	6	5	3	0	1	0	2	2
Cuba					0	0	1	1
Dom. Rep.	0	0	0	0	0	0	1	1
Ecuador	13	3	9	4	13	7	21	15
El Salvador	1	1	6	4	9	5	12	6
Guatemala	2	2	2	0	1	1	6	4
Honduras	2	0	0	0	1	0	2	0
Mexico	47	30	82	54	107	59	216	121
Nicaragua	0	0	0	0	0	0	1	1
Panama	4	3	2	1	1	0	1	0
Paraguay	3	1	3	1	3	2	7	7
Peru	43	24	33	16	105	87	485	321
Uruguay	1	0	9	5	5	2	8	4
Venezuela	73	33	28	11	31	19	69	56
Latin Am. total	2,196	1,192	2,179	1,309	4,442	3,020	8,668	5,549
World total	**53,689**	**29,425**	**58,232**	**32,046**	**82,526**	**48,479**	**174,570**	**105,702**
Latin Am. as % of world total	4.1%	4.1%	3.7%	4.1%	5.4%	6.2%	5.0%	5.2%
Latin Am. start as % of enrolled		54.3%		60.1%		68.0%		60.5%
World start as % of enrolled		54.8%		55.0%		58.7%		60.5%

Source: https://aei.gov.au/research/International-Student-Data/Documents/INTERNATIONAL%20
STUDENT%20DATA/2010/2010_basic_pivot_all.zip.

Table 2.8b: VET (2009–2012)

	2009		2010		2011		2012	
	Enrolled	Started	Enrolled	Started	Enrolled	Started	Enrolled	Started
Argentina	54	36	92	66	97	66	80	51
Bolivia	5	3	7	5	5	5	3	3
Brazil	5,967	3,677	5,938	3,862	5,620	2,798	5,306	3,603
Chile	292	175	333	215	414	292	458	298
Colombia	2,494	1,313	2,610	1,574	2,142	1,262	1,810	1,136
Costa Rica	3	2	6	4	2	2	6	5
Cuba	2	1	0	0	0	0	0	0
Dom. Rep.	2	1	2	1	1	0	1	0
Ecuador	32	21	30	16	23	16	30	22
El Salvador	22	16	42	31	46	36	23	23
Guatemala	7	4	7	5	4	3	0	0
Honduras	1	0	0	0	1	1	2	2
Mexico	237	148	245	173	280	202	292	207
Nicaragua	3	2	2	1	2	0	0	0
Panama	6	5	8	5	8	3	6	3
Paraguay	4	2	5	2	3	2	2	2
Peru	767	471	915	549	898	548	772	459
Uruguay	8	3	5	3	12	10	8	6
Venezuela	92	67	156	105	227	176	234	153
Latin Am. total	9,998	5,947	10,403	6,617	9,785	5,422	9,033	5,973
World total	**231,670**	**131,221**	**206,581**	**107,752**	**16,9634**	**97,369**	**145,540**	**85,317**
Latin Am. as % of world total	4.3%	4.5%	5.0%	6.1%	5.8%	5.6%	6.2%	7.0%
Latin Am. start as % of enrolled		59.5%		63.6%		55.4%		66.1%
World start as % of enrolled		56.6%		52.2%		57.4%		58.6%

Source: http://www.aei.gov.au/AEI/Statistics/StudentEnrolmentAndVisaStatistics/2010/2010_basic_ pivot_all_zip.htm.

As a series of press reports in 2010 highlighted, visas for VET programming were also used as a device to evade Australian immigration regulations. This resulted in the growth of exploitative schools that used VET programming and the associated visa permission to undertake limited paid employment as cover for migrant labour schemes. The global totals in 2009 show a dramatic spike in growth, surging from 24,425 in 2002 to 131,221 in 2009, which was the height of exploitation of this visa loophole. When combined with the decidedly cowboy nature of a handful of the registered VET programs, which gave only tacit acknowledgement to their putative educational function, the rapid policy redirection from the Australian government that took place in 2009–10 is hardly surprising.[27] The result was major changes in the number of VET and other student visas being offered, with particular emphasis being placed on tightening the list of occupations for which the government was willing to issue training visas.[28] These regulatory changes accompanied the global financial crisis, prompting a major drop in global uptake of VET places (Table 2.8a and 2.8b), going from 131,221 in 2009 to 85,317 by 2012. The parallel Latin American uptake of VET places was the reverse, rising 5,947 in 2009 to 6,617 in 2010 before receding to 5,973 in 2012. The disjuncture in these comparative statistics points to the different approach to pursuit of VET programming in Australia. While some countries use VET programs to access work in the Australian labour market, for Latin Americans the emphasis is more on the acquisition of skills that can be used upon return to the student's home country.

Challenges and opportunities

Education and intellectual collaboration represents an excellent area in which to build bilateral relations. In the Brazilian case, France continues to reap the rewards of the efforts it devoted to helping develop higher education in Brazil;[29] and the British are explicit regarding the role of education and research as a means of practising soft power in their Prime Minister's Initiative for International Education.[30] Education and research is an engagement area that builds the sorts of links sought by foreign ministries—deep person-to-

27   Department of Immigration and Citizenship, Government of Australia, 'Student convicted over Sydney college immigration fraud', Press Release, 12 July 2010; Department of Immigration and Citizenship, Government of Australia, 'Overview of Student Visa Changes to Assist International Education Sector', Press Release, 16 December, 2010.

28   Heath Gilmore with Nick O'Malley, 'Government, industry more concerned for selves than students', *The Sydney Morning Herald*, 29 March 2010, p. 15; Margaret Wehnam, 'Student visas denied', *The Courier-Mail*, 8 January, 2010, p. 18; Heath Gilmore, 'Overseas students as good as gold', *The Sydney Morning Herald*, 30 November, 2009, p. 3.

29   Thomas E. Skidmore, 'Lévi-Strauss, Braudel and Brazil: A Case of Mutual Influence', *Bulletin of Latin American Research* 22, 2003, (3): pp. 340–49.

30   Managed by the British Council: more information on the Prime Minister's Initiative for International Education can be found at http://www.britishcouncil.org/eumd-pmi2.htm.

person and institution-to-institution connections based upon commonalities and shared purposes—all of which serve as a strong foundation for expanded political and economic cooperation. In substantive terms all of the necessary elements are in place for a strong partnership. Recent research has quantified the extent to which a low-skilled workforce is negatively impacting Latin American development,[31] prompting a concentration from regional governments on programs that upgrade skills and general scientific and technical capacity within their respective countries. There is also a keen awareness in Latin America that long-term regional growth will require a high-value added economic core that builds around knowledge accrued from advanced research and university studies.[32] This is directly reflected in the increased funding that the Chilean, Colombian and Mexican governments are directing to their scholarship programs, including the Brazilian creation of 'sandwich' scholarships that allow PhD students to study abroad for a year, and more recently the 'Science Without Borders' scholarship program.

Australia thus possesses two of the things that Latin American governments see as essential for sustainable development: an established and reputable vocational skills sector and a world class university sector engaged in cutting-edge research. A significant number of institutions in Australia have worked to build upon this to attract international students as an income-generating device.[33] In the Latin American context perhaps the most active has been the University of Queensland with the support of the Queensland government, which has sought to marry cultural and linguistic studies with the institution's existing strengths in resource extraction industries. A similar phenomenon is occurring at The Australian National University, which is leveraging its policy sciences and Asia-Pacific expertise as the basis for expanded exchange and collaboration with Latin America, most notably through the launching of a Bachelor of Latin American Studies degree and the activities of the Australian National Centre for Latin American Studies.

When combined with the surges in ELICOS and VET enrolments from Latin America, the Australian government's November 2009 decision to transfer the international marketing and promotion of Australian education from AEI to Austrade emerges as both a challenge and an opportunity. Of particular note

---

31 Diego Restuccia, 'The Latin American Development Problem', *Serie Macroeconomía del Desarrollo* No. 81, Santiago, Chile: CEPAL, March, 2009.

32 Carlos Lordelo, Estadão.edu, e Mariana Mandelli, 'Até 2014, 75 mil alunos devem receber bolsa para estudar no exterior', O Estado de São Paulo, 7 June 2011; José Antonio Ocampo and Juan Martin, Globalization and Development: A Latin American and Caribbean Perspective, Palo Alto, CA: Stanford University Press, 2003.

33 On the process in Australia and in general, see Philip G. Altbach, 'Higher Education Crosses Borders', *Change*, March–April 2003; Philip G. Altbach and Jane Knight, 'The Internationalization of Higher Education: Motivations and Realities', *Journal of Studies in International Education* 11 (34), 2007: pp. 290–305; Naidoo, 'Repositioning Higher Education as a Global Commodity'; Marginson and Sawir, 'University Leaders' Strategies in a Global Environment'; Marginson, 'Dynamics of Global Competition in Higher Education'.

in this context was the decision to discontinue the AEI Education Counsellor position in Santiago, although a subsequent decision created a near-identical Austrade post. Posts were also established for locally engaged staff in São Paulo, Mexico City and Lima, with responsibilities also spreading to cover Venezuela, Colombia and Argentina. The unanswered question is whether this new structure will have the agility and contacts necessary not only to continue attracting new students to Australia in the face of stiff international competition, but also to set aside the commercial imperative and work in the opposite direction to impel Australian students and researchers to opportunities in Latin America.

The obvious danger with the change in the Australian government's engagement structure is that a wealth of contacts will be lost during the transition process. Austrade is hoping to offset this risk by providing a closer service to Australian entities seeking to enter the Latin American market by providing customised services that meet the specific needs of each educational institution. This will initially be directed through the articulation of a new strategy built on sector-wide consultations. In some respects the transfer of marketing management responsibility to Austrade can be seen as a test of how firmly Australian institutions have established themselves in the region—in the years before AEI took over regional management Austrade oversaw an approximately twenty per cent drop in Latin American enrolment in Australia. As some industry participants and observers noted, the concern with Austrade is that it focuses excessively on the trade aspect and not enough on relationship building, which is inimical to the sense of cooperative advancement that many feel is crucial to the education sector.[34] The flip-side is that Austrade has brought a wider set of engagement tools to the table, and began its approach to the issue by explicitly seeking counsel and advice from all sectors of the education industry in Australia and Latin America.

With respect to university-based research, of even greater interest to Latin American countries is Australian expertise in shared areas of economic importance such as mining, agro-industry, water and clean energy. It is thus not surprising that one of the priorities of the Latin American diplomatic corps in Canberra is building linkages with Australian universities and seeking ways of motivating Australian academics to engage their Latin American counterparts and encourage collaboration and exchange, which includes Australians travelling to the region for extended visits. This brings us to one of the primary barriers to expanded intercontinental relations in the education sector, namely the lingering vestiges of what can only be termed Australian parochialism.

Use of the term parochialism is sweeping and perhaps not entirely fair as a capstone descriptor, but it does capture the essence of the still-prevalent

---

34   Confidential interviews, Canberra, September 2010.

Australian attitude that sees Latin America as a developing, slightly lost region and more latterly as a new market ripe for exploitation. At its core rests the question of language and the perception that expanded engagement will not be possible until more Latin Americans speak English. The depth of this challenge was apparent at the 2010 COALAR-EAG Roundtable meeting, where the leader of one Australian VET provider operating in Chile was clear that one of the greatest barriers to expanding their business was the inability of Chilean students to follow the lessons in English. When asked why the program was not also delivered in Spanish, the reply was that this was not the comparative advantage of the firm and that Spanish firms would fill that function more efficiently. The idea of either developing Spanish skills in the firm's instructors or recruiting bilingual instructors was dismissed as unnecessary. Others at the Roundtable took a different view, with some working on creating Spanish-language programming for delivery in the region. The point is that pockets of parochialism persist, but are slowly being driven out by a mix of more aggressive entrepreneurship and a generational shift that is bringing to the fore a new generation of Australians fascinated with Latin America, which is reflected in the surge in individuals studying Spanish in post-secondary institutions.[35] While this is an initial positive sign, it does miss out on the region's leading economy and market of over 180 million, the Portuguese-speaking population of Brazil. It is also a far from certain indicator that the marketing spin of Australian universities will be matched by the concrete resources pushing for active and ongoing collaboration.

Unfortunately, this sense of cultural and linguistic parochialism continues to pervade key segments of the Australian government, civil society and academy. Government officials face a constant battle to direct political attention towards the Americas. This appeared to ease slightly with the regional interest shown by Foreign Minister Kevin Rudd in 2010 and 2011, and Prime Minister Julia Gillard's meeting with Brazilian President Dilma Rousseff, but the underlying reality is that the key decision-makers within the Australian government retain a narrow focus on the United States and China. There is little wider awareness within the Australian government machinery that there is much to learn from the Americas. More significantly for the subject of this chapter, the potential and actual academic contributions coming from Latin America are implicitly discounted by the assessment processes used for Australian Research Council grants, which do not include many important regional publications and thus effectively penalise researchers for publishing in these venues or entering into collaborative projects that will be published in Spanish or Portuguese. The resultant sense of isolation for Latin American students and scholars is further amplified by Australian government visa policies that seem to grant privileged

---

35   Jarvie, 'Latin America', *op. cit.*, note 7.

access to the richest countries irrespective of visa overstay rates from countries such as Canada, the UK and US, yet require onerous application processes from established professionals in the Americas seeking to collaborate with their antipodean colleagues.

In one sense these linguistic and cultural anecdotes simply reflect the risk aversion of many smaller Australian firms (in Brisbane, Melbourne and Sydney), to operations in countries that are not well understood. But they also point to a deeper Australian lack of understanding of the current realities in Latin America, which is certainly not a challenge unique to Australia, but also found in North America and Western Europe. One of the challenges Australian diplomats face when touring their political leaders through the region is how to prepare them for the reality that they are visiting sophisticated, developed urban economies, not ramshackle settlements drowning under oceans of starving poor. The same challenge faces inter-institutional agreements with Australian university administrators focusing upon the developing nature of Latin American economies rather than the sophistication of many sectors in these countries. While the succession of education tours conducted by Group of Eight university members is helping break down this lingering aspect of Australian parochialism, it has yet to translate into a wealth of substantial and sustained inter-continental research linkages. In particular, it is not yet leading to a widespread exchange of the postgraduate students and postdoctoral fellows that formed the foundation for the strong bilateral inter-institutional linkages found in France, Germany, the United Kingdom and the United States. Worse, this sort of attitude has coloured aspects of government-to-government discussions on mutual qualifications recognition, which at times have appeared to be dominated by an Australian view that Latin American post-secondary institutions are at best of mediocre quality, with Latin Americans—particularly Brazilians—responding in kind that they will not recognise the validity of the AQF. While in some cases this supposition is certainly true, a similar argument can also be made about some higher education institutions in Australia, Western Europe and North America. The more pressing reality is that bureaucratic structures in some Latin American countries designed to protect nascent post-secondary educational institutions are not keeping up with the increasingly globalised nature of knowledge generation and education.[36]

This brings us to the second aspect of Australian parochialism, namely the supposition that, in regard to education, Latin America needs Australia more than the obverse. As reports from DEEWR, COALAR and comments at the 2010 COALAR–EAG Roundtable make clear, Latin America is being viewed as a market

---

36   Juan Lucena, Gary Downey, Brent Jesiek, and Sharon Elber, 'Competencies Beyond Countries: The Re-Organization of Engineering Education in the United States, Europe, and Latin America', *Journal of Engineering Education* 97 (4), October 2008: pp. 433–7.

for Australian education providers. There is also a clear awareness in Australia that Latin America has alternatives which, as shown in the tables, become more cost-effective when the Australian dollar climbs in value relative to the US dollar, British pound and Euro. Indeed, as mentioned earlier, the United Kingdom is actively and explicitly seeking to exploit its weak currency and quality universities to capture the Latin American market. When the complications and perceived insults of Australian immigration policy and the logistics of travelling between the two continents are added to the equation, Australia's hold on its Latin American market share becomes even more tenuous. The mercantilist tenor of much of the Australian educational engagement with Latin America thus emerges as a challenge in itself. Simply put, a market-based focus leaves Australia as a service provider that may be dropped at a moment's notice in favour of a more attractive option. Creating a tighter hold on the Latin American market requires deep collaborative links that will cause the relationship to be viewed in more than just financial terms: this is what international relations scholars might call complex educational interdependence. While some limited progress is being made on this front, particularly through the MOUs that the Australian Group of Eight universities are negotiating with Latin American institutions, success will ultimately depend on individual researchers working together. Making this happen is challenging and will require a level of sustained institutional and financial support that does not yet appear to be in place.

Building partnerships between Australian and Latin American educational sectors and institutions thus emerges as a central challenge, and one that is complicated by the relatively low understanding in Australia of the opportunities beyond market-share available in Latin America. As this chapter highlights, much progress has been made in building concrete inter-continental links. It is also important to note that one of the major challenges facing expanded linkages—the last remaining vestiges of Australian parochialism—appears to be slowly fading as the next generation of Australian students and businesses embark on their own exploration of the world, leaving government and the academy to play catch-up. This is being further reinforced by a similar outreach from Latin America, which is looking for new partners beyond the United States and Europe. In short, some of the pre-conditions are in place for a further expansion of Australia–Latin American education relations, but success will only come if the hard work of the last decade is continued and expanded to include genuine collaborative work based on partnership, not service provision and market exploitation.

References

Altbach, Philip G. 'Higher Education Crosses Borders', *Change*, March–April 2003.

Altbach, Philip G., and Jane Knight, 'The Internationalization of Higher Education: Motivations and Realities', *Journal of Studies in International Education* 11, 2007, (3/4): pp. 290–305.

Antonio Ocampo, José, and Juan Martin, *Globalization and Development: A Latin American and Caribbean Perspective*, Palo Alto, CA: Stanford University Press, 2003.

'Australia Awards', http://www.australiaawards.gov.au/about.html, accessed 30 May 2011.

Boffey, Daniel, 'British bid to attract 10,000 Brazilian students', *The Observer*, 10 July 2011.

British Council, *Prime Minister's Initiative for International Education*, http://www.britishcouncil.org/eumd-pmi2.htm, accessed 6 October 2011.

Confidential interviews, Canberra, September 2010.

Council of Australian Governments, *International Student Strategy for Australia, 2010–2014* (2010), http://www.coag.gov.au/reports/docs/aus_international_students_strategy.pdf, accessed 23 October 2013.

Council on Australia–Latin American Relations, *Annual Report 1 July 2000–30 June 2004*, Canberra: Department of Foreign Affairs and Trade: p. 10.

———, *Annual Report, 2004–2005*, Canberra: Department of Foreign Affairs and Trade.

———, *Annual Report, 2005–2006*, Canberra: Department of Foreign Affairs and Trade.

———, *Annual Report, 2008–2009*, Canberra: Department of Foreign Affairs and Trade.

Craig, Natalie, 'Students From Abroad Treated Like Cash Cows', *Sunday Age*, 23 May 2010, p. 13.

Department of Immigration and Citizenship, Government of Australia, 'Student convicted over Sydney college immigration fraud', Press Release, 12 July 2010.

———, 'Overview of Student Visa Changes to Assist International Education Sector', Press Release, 16 December, 2010.

Doolette, Ann, 'Australian Qualifications Framework', Powerpoint Presentation to the 2010 COALAR–EAG Roundtable, Canberra, 10 September 2010.

El Tiempo (Colombia), 'Primera Feria Educativa Latino Australia Education', 2 September 2010.

'Estudar no exterior é tema de três eventos', *Folha de São Paulo*, 30 August 2009.

Gilmore, Heath, with Nick O'Malley, 'Government, industry more concerned for selves than students', *The Sydney Morning Herald*, 29 March 2010: p. 15.

Gilmore, Heath, 'Overseas students as good as gold', *The Sydney Morning Herald*, 30 November, 2009: p. 3.

Gonçalves, Glauber, 'Pré-sal provoca boom de cursos de petróleo', *O Estado de São Paulo*, 20 June 2010.

Group of Eight, *Memorandum of Understanding between the Council of Rectors of Chilean Universities and the Group of Eight, Australia*, Canberra, 2011: http://www.go8.edu.au/__documents/university-staff/international-collaboration/go8-chile_mou.pdf, accessed 30 May 2011.

Hilmer, Fred, 'The Dumb Blonde of International Education', *The Australian*, 1 November 2010: p. 14.

Jarvie, Wendy Katherine, 'Latin America: Opportunities and Risks in Education', *Global Education News, Australia*, 13 April 2011: http://www.austrade.gov.au/export_markets/industries/education/enewsletter, accessed 20 May 2011.

Lordelo, Carlos, Estadão.edu, e Mariana Mandelli, 'Até 2014, 75 mil alunos devem receber bolsa para estudar no exterior', *O Estado de São Paulo*, 7 June 2011.

Lucena, Juan, Gary Downey, Brent Jesiek, and Sharon Elber, 'Competencies Beyond Countries: The Re-Organization of Engineering Education in the United States, Europe, and Latin America', *Journal of Engineering Education,* 97 (4), October 2008: pp. 433–7.

Marginson, Simon, and Sawir, Erlenawati, 'University Leaders' Strategies in the Global Environment: A Comparative Study of Universities Indonesia and The Australian National University', *Higher Education*, 52, 2006: pp. 343–73.

Marginson, Simon, 'Dynamics of National and Global Competition in Higher Education', *Higher Education*, 52, 2006: pp. 1–39.

Meneghel, Stela, Debora Mello, Erasmo Gomes and Sandra Brisolla, 'The University–Industry Relationship in Brazil: Trends and Implications for University Management', *International Journal of Technology Management & Sustainable Development* 2 (3), 2004: pp. 173–90.

Mercer, Phil, 'Indian Students Claim Epidemic of Racist Violence in Australia', *Voice of America Online*, 4 June 2009; Andrew Harrison, 'Indian Students Grow Wary of Australia Following Attacks', *Wall Street Journal*, 3 June 2009.

Naidoo, Rajani, 'Repositioning Higher Education as a Global Commodity: Opportunities and Challenges for Future Sociology of Education Work', *British Journal of Sociology of Education* 24 (2), 2003: pp. 249–59.

Nelson, Brendan, Engaging the World through Education: Ministerial Statement on the Internationalisation of Australian Education and Training, Canberra: Department of Education, Science and Training, Australian Government, 2003.

Nye Jr., Joseph S. *The Paradox of American Power*, Oxford: Oxford University Press, 2002.

Owens, Jared, 'Coroner Condemns "Thuggish" Police Over Tazer Death of Brazilian Student Roberto Laudisio Curti', *The Australian*, 14 November, 2012.

Pamplona, Nicola, 'Um 'Vale do Sílico' para o pré-sal', *O Estado de São Paulo,* 7 March 2010.

————, 'Estatal investe para renovar quadro', *O Estado de São Paulo*, 1 November 2010.

Restuccia, Diego, 'The Latin American Development Problem', *Serie Macroeconomía del Desarrollo* No. 81, Santiago, Chile: CEPAL, March, 2009.

Skidmore, Thomas E. 'Lévi-Strauss, Braudel and Brazil: A Case of Mutual Influence', *Bulletin of Latin American Research* 22 (3), 2003: pp. 340–49.

UTS (University of Technology, Sydney), 'International Studies', http://www.internationalstudies.uts.edu.au/, accessed 23 October 2013.

Wehnam, Margaret 'Student visas denied', *The Courier-Mail*, 8 January, 2010, p. 18.

3. Australia's Foreign Aid to Latin America

John Minns

Introduction

The chapter outlines the background to the Latin America Program's launch by the Australian Agency for International Development (AusAID),[1] which manages the bulk of official development assistance (ODA) to the region. It also provides an overview of the Program's current and proposed activities. It reviews the current approach in the contexts of operation, especially focusing on the necessity for effective partnerships. It considers briefly a number of different forms of collaborative work, including trilateral engagements (i.e., third country delivery via channelling of funds through regional governments) and partnering with other donors, including the New Zealand Aid Programme; The United States Agency for International Development (USAID); the Canadian International Development Agency (CIDA); and the German International Cooperation Agency (GIZ).

Based on this investigation, it posits that a single issue should be championed in place of a widespread range of efforts. Reflecting on the region's specific needs, as well as lessons gleaned from review of the work of other actors, and finally considering Australia's comparative advantage, capabilities and national interests, the chapter suggests that the key focal point for the Program should be natural resource governance. Given this, it seeks to offer some brief pragmatic programming and policy advice in terms of modalities for delivery. The intention is to minimise the changes required to achieve this focusing of efforts, thereby avoiding time- and resource-consuming restructuring efforts.

The key purpose here is to provide consumable and pragmatic policy advice to decision-makers, bearing in mind the constraints within which they operate. While it pays tribute to much broader debates about aid and general international interactions, it does not seek to engage deeply in these. It is the hope of the author that the advice provided here might lead to more coherent strategy and activity in order to maximise this unique engagement in the Latin American region.

---

1   At the time of publication, new arrangements in the Australian government are being implemented to bring AusAID into DFAT, thereby removing its status as a separate agency. Recommendations later in this chapter for AusAID refer to the agencies functions and should be read as applicable to the area within DFAT that ultimately takes charge of Australia's aid program to Latin America.

Overview of aid context and AusAID's Latin America Program

Although under-publicised, in 2011–12 Australia was to provide some $A27.2 million in official development assistance (ODA) to the Latin American region.[2] This was largely managed by the Australian Agency for International Development (AusAID).[3] This is a significant increase from $A9.2 million in 2010–11—which comprised some $A5 million to Chile post-earthquake and $A0.5 million to Guatemala in humanitarian relief[4]—and $A2.1 million in the previous year (2009–10).[5]

Nonetheless, the 2012 sum is dwarfed by the overall increase in Australian aid from $A4,362 million in 2010–11 to $A4,836 million in 2011–12. This increase constitutes a scaling-up of the aid budget from 0.33 per cent to 0.35 per cent of gross national income (GNI). This was again proposed to almost double by 2015–16, with ODA forecast at that time to reach $A8–9 billion.[6] This increase was in line with Australian bipartisan commitment to the Millennium Development Goals (MDGs), which sets an aspirational goal for donors to increase their overseas aid to 0.5 per cent of GNI by the end of the 2015–16 MDG deadline.[7] Although the announced rise in aid was put on hold by the 2013 Federal Budget, it is nonetheless a significant increase by Australian historical and international standards.

As a proportion of the aid budget as a whole the commitment to Latin America is small, at well under one per cent of Australia's total ODA. Nonetheless, it constitutes a significant and unprecedented movement into the region. This is the first time in its history that the Australian aid program has featured a Latin American Program.

---

2   Australian Agency for International Development, the (AusAID), *Informal consultations with Latin America (LA) Program staff members eliciting 'open source' (public) information*, (May 2011). Defined as the 17 Spanish or Portuguese-speaking countries located in the Central or South America regions, excluding Caribbean states and CARICOM members. Namely: Argentina, Bolivia, Brazil, Chile, Colombia, Costa Rica, Cuba, El Salvador, Guatemala, Honduras, Mexico, Nicaragua, Panama, Paraguay, Peru, Uruguay, Venezuela.

3   Rudd, Kevin, 'Australia's International Development Assistance Program 2011–12: An Effective Aid Plan for Australia: Reducing Poverty, Saving Lives and Advancing Australia's National Interest—Statement by the Hon Kevin Rudd MP, Minister for Foreign Affairs 10 May 2011', Budget 2011–12. Australian Government, http://www.budget.gov.au/2011-12/content/ministerial_statements/ausaid/download/ms_ausaid.pdf, accessed 23 May 2011, p. 116.

4   *Ibid.* The $5 million to Chile was provided for emergency relief and reconstruction following the earthquake and tsunami in February 2010; the $0.5 million to Guatemala was for humanitarian assistance in the wake of the eruption of Pacaya and tropical storm Agatha.

5   Australian Agency for International Development, the (AusAID), *Caribbean and Latin America Program overview*, 2011: http://www.ausaid.gov.au/country/caribbean.cfm.

6   Rudd, *op. cit.*, note 3, p. iv.

7   Steven Smith, 'Budget 2009–10: Policy Statement on Australia's International Development Assistance', 2010: http://www.ausaid.gov.au/hottopics/topic.cfm?ID=872_6918_7937_5970_8092.

Given this substantial shift, what appears to be a general downplaying of the activity is at first confusing. For instance, reference to the Program is tucked away in the AusAID Annual Report 2010–11 within the indexed chapter *ODA—Africa, South and Central Asia, Middle East and Other*. Moreover, even mention of 'Other', under which the Program is ambiguously relegated, drops off in the referencing throughout the report to read: *Africa, South and Central Asia and Middle East*.[8] There is no mention at all in the Budget Highlights of the program's inception.

Australia's discreet camouflaging of this aid provision to Latin America is best explained as a means by which to dodge criticism. Public comments gathered by the Lowy institute—which has been managing the 'interpreting the aid review' blog for the recently completed Independent Review of Aid Effectiveness[9]—indicate that the Australian aid community, comprising individuals, organisations and institutes engaged in aid delivery work, is critical of Australian aid directed beyond the traditional geographic scope of the Asia-Pacific region.[10]

Criticisms levelled at the Program can largely be grouped into three clusters. The first relates to the reasons for entry into the region, especially those motivations of aid delivery which are tainted by undertones of diplomatic or national interest. The second questions the Latin American region's needs for aid vis-à-vis those of other regions. The third points to Australia's limited capacity to operate effectively in the region given budget constraints combined with a lack of experience and history of engagement from which to draw.

Purity of aid

> It is a very dangerous thing to justify aid only from the perspective of national interest. In fact, aid delivered with nation [sic] interest front of mind doesn't really deserve to be called aid at all… There is a role for the government in protecting our national interest and ensuring we have a

---

8 Rudd, *op. cit.*, note 3.

9 Independent Review of Aid Effectiveness, *Independent Review of Aid Effectiveness Official Website*, Commonwealth Government (of Australia), 2011: http://www.aidreview.gov.au/index.html. The Independent Aid Review's primary objective was to examine the effectiveness and efficiency of the Australian aid program and make recommendations to improve its structure and delivery.

10 Stephen Grenville, 'Aid Review: Narrow the geographic focus', *Lowy Institute for International Policy*, 20 January 2011: http://aidreview.lowyinterpreter.org/post/AusAID-Review-Narrow-the-geographic-focus.aspx; Jenny Hayward-Jones, 'Geographic focus or national interest?', *Lowy Institute for International Policy*, 25 January 2011: http://aidreview.lowyinterpreter.org/post/Geographic-focus-or-national-interest.aspx.

secure and stable region, but this should not be funded out of our aid program, which the majority of Australians agree should be used to help people living in poverty, not ourselves.[11]

Criticisms of Australia's strategic political reasons for expanding into Latin America indicate a somewhat naïve understanding of the nature of the Australian aid program or indeed that of any government. Enhancing Australia's national interest is explicitly articulated in AusAID's overarching aim:

[t]he objective of the Australian aid program is to assist developing countries reduce poverty and achieve sustainable development, in line with Australia's national interest.[12]

This intention was echoed in former Foreign Minister Stephen Smith's statement at the 2010 launch of the aid budget:

A strong and effective aid program advances Australia's reputation and our influence in the international community. Our aid program is not separate from our foreign policy. It is a crucial part of it.[13]

Similarly, commitment to the MDGs is justified by its contribution towards securing Australian national interests, as former Foreign Minister Rudd noted in the 2011 budget release:

It is for…humanitarian, national security and economic reasons that the Government is committed to increasing our aid to 0.5 per cent of our gross national income by 2015–16.[14]

While the Australian government generally frames entry into the Latin American region as relating to Australia's increasing commitment to meeting the MDG-based GNI aid commitment of 0.5 per cent—and hence the additional funds with which it might spread Australia's aid efforts—it is also not difficult to link the expansion to Australia's campaign at the time to win a temporary seat on the UN Security Council,[15] a particularly sore point of contention for those who object to linking aid to foreign policy objectives. Moreover, this campaign was successful, with Australia assuming its seat in 2013. Nonetheless, these debates around motivation for aid delivery in the Latin American region might equally be conducted for all Australian aid activities, in all regions.

11   Michael Wesley, 'Designing our foreign aid future: Interpreting the Independent Aid Review Blog', Lowy Institute for International Policy, 29 April 2011: http://aidreview.lowyinterpreter.org/.
12   Australian Agency for International Development, the (AusAID), About AusAID, 2011: http://www.ausaid.gov.au/about/default.cfm.
13   Smith, op. cit. note 7.
14   Rudd, op. cit., note 3. p.iii.
15   Nina Markovic (on behalf of the Department of Foreign Affairs and Trade), 'Australia, 2011, Budget 2011–12: Introduction', 2011: http://www.aph.gov.au/library/pubs/RP/BudgetReview2011-12/DFAT.htm.

Indeed, this is already the case with the concurrent and much greater move into Africa,[16] which continues to receive significant scrutiny and criticism for the political reasons prompting the expansion.

This chapter takes as a starting point the position that aid's linkage to the pursuit of national interests is inherent in contributions that are generated from tax revenues and managed by national governments. General debates about linkages between aid and politics, while important and necessary, are far too broad to be addressed by this chapter, which has the modest scope of providing targeted policy advice. That is, it takes the pragmatic view that the Australian aid program is inherently political and that policy advice ought, on the one hand, to acknowledge this given context, and, on the other seek, maximise ethical conduct within it.

The only gesture this chapter makes towards the much broader debate of aid motivations is to point out that the objectives of aid delivery—for the purpose of this chapter defined here as activities aimed at poverty alleviation and/or improving human living standards in recipient countries—are not, by necessity, at loggerheads with aims of furthering a donor's national interest. There is not necessarily a relationship of trade-off and indeed, in some instances, these two objectives and the activities they comprise can enhance one another. This is most clearly seen in examples of trade, wherein aid activities might support a more equal distribution of revenue generated from enhanced bilateral or multilateral trade relations. It is also apparent when activities funded by aid money offset the negative potential of the pursuit of 'national interests'. An example of this would be the funding of 'watch dog' or transparency mechanisms to monitor government or private industry activities, to ensure certain standards, such as those set in the Paris Declaration and the Accra Agenda for Action (AAA),[17] are adhered to.

In relation to providing policy advice, the most valuable point arising from this body of criticism is that, given the short-term political motivations prompting the Latin America expansion, the presence of Australian aid in Latin America might well be short-lived. This factor should be central to all programming decisions, both in terms of aid focus areas and delivery modalities.

---

16   Australian Agency for International Development, the (AusAID), *op. cit.*, note , p. 5. Australia's estimated ODA to the African region (targeting over 40 countries) for 2011–12 is $A291.3 million.
17   Organisation for Economic Co-operation and Development (OECD), 'Paris Declaration and Accra Agenda for Action', OECD Development Co-operation Directorate (DCD-DAC), 2011: http://www.oecd.org/document /18/0,3343,en_2649_3236398_35401554_1_1_1,00.html. Australia, like most major donors, is signature to the Paris Declaration (2005) and the related Accra Agenda for Action (2008). These outline five core principles, drawing on decades of lessons learnt from development activities. These refer to the need for: ownership (aid recipients establishing their own national development strategies with their parliaments and electorates); alignment (donor-support and compliance with the recipients' strategies); harmonisation (donor work to streamline their efforts in-country); results (the monitoring of aid activities toward articulated goals); mutual accountability (responsibility sharing between donors for realising the determined goals).

The deservedness of the Latin America region as an aid recipient

> The case for narrowing the geographic distribution is strong. There are plenty of poor people in the countries closer to us.... Almost half the Indonesian population lives on less than two dollars a day.... Thus there is plenty to do close to home.[18]

The more specific criticisms of Australia's expansion into Latin America relate to whether the region is a worthy recipient of aid money. Latin America is an area that has seen significant economic growth in the past decade. Furthermore, it is an area blessed with an abundance of natural resources, from which it derives much of its economic growth.[19]

The Human Development Index (HDI)[20] indicates that region-wide, Latin America enjoys a much higher standard of living than most countries of the African continent or South and South-East Asian regions.[21] Put in very crude terms, it is certainly true that few people in Latin America starve to death. That said, indications of plenty distract from the very harsh inequity of wealth distribution and the severe implications this engenders. It is a commonly cited fact that the region features the greatest levels of income inequity in the world.[22] Significant portions of its populations—ironically most especially in the advanced economies such as Brazil or Colombia—suffer under conditions of deprivation and, related to this, human insecurity. The region's average calculation of Gini coefficients [23] for income distribution is 51.3. This represents an average 65 per cent higher than high-income countries, 36 per cent higher than the income inequality observed in East Asian countries, and 18 per cent higher than that reported for Sub-Saharan Africa.[24] Hence, despite indications of strong national economic growth region-wide, there remain significant pockets

---

18   Wesley, op. cit., note 11.
19   Nancy Birdsall, Nora Lustig, and Darryl McLeod, 'Working Paper 251: Declining Inequality in Latin America: Some Economics, Some Politics', Center for Global Development, 19 May 2010: http://www.cgdev.org/content/publications/detail/1425092/?utm_source=nl_weekly&utm_medium=email&utm_campaign=nl_weekly_05242011&,.
20   United Nations Development Programme, The, (UNDP), 2010, *Human Development Index (HDI)—2010 Rankings*, 2010: http://hdr.undp.org/en/statistics/. The HDI is a single statistic allocated to each country. It is calculated from data about a wide range of social and economic conditions within each country and is used to rank a country's status on a spectrum between 0–1 to indicate their relative degree of development.
21   *Ibid.*
22   Luis F. López-Calva and Nora Lustig, (eds), *Declining Income Inequality in America: A Decade of Progress?* Baltimore, MD: Brookings Institution Press, 2010.
23   The World Bank, 2011. The Gini coefficient is a measure of the inequality of a distribution, a value of 0 expressing total equality and a value of 1 maximal inequality.
24   López-Calva, *et. al.*, *op. cit.*, note 22.

of deprivation throughout Latin America. This is a regional characteristic that must be considered in undertaking aid activities, which should in some form be aimed at correcting this inequity.

Putting aside equity issues, another significant point to redress is this criticism's implicit assumption that countries in the greatest desperation as defined by the HDI are also the countries where aid money will have the most impact. Unfortunately, this is rarely the case. Aid saturation occurs quickly in countries where infrastructure is limited, governance structures are poor, and human capacities are low.[25] There are numerous problems arising from pouring aid money into areas that are unable to absorb it properly. This approach is consistently linked to corruption and bypassing of government, as well as potentially fuelling existing or reigniting latent conflicts.[26] In other words, aid money often inadvertently funds activities that are in direct contradiction to the approaches espoused by the Paris Declaration and the AAA.

By way of contrast, aid money in many of the Latin American countries— when targeted appropriately—has been found to be highly effective in assisting communities to find and implement sustainable solutions to their challenges.[27] Additionally, the AusAID proposed modalities for aid delivery include south–south partnering between regional countries with strong GNIs and the necessary capacity, namely Chile and Brazil.[28]

For all these reasons, Latin America qualifies as a worthy recipient of aid. Furthermore, AusAID should identify and seek to understand regional characteristics as well as capitalise on the region's strengths, among them the presence of a relatively large highly educated middle class and numerous national organisations with strong aid-delivery capacity.

An example of such regional opportunity is the potential for donors to work in areas often overlooked when working to meet critical humanitarian needs, such as areas of environmental sustainability.

---

25 Matthew Clarke, 'How to deliver a doubling aid program?', *Lowy Institute for International Policy*, 6 April 2011, http://aidreview.lowyinterpreter.org/post/How-to-deliver-a-doubling-aid-program.aspx.

26 Hayward-Jones, *op. cit.*, note ; 'In our national interest—effective aid to the Pacific'; 'African gold rush: Aid and UN votes', *Lowy Institute for International Policy*, 4 May 2011: http://www.lowyinterpreter.org/post/2010/05/04/African-gold-rush-Aid-and-UN-votes.aspx.

27 Deutsche Gesellschaft für Internationale Zusammenarbeit (GIZ) GmbH, 2011: *GTZ in Honduras*, http://www.gtz.de/en/weltweit/lateinamerika-karibik/634.htm; 2011: *About GIZ*, http://www.giz.de/en/profile.html; (and) Canadian International Development Agency (CIDA)–ACDI, 2011: 'Statistical Report on International Assistance, Fiscal Year 2009–2010', *Her Majesty the Queen in Right of Canada*, http://www.acdi-cida.gc.ca/INET/IMAGES.NSF/vLUImages/stats/$file/Statistical_Report_2009-2010_eng.pdf.

28 Australian Agency for International Development (AusAID), *op. cit.*, note 2.

Australia's limited capacity for effective delivery

> The case for narrowing the geographic distribution is strong...the most powerful argument is about administering the program. Sure, aid funds are in short supply. The greater shortage, however, is effective and expert administration. Effective implementation requires detailed knowledge of the recipient country and a sharply focused experience of what can and can't be done with foreign aid.[29]

The final group of criticisms levelled at the Latin America Program's inception is that Australia lacks the engagement history and expertise to be effective in its aid delivery in the region. Bearing in mind the political reasons for engagement, and hence the likelihood of only short-term commitment to such work, this body of criticism is warranted in insisting that AusAID function realistically and strategically.

The AusAID team charged with managing the Latin America Program should undertake a realistic stock-take of its own capacity and consider this in light of the regional and country-specific needs and challenges.

The Latin America Aid Program in its current incarnation

The LA Program has identified four priority focus areas around which it will align its efforts. These are: Rural Development; Human Resource Development; Natural Resource Governance; and Climate Change and Environmental Stability.[30]

Rural Development is to be addressed via partnering with other donors. Within this focus area, Australia is to support work that improves agricultural productivity and financial services for the poor. The means of achieving this objective will be via provision of financial literacy training and programs that provide access to affordable, transparent and well-regulated financial service providers. These activities are expected to enable poor people to improve local enterprises and their overall standard of living. Additionally, AusAID will fund projects that improve small landholder agricultural production and access to markets so as to help poor rural dwellers secure sustainable livelihoods.[31]

---

29 Wesley, Michael, 'Designing our foreign aid future: Interpreting the Independent Aid Review Blog' 20 May 2011.

30 Rudd, *op. cit.*, note 3. p. 63.

31 *Ibid.*

Australia's contribution towards *Human Resource Development* is envisioned to be via sharing knowledge and technical expertise in sectors identified as supporting economic and social development. Activities relating to this will be: long-term scholarships; short courses and short-term professional development opportunities; volunteer programs; and small grant schemes. The expectation of such activities is that they will build capacity in the public and civil society sectors.[32]

Natural Resource Governance is intended to encompass those Australia-funded activities aimed at enhancing Latin American countries' capacity to manage their natural resource wealth effectively. This will be undertaken in close partnership with governments from the region as well as local stakeholders and other donors. Short courses, fellowships and scholarships will provide the means.[33]

The final priority focus is *Climate Change and Environmental Stability*. Work in this area will be aimed at assisting vulnerable Latin American countries' preparedness and ability to respond to increasingly common natural disasters. The modalities for work in this sector include support to projects and capacity-building activities aimed at climate change adaptation and disaster risk reduction (DRR), and will also likely involve the placement of some Australian volunteers.[34]

It would seem that despite the significant breadth of this program, few activities at the time of writing are underway. Current activities include: a commitment to an AUD$2 million microfinance project in Peru for financial literacy; and the initiation of two AUD$1 million microfinance projects in conflict-affected areas of Colombia.[35]

Logistics and staffing constraints may play a role in this slow beginning. The program is 'non-devolved', i.e., the high-level decision-making as well as the bulk of the administrative work is undertaken from Canberra. The only presence in the region has come about with the placement of an AusAID officer in Chile, Santiago in early 2010, later joined by a small team comprising only two nationally engaged employees. It is evidently an ambitious mandate for an office of this size to cover work in seventeen countries. The Canberra team also only numbers some five full-time staff positions.[36]

A slow initiation is hardly surprising for a recently launched program, and indeed might prove a prudent and sensible beginning; the more critical point in assessing the Program relates to an absence of coherence in its current and proposed activities. The breadth of the Program, in geographic as well as

---

32 *Ibid.*
33 *Ibid.*
34 *Ibid.*
35 Australian Agency for International Development (AusAID), *op. cit.*, note 2.
36 *Ibid.*

thematic scope, appears to exceed both the LA Program implementing team's budget and staff capacity for management. This overextension could easily result in fragmentation of activities, with tokenistic efforts to satisfy the current strategy's broad array of objectives and areas.

To maximise the given resources—namely time, budget and staffing—this chapter provides two recommendations for AusAID in developing its strategic approach. These are: to look to partners in order to address what to avoid and how to proceed; and to target efforts via championing a cause in which Australia has a comparative advantage, using existing partnerships and programs to do so.

Recommendation one: Look to partners

AusAID's Latin America Program has identified a range of modalities for aid delivery, among which various forms of partnering [37] play a crucial part. This approach is endorsed by key aid organisations that provided submissions to the Independent Aid Review,[38] and is supported by even a superficial glance at Australia's ambitions in the area, in contrast with its limited time, staffing and financial resources.

Nonetheless, prior to engagement, potential partners should first be assessed for what they can teach Australia about how—and how not—to go about delivering aid, as well as having their operations scrutinised for compatibility with those proposed by Australia.

Trilateral arrangements

Australia has reportedly begun investigations into trilateral arrangements, known as 'triangular aid' in Latin America, and the undertaking of some project work, most notably in delivering emergency relief to Haiti.[39] Triangular aid describes a collection of arrangements involving the partnering of the principal donor with the government of one of the region's stronger economies—generally

---

37 *Ibid.* Amongst them, multilateral partnering (with UN, INGOs and other OECD donors); bilateral partnering (in the form of trilateral cooperation including such initiatives as partnering with Brazil to deliver assistance in Haiti following the February 2010 earthquake); volunteering opportunities (via existing AusAID funded programs expansion of placements into the region); and scholarship programs (via the opening of existing opportunities to citizens from within the region—specifically including a *commitment* of 200 placements for regional scholars).

38 Oxfam Australia, 'Submission to Independent Review of Aid Effectiveness', Oxfam Australia, 2 February 2011: http://www.oxfam.org.au/resources/filestore/originals/OAus-IndependentAidReviewSubm ission-0211.pdf, p. 21.

39 Australian Agency for International Development (AusAID), *op. cit.*, note 2.

Chile, via the Agencia de Cooperación Internacional de Chile (AGCI), or Brazil, through the Agência Brasileira de Cooperação (ABC)—to provide assistance to a third country.[40]

These trilateral arrangements seem attractive as they embody the recommendations of the Paris Principles and the AAA, which guide donors towards more effective and sustainable aid delivery by, among other practices, ensuring host government involvement in activities.[41] Nonetheless, some caution should be taken with these partnerships. These agencies' publications indicate a highly technical vision of assistance: what may be termed a 'bricks and mortar' approach.[42] This is an approach that Australia, like most donors, has moved away from, preferring instead to enhance the capacities of the recipient country to undertake such work for themselves.[43] Furthermore, it is difficult to monitor funds channelled through a partner government's system. This approach also allows for little control over the speed of project delivery and limited input into operational decisions. As fledgling donors, the Brazilian and Chilean agencies will face inevitable bureaucratic, conceptual/policy and systemic establishment challenges, and hence operational delays. AusAID's limited resources, especially in terms of time, would be strained to overcome such constraints.

To avoid these obstacles, Australia ought to seek consortium-style partnerships that are led by experienced donors rather than rely on exclusive partnering with national governments via trilateral arrangements. The obvious donor–partner choice relies on those reputed donors working to similar objectives as Australia. Such partnerships should be selected with care, noting that donors enjoy distinct profiles and reputations.

The New Zealand government's Latin America Development Programme (LADP)

AusAID's Latin America Program would benefit from referring to the lessons learned by New Zealand's Latin America Development Programme (LADP). The New Zealand Aid Programme is often overlooked by Australia as an agency from which to learn because of its comparatively smaller ODA budget, which stands at about a quarter the size of Australia's. [44] Australia's regional neighbour has spearheaded aid provision in Latin America that parallels what the LA unit intends to implement.

---

40   Agência Brasileira de Cooperação (ABC), *Cooperação Técnica Introdução*, 2011: http://www.abc.gov.br/ct/introducao.asp; (and) Agencia de Cooperación Internacional de Chile (AGCI), 2011: *Cooperación Internacional*, http://www.agci.cl/cooperacion-internacional/.
41   Organisation for Economic Co-operation and Development (OECD), *op. cit.*, note 17.
42   Agência Brasileira de Cooperação (ABC), *op. cit.*, note 40.
43   Organisation for Economic Co-operation and Development (OECD), *op. cit.*, note 17.
44   New Zealand Agency for International Development, the, 'Latin America Regional', (official website page), June 2011: http://www.aid.govt.nz/programmes/r-latin-america.html. In 2010–11 the Australian

Among the similarities are those of the agencies' structures and objectives. Both the New Zealand Aid Programme and AusAID currently sit within their respective governments' departments of foreign affairs,[45] and therefore their activities are explicitly linked to foreign policy objectives.[46] Indeed, in the 2010 Independent Review of the LADP Program a congratulatory note is made that 'the LADP Strategy…has proved to be a valued foreign policy tool in the region over the past six years'.[47]

Both countries have a commitment to contributing towards reaching the MDGs, including scaling up their aid budgets to 0.5 per cent of their respective GNI. Moreover, the populations of Australia and New Zealand share many cultural traits—including national language, systems of government, and Commonwealth membership—and similar geographic concerns in that both are relatively remote from the major hubs of the other continents and possess a history of joint aid delivery primarily in Pacific states. Although neither country has a significant history of engagement with Latin America, New Zealand's modest aid provisions outdate and, until recently, exceeded in scale those of Australia.[48]

New Zealand's ODA contributions to the Latin America region date back to the 1970s.[49] The LADP manages only a modest portion of the overall ODA: over six years (2004/5–2009/10) the program received only NZ$28 million.[50] Nonetheless, this is more than that provided by Australia for the period up until 2009/10, when for the first time Australia's aid contributions exceeded those of New Zealand, and only then due to provision of unplanned humanitarian assistance.[51] With the AusAID Latin America Program's total ODA estimate set

---

government provided approximately $A4,349 million in total ODA, of which $A3,762 million was managed by AusAID. Whereas, for the same year, New Zealand's ODA totalled $NZ525 million [Marriott and Percy, 2010] a scaling up from the previous year's budget of $NZ500 million.

45   *Ibid*. Although for a period in the 1990s New Zealand's aid was delivered via a relatively autonomous agency, since 1 July 2002 this was converted into the New Zealand Aid Programme, which was established to manage New Zealand's ODA program with a central focus on poverty elimination and sits within New Zealand's department of foreign affairs.

46   *Ibid*. The objective of New Zealand's aid program is to: support sustainable development in developing countries in order to reduce poverty and to contribute to a more secure, equitable, and prosperous world. Nonetheless, the programme's position in the Ministry of Foreign Affairs and Trade (MFAT) is recognition that overseas development is an important pillar of New Zealand's foreign policy.

47   Sarah-Jane Marriott and Rachel Percy, 'Latin America Development Programme Strategy 2004–10: End Term Evaluation', The New Zealand Agency for International Development, Bristol (United Kingdom), May 2010: http://www.aid.govt.nz/what-we-do/review-and-evaluation-reports.html#2010, p. ix.

48   The New Zealand Agency for International Development, *op. cit.*, note 44.

49   Marriott and Percy, *op. cit.*, note 47, p. 4.

50   *Ibid*.

51   Australian Agency for International Development, the (AusAID), 'Submission to the Joint Standing Committee on Foreign Affairs, Defence and Trade, Inquiry into Australia's Relationship with the Countries of Africa', 18 March 2010: http://www.ausaid.gov.au/country/country.cfm?CountryID=95994596&Region=AfricaMiddleEast. NZAID's total support for Latin America in 2009-10 was $5.5 million [The New Zealand Agency for International Development, 2011]. For the same financial year, AusAID's country and regional program aid to Latin America totalled only $A2.1 million, although this was buffered somewhat by Australian humanitarian assistance, bringing the total ODA to an estimated $A9.3 million.

to peak at $27.2 million for the new fiscal year (2011-12),[52] now is the time to reflect on what might be learnt from a program with comparative scale and challenges in providing delivery.

The 2010 Independent Review of the LADP elicited some important findings.[53] It was critical of the combining of the LADP's geographic emphasis—on ten countries in the region, broken down into three sub-regions of Central America, the Andes, and the Southern Cone plus Brazil—with two thematic priorities—sustainable rural livelihoods for Central America and the Andes, and good governance for the Southern Cone and Brazil. The Review asserted that the LADP's geographic and thematic breakdown was inappropriate and ought instead to integrate the two key themes targeted in all three defined regions. It furthermore advised that the scope of the Program exceeds its implementing team's capacities.[54]

This second problem in particular is mirrored by the AusAID LA Program, which has a greater country scope than LADP, covering seventeen states in total. While LADP has fewer staff members [55] than the LA Program team, when this comparison is adjusted for aid scale—both budget and number of countries—AusAID emerges as only slightly better equipped than its neighbour to manage its work. This advantage is further reduced when Australia's far shorter program history is taken into consideration. In light of this similarly limited capacity, the AusAID team should look to mimic New Zealand's maximising of resources via leveraging off existing initiatives and programs. This approach circumvents the need to build up new versions of programs, costly both in time and staff resources and which typically take several years to reach full operation.[56] Indeed, the LA Program appears to have already recognised the value of this approach, having ensured that existing scholarship, fellowship and institutional–linkage program opportunities are made available to the Latin American region. Some examples of these include the Australian Leadership Award Scholarships (ALAS), the Australian Leadership Award Fellowships (ALAF) and the Government Partnerships for Development Program (GPFD).[57]

The most significant point made by the Review is in cautioning against dependency on partners to make up for their absence in the region. One of the key assumptions on which the Strategy appears to have been based—that the New Zealand government's lack of presence in the region could be mitigated through the appropriate selection of strategic partners—was found in need of

---

52   Rudd, *op. cit.*, note 3.
53   Marriott and Percy, *op. cit.*, note 47.
54   *Ibid.*
55   *Ibid.* This constitutes one full-time staff member operating from New Zealand and the only regional presence via four embassies.
56   Australian Agency for International Development (AusAID), *op. cit.*, note 2.
57   *Ibid.*

reappraisal.[58] There is not sufficient explanation in the Review for this warning, but it might be interpreted to imply that monitoring of project activities is made difficult by partner dependency. This is a valid point, and while limited resources and understanding of the region necessitate partnering, this must be done with trusted donors with compatible objectives.

USAID

The United States Agency for International Development (USAID) is the most prominent and well-established OECD donor in the region, having worked there for most of the 50 years of its existence. USAID's Bureau for Latin America and the Caribbean (LAC), which manages most US ODA-eligible funds, comprises sixteen bilateral missions, four regional programs, and several Washington-based programs for Cuba. Its total budget for FY09 was approximately $963 million.[59]

Despite the long history of its presence, USAID should be viewed with caution as a potential partner for AusAID due to its close associations with sensitive political issues. Although USAID is an independent federal government agency, it receives foreign policy guidance directly from the Secretary of State and explicitly acknowledges its interest in promoting US foreign policy. US foreign assistance has always had the two-fold purpose of furthering America's foreign policy interests in expanding democracy and free markets while improving the lives of the citizens of the developing world.[60] Specifically in the Latin American and Caribbean regions, US foreign policy aims to 'help governments respond to their citizens by promoting security, strengthening democracy, and creating widespread long-term economic growth'.[61] LAC's overriding objective is to 'consolidate and deepen democratic gains [in Latin America]'.[62]

Consequently, the reputation and profile of this heavyweight donor is tainted by the United States' long history of intervention in national affairs, at times with very tragic and long-lasting consequences. The view of USAID as a contributor to 'Banana Republics'[63] is widely held within the region and as such the political implications of its work—whether actual or only

---

58   Marriott and Percy, *op. cit.*, note 47.
59   USAID, 'Latin America and the Caribbean Program overview', USAID, 2011: http://www.usaid.gov/locations/latin_america_caribbean/.
60   *Ibid.*
61   *Ibid.*
62   *Ibid.*
63   Eduardo Galeano, *The Open Veins of Latin America*, (translation by Cedric Belfrage), New York and London: *Monthly Review Press*, 1973.

perceived—would be problematic for AusAID. If it is Australia's intention to foster strong diplomatic relationships in the region, partnering with USAID is best avoided.

The Canadian International Development Agency (CIDA)

Like USAID, the Canadian International Development Agency (CIDA) poses some advantages as a potential partner for AusAID, including a long history of operation in the region and a common national language. Furthermore, the Agency is not shadowed by the same negative historical, political and cultural associations of USAID.

CIDA sits within the Ministry of Foreign Affairs and Trade, which comprises several different agencies with international foci. CIDA's objective—to *Lead Canada's international effort to help people living in poverty*—is less overtly tied to forwarding national interest than is USAID's. Nonetheless, the Agency's position within the Ministry implies that its work is intended to harmonise with other international efforts such as trade negotiations and diplomacy.[64]

The Agency has significant experience in the Latin American region, its aid efforts dating back over 30 years. With a change of government in July 2007, these efforts were further scaled up.[65] During FY2009-10, CIDA's bilateral humanitarian—i.e., not all ODA—expenditure in the Americas, comprising 32 countries and including those that AusAID classifies as Caribbean states, totalled 200,750,000 Canadian dollars.[66] Despite this wide geographic spread in Latin America, CIDA's work concentrates on only five of these countries: Bolivia, Colombia, Haiti, Honduras and Peru, with very specific objectives relating to each context.[67] This is in line with the agency-wide policy implemented since February 2009 which directs CIDA to focus bilateral programming on only 20 countries so as to 'concentrate resources, intensify programming and improve coordination…in support of its commitment to the Paris Declaration and Accra Agenda for Action'.[68]

CIDA's substantial work in the region positions it well as an organisation from which Australia might learn. The most prominent example of this is CIDA's limited geographic approach to aid delivery. This should be seen as a strong

---

64   Canadian International Development Agency (CIDA), *op. cit.*, note 27.
65   *Ibid.*
66   Canadian International Development Agency (CIDA), 'Americas Program Overview,' *Her Majesty the Queen in Right of Canada*, http://www.acdi-cida.gc.ca/acdi-cida/ACDI-CIDA.nsf/eng/JUD-12911557-LVS, p. 15.
67   Canadian International Development Agency (CIDA), *op. cit.*, note 27, p. 4.
68   *Ibid.*

indication to Australia that its current LA Program objectives are over-ambitious and that a reduced country focus with related context-specific aims would be more appropriate.

Nonetheless, for partnering, CIDA may not prove the most appropriate choice, given that its areas of focus differ significantly from those of AusAID. CIDA has three key objectives in operating in Latin America: to promote basic democratic values; to strengthen economic linkages; and to meet new security challenges. As per the USAID example, these areas involve some political sensitivities which might prove harmful to diplomatic efforts—in accordance with Australia's national interests—and furthermore do not coincide with Australia's articulated areas of intended work. Hence, such partnering would not lend itself well to increasing LA Program coherence.

Deutsche Gesellschaft für Internationale Zusammenarbeit (GIZ) GmbH (The German International Cooperation Agency)

An alternative option for partnering is found in GIZ, the agency whose prime function is to provide support for the German government in the field of international cooperation for sustainable development. GIZ enjoys a strong reputation as an aid donor. [69] It has a history of over 45 years in the region and remains active in 21 countries.[70] Indeed, since 2000 GIZ has scaled up its efforts in Latin America and maintains a significant staff presence across the region. In 2009 GIZ directly employed some 155 seconded and 940 national personnel.[71] In particular, it is involved in numerous partnerships across the region, including collaborative aid projects typically involving a range of stakeholders from community groups, the private sector, international NGOs, the UN, and ministries of national governments.[72] Such consortium-style partnering appears to be a better option for AusAID's interests than triangular aid agreements, as it avoids the necessity for direct engagement with other governments' systems yet provides the potential for partnering with select ministries of these

---

69   William Easterly and Claudia R. Williamson, 'Rhetoric versus Reality: The Best and Worst of Aid Agency Practices', New York University: *Development Research Institute*, May 2011: http://williameasterly. files.wordpress.com/2010/08/61_easterly_williamson_rhetoricvsreality_prp.pdf. A recently released report ranked Germany in the top five of aid donors based on five criteria: aid transparency; minimal overhead costs; aid specialisation; delivery via effective channels; and selectivity of recipient countries based on poverty and good government.
70   Deutsche Gesellschaft für Internationale Zusammenarbeit (GIZ), *op. cit.*, note 27.
71   Deutsche Gesellschaft für Internationale Zusammenarbeit (GIZ) GmbH, *2009, Annual Report*, 2009: http://www2.gtz.de/dokumente/bib-2010/gtz2010-4000en-annual-report-2009.pdf.
72   Deutsche Gesellschaft für Internationale Zusammenarbeit (GIZ), *op. cit.*, note 27.

governments. Because of GIZ's record of success in the region it might be seen as a guarantor for the reliability of particular collaborative activities, thereby guiding AusAID's funding choices.

In addition to the advantages of its expertise, GIZ's areas of concern include those targeted by AusAID. These are identified as: democracy, civil society and public administration; crisis and conflict prevention; and, most significantly for AusAID, sustainable natural resource management and rural development. This final area covers three of AusAID's four identified pillars: Rural Development; Natural Resource Governance; and Climate Change and Environmental Stability.[73] Interestingly, the remaining Australian Program pillar, Human Resource Development, finds its parallel in GIZ's aid delivery means. That is, based on assessment of GIZ's Latin America projects,[74] the Agency sees capacity building and education as modes of realising these aid objectives rather than as ends in themselves. This suggests that AusAID's Human Resource Development would be more appropriately regarded as a modality for work than a Program end objective.

AusAID ought to consider adopting GIZ's amalgamation of the areas that the LA Program has separated into three pillars. This approach suggests that, at least in the Latin America region, they involve issues so interrelated that treating them together is a more appropriate strategy than tackling them separately. Similarly, GIZ's strategy should be reviewed more closely in order to obtain further useful knowledge that could inform the LA Program's strategy. The German International Cooperation Agency should also be recognised as an attractive partner for AusAID based on its expertise in the region, existing linkages with key actors and, of course, common thematic areas of interest.

Recommendation two: Championing a cause

> There is no doubt private sector investment can drive economic prosperity and reduce poverty in developing countries, provided appropriate regulation, transparency and accountability controls exist…[75]

The recommended focus: Natural resource governance

Australia's four-pillar strategy is problematic because it does not provide a clear ordering of priorities—and therefore direction—to those AusAID employees

---

73 Rudd, *op. cit.*, note 3.
74 Deutsche Gesellschaft für Internationale Zusammenarbeit (GIZ), *op. cit.*, note 27.
75 Andrew Hewett, 'Australian miners lacking transparency', *The Age*, 15 May, 2010: http://www. onlineopinion.com.au/view.asp?article=10456.

tasked with decision-making. In light of the potentially tight timeframe and scarce resources for a program intended to administer to as many as 17 countries, much greater coherence would be found via electing a single issue of key importance and setting the other issues as subsets of this, including where they contribute to meeting this targeted overarching objective.

In championing a single cause, Australia should elect an issue of significant importance to the region in which Australia has some comparative advantage. GIZ's focus on sustainable natural resource management and rural development, which encompasses most of the LA Program's current strategy, is a good starting point.

Within this, natural resource governance stands out due to its cross-cutting nature. Natural resources, where defined as extending beyond finite resources such as ore capable of being mined to include renewable resources such as forests, water sources, etc., are central to a vast array of important issues. These include: indigenous issues; environmental protection; distribution of wealth; human rights; transparency; governance; national and international trade; health; employment; conflicts; land tenancy; and agriculture. As well as being cross-cutting, natural resource governance is a multi-level sector in which work is required at all levels, from local through to the national and international.

Australia's competitive advantage in natural resource governance relates to its on-going engagement in Latin American primary resource extraction and trade. Australian companies have invested heavily in extractive industries in the region; much of Australia–Latin America trade is comprised of Australian exports of coal and Latin America's exports of copper and tin.[76]

Selection of natural resource governance as a key focus would support Australia's current engagement in the area and hence satisfy the necessity to promote 'national interest.' This is not to say, however, that aid should primarily constitute a vehicle for driving increased exploitation of natural resources. Rather, it might pose a means of enhancing accountability around such activities and the more equitable distribution of the benefits these generate. Australia's aid activities, directed by the necessity to meet standards enshrined in international accords that Australia has signed or ratified, might be a means of bringing an ethical element to Australia's engagement in the region.

The need for such work in this sector is critical and increasing. Latin America's history is often viewed through the prism of natural resources.[77] It was these riches that attracted the first conquistadors to the region and brought subsequent

76   Department of Foreign Affairs and Trade (DFAT), 'Australia's Trade with the Americas', 2009: http://www.dfat.gov.au/publications/stats-pubs/Australia-trade-with-the-Americas-2009.pdf.
77   Galeano, *op. cit.*, note 63.

waves of immigration, including the slave trade, the indentured labour for many natural resource sectors including gold mining and large-scale sugar and cocoa plantations. This long and complex history of natural resource exploitation in the region has involved a great many tragedies and been at the root of various protracted conflicts.[78]

Simultaneously, in one form or another, natural resources remain the basis for most economies and have offered some resilience to the region. The abundance of natural resources throughout Latin America significantly reduced the impacts of the global financial crisis. This buffer has even led to strong economic growth in some countries as a result of the post-crisis commodity boom.[79]

Indeed, appropriate governance of natural resources has been assessed as the key to sustainable reduction in income inequality in Latin America.[80] The Center for Global Development's working paper argues that decline in inequality is linked to an increase in natural resource exploitation and hence increased economic growth, but more importantly to social policies that redistribute wealth, especially in the form of educational expenditure and conditional cash transfers.[81] In this comparative study of several countries with unique profiles, the paper concludes that the political regime and governance at all levels from local through to international are more determinant of the decline than is the presence of resources.[82]

While the instances of good social policy are promising signs of the potential for good natural resource governance, there is some question as to whether these will be submerged in the growing wave of international investment in commodities from states with growing economies, such as China. In other words, will protection of vulnerable communities and the natural environment be sacrificed by governments in favour of the short-term gains of natural resource exploitation? Or can the two objectives be simultaneously realised? Finally, and more pertinent to the argument of this chapter, could the presence of aid reduce the negative impacts of such activities and enhance the positives? This presence might occur, for instance, by collaborating with companies on corporate–social responsibility activities and holding international investors accountable to codes of conduct, or critically publicising instances when organisations fail to do so.

While the responses to these questions should be the subject of ongoing attention beyond the scope of this chapter, one thing is certain: the investment wave is growing and the world's emerging economies are dependent on either

---

78 *Ibid*; (and) Birdsall *et al., op. cit.*, note 19, p. 5.
79 Birdsall *et al., op. cit.*, note 19.
80 *Ibid.*
81 *Ibid.*
82 *Ibid.*

the purchase or sale of natural commodities.[83] In acknowledging this reality, aid actors including major NGOs are advocating engagement in—and hence potential influence of—this process, rather than limiting responses to mere criticism.[84]

How to focus the LA Program efforts

Promoting improved natural resource governance should be as resource-light as possible, undertaken via two mechanisms: first, the partnering model as outlined above, namely the consortium arrangements spearheaded by a reputable donor such as GIZ; and secondly, via existing AusAID programs and linkages.

An example of the former mechanism would be that of seeking collaboration via co-funding on a project in a Latin American country where Australia and Germany's objectives overlap, such as in Honduras. Here, GIZ specifically aims at natural resource governance, and the projects it supports have strong national government involvement. Furthermore, as outlined in the country strategy, in Honduras GIZ actively seeks to coordinate its efforts with those of other donors and bring in a range of stakeholders from the private sector.[85]

An example of the latter mechanism is in the selection of scholarship, fellowship or organisation recipients in AusAID programs such as the previously mentioned: ALAS, ALAF and GPFD. That is, strong applications that identify a pertinent natural resource governance issue as their core would be prioritised for funding.

The Program team could easily reconfigure the current four-pillar structure into a pointed strategy with the pillar of Natural Resource Governance at the head and the aims of the Rural Livelihoods and Climate Change pillars as subcomponents, included as they relate to the overarching aim. In this proposed model the pillar of Human Resource Development would be more appropriately treated as a modality. That is, aid activities should involve capacity building with the objective of enhancing natural resource governance.

The focus areas currently grouped under the pillars of Rural Livelihoods and Climate Change/Environmental Stability might both sit comfortably beneath Natural Resource Governance. For instance, a quick glance at demographic trends across the region demonstrates that the populations typically located in areas of large-scale natural resource exploitation are overwhelmingly poor.[86]

---

83 Maxwell Strachan, '"Six Emerging Economies Will Account For Over Half Of Economic Growth By 2025", World Bank Says', *The Huffington Post*, 2011: http://www.huffingtonpost.com/2011/05/17/us-dollar-dominance-world-bank-currency_n_863248.html.

84 World Wildlife Fund, 'WWF–Australia's submission to the Independent Review of Australian Aid Effectiveness', *WWF–Australia*, 2 February 2011: http://www.aidreview.gov.au/publications/sub-wwf.pdf.

85 Deutsche Gesellschaft für Internationale Zusammenarbeit (GIZ) GmbH, *op. cit.*, note 27.

86 International Fund for Agricultural Development, the (IFAD), 'IFAD strategy for rural poverty reduction: Latin America and the Caribbean', 2002: http://www.ifad.org/operations/regional/2002/pl/pl.htm.

These groups fail to receive any benefits from natural resources in the form of revenue, employment opportunities, or otherwise, and in fact all too often suffer negative impacts, including contamination of water sources and soil, and displacement from their lands. In other instances, the problems around poor natural resource governance might result from small-scale exploitation of natural resources in environmentally damaging ways by the rural poor themselves, including mining and high-impact agricultural practices.[87]

In both instances, addressing rural livelihoods is of vital importance. For instance, this focus might see the push towards job creation within large-scale activities or, alternatively, the training of small-scale miners, farmers, etc., in practices that minimise environmental damage or even provide them with alternative skill-sets and hence employment opportunities.

Similarly, in all LA Program work, consideration should be given to environmental protection and anticipated climate change impacts, including increased natural disasters. Such activities might involve research into possible adaptation responses. It would presumably also include activities supporting alternative energy generation and national-scale initiatives such as carbon trading schemes, as well as promising resource management initiatives such as Benefit Sharing Mechanisms (BSM) and Payments for Environmental Services (PES).[88]

Concluding remarks

AusAID's expansion into Latin America has been criticised first for its political motivations; secondly for the region being undeserving as an aid recipient—given several already strong and increasingly growing economies; and thirdly for the

---

87 United Nations Environmental Programme, the, (UNEP), 'Payments for Ecosystem Services: Getting Started', Nairobi, Kenya, 2008: http://www.unep.org/pdf/PaymentsForEcosystemServices_en.pdf.

88 *Ibid*. Past debates about prioritising environmental protection above 'the right to development' have pitted 'conservationists' against 'humanitarians'. However, the last decade, particularly in the LA region, has seen these debates reconfigured with recognition that both objectives can and should be realised concurrently. This perspective was encapsulated in the 1992 Rio Declaration on Environment and Development, whose first principle states that '[h]uman beings are at the centre of concern for sustainable development' [UN, 1992]. This Declaration built on earlier foundations established at the Stockholm Conference (considered the first major conference on environmental issues at the international level) [UN, 1992] and propelled the emergence of initiatives aimed at enhancing human wellbeing via their involvement in environmental protection. Examples of such initiatives include 'Benefits Sharing Mechanisms' (BSMs) which seek the more equitable distribution of the benefits derived from natural resource systems (often referred to as Ecosystem Services—ES) and simultaneous protection of the ES. These may take the form of Payment for Environmental Services (PES) or in other cases non-monetary benefit-sharing. These are found in various forms throughout the world and not exclusively in 'developing' countries. Indeed, because they typically require involvement of various levels of government in the context in which they are implemented, they require reasonably high levels of capacity within the host governments. Because many Latin American countries qualify on this count, in addition to the abundance of their natural resources and situations of inequitable distribution, they are often seen as perfect potential sites for BSM implementation [UNEP, 2008 (and) Fundación Natura Bolivia, 2011].

new Program's overambitious scope given its relatively modest funds—AUD$100 million over four years, the expansive seventeen-country reach, and Australia's lack of history or expertise in engaging in the region.

The first group of these criticisms is not easily dealt with by a chapter most directly concerned with policy advice in a particular context, rather than in questioning the very foundations and nature of international aid. However, it is nonetheless useful to note that Australia's aid delivery, like that of most OECD donors, is explicitly and inherently intended to uphold national interests, as is spelled out in the Agency's overarching objective. The political motivations accompanying the expansion into Latin America are by no means unique. Nor, as this chapter argues, does this political context necessarily undermine the value of what aid activities might achieve. Rather, taking 'forwarding Australian national interest' as read, the presence of aid actors in national or international engagements—such as in trade or negotiations regarding natural resource management and/or exploitation—might serve as a watch-dog on such activities.

At the time of writing, the future of the LA Program is uncertain—whether future governments will continue to support it is unclear. It certainly seems, at the very least, that a major expansion of the program is unlikely. Hence, the Program strategy should accordingly work to short timeframes, and focus on enhancing existing initiatives, especially scholarship, fellowship and organisational linkages programs, rather than beginning these from scratch.

Likewise, criticisms about the region's deservedness as an aid recipient are relatively easily dealt with. Certainly, Latin America is a region characterised by the strong growth of national economies, a burgeoning middle class in many countries, and relatively strong average HDI vis-à-vis those of Africa and South-East Asia. Nonetheless, the region is also consistently ranked as the most unequal in terms of wealth distribution. Large sectors of populations continue to live in abject poverty despite the growth of their countries' economies, and many communities are affected by situations of insecurity largely generated by unequal resource allocation. Furthermore, unlike some countries saturated by aid provisions, Latin America's capacity to use aid flows means that if programming is undertaken strategically, increased aid provisions via the scaling-up of the Australian aid program to meet MDG commitments might see a significant impact within the region. Just as the criticisms about political interests indicate the need for short-term planning, responding to criticisms about deservedness leads to the conclusion that Australia's focus should be appropriate for the needs of the region.

The final and most compelling group of criticisms points to Australia's limited capacity in terms of time, budget and staffing to deliver effective aid in an area where it has no history of engagement. Noting these constraints, the chapter posits two recommendations. The first is that AusAID should seek partnerships to guide its work strategically as well as operationally; and the second is that AusAID ought to refine its objectives to a single priority area.

In relation to the first of these recommendations, GIZ stands out as the most valuable potential partner for the LA Program, given its similar program focus and its large-scale, long-term and well-received regional presence. A partner to whom AusAID might look for lessons learnt and on which to model its strategy as a fledgling and lightweight donor is neighbouring New Zealand.

In relation to the second of these recommendations, the stand-out issue for the Latin America region is the protection of the abundant but all too often mismanaged natural resources upon which all communities in the region depend in one form or another.

Championing improved natural resource governance would see the LA Program orient all activities in a cohesive manner and permit collaboration with GIZ, which works extensively in this theme. Furthermore, it would support fulfilment of the ethical responsibility that ought to accompany Australia's involvement, namely, mining investments and trade based on primary commodities. That is, in this way Australian aid might assist the reduction in environmental damage associated with the extractive industries, and furthermore might support the more equitable sharing of benefits generated by natural resources with otherwise marginalised communities. Given that Australia is likely to be involved in rising investments in extractive industries in Latin America in the future, the country's reputation can only be enhanced by aid designed to produce the best possible local outcomes in these industries.

The importance of the Program's reconfiguration is more than one of semantics. Clear prioritisation within an aid program's strategy is of utmost importance as this will inform the decisions made about activities funded and increase the likelihood that these might complement or strengthen one-another. The strategy outlined in this chapter—of championing natural resource governance, in partnership with GIZ and via established programs—would satisfy the necessary obligations of forwarding Australian national interest by promoting Australia as a good international citizen with concern for issues of international relevance. Moreover, this proposed strategy would concentrate modest aid provisions towards an area which sees the intersection of two areas of vital importance across all of Latin America: enhancing environmental protection and improving equity.

References

Agência Brasileira de Cooperação, *Cooperação Técnica Introdução*, http://www.abc.gov.br/ct/introducao.asp, accessed 24 May 2011.

Agencia de Cooperación Internacional de Chile,, *Cooperación Internacional*, http://www.agci.cl/cooperacion-internacional/, accessed 23 May 2011.

Australian Agency for International Development, *About AusAID*, http://www.ausaid.gov.au/about/default.cfm, accessed 20 May 2011.

Australian Agency for International Development, Informal consultations with Latin America Program staff members eliciting 'open source' (public) information, (May 2011).

Australian Agency for International Development, 2011, *Caribbean and Latin America Program overview*, http://www.ausaid.gov.au/country/caribbean.cfm, accessed 20 May 2011.

Australian Agency for International Development, 18 March 2010, Submission to the Joint Standing Committee on Foreign Affairs, Defence and Trade, Inquiry into Australia's Relationship with the Countries of Africa, http://www.ausaid.gov.au/country/country.cfm?CountryID=95994596&Region=AfricaMiddleEast, accessed 26 May 2011.

Birdsall, Nancy, Nora Lustig, and Darryl McLeod, 'Working Paper 251: Declining Inequality in Latin America: Some Economics, Some Politics', *Center for Global Development*, 19 May 2010, http://www.cgdev.org/content/publications/detail/1425092/?utm_source=nl_weekly&utm_medium=email&utm_campaign=nl_weekly_05242011&, accessed 23 May 2011.

Canadian International Development Agency, 'Americas Program Overview,' *Her Majesty the Queen in Right of Canada*, http://www.acdi-cida.gc.ca/acdi-cida/ACDI-CIDA.nsf/eng/JUD-12911557-LVS, accessed 24 May 2011.

Canadian International Development Agency, 2011, 'Statistical Report on International Assistance, Fiscal Year 2009–2010', *Her Majesty the Queen in Right of Canada*, http://www.acdi-cida.gc.ca/INET/IMAGES.NSF/vLUImages/stats/$file/Statistical_Report_2009-2010_eng.pdf, accessed 24 May 2011.

Clarke, Matthew, 'How to deliver a doubling aid program?', *Lowy Institute for International Policy*, 6 April 2011, http://aidreview.lowyinterpreter.org/post/How-to-deliver-a-doubling-aid-program.aspx, accessed 16 May 2011.

Deutsche Gesellschaft für Internationale Zusammenarbeit GmbH, *2009,Annual Report*, http://www2.gtz.de/dokumente/bib-2010/gtz2010-4000en-annual-report-2009.pdf, accessed 25 May 2011.

Deutsche Gesellschaft für Internationale Zusammenarbeit GmbH, 2011, *GIZ in Honduras*, http://www.gtz.de/en/weltweit/lateinamerika-karibik/634.htm, accessed 30 May 2011.

Deutsche Gesellschaft für Internationale Zusammenarbeit, GmbH, 2011, *About GIZ*, http://www.giz.de/en/profile.html, accessed 24 May 2011.

Department of Foreign Affairs and Trade, 'Australia, Australia's Trade with the Americas', 2009, http://www.dfat.gov.au/publications/stats-pubs/Australia-trade-with-the-Americas-2009.pdf, accessed 24 May 2011.

Easterly, William, and Claudia R. Williamson, 'Rhetoric versus Reality: The Best and Worst of Aid Agency Practices', New York University: *Development Research Institute*, May 2011, http://williameasterly.files.wordpress.com/2010/08/61_easterly_williamson_rhetoricvsreality_prp.pdf, accessed 30 May 2011.

Fundación Natura Bolivia, *Fundación Natura Bolivia* Website, 2011, http://www.naturabolivia.org/indexI.htm, accessed 25 May 2011.

Galeano, Eduardo, *The Open Veins of Latin America*, (translation by Cedric Belfrage), New York and London: *Monthly Review Press*, 1973.

Grenville, Stephen, 'Aid Review: Narrow the geographic focus', *Lowy Institute for International Policy*, 20 January 2011, http://aidreview.lowyinterpreter.org/post/AusAID-Review-Narrow-the-geographic-focus.aspx, accessed 22 May 2011.

Hayward-Jones, Jenny, 'African gold rush: Aid and UN votes', *Lowy Institute for International Policy*, 4 May 2011, http://www.lowyinterpreter.org/post/2010/05/04/African-gold-rush-Aid-and-UN-votes.aspx, accessed 20 May 2011.

Hayward-Jones, Jenny, 'Geographic focus or national interest?', *Lowy Institute for International Policy*, 25 January 2011, http://aidreview.lowyinterpreter.org/post/Geographic-focus-or-national-interest.aspx, accessed 21 May 2011.

Hayward-Jones, Jenny, 'In our national interest—effective aid to the Pacific', *Lowy Institute for International Policy*, 25 April 2011, http://aidreview.lowyinterpreter.org/post/Geographic-focus-or-national-interest.aspx, accessed 20 May 2011.

Hewett, Andrew, 'Australian miners lacking transparency', *The Age*, 15 May, 2010, http://www.onlineopinion.com.au/view.asp?article=10456, accessed 28 May 2011.

Independent Review of Aid Effectiveness, *Independent Review of Aid Effectiveness Official Website*, 2010, Commonwealth Government (of Australia), http://www.aidreview.gov.au/index.html, accessed 20 May 2011.

International Fund for Agricultural Development, 'IFAD strategy for rural poverty reduction: Latin America and the Caribbean', http://www.ifad.org/operations/regional/2002/pl/pl.htm, accessed 30 May 2011.

López-Calva, Luis F. and Nora Lustig (eds), *Declining Income Inequality in America: A Decade of Progress?* Baltimore, MD: Brookings Institution Press, 2010.

Markovic, Nina (on behalf of the Department of Foreign Affairs and Trade), 'Australia, 2011, Budget 2011–12: Introduction', http://www.aph.gov.au/library/pubs/RP/BudgetReview2011-12/DFAT.htm, accessed 25 May 2011.

Marriott, Sarah-Jane, and Rachel Percy, 'Latin America Development Programme Strategy 2004–10: End Term Evaluation', The New Zealand Agency for International Development, Bristol (United Kingdom), May 2010, http://www.aid.govt.nz/what-we-do/review-and-evaluation-reports.html#2010, accessed 24 May 2011.

New Zealand Agency for International Development, The, 'Latin America Regional', (official website page), June 2011, http://www.aid.govt.nz/programmes/r-latin-america.html, accessed 24 May 2011.

Organisation for Economic Co-operation and Development, 'Paris Declaration and Accra Agenda for Action', OECD Development Co-operation Directorate, http://www.oecd.org/document/18/0,3343,en_2649_3236398_35401554_1_1_1_1,00.html, accessed 25 May 2011.

Oxfam Australia, 'Submission to Independent Review of Aid Effectiveness', Oxfam Australia, 2 February 2011, http://www.oxfam.org.au/resources/filestore/originals/OAus-IndependentAidReviewSubmission-0211.pdf, accessed 23 May 2011.

Rudd, Kevin, 'Australia's International Development Assistance Program 2011–12: An Effective Aid Plan for Australia: Reducing Poverty, Saving Lives and Advancing Australia's National Interest—Statement by the Hon Kevin Rudd MP, Minister for Foreign Affairs 10 May 2011', *Budget 2011-12*. Australian Government, http://www.budget.gov.au/2011-12/content/ministerial_statements/ausaid/download/ms_ausaid.pdf, accessed 23 May 2011.

Smith, Hon Steven (MP, Minister for Foreign Affairs), 'Budget 2009–10: Policy Statement on Australia's International Development Assistance', http://www.ausaid.gov.au/hottopics/topic.cfm?ID=872_6918_7937_5970_8092, accessed 24 May 2011.

Strachan, Maxwell, '"Six Emerging Economies Will Account For Over Half Of Economic Growth By 2025", World Bank Says', *The Huffington Post*, 2011, http://www.huffingtonpost.com/2011/05/17/us-dollar-dominance-world-bank-currency_n_863248.html, accessed 24 May 2011.

United Nations Development Programme, *2010, Human Development Index (HDI)—2010 Rankings*, http://hdr.undp.org/en/statistics/, accessed 20 May 2011.

United Nations Environmental Programme, 'Payments for Ecosystem Services: Getting Started', Nairobi, Kenya, 2008. http://www.unep.org/pdf/PaymentsForEcosystemServices_en.pdf, accessed 28 May 2011.

World Bank, The, 'Measuring Inequality', 2011, http://web.worldbank.org/WBSITE/EXTERNAL/TOPICS/EXTPOVERTY/EXTPA/0,,contentMDK:20238991~menuPK:492138~pagePK:148956~piPK:216618~theSitePK:430367,00.html, accessed 24 May 2011.

United Nations, The, 'Rio Declaration on Environment and Development', Rio de Janeiro, The United Nations Conference on Environment and Development, June 1992, http://www.unep.org/Documents.Multilingual/Default.asp?DocumentID=78&ArticleID=1163&l=en, accessed 30 May 2011.

USAID, 'Latin America and the Caribbean Program overview', USAID, 2011, http://www.usaid.gov/locations/latin_america_caribbean/, accessed 28 May 2011.

Wesley, Michael, 'Designing our foreign aid future: Interpreting the Independent Aid Review Blog', *Lowy Institute for International Policy*, 29 April 2011, http://aidreview.lowyinterpreter.org/, accessed 20 May 2011.

World Wildlife Fund, 'WWF–Australia's submission to the Independent Review of Australian Aid Effectiveness', *WWF–Australia*, 2 February 2011, http://www.aidreview.gov.au/publications/sub-wwf.pdf, accessed 20 May 2011.

4. Australia, Latin America and the Environment

James R. Levy and Peter Ross

Introduction

Environmental issues have taken centre stage in the globalised world of the 21st century. There is a growing awareness and acceptance of the interconnectedness of nation states, not just at the level of trade, investment and ideas, but also at the level of the shared environmental consequences stemming from the types of development undertaken. Environmental damage in one nation state can directly affect contiguous nation states, as has been observed in the past with events such as acid rain, flooding, and nuclear fallout, but a far greater problem is the global nature of the current environmental crisis as manifested by—but not limited to—climate change and pressure on finite resources shared by various nation states. A major consequence is that the concept of national strategic interest needs to be considerably broadened. If national interest means anything then it is about the wellbeing and security, in the broadest sense, of the people who comprise a nation state. This can no longer be limited to military defence and rising living standards as measured by GDP per capita, education levels and increasing longevity, the components of the United Nations' Human Development Index (HDI). The health of the planet also needs to be included. And no one nation state can take responsibility for that. Cooperation is essential—and that cooperation must be as global as possible.

Cooperation among nation states depends upon a clear understanding of similarities and differences. A major difficulty in analysing Australian–Latin American relations in any sphere, including the environment, is that Latin America is comprised of about 20 nation states,[1] each with its own peculiarities and developmental pattern, with significant differences with regard to living standards, population, natural resources, and degree of industrialisation and urbanisation. Moreover, these nation states stretch from the northern hemisphere

---

1   Latin America is a vague term and is generally used to refer to those countries in the Americas in which Spanish and Portuguese are official languages. Sometimes French-speaking countries are included. If all countries in the Americas south of the United States and including all of the Caribbean nations are thought of as Latin American, then the total rises to 42. For the purposes of this chapter we use Latin America to refer only to the Spanish and Portuguese speaking countries.

to the Antarctic. None of them approach Australia in terms of living standards as measured by the HDI. Australia is currently ranked number two in the world, while the first Latin American country to be listed is Chile at number 43.

On the other hand, Australia and most of Latin America are situated in the southern hemisphere; many of the environmental problems the globe confronts, from climate change to serious marine pollution, emanate from the northern hemisphere. Whether the source is a poor nation, such as China, or a rich nation, e.g., the United States, the fact remains that the problem derives very largely from the northern hemisphere, not the southern. The north contributes far more than its fair share of environmental degradation and dominates such practices as polluting both the atmosphere and the oceans; the illegal, unreported, and unregulated fishing that is adding to the crisis of fish stocks; warming the climate; and enforcing economic policies that result in increasing rates of deforestation in the south.

The environment below the equator is cleaner, less polluted and possibly less exploited than that of the north. The obvious question is: why do the nations of the south allow their resources and their environment to be plundered and ruined while simultaneously suffering the deterioration of their own living conditions? The answer involves not only the political and economic: it also requires a moral understanding of just who possesses rights over the earth. Thus, the solution must involve more than Australia and Latin America: it requires a larger consensus. Fish, for example, do not know whether they are swimming in territorial waters or in the open seas. But Australia and Latin America together and with other partners can begin to articulate a common political and moral position that could serve notice that narrow economic and material interest is no longer acceptable to the southern hemisphere in protecting and managing its environment for all stakeholders.

In this chapter, we consider two issues—deforestation and the marine environment, particularly fishing—that directly affect the lives of Latin Americans and Australians. Given the overwhelming and immediate importance of addressing global warming, deforestation is the more central if not the more contentious issue because of its direct relationship to carbon emissions. As will become evident below, the possibilities of achieving cooperation between the many Latin American states and Australia on deforestation will be conditioned by the economic needs and specific strategies related to producing less carbon. As for the marine environment, the focus on fishing and the protection of whales dramatises the prospects of a finite resource seriously threatened. Much research currently concentrates on the relationship between global warming and the deterioration of the oceans. The absorption by the oceans of some 20 to 30 per cent of the carbon dioxide emitted has resulted in acidification that will affect food security, coral reef ecosystems and the deaths of some marine organisms.[2] In addition, sea levels are rising, low-lying islands are facing submersion, and coastal environments such as salt marshes and mangroves confront severe deterioration.

Although much research is being done, the main focus is on pollution and conservation of fish stocks and whales. Nevertheless, just because the deteriorating marine environment may not be as directly determined by global warming as the terrestrial environment, the oceans remain the source of much life on the planet including, of course, our food.

Despite the obvious difficulties in achieving and maintaining cooperation between Australia and Latin America, the record is clear that both the institutions and the policies for a common southern hemisphere position on the environment can be formed. Australia and most Latin American nations cooperate on many issues in such forums as the United Nations, APEC and the World Trade Organization. Within the UN framework, for example, Australia signed the Antarctic Treaty in 1959, joining with Argentina, Brazil, Chile, Ecuador, Peru and Uruguay. These nations were among the 27 that wrote the Treaty. Australia continues as host of the Commission for the Conservation of Antarctic Marine Living Resources and has signed the Convention on International Trade in Endangered Species and the International Tropical Timber Agreement. Notably, in 1995 it convened the Valdivia Group, formally named the Group of Temperate Southern Hemisphere Countries on Environment, which includes New Zealand, Chile, Argentina, Uruguay, Brazil and South Africa. More will be said about this below. But Australia does not always cooperate on behalf of the planet. Particularly egregious examples include its stance on carbon emissions and its membership of the Miami Group of nations—Canada, Argentina, Uruguay and the United States—which has successfully frustrated the formulation of the Biosafety Protocol to the Convention on Biodiversity.[3]

Forest management and carbon sequestration

As a response to global warming, forest conservation, management and expansion are areas of common interest to Australia and Latin America. Carbon released as a result of deforestation constitutes about 17.3 per cent of global greenhouse gas emissions. Deforestation is most prevalent in developing countries but, until relatively recently, has also been a feature of Australian development. The causes

---

2   See 'Summary of the Oceans Day at Cancún, 4 December 2010', www.iisd.ca/climate/cop16, accessed 27 October 2013.
3   The Miami Group of exporting agricultural nations refuses to sign the Protocol because it seeks to restrict the trade in genetically modified crops. The irony here, of course, is Australia's ostensible cooperation with Argentina and Uruguay. Sectoral economic interests invariably trump morality and perhaps safety.

result from the need or desire to increase production to make profits, improve living standards, pay foreign debt, and/or offset the cost of imports by means of the use and commercialisation of such natural resources as land, timber, water, minerals and oil and gas deposits.

Both Latin America and Australia possess considerable tracts of forest, a consequence of relatively late development and of relatively low population densities. These forests not only store carbon and act as carbon sinks, they are also the most bio-diverse of terrestrial environments. Even without the threat posed by global warming, a case for forest preservation is easily mounted based on the importance of biodiversity and the wellbeing of humans—many of them indigenes—currently living in, and off, the forests. This analysis, however, will focus on the issues raised by the world's response to global warming and the commonalities and differences that have resulted in Australian and Latin American initiatives with regard to forests.

All Latin American countries ratified the 1997 Kyoto Protocol. Australia did not do so until late 2007, after the election of the Labor Party to office. The reluctance of the Liberal–National Coalition government to ratify the Protocol, as distinct from signing up to it, stemmed from its belief that as a developed nation (an Annex 1 country), Australia would ultimately be required to reduce its greenhouse gas emissions. This could result in lower or negative GDP growth, and hurt the economic wellbeing of the population. The Latin American nations, on the other hand, were not required to reduce emissions since they were classified as developing countries (Non-annex 1), although by the terms of the 2007 Bali Action Plan of the Thirteenth Conference of Parties (COP) under the UN Framework Convention on Climate Change, the developing countries were strongly encouraged to take nationally appropriate mitigation actions (NAMAs). These actions, unlike those of the developed countries that ratified the Kyoto Protocol, were voluntary, in line with the principle of shared but differentiated responsibilities.

This division of the world into developed or industrialised, and developing or non-industrialised, placed Australia and Latin American nations on opposite sides of the negotiating table in climate change forums. This was most apparent at the Fifteenth COP held in Copenhagen in December 2009. The Australian negotiators, headed by Prime Minister Kevin Rudd, cooperated with the chair of the conference, the Danish Prime Minister, in an attempt to draft an agreement by which both developed and developing countries would be obliged to reduce emissions. They were not successful. Instead, in talks with Brazil, South Africa, India and China, the United States produced the non-binding Copenhagen Accord, to which some of the Latin American countries, particularly those in the Bolivarian Alternative for the Americas (ALBA) took strong exception on a number of grounds, including that the Accord was not arrived at democratically and that the target greenhouse gas reductions were not sufficient.

That Brazil helped to pen the final accord, even while its President, Lula da Silva, expressed the view that it was an inadequate outcome, underlines the differences amongst the Latin American countries. Of the fifty-five nation states that formally associated themselves with the Accord by submitting reduction targets for 2020 by the deadline of 31 January 2010, only two were Latin American, namely Brazil and Costa Rica. Cuba specifically stated that it would not associate. The Australian letter of association guaranteed that it would cut year-2000 emissions by five per cent, and by up to 15 to 20 per cent if major developing and developed countries committed to reduce their emissions substantially.[4] Australia's position on the necessity to include all of the major national economies, whether developed or developing, in a binding agreement on the reduction of emissions of greenhouse gases has been fairly consistent over the period of the 1990s to the present. Latin American countries, while not having any unified policy on the issue, have generally not been opposed to a binding agreement, but they have all maintained that, as developing countries, the same rules should not apply to them as to the developed world. On this matter Australia and Latin America have divergent positions. However, both have a common interest in the inclusion of forest conservation and land management in the calculation of carbon emissions and sequestration for individual nation states.

The Kyoto Protocol did not approve a mechanism by which forest conservation and most land use changes could be used to generate carbon credits. This was mainly due to the technical difficulties of measuring carbon sequestration, and to the fact that deforestation was not regarded as an important source of greenhouse gas emissions in the developed world. On the other hand, afforestation and reforestation projects could qualify as carbon emission reduction schemes under the Clean Development Mechanism (CDM). Australia, however, managed to secure a special deal at Kyoto due to hard bargaining on its part, and to the determination of other countries to get as many nation states on board as possible. Whereas the average reduction of greenhouse gas emissions for developed countries for the first commitment period was 5.2 per cent below the baseline of 1990 emissions, Australia was permitted to increase its emissions by eight per cent. Moreover, Australia secured the right to include any improvements in its deforestation rate within its target. As it happened, 1990 was a peak for deforestation in Australia and represented some 30 per cent of the country's carbon emissions. Already by the time of Kyoto the deforestation rate was much lower and continued to decrease as the Federal government, in concert with state

---

4   UNFCCC, 'Appendix 1—Quantified economy-wide emissions targets for 2020', http://unfccc.int/files/parties, accessed 2 February 2010.

governments, made the reduction of deforestation the central plank in its drive to achieve its Kyoto target, despite not having ratified the Protocol. Reductions in greenhouse gas emissions in this sector permitted increased emissions from other areas including agriculture, industry, transport, mining, households and energy generation, which is heavily dependent on coal-fired power stations. In fact, such emissions increased by 26 per cent between 1990 and 2007. However, because of the offset provided by reduced deforestation, the official figures for emissions increase between 1990 and 2008 was nine per cent, very close to the target of eight per cent set for Australia at Kyoto.[5] Since 2008 Australia's greenhouse gas emissions have declined slightly, keeping it within its set target.

Following Kyoto, Australia mounted a strong campaign to have the special deal it secured with regard to forest management institutionalised within the framework of the strategies endorsed by the United Nations Framework Convention on Climate Change. Many of the developed countries joined this campaign. On the one hand they were concerned about the substantial amount of greenhouse gas emissions generated by deforestation; on the other they could offset some of their own emissions by investing in forest conservation and other forestry projects in the developing countries, a strategy endorsed in a limited way at Kyoto via the 'flexible mechanisms' of emissions trading and the clean development mechanism (CDM).[6] Developing countries with deforestation problems were also enthusiastic about the inclusion of forest preservation and augmentation within the parameters of the Kyoto Protocol. These pressures from both developed and developing countries resulted in the 2007 Bali Action Plan, which included the formulation of strategies for reducing emissions from deforestation and forest degradation in developing countries (REDD).

Understandably, Australia welcomed the REDD initiative because the reduction of deforestation within its own borders was the key element in its strategy to reach the targets set for it at Kyoto, and any institutionalisation of the special deal it had secured validated its environmental policies. The Bali Roadmap might also constitute a first step towards the inclusion of the developing countries into the sort of binding agreements to which most of the developed countries had agreed at Kyoto. Moreover, Australia asserted that it was in the forefront of technological development with regard to the measurement of the mitigation of climate change by means of the reduction of deforestation and of efforts made in the areas of reforestation and afforestation (REDD-plus). Australia therefore considered it was in an advantageous position to help developing countries become REDD ready and initiated bilateral International Forest Carbon projects

---

5   Andrew Macintosh, 'Reducing emissions from deforestation and forest degradation in developing countries: A cautionary tale from Australia', the Australia Institute, *Policy Brief*, No. 12, 2010, p. 4.

6   The Eliasch Review, commissioned by British Prime Minister Tony Blair is a good example of the developed world's concerns regarding deforestation. See Johan E. Eliasch, *Climate Change: Financing Global Forests*, London, Earthscan, 2008.

with Indonesia (the Kalimantan Forests and Climate Partnership) and with Papua New Guinea, providing scientific, technical and analytical support to both countries. Australia also participated with the World Bank in the Forest Carbon Partnership Facility and the Forest Investment Program, hosted the second world workshop on REDD in Cairns in March 2007, and cooperated with the Clinton Climate Initiative in efforts to establish efficient and effective forest carbon measurement systems in developing countries.[7] The efforts of Australia and other nations to have REDD-plus accepted as a legitimate means of reducing greenhouse gas emissions were recognised at the Copenhagen meeting, which effectively gave the green light to the strategy.

Latin American countries were also active in the push for the validation of REDD and REDD-plus. In 2005, on the initiative of Papua New Guinea's President, Michael Somare, a loose coalition of developing countries established the Coalition for Rainforest Nations to secure finance from developed countries to preserve rainforests. Of the 33 countries listed as participants, 13 are Latin American. The Coalition was instrumental in the formation of the World Bank's Forest Carbon Partnership Facility and in the push for the acceptance of the REDD program. Various developed countries, including Australia, have pledged US$3 billion to build capacity and provide incentives to reduce rainforest destruction. The UN has commenced REDD readiness programs in Panama, Bolivia and Paraguay.[8]

Brazil, not a member of the Coalition, has also been active in becoming REDD ready. In the Brazilian state of Amazonas, the Juma project aims to halt deforestation, improve the wellbeing of locals, avoid the degradation of 366,151 hectares of rainforest and the accompanying release of 210,885,604 million tons of carbon dioxide by 2050, and generate carbon credits equivalent to 189,767,027 tons of carbon dioxide. Finance for the project comes from the state government and a range of private corporations including the Bradesco Bank and the Marriott hotel chain.[9] In joining the Copenhagen Accord, Brazil pledged to reduce its carbon emissions by about 39 per cent by 2020. In effect this would be done by following the Australian path of reducing deforestation and taking other measures approved by the UN in the areas of afforestation, reforestation and land change. By 2013 government initiatives to control deforestation had had notable success, leaving Brazil well on track to meet its Copenhagen target.

---

7   Australian Government, Department of Climate Change, 'International Forest Carbon Initiative', http://www.climatechange.gov.au/government/initiatives/international-forest-carbon-initiative.aspx, accessed 22 January 2010. See also Australian Government, Department of Climate Change and Energy Efficiency, 'Action under the International Forest Carbon Initiative', http://www.climatechange.gov.au/government/initiatives/international-forest-carbon-initiative/action.aspx, accessed 14 December 2010.

8   Latin American and Caribbean Forestry Commission, 'Forests and Climate Change—With a Special Focus on Climate Change Adaptation', Twenty-Sixth Session, Guatemala City, 24–28 May 2010, FO:LACFC/2010/6, www.rlc.fao.org/es/comisiones/coflac/2010/pdf/lacfc-6e.pdf, accessed 20 June 2010.

9   Virgilio Viana, 'Seeing REDD in the Amazon', *Tiempo*, 73, 2009, p. 5.

Costa Rica aims to become carbon neutral by 2020, again largely based on reducing deforestation and by planting trees. Since 2005, landowners have been paid from a variety of state revenues including a tax on fuel to conserve trees and to plant new trees. Costa Rica's policy is also predicated on both domestic and foreign corporations using carbon sequestration in the country as a means of offsetting carbon emissions within Costa Rica and abroad.

On the face of it, therefore, Australia and many of the Latin American countries have a common interest in reducing their greenhouse gas emissions by means of carbon sequestration and carbon capture associated with forests and land use. However, there are major differences that hinder cooperation. The most important of these is the nature and role of financing. Australia wants to anchor the process in a global carbon market, arguing that only a market-based approach can provide the finance and investment on the scale needed to address forest emissions. At the same time, Australia does recognise that some countries might prefer to stay with the offset system of the Clean Development Mechanism as established at Kyoto. Australia also accepts that public financing—domestic and international—is essential, especially in the early stages of countries becoming REDD ready. However, in the long term, only a carbon market will work.[10] The Latin American countries in general do not agree with this stance. The most extreme position is that adopted by Bolivia and enshrined in the Cochabamba People's Agreement produced at the World People's Conference on Climate Change and the Rights of Mother Earth, held at Cochabamba in April 2010. That document absolutely rejects the use of market mechanisms to reduce deforestation and forest degradation. Moreover, it argues that the developed world is responsible for global warming and therefore owes a climate debt to the developing countries. It states that the developed countries have colonised the atmosphere. To make amends and to remedy the situation, the rich countries should pay about six per cent of their GDP to the developing countries so that they can achieve sustainable development. The developed countries should also be obliged to transfer technology associated with climate change to the developing countries free of intellectual property rights. The Agreement sheets home the blame for the environmental crisis to the capitalist mode of production.[11]

Bolivia's stance is undeniably extreme within Latin America; however, almost all Latin American nations reject the notion that a global carbon market will be beneficial to them. From Mexico to Brazil, governments have voiced their belief that there needs to be a transfer of funds and technology from the developed to the developing world if forests are to be saved and forest degradation reversed.

---

10 Australian Government, 'Australia's proposal for a forest carbon market mechanism', March 2009, http://www.climatechange.gov.au/government/initiatives/unfccc/submissions.aspx, accessed 22 February 2010.

11 World People's Conference on Climate Change and the Rights of Mother Earth, http://pwccc.wordpress.com/, accessed 17 August 2010.

Even the Copenhagen Accord recognised this, at least to some extent, and promised the transfer of some US$30 billion to the developing world over the period 2010–2012, and US$100 billion annually by 2020, only half of which would be derived from the carbon market. In 2008 Brazil unilaterally established an Amazon Fund, and called on the developed nations to deposit US$21 billion to fund rainforest preservation. Only Norway responded, promising some US$1 billion. Funds advanced to date have been used to control bushfires, compensate landowners, resolve land ownership disputes, and educate landowners on sustainable farming and pastoral activities.

The COP16 global climate summit held at Cancún towards the end of 2010 essentially reiterated the determinations of Copenhagen. With regard to forests, the objective of Australia and of many of the Latin American countries to have REDD made a fully accepted part of the world's strategy for greenhouse gas reduction was achieved. How REDD projects would be funded, however, was not clarified. The most recent climate summit held in Dohar in November 2012 again did not resolve disputes over funding.

There is now an opportunity for Australia and Latin America to forge a much greater bond in the pursuit of carbon sequestration and carbon capture by means of forest and land management. Australia has considerable scientific expertise in the measurement of carbon sequestration and could transfer this technology to the Latin American countries. Such transfers were called for in the final documents of the Cancún talks, but how these would be financed was not made clear. To date, Australia has made such transfers only to its immediate neighbours of Indonesia and Papua New Guinea. However, in the interest of forging closer relations within the southern hemisphere, Australia would do well to shore up and expand its connections with the Latin American countries by means of the transfer of clean energy knowledge, especially in the domain of forest management.

Australia could also take note of some of the concerns raised by Bolivia and others, especially with regard to the treatment of forest peoples, including indigenes. In pushing for a carbon market, Australia favours private ownership or control of resources. This is far from the position of the Bolivian government, which supports state and communal ownership. Bolivia has also raised the issue of the treatment of environmental refugees and is concerned about the barriers placed in their way in accessing other countries, particularly by the developed nation states. Given that Australia has one of the highest per capita greenhouse gas emissions of all the nation states, and that it has been recently reprimanded by the United Nations for discrimination against its Aboriginal population and for its treatment of refugees, it is hardly in a position to adopt a morally superior position, as it has a tendency to do. Moreover, there is much to be learnt from

Latin America with regard to the sustainable use of forests, and a fruitful interchange among the countries of the southern hemisphere, unhindered by free market ideology, is imaginable and desirable.

The marine environment

Perhaps the most obvious place where Australia, Latin America and other nations in the south can meet is in the Pacific, Indian and southern oceans. Among the critical issues we confront in these spaces are whaling, over-fishing, pollution of the marine environment, illegal, unreported and unregulated fishing, and threats to the survival of fish and bird species. With the possible exception of shipping, fishing is economically the most important oceanic activity to Australia, which may help to explain the government's keen interest in the marine environment.

Although the fishing industry is not a huge contributor to the nation's total production it is nevertheless a significant participant. According to the most recent figures available, in 2010–11 the gross value of Australian fisheries amounted to $A2.23 billion, of which $A948 million came from aquaculture and $A1.3 billion derived from the wildcatch sector. The contribution of aquaculture has increased at the expense of wildcatch.[12]

Australian fish exports are almost entirely of edible products sent to Hong Kong and worth $A539 million; to Japan worth $A269 million; and to China $A146 million. Pearls are the second most important export by value ($A241 million) after rock lobster ($A369 million).[13] The sources of imports are Thailand ($A297 million), New Zealand ($A207 million), Vietnam ($A142 million) and China ($A133 million). The imported products include canned fish, frozen fish fillets, fresh, chilled or frozen prawns, pearls and canned crustaceans and molluscs.[14] These statistics suggest the limited importance of fishing to the Australian economy; in fact the industry has stagnated during the last decade. One welcome statistic is the decline in the number of foreign fishing vessels caught illegally in Australian waters during 2011–12: it is at a 19-year low.[15] Based on available evidence it would appear that within the waters administered by the Australian Fisheries Management Authority, the fishing industry is carefully supervised, thanks in part to border security, in cooperation with private industry. Consequently, the *Fishery status reports* of the Department of Fisheries and Aquaculture assures us that of the fish stocks assessed, 77 were not subject

---

12   Australian Bureau of Agriculture and Resource Economics, *Australian Fisheries Statistics 2011*, December 2012, p. 1. abare.gov.au. Since 2000–01, the 'real values of Australian fisheries exports fell by 57 per cent ($A1.6 billion)'.

13   *Ibid*.p. 22.

14   *Ibid*.p. 23.

15   Australian Fisheries Management Authority, *Annual Report 2008-09*, Canberra, 2009, p. 2.

to overfishing, 58 were not overfished, six were subject to overfishing, and 11 were overfished. In short, Australian fish stocks are carefully monitored and ecologically in relatively good condition—that is, their biomass quantity in general is at low or moderate risk.[16]

Fishing plays an important part in the economies of several Latin American nations, particularly in Chile and Peru. In 2009, Chile claimed seventh place among the world's largest exporters of fish and fish products by value ($US3,606,328,000) and Peru came in at fourteenth ($US2,208,874,000). Among the nations that concern us in this chapter, Ecuador, Argentina, Australia, New Zealand, Mexico, South Africa and Brazil followed in that order according to the value of exports among the world's 50 principal fishing nations.[17] Chile's exports include both fish and processed products, mostly fishmeal, while those of Peru are almost entirely of fishmeal. Thus, the contribution of fishing to the economies of both countries is significant—it is no wonder that Chile and Peru along with Ecuador initiated the movement to establish the 200-mile territorial limit for fishing in the early 1950s.

However, there are difficulties and challenges facing the Australian industry and fishing industries elsewhere that cannot be easily overcome. For example, climate change: the *Annual Report 2008–2009* of the Australian Fisheries Management Authority noted that it is carefully monitoring research on the marine environment and fisheries because the science predicts that 'climate change will affect the distribution of fish stocks over time'.[18] In its *Annual Report 2011–2012* the Authority said that climate change is 'already affecting fishers', although at present it does not anticipate any immediate action due to present management of the fisheries.[19]

Another issue concerns floating marine debris that accumulates in 'the eastern-centre region of the South Pacific subtropical gyre' and is locked in.[20] The debris is not only an aesthetic issue: the authors cite an article that estimates the deaths of more than 100,000 sea creatures, including turtles, because they have consumed or been entrapped by plastic bags or other debris. Nor is there any certainty of what happens to the marine environment when the debris slowly disintegrates and chemicals are released into the ocean. The pollution problem that threatens fishing extends also to birds and indeed much of the marine ecosystem. An example close to home is the effects on the Great

---

16   Australian Government, Department of Agriculture, Fisheries and Aquaculture, *Fishery status reports 2011*, 18 December 2012 www.daff.gov.au/abares/publications_remote_content/public, accessed 27 October 2013.
17   See FAO *Yearbook of Fishery Statistics 2010, Summary Tables*, p. 15. ftp://ftp.fao.org/fi/stat/summary, accessed 27 October 2013.
18   Australian Fisheries Management Authority, *Annual Report 2008–2009*, Canberra, 2009, p. 3.
19   Australian Fisheries Management Authority, *Annual Report 2011–2012*, Canberra, 2012, p. 4.
20   Elodie Martinez, *et al.*, 'Floating marine debris surface drift: Convergence and accumulation toward the South Pacific subtropical gyre', *Marine Pollution Bulletin*. 58, 2009, pp. 1347–55.

Barrier Reef of herbicide, pesticide and fertilizer run-off from farming. Even mining contributes to the threat.[21] Another pollutant particularly serious for sea creatures is discarded fishing gear, especially nets that entrap their victims. But the greatest criminal by far is plastic; a survey of the ten most common items collected in South America in 2005 found plastic containers and lids at the top: in Peru they accounted for 49 per cent of the debris, in Chile about 70 per cent, while in Ecuador cigarettes and their filters made up over 55 per cent.[22] Much of the plastic found as waste originated in the northern hemisphere. Europe, North America and Japan account for about 60 per cent of plastic production, but developing countries find that their lower wages are increasingly attractive to plastics producers who are shifting operations to such nations: '[I]n the south-eastern Pacific Ocean, surveys of plastic pollution near the coast, including fragments of foamed polystyrene, plastic bags, and food sacks from salmon farms identified aquaculture as the most significant contributor'.[23] On the most remote beaches of Tasmania clean-up volunteers collected 35,777 bits of debris in one week, including an Argentine rugby ball, a Brazilian Coca-Cola bottle cap, and plastic energy drink bottles from South Korea.[24]

Overfishing threatens the economic survival of the populations who depend on this finite resource. The notion that fisheries policies should reflect social needs is all but lost among the countries of the north. As David Symes and Jeremy Phillipson write:

> Unlike most Third World countries where social issues—including food security, employment, fair trade and the protection of individual and community fishing rights—are very much to the forefront of fisheries development, in Europe, North America and Australasia the social objectives of fisheries policy have all but disappeared from view. Although disturbing, this turn of events is not altogether surprising. One does not have to look very far for an explanation of the obscuring of the social dimension in fisheries policy.

21   'From Catchment-to-reef continuum: Case studies from the Great Barrier Reef. A special issue', Editorial, *Marine Pollution Bulletin 2012*, 65, 2012, p. 77. Elsevier: www.elsevier.com/locate/marpolbul, accessed 27 October 2013.

22   Scientific and Technical Advisory Board, *Marine Debris as a Global Environmental Problem*, Washington, DC November 2011, p. 8.

23   Marcus Erikson, *et al.*, 'Plastic pollution in the South Pacific subtropical gyre', *Marine Pollution Bulletin*, 68, 2013, pp. 71–2, www.elsevier.com/locate/marpobul, accessed 27 October 2013.

24   Andrew Darby, 'Fight to turn tide of trash crashing on wild shores', *The Sydney Morning Herald*, 12–13 April, 2013, p. 7. http://www.smh.com.au/environment/conservation/fight-to-turn-tide-of-trash-crashing-on-wild-shores-20130412-2hquu.html, accessed 27 October 2013.

Even in the developed world formal fisheries policies and comprehensive management systems, as distinct from piecemeal regulation, are little more than 30 or 40 years old. They were born of a growing concern for the depletion of commercially valuable fish stocks through overfishing.[25]

Perhaps the greatest barrier to doing anything about the situation is the law of the sea that enshrines equal access to the oceans beyond the 200-mile limit. Increasingly in various international forums, however, discussions address the need to find a way of reconciling the oceans as 'commons' with the requirements of sustaining and improving the marine environment.[26]

A list of just the major issues relating to fishing reveals the daunting complexity of the matter as well as the precarious future of the entire marine environment. Overshadowing all the subsidiary problems is that of over fishing and the probability that about 60 per cent of fish species are in great or significant danger of extinction. In spite of the United Nations Fish Stocks Agreement adopted on 4 August 1995, the situation is deteriorating due to illegal, unreported and unregulated fishing, the flag of convenience vessels that permit irresponsible fishing, the huge quantities of unwanted marine life that are destroyed and thrown back into the sea—so-called by-catch—and freedom of the high seas that raises all sorts of problems in the regulation and enforcement of agreements among states and multinational bodies. And if these problems are not difficult enough, then there are debates over technical issues such as obtaining reliable data on the biomass of species; use of proper fishing equipment; differences between developed and developing nations over what, if any, advantages should be allowed the latter in fishing on the high seas; the difficulties of reconciling the conservation measures between those applicable to a country's exclusive economic zone—the 200-mile limit—and the high seas; and conflicts between artisanal and industrial fishers.

The solutions are as difficult as the problems. For example, on the question of whaling—discussed below—Australia and the Buenos Aires Group of nations together resisted the attempt to reintroduce commercial whaling at the June 2010 meeting of the International Whaling Commission. Instead, they supported the establishment of a South Atlantic sanctuary for whales. Another recent example of the common search for solutions is the agreement on Port State Measures to prevent, deter and eliminate illegal, unreported and unregulated fishing.[27] This

---

25   David Symes and Jeremy Phillipson, 'Whatever became of social objectives in fisheries policy?', *Fisheries Research*, 95, 2009, pp. 1–5. http://www.elsevier.com/locate/fisheries, accessed 27 October 2013.

26   See, for example, UN General Assembly, Sixty-fifth session, Agenda item 75 (a), Oceans and the law of the sea, 'Letter dated 16 March 2010 from the Co-Chairpersons of the Ad Hoc Open-ended Informal Working Group to the President of the General Assembly'. A/65/68.

27   'Port State' refers to the port of the country where the catch is landed. See UN, FAO, Fisheries and Aquaculture Department, 'Port State Measures Agreement.' http://www.fao.org/fishery/topic/166283/en. The following countries have acceded: Myanmar and Sri Lanka; Norway has ratified, and the EU has approved. Twenty-five States and the EU have signed, as has Australia. Signing is insufficient to give the agreement force.

agreement establishes a regime that will make it possible to refuse port entry to fishing vessels that cannot meet certain specifications regarding the origins of the catch, the kind of equipment used, authorisation to fish in certain waters, and so on. Approved in November 2009, the original signatories included Australia, Brazil, Chile, New Zealand, Peru and Uruguay. Since then, only Chile has ratified the agreement that requires the ratification, acceptance, approval or accession of the 25 states and regional economic integration organisations. Effective administration by port states is seen as one of the best strategies available to control illegal, unreported and unregulated fishing—if, of course, the port states possess the capacity and the will to enforce the agreement.

Although published by the Australian Department of Agriculture Fisheries and Forestry in 2005, the more detailed description and analysis of widespread illegal, unreported and unregulated fishing on the high seas retains its validity even today.[28] The declining, even threatened, stocks of popular edible fish including Atlantic, Pacific and Indian Ocean tuna, and the Patagonian toothfish in the southern ocean, entice fishers to defy governments, international agreements and legitimate fishing enterprises in search of the highly priced fish. Many, probably most, of the vessels involved are registered under flags of convenience issued primarily by Belize and followed by Honduras, Panama, and St. Vincent and the Grenadines. However, even the landlocked countries Bolivia and Mongolia have issued such flags, albeit in minor quantities.[29] By mid-2005, over 1,000 large-scale fishing vessels sailed under flags of convenience, while the group for which flags are unknown to insurers increased in number since 1999 by 50 per cent. Altogether, about 15 per cent of the global large-scale fishing vessel fleet flew under flags of convenience, with Spain and Taiwan being the major profiteers. This illegal, unreported and unregulated fishing has become widespread as coastal waters are fished out or are declared highly protected. The report concludes: 'Unfortunately, with some exceptions, the international community is losing the battle to effectively conserve and manage fisheries on the high seas'.[30] The Australian fishing industry and the government have worked hard to protect their own region: during 2011–12, some 12 foreign fishing vessels were caught, down from 14 during 2010–11, 23 in 2009–10, and 27 in 2008–09.[31] Of the 12 fishing vessels apprehended in 2011–12, five were destroyed in the Authority's land-based facilities, six were disposed of at sea, and one sank after the crew was removed.

---

28 See M. Gianni and W. Simpson, 'The Changing Nature of High Seas Fishing: how flags of convenience provide cover for illegal, unreported and unregulated fishing', Australian Department of Agriculture, Fisheries and Forestry, Canberra, 2005.

29 *Ibid.* p. 4.

30 *Ibid.* p. 6.

31 Australian Fisheries Management Authority, *Annual Report 2011-2012*, Canberra, 2012, pp. 19, 26.

As southern hemisphere countries that border the Pacific Ocean, both Peru and Chile possess fishing industries that suffer periodic crises related to the availability of fish stocks; when these stocks decrease, they cause industrial over-capacity, especially in the production of fishmeal. This, in turn, causes conflict between local, artisan fishers and the large, industrial firms. In the case of Peru, since the 1960s fishing interests and the government have experienced great difficulties in finding a compromise because of nationalism, private sector demands over the size of quotas and profitability in general, and the government's interests to maintain the stocks of anchovies that produce state revenues. In 1998, the Peruvian government allowed local artisan fishers to catch anchovies and, although strict limits were placed on the size of the catch, it nevertheless led to over-capacity. That challenged the profitability of the large industrial fishers.[32]

In Chile local fishers criticised the government during 2007 for allowing industrial fishers to over-fish the stocks of hake, the biomass of which in 2002 was estimated to be roughly 1.5 million tons, but by 2007 had fallen to 272,000 tons. The spokesperson for the artisan fishers called for the government to protect both the fish and the small enterprises. The Chilean senator who attended the protest meeting agreed that the problem existed but made very clear that nothing would be done about it in the foreseeable future. He commented: 'There is a lack of political will to resolve the problems of the fishing industry because the state is trapped in a tangle of interests. Conservation today is not oriented to the fish, but instead to the industrial fishing companies.'[33]

At the moment of writing, the marine issue of greatest popular interest in the southern hemisphere is whaling. It attracts a huge audience in Australia and the three major political parties agree that whaling should be stopped. Because Japan is seen as the major whaling nation, along with Norway and Iceland, the tension between the pro- and anti-whaling nations also suggests strong differences between the hemispheres. On the question of whaling, the once solid front of southern hemisphere nations that called for immediate cessation of whaling in the International Whaling Commission has broken down because of the whaling nations' enduring refusal to cease killing whales. Thus, in order to break the deadlock and the continued whaling activity, the government of New Zealand recently proposed a compromise that would allow phasing-out of whaling over a ten-year period. The Australian government's position is based

---

32 Martín Aranda, 'Developments on fisheries management in Peru: The new individual vessels quota system for the anchoveta fishery', *Fisheries Research*, vol. 96, issues 2–3, March 2009, pp. 308–12. For an earlier but more comprehensive statement of the problem, see Alonso Aguilar Ibarra, Chris Read and Andy Thorpe, 'The Political Economy of Marine Fisheries Development in Peru, Chile and Mexico', *Journal of Latin American Studies*, vol. 32, 2000, pp. 503–27.
33 Steve Anderson, 'Chilean coastal fishermen protest depletion of hake', *The Santiago Times,* 26 October, 2007. http://www.santiagotimes.cl/index, accessed 2 October 2011.

on former Prime Minister Kevin Rudd's promise to take the Japanese government to the International Court of Justice (ICJ) to stop scientific whaling while phasing out commercial whaling altogether over a five-year period. Although according to Canberra the New Zealand compromise would undermine the case before the International Court,[34] the Australian government has since taken the case to the ICJ, with closing arguments heard on 16 July and judgement expected in late 2013.[35]

A strong base now exists for cooperative action between Australia and the South American nations. Since 2000 Australia and New Zealand have supported a proposal for a South Pacific Whale Sanctuary and, more recently, a similar proposal for a South Atlantic Sanctuary instigated by Argentina and Brazil. In February 2009, the then Australian Minister for the Environment, Heritage and the Arts, Peter Garrett, offered a package of proposals that included reform of the gridlocked International Whaling Commission, the funding of a six-year program to improve non-lethal research on whales, and the establishment of a Southern Ocean Research Partnership to which Argentina, Brazil, Chile and New Zealand are committed.[36] Meanwhile, the Buenos Aires Group is 'setting broad and joint research priorities for marine mammals in South America'.[37] Among the participants in the Workshop that convened to plan research activities were Argentina, Brazil, Chile, Costa Rica, Mexico, New Zealand, South Africa and Uruguay. Also attending were scientists from France, Italy and the United States.[38]

Cooperative research progresses: for example, the Southern Ocean Research Partnership convened the Living Whales Symposium and Workshop in Puerto Varas, Chile during 27–29 March 2012, which attracted 124 participants, some of whom came from Colombia, Ecuador, Mexico, Panama and even land-locked Paraguay. The conference dealt with the development and application of new non-lethal research methods in a variety of activities related to whales. Current

34   Lenore Taylor, 'Whaling compromise would break election promise', *The Sydney Morning Herald*, 3 April 2010, http://www.smh.com.au/environment/whale-watch/whaling-compromise-would-break-election-promise-20100402-rjy5.html, accessed 27 October 2013.

35   Andrew Darby, 'Decision will bring tectonic shift in whaling politics.' *The Age*, 17 July 2013, http://www.theage.com.au/federal-politics/political-opinion/decision-will-bring-tectonic-shift-in-whaling-politics-20130717-2q351.html#ixzz2cYh2HIWE, accessed 27 October 2013. At time of publication (December 2013), no judgement had been rendered —ICJ, 'Whaling in the Antarctic (Australia v. Japan: New Zealand Intervening): Conclusion of the Public Hearings: Court to Begin its Deliberations', Press Release No. 2013/16, International Court of Justice, The Hague, 17 July 2013: http://www.icj-cij.org/docket/files/148/17464.pdf, accessed 6 December 2013.

36   Peterr Garrett, 'Speech: The Future of International Whale Conservation, Lowy Institute', Sydney, http://www.petergarrett.com.au, 18 February 2009.

37   Draft Report of the Planning Workshop of the Southern Ocean Research Project, p. 4. Workshop held in Sydney, 23–6 March 2009.

38   Australian Marine Mammal Centre: Southern Ocean Research Partnership. http://www.marineanimals.gov.au/southern-ocean-research-partnerships-sorp, accessed 27 October 2013.

research projects of the Partnership involve the Antarctic blue whale, the foraging ecology and predator–prey relations between whales and krill, and the behaviour and abundance of humpback and killer whales in the Southern Ocean.[39]

At the International Whaling Commission meeting in Morocco in June 2010, Australia staved off the threat to abandon the moratorium on commercial whaling. Minister Garrett's press release revealed his satisfaction with the results of the tense and difficult meeting while emphasising the role of the southern hemisphere nations in the cause of further research and conservation. He noted the progress in the formulation of the IWC's whale conservation management plans and the development of a research program focused on non-lethal scientific research: 'We will continue to work closely with other conservation-minded countries to finalise regional whale conservation management plans for some of the world's most threatened whale species, including South American southern right whales and western gray whales.'[40]

Having surveyed some of the environmental issues concerning fishing and whaling that affect Australia and Latin America, and the mechanisms employed to deal with them, we turn now to the means by which more effective action can be taken to protect the environmental interests of Australia and Latin America. It is not as if the Latin American nations with maritime interests have neither the experience nor the capacity to protect their resources. They are, of course, parties to many of the same international agreements as Australia. Moreover, these countries have developed national institutions to protect and manage their own maritime resources within territorial waters. Notably, the most important of such instruments, the 200-mile limit, was the result of a collective effort between Ecuador, Peru and Chile that issued the Santiago Declaration in 1952 claiming a 200-mile boundary for fishing activities. This limit is now widely accepted.

The constitutions of Latin American states generally recognise the subsoil as inalienable to private ownership, a principle extended to the seabed under the territorial waters up to 12 miles from shore. Thus, it is clear that national governments in Latin America are responsible for the management of coastal waters and are allowed to concede to private interests rights to exploit resources, as well as to protect them. As might be expected, the arrangements vary from state to state according to the situation, but the machinery for managing the marine environment in Latin America clearly exists.

Ecuador, for example, with a major fishing industry and the treasured Galapagos, has established seven *Zonas Especiales de Manejo* (Special Management Zones) wherein any activities such as fishing must conform to the zone's management

---

39   Australian Government, Department of Sustainability, Environment, Water, Population and Communities, Australian Marine Mammal Centre. www.marinemammals.gov.au/home, accessed 27 October 2013.

40   Garrett, Peter, http://www.environment.gov.au/minister/garrett/2010. Media release 28 June 2010.

plan.[41] Mangroves cannot be commercially exploited, although local ancestral communities can develop aquaculture under agreements known as Sustainable Use and Custody of the Mangroves. As for the Galapagos, a marine reserve, the only fishing permitted is limited to artisanal, local fishers for sustainable consumption. Larger vessels are allowed under a license system but all fishermen must be members of the applicable trade union.

Chile's very long Pacific Ocean coastline, its Antarctic claims, and Easter Island render it largely unable to manage the exclusive economic zone and its proximate high seas. The management of resources up to 12 miles out to sea and the implementation of controls over pollution are assigned to the Marine Subsecretary under the Ministry of National Defence and to the General Directorate of the Marine Territory and Merchant Navy. Responsibility for the protection of marine fauna and aquaculture development lies with the National Fishing Service. Chile actively involves the private sector in development of ecotourism and conservation of the ecosystem through a system of concession and authorisation. The Marine Coastal Protected Areas program is a government-backed initiative collaborating with the private sector to implement a project entitled Conservation of the Biodiversity of Global Importance along the Length of the Chilean Coast.[42] The examples of Chile and Ecuador are but two among the Latin American states that have evolved means for protecting their marine environment and that suggest possibilities for cooperation with Australia not only in scientific research but also perhaps in management practices and in technological exchange.

In May 2010, the UN hosted in New York a review of the current situation related to the Agreement on the Conservation and Management of Straddling Fish Stocks and Highly Migratory Fish Stocks.[43] The summary of the review reveals clearly the current situation: there is some hope and many perils for straddling and migratory fish. Crucial to the hopes for achieving satisfactory outcomes for arresting the decline in fish stocks are the performance of the Regional Fisheries Management Organizations. Numbering 17 at last count, these organisations are responsible for implementing the Agreement on the Conservation and Management of Straddling Fish Stocks and Highly Migratory Fish Stocks, which entered into force in 2001. As of March 2010, 77 states have ratified it, including Argentina, Australia, Brazil, Costa Rica, New Zealand, Panama, South Africa and

---

41   See 'Ecuador Analysis', *Marine Conservation Agreements: a Practitioner's Toolkit*, http://www.mcatoolkit.org/Country_Analyses/Ecuador.html, accessed 27 October 2013.

42   *Ibid.*

43   The summary of the meeting can be found in 'Summary of The Resumed Review.

Conference of the UN Fish Stocks Agreement: 24–28 May 2010', *Earth Negotiations Bulletin*, vol. 7, no. 65, 31 May 2010. http://www.iisd.ca/download/pdf/enb0765e.pdf, accessed 27 October 2013.

Uruguay.[44] There was agreement that a number of the Management Organizations needed to improve their performance, but some disagreement emerged as to how this might be achieved. The vigorous participation of the Latin American nations, particularly Argentina, Brazil, Chile and Peru, revealed: the need for improvement and expansion of scientific information—something many developing countries cannot afford; the complexity of reconciling the conservation measures in the exclusive economic zones with their high seas obligations; the need to expand membership of the South Pacific Regional Management Organization; and the responsibility of states over fishing vessels flying their flags. Two issues elicited clear conflict: the allowances made to developing countries in fishing on the high seas for which Brazil and Peru argued strongly—Australia was opposed; and the question of how to monitor, control, survey and enforce agreements. The Latin American participants asserted that they do not have the resources, financial or technological, to be as effective as required. In addition, they face domestic divisions between the demands of local industries, artisanal fishers, state revenues and the power of the major industrial fishers including China, Japan and Taiwan. The Latin American countries called for financial assistance to develop their capacities in these areas and resented the admonitions of some of the developed nations to strengthen the performance of the applicable Regional Fisheries Management Organization. Indeed, the Argentine delegate declared the recommendations adopted at the meeting unacceptable partly because there was no discussion of the provisions of the original Agreement. On this specific criticism the delegates of Mexico and Ecuador voiced agreement.

Despite the tensions, however, the participants achieved substantive accord on many issues such as collecting and submitting data on fisheries, the implementation of an ecosystem approach to assess and manage fish stocks, the enforcement of the existing prohibition of shark finning, improving the structures and performances of the Regional Management Organizations, the support of measures to prevent the landing of illegally caught fish, and control of the trans-shipment of catch on the high seas that evades the landing of catch at ports, thereby enforcing the agreements concerning illegal, unreported and unregulated fishing.

Conclusion

To assert a political and moral position regarding the environment of the south, a potentially powerful and effective institution already exists that deserves far more nurturing and attention than it presently receives: the Group of Temperate

44   Patricia Lee Devaney, 'Regional Fisheries Management Organizations: Bringing Order to Disorder', http://www.pon.org/downloads/ien14_4Devaney, accessed 27 October 2013.

Southern Hemisphere Countries on Environment, known also as the Valdivia Group after the city in Chile where the members first met. Formed in response to an initiative of the Australian government in 1995, its membership included New Zealand, Chile, Argentina, Uruguay and South Africa. Brazil joined the Group in 1997.[45] At the inaugural meeting, six working groups were formed to work on biodiversity, climate change, forests, ozone, chemicals and desertification.

Implied in the formal title of the Group are a number of ideas worthy of analysis here. First is the notion that the member nations recognise a kind of stewardship over the southern hemisphere environment. When opening the fourth meeting of the Group's Coordinating Committee in Wellington, New Zealand in 1998, Don MacKay, then Deputy Secretary of the Ministry of Foreign Affairs and Trade, noted that the Group's geographical position in the world provided members with a unique outlook in comparison with northern hemisphere neighbours.[46] Second, the name of the Group defines the existence of a southern hemisphere community that possesses its own characteristics and interests. On environmental issues, the implications are clear not only for the economies of the members of the Group and of the hemisphere, but also for the globe in such activities as fishing and forestry: resources must be carefully managed; consumption by the rich needs to be restricted. A third implication in the title concerns use of the word 'Temperate'. It refers to more than the climate; rather, in historical and development studies, these nations have been called 'lands of recent settlement,' associated with a temperate environment which in turn seeks to imply that they are more European, more developed economically than tropical southern hemisphere countries. Thus, Australia is not as different from its South American temperate partners as language and culture may indicate.[47]

All this could mean, if explored, the beginnings of a political community centred on issues of environmental protection and security. Alexander Downer, then Minister of Foreign Affairs and Trade in the Coalition government under Prime Minister John Howard, was an enthusiastic supporter of the Group in the mid-1990s. As recently as 2004, the Australian Labor Party endorsed the Group in its national platform: 'Labor will work to enhance the role of the Valdivia Group of Temperate Southern Hemisphere Countries in giving voice to southern hemisphere interests in international environment meetings'.[48] Unfortunately, the Valdivia Group has disappeared from view. We have been unable to find

---

45   To date, the only comprehensive article concerning the Valdivia Group is by Klaus Dodds, 'The geopolitics of regionalism: the Valdivia Group and southern hemispheric environmental co-operation', *Third World Quarterly*, vol. 19, no. 4, 1998, pp. 725–43.

46   Closing Statement of the Fourth Meeting of the Coordinating Committee of the Valdivia Group, Wellington, 24–5 June 1998. http://www.dfat.gov.au/environment/valdivia, accessed 27 October 2013.

47   Strictly speaking, Brazil, Peru and Chile are not considered 'regions of recent settlement' although Brazil might be. Among the qualifications is heavy European immigration during the 19th and early 20th centuries.

48   Australian Labor Party, *National Platform and Constitution 2004*, p. 243. http://www.alp.com, accessed 27 October 2013.

any documentation related to its activities in recent years. It has achieved limited success: on the issue of ozone depletion the campaign resulted in the production of a clean technology that admittedly was the initiative of the north. The Group also produced an Agreement on the Conservation of Albatrosses and Petrels. Although the problem of bird mortality caused principally by long-line fishing was recognised in the early 1990s, not until 1998 did serious work begin after the Wellington meeting of the Valdivia Group heard a paper on the topic presented by Australian scientists.[49] By 2001 the Agreement opened for signatures, and by 2004 the necessary signatories to enter the Agreement into force existed: Australia, New Zealand, and South Africa within the Valdivia Group, and joined by Ecuador and Spain. In 2006 Chile, Peru, France and the United Kingdom signed, and Argentina's signature was imminent.

In the light of the Agreement and in the aftermath of Copenhagen it is time to revisit the Valdivia Group, to explore the possibilities of using it to forge stronger political and environmental ties with Latin America and, at the same time, to define a community of the south in which common interests are acknowledged and made known to the polluters of the north. This requires Australian leadership through a commitment to invest resources in sharing technology, for example, and the development of research capacities among the members, and even the development of means to enhance compliance with the laws and agreements that already exist. The environmental issue cannot be neatly split off from the political, economic and social issues—or, indeed, from the moral and ethical. If an expanded Valdivia Group can marshal its strengths—at this moment, primarily scientific—to articulate a strong message, both political and moral, very likely it would have a significant effect on the entire world.

In light of the catastrophe in the Gulf of Mexico caused by careless oil drilling practices, attention should be drawn to recent exploratory drilling in the waters off the Malvinas (Falklands) in the southern Atlantic Ocean.[50] It is dangerous on environmental grounds and, given the turbulent history of the islands, politically short-sighted. This is a moment when the south needs the Valdivia Group.

49   J. Cooper, et al., 'The Agreement on the Conservation of Albatrosses and Petrels: Rationale, History, Progress and the Way Forward', *Marine Ornithology*, vol. 34, 2006, pp. 1–5.
50   *The Sydney Morning Herald*, 3 June 2010, Business Day, p. 4.

References

Aguilar Ibarra, Alonso, Chris Read and Andy Thorpe, 'The Political Economy of Marine Fisheries Development in Peru, Chile and Mexico', *Journal of Latin American Studies*, vol. 32, 2000, pp. 503–27.

Anderson, Steve, 'Chilean coastal fishermen protest depletion of hake', *The Santiago Times,* 26 October, 2007. http://www.santiagotimes.cl/index, accessed 2 October 2011.

Aranda, Martín, 'Developments on fisheries management in Peru: The new individual vessels quota system for the anchoveta fishery', *Fisheries Research*, vol. 96, issues 2–3, March 2009, pp. 308–12.

Australian Bureau of Agriculture and Resource Economics, *Australian Fisheries Statistics 2011*, December 2012, p. 1. http://abare.gov.au, accessed 27 October 2013.

Australian Fisheries Management Authority, *Annual Report 2008-09*, Canberra, 2009.

————, *Annual Report 2008–2009*, Canberra, 2009.

————, *Annual Report 2011-2012*, Canberra, 2012.

————, *Annual Report 2011–2012*, Canberra, 2012.

Australian Government, 'Australia's proposal for a forest carbon market mechanism', March 2009, http://www.climatechange.gov.au/government/initiatives/unfccc/submissions.aspx, accessed 22 February 2010.

Australian Government, Department of Agriculture, Fisheries and Aquaculture, *Fishery status reports 2011*, 18 December 2012, http://www.daff.gov.au/abares/publications_remote_content/public, accessed 27 October 2013.

Australian Government, Department of Climate Change and Energy Efficiency, 'Action under the International Forest Carbon Initiative', http://www.climatechange.gov.au/government/initiatives/international-forest-carbon-initiative/action.aspx, accessed 14 December 2010.

————, 'International Forest Carbon Initiative', http://www.climatechange.gov.au/government/initiatives/international-forest-carbon-initiative.aspx, accessed 22 January 2010.

Australian Government, Department of Sustainability, Environment, Water, Population and Communities, Australian Marine Mammal Centre, http://www.marinemammals.gov.au/home, accessed 27 October 2013.

Australian Labor Party, *National Platform and Constitution 2004*, http://www.alp.com, accessed 27 October 2013.

Australian Marine Mammal Centre: Southern Ocean Research Partnership. http://www.marineanimals.gov.au/southern-ocean-research-partnerships-sorp, accessed 27 October 2013.

'Closing Statement of the Fourth Meeting of the Coordinating Committee of the Valdivia Group, Wellington', 24–5 June 1998. http://www.dfat.gov.au/environment/valdivia, accessed 27 October 2013.

Cooper, J., *et al.*, 'The Agreement on the Conservation of Albatrosses and Petrels: Rationale, History, Progress and the Way Forward', *Marine Ornithology*, vol. 34 2006, pp. 1–5.

Darby, Andrew, 'Decision will bring tectonic shift in whaling politics.' *The Age*, 17 July 2013, http://www.theage.com.au/federal-politics/political-opinion/decision-will-bring-tectonic-shift-in-whaling-politics-20130717-2q351.html#ixzz2cYh2HIWE, accessed 27 October 2013.

Darby, Andrew, 'Fight to turn tide of trash crashing on wild shores', *The Sydney Morning Herald*, 12–13 April, 2013, p. 7. http://www.smh.com.au/environment/conservation/fight-to-turn-tide-of-trash-crashing-on-wild-shores-20130412-2hquu.html, accessed 27 October 2013.

Devaney, Patricia Lee, 'Regional Fisheries Management Organizations: Bringing Order to Disorder', http://www.pon.org/downloads/ien14_4Devaney, accessed 27 October 2013.

Dodds, Klaus, 'The geopolitics of regionalism: the Valdivia Group and southern hemispheric environmental co-operation', *Third World Quarterly*, vol. 19, no. 4, 1998, pp. 725–43.

Draft Report of the Planning Workshop of the Southern Ocean Research Project, Workshop held in Sydney, 23–26 March 2009.

'Ecuador Analysis', *Marine Conservation Agreements: a Practitioner's Toolkit*, http://www.mcatoolkit.org/Country_Analyses/Ecuador.html, accessed 27 October 2013.

Eliasch, Johan E. *Climate Change: Financing Global Forests*, London, Earthscan, 2008.

Erikson, Marcus, *et al.*, 'Plastic pollution in the South Pacific subtropical gyre', *Marine Pollution Bulletin,* 68 (2013): 71–2, http://www.elsevier.com/locate/marpobul, accessed 27 October 2013.

FAO, *Yearbook of Fishery Statistics 2010, Summary Tables*, p. 15. ftp://ftp.fao. org/fi/stat/summary, accessed 27 October 2013.

'From catchment-to-reef continuum: Case studies from the Great Barrier Reef. A special issue', Editorial, *Marine Pollution Bulletin 2012*, 65, 2012, p. 77. Elsevier: http://www.elsevier.com/locate/marpolbul, accessed 27 October 2013.

Garrett, Peter, 'Progress made at the International Whaling Commission', Media release, Australian Government, 28 June 2010, PG/74, http://www. environment.gov.au/minister/archive/ env/2010/mr20100628.html accessed 25 May 2011.

Garrett, Peter, 'The Future of International Whale Conservation', Speech: Lowy Institute, Sydney, 18 February 2009, http://www.petergarrett.com.au.

Gianni, M., and W. Simpson, 'The Changing Nature of High Seas Fishing: how flags of convenience provide cover for illegal, unreported and unregulated fishing', Australian Department of Agriculture, Fisheries and Forestry, Canberra, 2005.

ICJ, 'Whaling in the Antarctic (Australia v. Japan: New Zealand Intervening): Conclusion of the Public Hearings: Court to Begin its Deliberations', *Press Release No. 2013/16*, International Court of Justice, The Hague, 17 July 2013: http://www.icj-cij.org/docket/files/148/17464.pdf, accessed 6 December 2013.

Latin American and Caribbean Forestry Commission, 'Forests and Climate Change —With a Special Focus on Climate Change Adaptation', Twenty-Sixth Session, Guatemala City, 24–8 May 2010, FO:LACFC/2010/6, http:// www.rlc.fao.org/es/comisiones/coflac/2010/pdf/lacfc-6e.pdf, accessed 20 June 2010.

Macintosh, Andrew, 'Reducing emissions from deforestation and forest degradation in developing countries: A cautionary tale from Australia', the Australia Institute, *Policy Brief*, No. 12, 2010.

Martinez, Elodie, *et al.*, 'Floating marine debris surface drift: Convergence and accumulation toward the South Pacific subtropical gyre', *Marine Pollution Bulletin*. 58, 2009, pp. 1347–55.

Scientific and Technical Advisory Board, *Marine Debris as a Global Environmental Problem*, Washington, DC November 2011.

'Summary of the Oceans Day at Cancún, 4 December 2010', http://www.iisd.ca/ climate/cop16, accessed 27 October 2013.

'Summary of the Resumed Review Conference of the UN Fish Stocks Agreement: 24–28 May 2010', *Earth Negotiations Bulletin*, vol. 7, no. 65, 31 May 2010. http://www.iisd.ca/download/pdf/enb0765e.pdf, accessed 27 October 2013.

Symes, David, and Jeremy Phillipson, 'Whatever became of social objectives in fisheries policy?', *Fisheries Research*, 95, 2009, pp. 1–5, http://www.elsevier.com/locate/fisheries, accessed 27 October 2013.

Taylor, Lenore, 'Whaling compromise would break election promise', *The Sydney Morning Herald*, 3 April 2010, http://www.smh.com.au/environment/whale-watch/whaling-compromise-would-break-election-promise-20100402-rjy5.html, accessed 27 October 2013.

UN General Assembly, Sixty-fifth session, Agenda item 75 (a), Oceans and the law of the sea, 'Letter dated 16 March 2010 from the Co-Chairpersons of the Ad Hoc Open-ended Informal Working Group to the President of the General Assembly'. A/65/68.

UN, FAO, Fisheries and Aquaculture Department, 'Port State Measures Agreement'. http://www.fao.org/fishery/topic/166283/en, accessed 27 October 2013.

UNFCCC (United Nations Framework Convention on Climate Change), 'Appendix 1—Quantified economy-wide emissions targets for 2020', http://unfccc.int/files/parties, accessed 2 February 2010.

Virgilio, Viana, 'Seeing REDD in the Amazon', *Tiempo*, 73, 2009, p. 5.

World People's Conference on Climate Change and the Rights of Mother Earth, http://pwccc.wordpress.com/, accessed 17 August 2010.

5. Australia–Latin America Trade and Business Relations

Pierre van der Eng and Don Kenyon

Introduction

Australia and the countries of Latin America are situated in the most economically dynamic part of the globe that has been exposed to the effects of significant economic growth in East Asia.[1] Nevertheless, trade and investment flows across the South Pacific have long held a promise that has not yet been fully realised. Both remained relatively marginal until quite recently. Chief among the casual answers for this fact is the notion that the respective economies lack complementarity, as Australia and its Latin American counterparts have traditionally been competitive exporters of primary products, primarily agricultural goods, but also minerals.

The purpose of this chapter is to take stock of the development of business relations between Australia and Latin America during the past two decades. It will argue that both parts of the world lack complementarity is no longer accurate; trade and investment flows between both continents have grown considerably in recent years, despite various factors that continue to dampen business relations across the Pacific. For example, the total value of goods trade between Australia and Latin America in 2012 was A$8.5 billion, six times more than the A$1.3 billion in 1990.

Sections two and three will establish the orders of magnitude of change in trade and business relations. They will demonstrate that intercontinental trade flows have diversified away from basic commodities to include a wider range of manufactured products and services. This significant growth and diversification, in combination with the relatively low level of existing trade and investment flows, substantiates the conclusion of this chapter that substantial potential for further growth of trans-Pacific business relations still remains.

---

1   For the purpose of this chapter, Latin America is broadly defined to comprise South America and Central America, including the Caribbean, although further discussion will focus on Australia's main business partners in Latin America.

Section four will examine remaining differences in the business environments of Australia and the countries of Latin America that may help to explain why Australia's trade and business relationships across the Pacific have not developed as fast as those with some of Australia's other trading partners.

Recent trends: Trade relations

The trends in bilateral business relations between Latin America and Australia are most easily captured with statistics on trade and investment. Table 5.1 gives an overview of the development of trade relations between Australia and Latin America during the last 20 years. It shows annual averages for different periods in order to exclude year-to-year fluctuations from the analysis. In terms of goods, the balance of goods trade has shifted in favour of Latin America during the past ten years, as Australian imports exceeded exports. The balance of services trade has shifted in Australia's favour over the last eight years, but the margin is small. The table also shows that trade relations grew significantly by a factor of five, six in the case of exports and imports of goods during the past 23 years. This rate of growth was higher than that of Australia's trade with the rest of the world, indeed Latin America's shares in Australia's goods exports and imports increased to 1.4 per cent and 2.2 per cent respectively. During the past 12 years Australia's services exports to Latin America increased by a factor of 3.8, significantly higher than goods exports, which increased by a factor of 1.5. This indicates that Australia's business relations with Latin America are diversifying to accommodate services to a greater degree.

Nevertheless, the shares in Table 5.1 indicate that Latin America is in relative terms still of significantly lower importance to Australia's foreign trade relations than other parts of the world, particularly the European Union, East Asia and North America. From a Latin American perspective, trade data reveal that the average share of Australia in Latin America's goods trade was on average 0.3 per cent during 2002–11, the same as during 1992–2001.[2] Hence, despite significant growth in Latin America's trade relations with Australia, its trade with the rest of the world increased just as fast.

---

2   Calculated from the UN Comtrade database (http://comtrade.un.org) with trade data for Argentina, Brazil, Chile, Colombia, Costa Rica, El Salvador, Mexico, Peru and Uruguay.

Table 5.1: Australia–Latin America trade relations, 1990–2012 (annual averages)

	Australian exports to Latin America				Australian imports from Latin America			
	Goods		Services		Goods		Services	
	(mln A$)	% of total	(mln A$)	% of total	(mln A$)	% of total	(mln A$)	% of total
1990–94	655	1.1%	na	-	829	1.5%	na	-
1995–99	1,060	1.3%	na	-	1,061	1.2%	na	-
2000–04	1,473	1.3%	599	1.7%	1,732	1.4%	479	1.4%
2005–09	2,611	1.5%	1,635	3.4%	3,344	1.8%	751	1.6%
2010–12	3,339	1.4%	2,259	4.4%	5,061	2.2%	705	1.1%

Notes: na = not available. 2010–12 services trade average refers to 2010–11. 2000–12 services exports re-estimated, using travel exports to Latin America from ABS 5368.055.004 Table 9, not Table 5.

Sources: Calculated from ABS 5368.0 and ABS 5368.055.004.

Table 5.2: Australia's main trade partners in Latin America, 2007–11 (annual averages)

	Australia's goods exports			Australia's goods imports	
	(mln A$)	% of total		(mln A$)	% of total
Brazil	1,267	41.4%	Mexico	1,377	32.5%
Mexico	804	26.3%	Brazil	876	20.7%
Chile	304	9.9%	Chile	705	16.6%
Argentina	266	8.7%	Puerto Rico	520	12.3%
Peru	104	3.4%	Argentina	366	8.6%
Trinidad & Tobago	48	1.6%	Peru	125	3.0%
Colombia	41	1.3%	Costa Rica	101	2.4%
Costa Rica	31	1.0%	Colombia	34	0.8%
El Salvador	31	1.0%	Dominican Rep.	21	0.5%
Guatemala	25	0.8%	Uruguay	18	0.4%
Jamaica	21	0.7%	Ecuador	16	0.4%
Other	117	3.8%	Other	76	1.8%
Total	3,059	100%	Total	4,235	100%

Source: Calculated from ABS 5368.0.

Table 5.2 identifies Australia's main trade partners in Latin America during the past five years. It is very clear that four countries dominate: Brazil, Mexico, Chile and Argentina. Together they occupy about 80 to 85 per cent of Australia's trade with Latin America, a share that has not changed much since the 1990s. The dominant four countries include Latin America's three most populous nations, with Chile being geographically closest to Australia and having the most open economy of the four. Puerto Rico also has a significant role in Australia's imports from Latin America, largely due to the imports of products from that country's prominent pharmaceutical industry. Of the other countries, Peru and Colombia can be mentioned.

Table 5.3 disaggregates Australia's goods trade with the four key Latin American countries. Australia's trade statistics contain a significant share of unidentified 'confidential items', which is around 20 per cent of exports to Argentina and Brazil.[3] The shares in Australia's exports were therefore estimated on the basis of the trade statistics of the partner countries. Table 5.3 reveals that primary commodities (categories 0–3) dominated Australia's exports to Latin America, followed by a diverse range of machinery and mechanical appliances (included in SITC category 7). Coal (included in category 3) features prominently in Australia's exports, even though all four Latin American countries are coal-producing countries themselves.

Australia's imports from Latin America were dominated by machinery and mechanical appliances (category 7). This is particularly the case with Mexico.[4] A closer look reveals that this category largely comprises internal combustion engines, car parts and cars, as well as personal computers, computer peripherals and communication equipment. The share of Brazil's exports of manufactured products to Australia is also high, particularly transport equipment (category 7), due to the delivery of 20 Embraer aeroplanes to Virgin Blue in 2008. Australia also imports basic manufactured products from Latin America, particularly refined copper and copper products in the case of Chile (categories 2 and 6), as well as assorted food products (category 0), particularly animal feed from Argentina.

---

3   It is unclear what 'confidential items' Australia exports to Latin America. They could be exports of nickel and nickel products, which the ABS does not report in Australia's foreign trade statistics: see DFAT, *Exports of Primary and Manufactured Products, Australia 2008–09*, 2010, pp. 10–14. But a range of other commodities, such as coal, toothfish and animal hides, are or have been included as well: see ABS 5372.0.55.001.
4   Australian trade statistics with Mexico may be understated by transit trade through the United States: see JEG, *Australia–Mexico Joint Experts Group on Strengthening Bilateral Economic Relations*, 2009, pp. 49–50.

Table 5.3: Shares of product groups in Australia's goods trade with Latin America, 2007–11 annual averages

	Australia's exports to					Australia's imports from				
SITC Rev.3 category	Argentina	Brazil	Chile	Mexico	Average	Argentina	Brazil	Chile	Mexico	Average
0 Food and live animals	0.6%	4.0%	13.4%	3.7%	5.4%	43.7%	18.5%	6.1%	1.7%	17.5%
1 Beverages and tobacco	0.1%	0.2%	0.0%	0.2%	0.1%	0.6%	3.9%	0.7%	6.5%	2.9%
2 Crude materials, inedible, except fuels	7.2%	3.3%	1.6%	12.0%	6.0%	3.7%	17.4%	17.3%	3.5%	10.5%
3 Mineral fuels, lubricants and related materials	71.0%	61.8%	37.6%	51.9%	55.6%	0.6%	0.0%	0.0%	0.0%	0.1%
4 Animal and vegetable oils, fats and waxes	0.4%	0.1%	0.0%	0.0%	0.1%	12.2%	1.2%	0.1%	0.0%	3.4%
5 Chemicals and related products, n.e.s.	6.3%	4.2%	7.0%	6.2%	5.9%	6.9%	7.4%	4.3%	7.7%	6.6%
6 Manufactured goods classified chiefly by material	4.6%	7.3%	11.2%	9.3%	8.1%	12.1%	13.6%	69.9%	6.2%	25.6%
7 Machinery and transport equipment	7.4%	14.8%	20.9%	12.3%	13.9%	18.6%	32.3%	1.5%	61.8%	28.6%
8 Miscellaneous manufactured articles	2.3%	2.5%	8.2%	2.9%	4.0%	1.6%	4.6%	0.2%	12.5%	4.7%
Other and confidential items	0.1%	0.8%	0.0%	1.4%	0.6%	0.1%	1.1%	0.0%	0.2%	0.3%
Total	100%	100%	100%	100%	100%	100%	100%	100%	100%	100%
Total value (mln US$)	237	1,103	270	707	2,316	328	767	634	1,230	2,959

Notes: Shares in Australia's exports are based on partner country trade data (see main text). The averages are unweighted.

Source: Calculated from UN Comtrade database, http://comtrade.un.org.

Table 5.4 summarises change in the composition of Australia's goods trade with its four key trade partners in Latin America.[5] On average, the share of manufactures in Australia's imports rose from 56 per cent in 1990–94 to 66 per cent in 2007–11. The average share of manufactured products in Australia's exports increased somewhat from 26 to 32 per cent, but this was largely due to the decrease in the share of manufactured exports to Argentina. Excluding Argentina, the average share increased to 36 per cent. Table 5.4 therefore reveals that manufactured products now play a greater role in Australia's trade with Latin America than 20 years ago. Australia's goods trade with Latin America has clearly diversified away from primary commodities.

Table 5.4: Share of manufactures in Australia's goods trade with Latin America, 1990–94 and 2007–11 annual averages

	Argentina	Brazil	Chile	Mexico	Average
A. Australia's exports					
1990–94	48.0%	8.0%	34.6%	14.8%	26.4%
2007–11	20.6%	28.8%	47.4%	30.7%	31.9%
B. Australia's imports					
1990–94	45.3%	75.9%	22.8%	80.1%	56.0%
2007–11	39.2%	57.9%	75.9%	88.1%	65.6%

Notes: Manufactures are defined as SITC Rev.3 categories 5–8. Australia's export shares for 2007–11 are based on partner country trade data (see main text). The averages are unweighted.

Source: Calculated from UN Comtrade database, http://comtrade.un.org.

Australia's services exports to Latin America consist largely of travel-related services, particularly personal travel (tourism) and education-related services, which occupy 76 per cent, as Table 5.5 shows. Vice versa, Australia's imports of services from Latin America are clearly dominated by unspecified business services, followed by tourism and transport. Unfortunately, the source is too incomplete to allow a very specific disaggregation of services trade according to countries of direction and origin—except that over two-thirds of the large share of unspecified imported business services are imported from Central America and the Caribbean. It is likely that this is related to the significant portfolio and direct investment transactions between Australia and countries such as the British Virgin Islands, the Cayman Islands and Bermuda (see below).

---

5   Australia's export data to Latin America did not contain such 'confidential items' for 1990–1994.

Table 5.5: Shares in Australia's services trade with Latin America, 2007–11 (annual averages)

	Australia's services exports			Australia's services imports	
	(mln A$)	% of total		(mln A$)	% of total
Travel, personal	864	40.5%	Business	312	38.8%
Travel, education	768	36.0%	Travel, personal	238	29.6%
Business, nes	198	9.3%	Transport	135	16.8%
Travel, other	119	5.6%	Intellectual property	32	4.0%
Transport	80	3.7%	Government	23	2.9%
Financial	48	2.2%	Travel, other	21	2.6%
ICT	34	1.6%	ICT	14	1.7%
Intellectual property	12	0.6%	Financial	13	1.6%
Government	5	0.2%	Travel, education	12	1.5%
Construction	1	0.0%	Insurance, pensions	2	0.2%
Other	6	0.3%	Other	2	0.2%
Total	**2,135**	**100.0%**	**Total**	**804**	**100.0%**

Note: ICT refers to Information, Computer and Telecommunications services. 2007–11 services exports re-estimated, using travel exports to Latin America from ABS 5368.055.004 Table 9, not Table 5.

Source: Calculated from ABS 5368.055.004.

Regarding travel-related services, Table 5.6 shows short-term arrivals and departures between Australia and Latin America, presumably for purposes that include tourism, family visits, business and education. The table confirms the broad trends in Table 5.1. In relative terms, the share of citizens of Latin American countries on short-term visits to Australia almost trebled from 0.5 per cent of the total number of visitors during 1991–94 to 1.3 per cent during 2010–12, while the share of Australian residents visiting Latin American countries increased from 0.8 per cent to 1.2 per cent. In all, such intercontinental visits are still marginal compared to visits between Australia and other continents, but they have grown significantly in recent years to the extent that Australia in 2012 hosted 84,700 short-term visitors from Latin America, particularly from Brazil, while 99,000 Australian residents visited Latin America, particularly Brazil, Argentina and Chile.

Table 5.6: Travel between Australia and Latin America, 1991–2012 (annual averages)

	Brazil	Mexico	Argentina	Chile	Other	Total, Latin America	As % of Australia total
A. Short-term arrivals in Australia of Latin American citizens							
1991–94	2,925	1,950	na	na	8,625	13,500	0.5%
1995–99	7,480	2,700	na	na	15,380	25,560	0.6%
2000–04	10,740	5,380	na	na	18,020	34,140	0.7%
2004–09	17,400	5,520	na	na	23,440	46,360	1.0%
2010–12	29,067	6,333	na	na	39,433	74,833	1.3%
B. Short-term departures of Australian residents to Latin America							
1991–94	2,000	2,100	3,625	4,450	5,300	17,475	0.8%
1995–99	3,520	3,000	5,520	5,140	9,160	26,340	0.9%
2000–04	5,580	5,060	5,760	7,040	14,880	38,320	1.1%
2004–09	8,720	6,800	8,960	9,100	20,540	54,120	1.2%
2010–12	16,300	11,400	15,667	12,333	34,267	89,933	1.2%

Notes: na = not available, Latin America includes South and Central America, and the Caribbean.

Source: Calculated from ABS 3401.0.

A special group of short-term visitors are international students. On average there were 23,000 students in Australia during 2012 who held Latin American or Caribbean citizenship, a number that had almost quadrupled from around 6000 in 2002.[6] In 2012, 15 per cent of these students were enrolled in higher education, 29 per cent in vocational education, 52 per cent attended English language courses, and three per cent schools and other educational institutions. The growth of the total number of Latin American students was mainly fuelled by enrolments in vocational and English language programs. In 2012, 46 per cent of these students were from Brazil, 31 per cent from Colombia, seven per cent from Chile, six per cent from Peru, and five per cent from Mexico. The share of Latin American students in the total population of international students in Australia increased from three per cent in 2002 to six per cent in 2012.

To summarise, this section has shown that Australia's business relations with Latin America are very much focused on Argentina, Brazil, Chile and Mexico. While in the past these relations may have been dominated by primary commodities, the share of manufactured products and services has increased in Australia's trade relations with key Latin American countries. This indicates that business relations have diversified and it is likely that this diversification has driven a rate of growth of trade relations. In the case of merchandise trade,

---

6   AEI, International Student Data, 2002–2012, 2012.

this growth is higher than Australia's trade with the rest of the world. It truly appears that business relations between Australia and Latin America are on the move, albeit gradually. The next section will establish the degree to which the change in trade relations is also reflected in investment relations.

Recent trends: Investment relations

Table 5.7 shows the stock of Australian investment in Latin America and of investments from Latin America in Australia. The Australian Bureau of Statistics (ABS) does not publish details of investments for most Latin American countries for reasons of confidentiality, while the published data for other countries are incomplete. Hence, some of the data in the table are only estimates based on information for previous years and on the distribution of investment. Nevertheless, it is clear from Table 5.7 that the accumulated investment flows to and from Latin America are relatively marginal from an Australian perspective, as less than three per cent of Australian outward investment found its way to Latin America. Likewise, Latin America was the source of just two per cent of foreign investment in Australia; more so for portfolio investment than for direct participation in foreign ventures, or Foreign Direct Investment (FDI).

Table 5.7: Stock of investment between Australia and Latin America, 2011 (mln A$)

	Australian foreign investment			Foreign investment in Australia		
	Direct	Portfolio	Total	Direct	Portfolio	Total
Argentina	914	18	932	10	240	250
Bermuda	7,000	3,257	10,257	7,791	1,500	9,291
Brazil	1,000*	3,085	4,085	350	650	1,000
British Virgin Islands	na	na	na	20,000	0	20,000
Cayman Islands	360	500	860	1,500	468	1,968
Chile	1,325	229	1,554	na	na	na
Mexico	1,900	1,345	3,245	1	41	42
Total, these countries	**24,400**	**8,434**	**20,933**	**29,652**	**2,899**	**32,551**
As % of Australia total	7.2%	1.9%	2.7%	5.8%	0.2%	1.9%

* The source lists a stock of Australian outward FDI in Brazil of about A$12.9 billion, compared with A$1 billion in 2008, and around A$1 billion in the Brazilian statistics (BCB, *Census of Foreign Capitals in Brazil, 2000 Base-Year*, 2010). Australian FDI flows to Brazil did not increase significantly in 2009. The increase is therefore likely to be caused by changes in the FDI portfolio of Australian firms that brought interests in other countries under the control of their subsidiaries in Brazil.

Notes: na = not available. Numbers in italics are estimates. Total is for identified partner countries only.

Source: Estimated from ABS 5352.0.

If it weren't for the fact that a considerable amount of investment was channelled through financial institutions and holding companies in Bermuda, the British Virgin Islands, and the Cayman Islands, FDI would have been even more marginal. It is very likely that the ultimate destinations of this Australian investment were not other countries in Latin America, while Latin America was not the original source of this investment in Australia. For example, in 2006 Telstra acquired 51 per cent of SouFun Holdings for US$254 million, which is a Chinese company registered in the Cayman Islands.[7] Likewise, in 2008 CopperCo acquired 74 per cent in Mineral Securities for $536 million, a British company registered in the Virgin Islands. In the other direction, Cheung Kong Infrastructure Holdings in Bermuda acquired 51 per cent of Victorian electricity distributors Powercor Australia and CitiPower in 2000 and 2002 respectively, on behalf of Cheung Kong Infrastructure and Hong Kong Electric Holdings, two companies in the Hong Kong-based Cheung Kong business group.

Two other ABS publications confirm the impression that Table 5.7 does not fully represent the investment relations between Australia and Latin America. One reveals that there was no significant presence of Latin American companies in Australia in 2000–01.[8] This may have changed somewhat in recent years, but not drastically. Many Latin American firms have internationalised their operations to become the so-called 'Multilatinas' and more recently 'Global Latinas',[9] but most of them still have to find their way to Australia. A further ABS publication shows that there were 39 Australian-owned affiliates in Brazil in 2002–03—27 in Chile and 25 in Mexico—that altogether employed 6300 people, plus another 22 in other Latin American countries.[10] Many of these companies are likely to have been subsidiaries of Australia's mining and mining supplies and service companies. Given significant FDI inflows in Latin America's booming mining sector, it is likely that the number of Australian firms in Latin America has increased significantly in recent years.

Excluding the investments by Australian firms in small Central American countries,[11] as well as by companies from those countries in Australia, Table 5.8 summarises information on company acquisitions between Australia and Latin America up to 2010. The most prominent acquisition in Latin America was Nufarm's purchase of Agripec in Brazil in 2007. Of greater significance was the acquisition of the Rinker group—including Readymix and Humes—in Australia

---

7   Telstra divested its interest in SouFun Holdings for US$433 million in September 2010.
8   ABS (ABS 5494.0), Economic Activity of Foreign Owned Businesses in Australia, 2004.
9   Lourdes Casanova and Matthew Fraser, (eds), *From Multilatinas to Global Latinas*, 2009; Andres Hatum and Josefina Michelini, 'Going Global: The Process of Internationalisation of Latino Multinational Firms', *International Journal of Business and Emerging Markets*, 2011, 3: pp. 36–56.
10   ABS (ABS5495.0), Australian Outward Foreign Affiliates Trade: Experimental Results, 2004; Frances van Ruth, The Internationalisation of Australian Firms, PhD Thesis, 2008, p. 13.
11   Specifically, acquisitions from and sales to the Netherlands Antilles, Bermuda, Belize, Cayman Islands, Panama, British Virgin Islands, and Antigua and Barbuda were excluded from Table 5.8.

by construction materials firm Cemex of Mexico in 2007, although Cemex sold Rinker two years later to Holcim, a Swiss cement firm. Also significant was the 2007 purchase of coal-mining company AMCI Holdings by Brazil's iron ore-mining company Vale. Brazil's JBS Friboi group gained control over meat packer Australia Meat Holdings when it acquired its US parent firm Swift in 2007. Renamed Swift Australia, this JBS subsidiary purchased the Tatiara Meat Company in 2010.

Table 5.8 suggests that mining, mining services and utilities companies dominate the interests of Australian companies in Latin America. BHP Billiton has a 100 per cent interest in the Cerro Colorado copper mine in Chile, joint venture interests in refining plants and coal and nickel mining in Brazil and Colombia, as well as in the Antemina copper and zinc mine in Peru. Several Australian mining supplies and service companies have followed in the wake of the mining companies. For example, Austin Engineering purchased Conymet in Chile in 2009 to produce dump-truck bodies for mining ventures throughout South America. Several non-mining firms have also found their way to Latin America. For example, Australia's Pacific Hydro used its expertise in hydro and wind electricity to take advantage of privatisation in Chile's energy sector to enter the market for hydro-electricity in 2004, and invest in wind electricity projects in Brazil. Packaging producer TNA established subsidiaries in Chile and Mexico. A number of Australian companies (such as the mining services and chemicals divisions of Orica), have also been attracted by the openness of the Chilean economy to choose it as their base in Latin America. It is difficult to provide a comprehensive overview of business interactions between Australia and Latin America: several of the interests of Australian mining companies are not included in Table 5.8, which can only offer an incomplete impression of bilateral investment for the following four reasons.

Table 5.8: Company acquisitions between Australia and Latin America, 1997–2012

Australian firm	Latin American firm	Country	Year	Industry	Stake	Deal value (mln $)
By Australian firms in Latin America						
Nufarm Ltd	Agripec Química e Farmacêutica SA	Brazil	2004, 2007	Manufacturing	100%	389
QBE Insurance Group Ltd	HSBC Argentina Holdings SA	Argentina	2012	Insurance	99%	215
Pacific Hydro International Pty Ltd	Pacific Hydro Chile SA	Chile	2008	Utilities	>50%	118
Superannuation funds consortium	GasValpo SA	Chile	2008	Utilities	100%	101
SEEK Ltd	Brasil Online Holdings Coöperatief UA	Brazil	2008, 2012	ICT	51%	160
Beadell Resources Ltd	Mineração Pedra Branca do Amapari Ltd a	Brazil	2010	Mining	100%	68
SEEK Ltd	Ontime Career Centre Mexico SA de CV	Mexico	2010, 2012	ICT	47%	63
Australis Mining Ltd	SCM Vallenar Iron Company	Chile	2010	Mining	60%	50
Strike Resources Ltd	Apurímac Ferrum SA	Peru	2008	Mining	51%	39
QBE Insurance Group Ltd	Optima Insurance Group	Puerto Rico	2012	Insurance	100%	38
Admiralty Resources NL	Compania Minera Santa Barbara SA	Chile	2005, 2008 b	Mining	60%	28
QBE Insurance Group Ltd	Compañía Central de Seguros SA	Colombia	2005	Insurance	97%	26
Tamaya Resources Ltd e	Latin American Copper Chile SA	Chile	2007	Mining	100%	24
Austin Engineering Ltd	Conymet Ltd a	Chile	2009	Mining services	100%	23
BHP Billiton Ltd	Jaguar Nickel SA	Guatemala	2005 d	Mining	100%	22
Voicenet (Aust) Ltd	Rimpex International SA	Chile	2000	ICT	100%	11
Natasa Mining Ltd c	Puquios copper project	Chile	2007	Mining	92%	10
Coffey International Ltd	Geoexplore Consultoria e Servicos Ltd a	Brazil	2007	Mining services	100%	8
Tamaya Resources Ltd e	Compañía Minera Tamaya SA	Chile	2003	Mining	100%	8
Orica Ltd	Andean Chemicals Group	Chile, Peru	2005	Manufacturing	51%	8
By Latin American firms in Australia						
Rinker Group Ltd	Cemex SAB de CV	Mexico	2007 d	Construction	100%	19,392
AMCI Holdings Australia Pty Ltd	Companhia Vale do Rio Doce Ltd a	Brazil	2007	Mining	100%	986
Tatiara Meat Company Pty Ltd	JBS SA	Brazil	2010	Food processing	100%	35
Rositas Investments Pty Ltd	Gruma SA de CV	Mexico	2006	Food processing	100%	18

Notes: Only deals with a disclosed value of over A$8 million. The deal value may vary from announcements, due to exchange rate differences between announcements and settlements in US$. a. Divested in 2008. b. Divested in 2010. c. Previously Investika Ltd. d. Divested in 2009. e. Previously SMC Gold Ltd. f. Previously Icarus Derivatives, and now registered in the British Virgin Islands.

Sources: Bureau van Dijk, Zephyr database, May 2010; company public announcements.

(1) The value of deals is not always disclosed. For example, QBE's acquisition of insurance firm Cumbre Seguros in Mexico in 2007, or Ansell's purchase of Blowtex in Brazil in 2007, are not included for that reason.

(2) Systematically collected information on Greenfield investments is not readily available. For example, Agrichem's establishment in 2000 of a joint venture fertiliser production and distribution plant in Brazil is not included, nor is Orica's joint venture with Grupo Merand in Venezuela that since 2000 operates two explosives plants. For the same reason, many of the smaller interests of Australian firms are not included, such as the Nufarm-owned subsidiary companies in ten Latin American countries that distribute Nufarm's products.

(3) Many Australian construction, mining and mining services companies operate in Latin America on a project basis and have either specific project-based subsidiaries or representative offices in Latin America. A relatively large number of Australia-based mining companies have ventures in Latin America that are in different stages of development. They may have concessions for exploration of mineral deposits, or are in the process of acquiring funding for that purpose. Others are still awaiting permissions to commence mining operations and/or are in the process of securing funding for that purpose on Australian or international capital markets. Or they are in the process of creating joint-venture operations for that purpose. Brambles and Bovis Lend Lease have a presence in Argentina, Brazil, Chile and Mexico for the purpose of securing or carrying out construction projects. Queensland engineering company Cullen Grummit and Roe has a presence in Argentina and Peru and conducts port development projects in different Latin American countries. Likewise, mining services companies Maptek in Adelaide and Mincom in Brisbane conduct IT projects in several places in Latin America.

(4) Several Australian companies arranged the acquisitions of firms in Latin America through their other foreign subsidiaries. For example, Amcor acquired a significant presence in Latin America in 2003 through a US$115 million purchase of nine PET container production facilities from global competitor Alcoa, but the acquisition was completed by its US subsidiary Amcor Holdings. The large mining companies in particular conduct their operations in this way. For example, BHP Billiton invested in Chile via one of its US subsidiaries.[12] Consequently, Australian mining companies, particularly BHP Billiton, Rio Tinto, and Xtrata—an Australian firm since its purchase of MIM Holdings in 2003—have established multiple operations in Latin America that are not captured in Table 5.8. Similarly, the purchase of Rinker was financed through the foreign operations of Cemex rather than by its headquarters in Mexico, but this deal is included in Table 5.8.[13]

---

12   Van Ruth, *op. cit.*, note 10, p. 13.
13   ECLAC, Foreign Direct Investment in Latin America and the Caribbean, 2007, p. 55.

These four factors help in understanding that the investment stock data in Table 5.7, as well as the acquisitions data in Table 5.8 only offer a partial impression of the business relations between Australia and Latin America. On the other hand, it should be kept in mind that Australian firms are altogether not major investors in Latin America. For example, at the end of 2008 FDI from Australia was only three per cent of the total stock of FDI in Chile,[14] and only two per cent of the stock of FDI in Brazil.[15]

Nevertheless, sections two and three have together underlined that Australia's business relations with Latin America have grown, but remain of lower significance compared with those with other parts of the world, and vice versa. This impression is confirmed by other sources of information, such as the three 2008–10 surveys among Australian companies by Australia's Export Finance Insurance Corporation (EFIC). They consistently rated Central and South America last among all continents in the world, including Africa, in terms of foreign revenues (14 per cent in 2008), export destinations (12 per cent in 2009; ten per cent in 2010), expected future export destinations (14 per cent in 2009 and 2010), offshore operations (nine per cent in 2008; six per cent in 2009, four per cent in 2010, particularly mining companies), and expected future offshore operations (six per cent in 2008, ten per cent in 2009, seven per cent in 2010).[16] This suggests that there are still ample opportunities for further expansion of trade and business relations. Before analysing how this expansion may be fostered, it would be relevant first to probe the factors that help to explain why Australian companies currently take only a relatively marginal interest in business relations with Latin America.

Business environments: How important are the remaining differences?

Distance across the Pacific Ocean is sometimes identified as a major impediment to Australia's business relations with Latin America. For example, a 2001 DFAT report noted that the long distance between Australia and Latin America increases the share of transport costs, especially for Australia's low-value bulk export commodities.[17] However, physical distance is not necessarily an

---

14   INE, *Estatuto de la Inversión Extranjera* (DL600), Santiago de Chile: Institutio Nacional de Estadísticas de Chile, 2009. http://www.ine.cl, accessed 11 November 2013.

15   BCB, *Census of Foreign Capitals in Brazil, 2000 Base-Year*. Brasilia: Banco Central do Brasil, 2010. http://www.bcb.gov.br/, accessed 11 November 2013.

16   EFIC, *Global Readiness Index: National Report*, Canberra: Export Finance and Insurance Corporation, 2008–2010: EFIC 2008, pp. 16, 24, 30; EFIC 2009 pp. 18, 24, 30, 46; EFIC 2010, pp. 28, 32, 42, 52.

17   DFAT, Investing in Latin American Growth: Unlocking Opportunities in Brazil, Mexico, Argentina and Chile, Canberra: Department of Foreign Affairs and Trade, 2001, pp. 20–21.

impediment. After all, for centuries Australia has conducted long-distance trade with the United Kingdom over distances that span half the globe. Physical distance was overcome through efficient transport connections—shipping and air transport—for goods and people; as well as communications, finance, long-term accumulation of personal and business connections; similarities in institutions relevant to business relations—social and legal; and similarities in living standards. If physical distance is not necessarily an issue, what issues then sustain the notion of 'distance' between Australia and Latin America?

Analyses of international business relations tend to use notions of 'economic', 'institutional' and 'psychic' distance, rather than simply geographic distance, to explain the degree of trade and business contacts between two countries.[18] Economic distance relates to differences in the economic situation between Australia and the countries of Latin America. This notion can be captured with some basic numbers, such as those in Table 5.9. It shows that Australia is small relative to the main countries of Latin America in terms of its population. However, GDP per capita indicates that Australia's standard of living is high relative to Latin America. Despite its significantly smaller population, Australia's GDP is therefore large relative to the larger Latin American economies. The degree to which the Australian economy depends on foreign trade is broadly comparable to Latin America as a whole, which of course implies that trade per capita is significantly higher than in Latin America, as Table 5.9 confirms.

The difference between the levels of GDP per capita is in itself an indication of a significant economic distance between Australia and Latin American countries. These levels could be broad indicators of the low maturity of markets for advanced goods and services. However, the size of the population in several Latin American countries, particularly Brazil, Mexico and Argentina, combined with significant and persistently high income inequalities,[19] suggests that there could be sizeable mature markets in Latin America. If, for example, only ten per cent of the population in Latin American countries maintains an average level of income comparable to Australia, it would still comprise a potential market of over 50 million people. This market may be imperfectly integrated, but its size would be well in excess of Australia's.

---

18   Van Ruth, *op. cit.*, note 10, pp. 19–62, offers an extensive discussion of this literature, as well as the measurable differences in the business environments of Latin American countries.
19   Ewout Frankema, *Has Latin America Always Been Unequal? A Comparative Study of Asset and Income Inequality in the Long Twentieth Century*, Leiden: Brill Publications, 2009.

Table 5.9: Basic economic indicators, Australia and Latin America, 2009-2011

	Population (mln, 2011)	GDP (bln US$, 2011)	GDP per capita (US$, 2011)	Trade per capita (US$, 2009–11 av.)	Trade to GDP ratio (2009–11 av.)
Australia	22.6	1,371.7	60,695	22,764	44
Brazil	196.7	2,476.6	12,591	2,423	23
Mexico	114.7	1,155.3	10,072	5,525	61
Colombia	46.9	331.6	7,070	2,107	34
Argentina	40.8	446.0	10,940	3,706	40
Peru	29.4	176.7	6,009	2,612	50
Venezuela	29.3	316.5	10,810	4,379	36
Chile	17.3	248.6	14,394	8,537	69
Guatemala	14.8	47.0	3,184	1,817	62
Ecuador	14.7	67.0	4,569	2,892	71
Bolivia	10.1	24.4	2,421	1,389	67
Dominican Rep	10.1	55.7	5,535	2,888	56
Honduras	7.8	17.3	2,226	2,231	109
Paraguay	6.6	23.9	3,635	3,104	106
El Salvador	6.2	23.1	3,702	2,408	69
Nicaragua	5.9	7.3	1,243	1,618	140
Costa Rica	4.7	41.0	8,675	6,148	81
Uruguay	3.4	46.7	13,865	6,148	53
Jamaica	2.7	15.1	5,563	4,019	79
Trinidad & Tobago	1.3	22.5	16,704	16,385	96
Total, average	563.2	5,542.1	9,841	3,498	40

Note: The average trade–GDP ratio for Latin America is unweighted.

Source: WTO Trade Profiles, http://stat.wto.org/.

Market size matters to business relations, but so does a range of other aspects of the business environment, such as economic stability. During the past 20 years, major countries in Latin America have experienced significant macro-economic crises, particularly Mexico in 1982, 1990 and 1994–95, Brazil in 1994–95 and Argentina in 2002–03 (see Chapter 6). Such instability found its expression in drastic exchange rate fluctuations that enhanced the risk of doing business with these countries. Memories of the specifics of such episodes of economic crisis may now be fading, but they are likely to feed lingering general impressions of economic instability.

Fluctuating exchange rates, lack of full convertibility in some cases, and economic instability are factors that determine impressions of economic distance. A range of other factors impact on business relations also. For trade relations, exchange rate stability may be less relevant because international transactions are generally denominated in relatively stable international currencies, and firms can hedge adverse exchange rate movements. More important in this case is the likelihood that foreign business partners will pay for deliveries, or will deliver goods upon receipt of payment. Normally, the letter of credit and bill of exchange mechanism is sufficient for this purpose. But for transactions involving partners located in countries with higher risk ratings, companies tend to secure the services of government-sponsored agencies that offer export credit insurance and finance for export activities in case private financial companies do not. In Australia, EFIC offers this service. As with similar agencies in other countries it uses the country risk classifications of the Organisation for Economic Cooperation and Development (OECD) as one of the foundations for its activities. These classifications are summarised in Table 5.10.

The OECD consistently ranks Australia, together with most other OECD countries, among the countries where the risk of non-repayment of export credits is very low. This implies that companies can be assured that payments for exports will eventuate and that goods will be delivered for import upon payment. It also implies that there are reasonably effective legal mechanisms available to seek redemption in case payments or deliveries do not eventuate. Table 5.10 indicates that most Latin American countries are in the medium to high risk category. Some countries are perceived as less risky than others, particularly Chile, Trinidad and Tobago, and Mexico, but others such as Argentina and Ecuador are considered to be high-risk. Table 5.10 also shows that some countries have reduced their risk ranking during the past decade; particularly Mexico and Brazil for reasons that will be discussed in Chapter 6. In broad terms, we can expect that there is a positive correlation between the reluctance among Australian companies to export to or import from these countries and their risk rating. Australian firms can of course seek to minimise transaction risks, for example by dealing exclusively with trusted business partners, or purchasing export credit insurance from financial institutions or possibly EFIC, but such actions increase their transaction costs.

Table 5.10: OECD country risk classifications, Australia and Latin America, 1999–2013

	1999–03	2004–08	2009–13
Australia	0.0	0.0	0.0
USA	0.0	0.0	0.0
Chile	2.0	2.0	2.0
Trinidad and Tobago	2.3	2.0	2.0
Mexico	3.3	2.3	2.9
Brazil	6.0	4.4	3.0
Costa Rica	3.4	3.0	3.0
Panama	4.0	3.7	3.0
Peru	5.1	4.2	3.0
Uruguay	4.1	5.2	3.6
Colombia	5.1	4.6	4.0
El Salvador	4.0	4.0	4.0
Guatemala	6.0	5.5	5.0
Paraguay	5.8	6.2	5.0
Honduras	6.9	6.7	6.0
Jamaica	5.1	6.0	6.2
Bolivia	6.7	7.0	6.4
Venezuela	5.1	6.2	6.9
Argentina	6.1	7.0	7.0
Cuba	7.0	7.0	7.0
Ecuador	6.9	7.0	7.0

Note: The classifications are for export credit risk assessment. The scale is from 0 (low risk) to 7 (high risk). The data shown are calculated from quarterly data.

Source: Calculated from OECD, http://www.oecd.org/tad/xcred/cre-crc-historical-internet-english-[25-0-2013].pdf.

The authoritative OECD risk indicators summarised in Table 5.10 are based on the OECD's considerations of the payment experiences of partner countries, as well as the financial and economic situation of assessed countries. The OECD does not publish the details of its deliberations, but they are most likely based on an amalgam of factors. McCoy and McLendon offer an intricate discussion of factors that shape the business environment in 18 Latin American countries.[20] Key factors are also captured in composite indices that rank countries on the

---

20   McCoy, Terry L. and Timothy McLendon, *2009 Latin American Business Environment Report*, Gainesville FL: Center for Latin American Studies, University of Florida, 2009.

basis of various aspects of their business environment. For example, the annual Heritage Foundation's Index of Economic Freedom is based on publicly available statistical information that captures aspects of a country's legal, economic, regulatory and governance structures that can confound investment and commerce. *Euromoney*'s annual Country Risk rankings of countries uses similar data, but combines them with surveys among company executives into their perceptions of the risks of doing business in other countries. Table 5.11 shows the most recent results for Australia and Latin American countries.

Table 5.11: Diversity in the business environments of Australia and Latin America, 2013

	Index of Economic Freedom	Euromoney Country Risk Index
Australia	82.6	81.2
USA	76.0	74.9
Chile	79.0	74.6
Brazil	57.7	60.2
Mexico	67.0	58.9
Colombia	69.6	58.6
Trinidad and Tobago	62.3	58.2
Peru	68.2	57.0
Uruguay	69.7	51.9
Costa Rica	67.0	50.1
El Salvador	66.7	43.6
Paraguay	61.1	41.3
Bolivia	47.9	39.4
Honduras	58.4	38.0
Guatemala	60.0	37.4
Ecuador	46.9	35.5
Argentina	46.7	33.6
Venezuela	36.1	33.4
Jamaica	66.8	32.0
Nicaragua	56.6	28.4

Note: The scales are from 0 (respectively low opacity, low economic freedom or high risk) to 100 (respectively high opacity, high economic freedom or low risk).

Sources: Miller, Holmes and Feuler 2013; *Euromoney* (January 2013) http://www.euromoney.com.

The choice and weighting of the different indicators on which these indices have been based contain an element of arbitrariness. It is possible that the indicators are not able to capture all elements of country risk that are relevant to business decisions. And, for that matter, it is possible that the indicators also fail to take account of any actions that foreign firms may implement to assess and absorb the risk they face in countries that are ranked low in Table 5.11. Nevertheless, in broad terms, there is a positive correlation between these rankings and the last column in Table 5.10. Table 5.11 therefore confirms that there are very significant differences between the business environments of Australia and most countries of Latin America, as well as between Latin American countries themselves. It also confirms that those differences inform perceptions of risk that companies take into account when considering whether or not to take advantage of foreign business opportunities through trade and investment. For example, research for Latin American countries found that greater economic freedom, as well as minimisation of expropriation risk, financial and trade reforms, good governance and institutional improvements are all positively correlated with greater inflows of FDI.[21]

Most pertinent to companies engaged in international business are issues that the World Bank captures in its annual survey of the business environment in countries around the world.[22] The results for 2012 are summarised in Table 5.12. They show that Australia is not necessarily the easiest country in which to conduct business, depending on the indicator used. However, compared with most countries in Latin America, Australia ranks on average highly, as do most other OECD countries. Hence, it is not just on the basis of the opinions of company executives and/or macro-economic and financial indicators that Latin American countries can be regarded as difficult and risky countries for the purposes of international business. A range of micro-economic regulatory issues relevant to business operations points in the same direction, although it needs to be emphasised that there are significant differences between countries in the region.

As mentioned, private companies can find ways to overcome such difficulties in foreign business environments. For example, with specific reference to Australian firms in Latin America, Van Ruth found that person-to-person contact and the creation of networks based on such personal contacts can help to overcome the difficulties that underlie the 'psychic distance' between Australia and Latin America.[23] She determined that networks mitigated risk and thus expedited the

---

21   Marta Bengoa and Blanca Sánchez-Robles, 'Foreign Direct Investment, Economic Freedom and Growth: New Evidence from Latin America', *European Journal of Political Economy*, 2003, 19, pp. 529–45; Len J. Treviño, and Franklin G. Mixon, 'Strategic Factors Affecting Foreign Direct Investment Decisions by Multi-National Enterprises in Latin America', *Journal of World Business*, 2004, 39, pp. 233–43; Glen Biglaiser and Karl De Rouen, 'Economic Reforms and Inflows of Foreign Direct Investment in Latin America', *Latin American Research Review*, 2006 41(1), pp. 51–75.

22   Brenes *et al.*, 'Latin America: Environmental and Firm-Level Challenges', *Journal of Business Research*, 2009, 62, pp. 849–53, offer a firm-level perspective of the importance of some of these impediments; while Patricio Donoso and Victoria L. Crittenden, 'Strategic Management in Latin America', *Journal of Business Research*, 2008, 61, pp. 587–9, explain the ample opportunities for further research on the international competitiveness and strategic management of firms in Latin America.

23   Van Ruth, *op. cit.,* note 10.

internationalisation of Australian firms in Latin America by providing access to relevant business information that would otherwise be difficult to obtain, e.g., in finding employees, agents or local partners, providing access to customers and suppliers, as well as reassurance and credibility, and an opportunity to share and learn from experiences. It could be argued that networks are particularly relevant to the business environment in Latin American countries, given the opacity and the uncertainties caused by the presence in most of weak formal institutions, but also because of a culturally ingrained penchant for personal relationships that is arguably much stronger than in the United States or Australia.[24]

While networks may be a solution to overcoming the difficulties posed by unfavourable business environments, a likely problem is that few Australian companies are prepared or able to invest time and effort in the long-term strategy of building them by accumulating and maintaining intercontinental personal and business relations. Creating functional networks that foster business relations on the basis of interpersonal trust tends to be a long cumulative process. Spanish may still be a difficult language for many Australian business people. Although English is likely to be a second language for most business people in Latin America, speaking the same language does not necessarily mean that people entirely understand each other's intentions, as arguably over 90 per cent of interpersonal communication tends to be of a non-verbal nature.[25] If so, cultural differences may have an impact on the perceived 'distance' between the business environments of Australia and Latin American countries, and may thus be a barrier to business contacts.

---

24   Joyce S. Osland, *et al.*, 'Organizational Implications of Latin American Culture', *E&G Economiae Gestào*, 2008, 7(14), pp. 109–20, 111.
25   Merabian, Albert, *Silent Messages: Implicit Communication of Emotions and Attitudes,* 1981.

Table 5.12: Australia and Latin American countries in global ranking of 185 countries by ease of doing business, 2012

	Total	Starting a business	Dealing with construction permits	Getting electricity	Registering property	Getting credit	Protecting investors	Paying taxes	Trading across borders	Enforcing contracts
United States	4	13	17	19	25	4	6	69	22	6
Australia	10	2	11	36	37	4	70	48	44	15
Puerto Rico	41	12	156	37	128	12	19	104	96	101
Peru	43	60	86	77	19	23	13	85	60	115
Colombia	45	61	27	134	52	70	6	99	91	154
Mexico	48	36	36	130	141	40	49	107	61	76
Trinidad & Tobago	69	71	101	11	176	23	25	90	75	170
Uruguay	89	39	158	20	164	70	100	140	104	102
Jamaica	90	21	50	123	105	104	82	163	106	129
Guatemala	93	172	94	34	20	12	158	124	117	96
Paraguay	103	111	71	26	67	83	70	141	155	106
Costa Rica	110	128	128	45	46	83	169	125	51	128
El Salvador	113	139	146	131	56	53	169	153	80	71
Nicaragua	119	131	154	129	123	104	100	158	81	55
Argentina	124	154	171	74	135	70	117	149	139	48
Honduras	125	155	65	117	92	12	169	139	90	179
Brazil	130	121	131	60	109	104	82	156	123	116
Ecuador	139	169	104	146	101	83	139	84	128	99
Bolivia	155	174	114	126	139	129	139	180	125	136
Venezuela	180	152	109	160	90	159	181	185	166	80

Source: World Bank, http://www.doingbusiness.org/rankings.

Table 5.13 illustrates the extent to which cultural differences between Australia and the countries of Latin America are substantial, while those between Australia and the United States are small. The indicators in this table are based on an aggregation of large numbers of survey responses. The results are not beyond debate, but the existence of measurable cultural differences has been confirmed in later research.[26] For example, the table shows an Australian score of 90 on the individualism index, while the average score for 14 Latin American countries is 22. This indicates that Latin American individuals are inclined to establish strong, cohesive in-groups on the basis of personal relationships, while in Australia ties between individuals tend to be very loose. Another example is that Australia scores low on uncertainty avoidance, while most Latin American countries have a high score. This indicates that Australians are more tolerant of the uncertainty and ambiguity of new situations and experiences, while in Latin American countries people prefer to avoid uncertainty. Hence, the results in Table 5.13 reveal significant differences in the norms and values that Australians and people in Latin America tend to evince. They could be a source of miscommunication at an interpersonal level between individuals. Nevertheless, only 15 per cent of all Australian companies identified cultural differences as a major barrier to international expansion, the lowest of all perceived barriers.[27] And the difference between companies with and without international experience was marginal in this respect.[28] A further 57 per cent regarded cultural differences to be a minor barrier.

Awareness of the relevance of cultural differences tends to be a personal experience that only comes with sustained immersion in a different culture. While large companies may be able to reserve resources to help their key managers to develop ways to overcome cultural differences, small and medium-sized enterprises (SMEs) do not, notwithstanding the increasing ease of communications by internet across the globe. In Australia, SMEs particularly face a steep learning curve when they seek to engage in international business. Consequently, only 10 per cent of Australian SMEs engages in exporting,[29] lower than in other country.[30]

26   Robert J. House, *et al.*, (eds), Culture, Leadership, and Organizations: The GLOBE Study of 62 Societies, Thousand Oaks: Sage, 2004.
27   EFIC, *Global Readiness Index, op. cit.*, note 16, 2008, pp. 42, 52.
28   EFIC, *Global Readiness Index, op. cit.*, note 16, 2009, p. 62.
29   Sensis, Sensis Business Index: Small and Medium Sized Enterprises, Melbourne: Sensis, August 2010, p. 17.
30   Austrade, *Knowing and Growing the Exporter Community*, Canberra: Australian Trade Commission, 2002, p. 9.

Table 5.13: Cultural differences between Australia, United States and Latin America

	Power Distance Index	Individualism Index	Masculinity Index	Uncertainty Avoidance Index
Australia	36	90	61	51
USA	40	91	62	46
Latin America, average	68	22	49	80
Guatemala	95	6	37	101
Panama	95	11	44	86
Mexico	81	30	69	82
Venezuela	81	12	73	76
Ecuador	78	8	63	67
Brazil	69	38	49	76
Colombia	67	13	64	80
El Salvador	66	19	40	94
Peru	64	16	42	87
Chile	63	23	28	86
Uruguay	61	36	38	100
Argentina	49	46	56	86
Jamaica	45	39	68	13
Costa Rica	35	15	21	86

Note: Averages for Latin America are unweighted.

Source: Hofstede (1997: pp. 26, 53, 84, 113).

Lastly, the perception of significant physical distance across the Pacific Ocean is enhanced by the fact that communications are cumbersome. Telephone and internet connections may now be well-developed, but there are still limited direct shipping connections between Australian and Latin American ports. For example one per cent of the value of outward freight loaded in Australian ports is destined for South America, and 1.4 per cent of freight unloaded in Australian ports originated from South America,[31] which is lower than the share of Latin America as a whole in the value of trade (Table 5.1). Most of the cargo is transhipped in containers via other ports. For example, shipping company Maersk ships containers between Australia and Latin America via Manzanillo and Balboa in Panama and Cartagena in Colombia, while Evergreen ships them via ports in Asia, such as Hong Kong and Singapore to the East Coast, and via

---

31 BITRE, *Statistical Report: Australian Sea Freight 2010–11*, Canberra: Bureau of Infrastructure, Transport and Regional Economics, 2012, pp. 8–9.

Colon in Panama to the West Coast of Latin America. Facilities in container ports may be efficient, but transhipments add costs and increase delays in deliveries. Direct air transport routes are few, although they have increased in recent years. Qantas commenced thrice-weekly non-stop flights from Sydney to Buenos Aires in 2008. Codesharing with LAN Airlines, Qantas now offers daily flights via Auckland to Santiago de Chile, connecting there to LAN's extensive network in Latin America. Until mid 2014 Aerolíneas Argentinas flew two to three times a week from Sydney to Buenos Aires, where there were connections throughout South America. Other air transport routes are via the United States, South Africa and Europe.

The fact that the business environment in Latin America poses significant challenges to Australian firms does not mean that it deters all business relations. As Sections 2 and 3 explained, trade and business relations have grown during the last 20 years. However, these relations are largely the result of Australian companies seizing opportunities and finding ways to deal with the elements of risk that exist. Potter discussed the significant difficulties that Australian firms, such as RYCO Hydraulics, had to overcome in Brazil, before their ventures succeeded.[32] On the other hand, there are examples of firms whose ventures in Latin America did not live up to expectations. For example, in 1994 Village Roadshow created a subsidiary venture to establish and manage cinemas in Argentina, which it divested in 2005 when the venture became unprofitable. Likewise, in 2000 AGL took a controlling share in gas distributor GasValpo in Chile, which it divested in 2008.

Australian government agencies can assist firms in overcoming the real or imagined risks that firms perceive when considering business relations with Latin America. Three-quarters (76 per cent) of Australian firms identified their lack of local business and market knowledge in foreign countries as an impediment to engagement in international business.[33] About a third (32 per cent) had used the services of Austrade to overcome this impediment, and 15 per cent had consulted EFIC.[34] Austrade maintains six offices, i.e., 'posts' and 'sub-posts', in Latin America—Argentina, Brazil, Chile, Colombia, Mexico and Peru—where around 25 business development managers are active.[35] In addition, Austrade employs around five officers based in Australia who focus on Latin America.

EFIC's expertise with Latin America appears limited. For example, it does not issue any profiles on the countries of that global region, but refers potential

---

32   Potter, Ben, 'Bulls on Brazil', *Australian Financial Review Magazine*, 31 July 2009.

33   EFIC, *Global Readiness Index, op. cit.*, note 16, 2008, p. 53.

34   EFIC, *Global Readiness Index, op. cit.*, note 16, 2009, p. 66.

35   Austrade, *Australian Trade Commission, Annual Report 2011–12*, Canberra: Australia's Trade and Investment Development Agency, 2012, p. 9; Austrade communication to authors.

customers to the OECD country risk grades mentioned above. EFIC's annual reports indicate that the share of South America in the agency's total exposure increased from 0.4 per cent in mid-2006 and 2007 to 2.8 per cent in mid-2008 and 2009. Although still marginal, it suggests that firms have increased their appeal to EFIC for support of their undertakings in Latin America, which is possibly related to the increased activity of Australian mining companies in Latin America. But it should be noted that most firms don't engage EFIC's services at all, which means that they may have only a small number of transactions with Latin America.

The key Latin American countries all have government agencies that are equivalent to Austrade.[36] Their websites suggest that they focus on promoting their countries as destinations for inward foreign investment. Where these agencies generate information for the purpose of supporting exports from their countries, they do not specifically dispense information on Australia. This suggests that there is little Australia-specific expertise at these agencies that may foster bilateral business relations.

This section has demonstrated that there are still significant differences between the business environments of Australia and the countries of Latin America; though the latter are far from homogenous. These differences have not deterred several Australian companies from establishing business relations with partners in Latin America. It also did not deter Australian firms from investing in Latin America. In particular, Australia-based multinational mining companies have done so, possibly in response to the tripling of the prices of metals and energy on global markets during 2004–2011.[37] The gains became so high in this sector that these firms were able to muster the relevant resources to overcome difficulties of conducting business in Latin America, and absorb the cost of minimising risk. Outside the mining sector there are far fewer examples of Australian firms that have invested in Latin America. There are also few examples of Latin American companies that invested in Australia. Hence, while non-mining companies can in principle also take initiatives to mitigate risk in international business, the differences in the business environments of Australia and Latin America most likely still deter business relations.

---

36   The agencies are: Brazil, ApexBrasil (Business Intelligence Unit, Unidade de Inteligencia Comercial), and the Ministry of External Relations (Trade and Investment Promotion Department, Departamento de Promocao Comercial); Argentina, ProsperAr; Mexico, Secretaría de Promoción Económica (Jalisco); Chile, Chilean Economic Development Agency (InvestChile CORFO).

37   IMF, *IMF Primary Commodity Prices*, Washington DC: International Monetary Fund, 2013. http://www.imf.org/external/np/res/commod/index.asp, accessed 12 November 2013.

Conclusion

The scope for closer trade and business relations between Australia and Latin America—particularly over the past 20 years—appears to have slowly materialised. The rates of growth have been slow and the results meagre, with Australian merchandise imports from and exports to Latin America still only accounting for 2.2 per cent and 1.4 per cent respectively of Australia's total merchandise trade. Nevertheless, trade and business relations between Australia and Latin America are on the move. An especially interesting factor is the growth in operations of the large multinational mining companies such as BHP, Rio Tinto, Vale and Xtrata on both sides of the Pacific. A number of other Australian mining companies and mining technology and services companies are also showing increasing interest in Latin America.

Australia's business relations with Latin America are still very much focused on Argentina, Brazil, Chile and Mexico, which indicates that there are still underexplored opportunities in other countries in the region, particularly Peru, Colombia, Guatemala and Ecuador. The share of manufactured products and services has increased in Australia's trade relations with key Latin American countries, but primary commodities and simple manufactured products still dominate. As diversification has driven a rate of growth of trade relations, there appears to be scope for additional growth in further diversification.

Nevertheless, this chapter has revealed that the business environments of Australia and Latin America are dissimilar in many ways, some to a greater degree than others. Several Australian companies have defied these differences by establishing business relations with partners in Latin America, or by investing there. However, most Australian companies have no intentions to do so, and are focused on traditional markets and host countries in Europe, North America and East Asia. In response to high international prices of minerals during the last ten years, Australia-based multinational mining companies have taken a keen interest in the business opportunities in Latin America and have found ways to overcome real or perceived difficulties of doing business in Latin America, and absorb the cost of minimising risk to assets. Outside the mining sector, there are fewer examples of Australian firms that have invested in Latin America, and even fewer examples of Latin American companies that invested in Australia. This suggests that firms on both sides of the Pacific are still reluctant to take up business opportunities, and that further growth of business relations will be a slow but possibly consistent process.

References

Serials

ABS 3401.0, *Overseas Arrivals and Departures, Australia*, Canberra: Australian Bureau of Statistics.

ABS 5352.0, *International Investment Position Australia: Supplementary Country Statistics*, Canberra: Australian Bureau of Statistics.

ABS 5368.0, *International Trade in Goods and Services, Australia*, Canberra: Australian Bureau of Statistics.

ABS 5368.0.55.004, *International Trade in Services by Country, by State and by Detailed Services Category*, Canberra: Australian Bureau of Statistics.

ABS 5372.0.55.001, *International Merchandise Trade: Confidential Commodities List*, Canberra: Australian Bureau of Statistics.

Other

ABS, ABS 5494.0, *Economic Activity of Foreign Owned Businesses in Australia*, Canberra: Australian Bureau of Statistics, 2004.

ABS, ABS5495.0, *Australian Outward Foreign Affiliates Trade: Experimental Results*, Canberra: Australian Bureau of Statistics, 2004.

AEI, *International Student Data, 2002–2012*, Canberra: Australian Education International, 2012. https://aei.gov.au/research/International-Student-Data/, accessed 12 November 2013.

Austrade, *Knowing and Growing the Exporter Community*, Canberra: Australian Trade Commission, 2002.

Austrade, *Australian Trade Commission, Annual Report 2011–12*, Canberra: Australia's Trade and Investment Development Agency, 2012.

BCB, *Census of Foreign Capitals in Brazil, 2000 Base-Year*. Brasilia: Banco Central do Brasil, 2010. http://www.bcb.gov.br/, accessed 12 November 2013.

Bengoa, Marta and Blanca Seanchez-Robles, 'Foreign Direct Investment, Economic Freedom and Growth: New Evidence from Latin America', *European Journal of Political Economy*, 2003, 19, pp. 529–45.

Biglaiser, Glen and Karl De Rouen, 'Economic Reforms and Inflows of Foreign Direct Investment in Latin America', *Latin American Research Review*, 2006, 41(1), pp. 51–75.

BITRE, *Statistical Report: Australian Sea Freight 2010–11*, Canberra: Bureau of Infrastructure, Transport and Regional Economics, 2012.

Brenes, Esteban R. Jerry Haar and Bernardo Requena, 'Latin America: Environmental and Firm-Level Challenges', *Journal of Business Research*, 2009, 62, pp. 849–53.

Casanova, Lourdes and Matthew Fraser, (eds), *From Multilatinas to Global Latinas: The New Latin American Multinationals (Compilation Case Studies)*, Washington DC: Inter-American Development Bank, 2009.

DFAT, *Investing in Latin American Growth: Unlocking Opportunities in Brazil, Mexico, Argentina and Chile*, Canberra: Department of Foreign Affairs and Trade, 2001.

DFAT, *Exports of Primary and Manufactured Products, Australia 2008–09*, Canberra: Department of Foreign Affairs and Trade, 2010.

Donoso, Patricio and Victoria L. Crittenden, 'Strategic Management in Latin America', *Journal of Business Research*, 2008, 61, pp. 587–9.

ECLAC, *Foreign Direct Investment in Latin America and the Caribbean, 2007*. Santiago: UN Economic Council for Latin America and the Caribbean, 2007.

EFIC, *Global Readiness Index: National Report*, Canberra: Export Finance and Insurance Corporation, 2008–2010.

Frankema, Ewout, *Has Latin America Always Been Unequal? A Comparative Study of Asset and Income Inequality in the Long Twentieth Century*, Leiden: Brill Publications, 2009.

Hatum, Andres, and Josefina Michelini, 'Going Global: The Process of Internationalisation of Latino Multinational Firms', *International Journal of Business and Emerging Markets*, 2011, 3, pp. 36–56.

Hofstede, Geert, *Cultures and Organizations: Software of the Mind*. New York: McGraw-Hill, 1997.

House, Robert J. Paul J. Hanges, Mansour Javidan, Peter W. Dorfman and Vipin Gupta, (eds), *Culture, Leadership, and Organizations: The GLOBE Study of 62 Societies*, Thousand Oaks: Sage, 2004.

IMF, *IMF Primary Commodity Prices*, Washington DC: International Monetary Fund, 2013. http://www.imf.org/external/np/res/commod/index.asp, accessed 12 November 2013.

INE, *Estatuto de la Inversión Extranjera* (DL600), Santiago de Chile: Instituto Nacional de Estadísticas de Chile, 2009. http://www.ine.cl, accessed 12 November 2013.

JEG, *Australia–Mexico Joint Experts Group on Strengthening Bilateral Economic Relations: Joint Report*, Canberra/Mexico City: Department of Foreign Affairs and Trade/Ministry of the Economy, 2009.

McCoy, Terry L. and Timothy McLendon, *2009 Latin American Business Environment Report*, Gainesville FL: Center for Latin American Studies, University of Florida, 2009.

Merabian, Albert, *Silent Messages: Implicit Communication of Emotions and Attitudes*, Belmont CA: Wadsworth, 1981.

Miller, Terry, Kim R. Holmes, and Edwin J. Feuler, *2013 Index of Economic Freedom: Promoting Economic Opportunities and Prosperity*, Washington DC: The Heritage Foundation, 2013.

Osland, Joyce S., Silvio De Franco, and Asbjorn Osland, 'Organizational Implications of Latin American Culture: Lessons for the Expatriate Manager', *E&G Economiae Gestào*, 2008, 7(14), pp. 109–20.

Potter, Ben, 'Bulls on Brazil', *Australian Financial Review Magazine*, 31 July 2009.

Sensis, *Sensis Business Index: Small and Medium Sized Enterprises*, Melbourne: Sensis, August 2010.

Treviño, Len J. and Franklin G. Mixon, 'Strategic Factors Affecting Foreign Direct Investment Decisions by Multi-National Enterprises in Latin America', *Journal of World Business*, 2004, 39, pp. 233–43.

Van Ruth, Frances, *The Internationalisation of Australian Firms: How Networks Help Bridge the 'Psychic Distance' Between A Firm and A Market*, PhD thesis, Department of Management and Marketing, University of Melbourne, 2008.

6. Australia and Latin America: Shared experiences and prospects for a new partnership

Don Kenyon and Pierre van der Eng

Introduction

Chapter 5 surveyed the development of the trade and business relations between Australia and the countries of Latin America during a period of more than 20 years.[1] Apart from pointing to the fact that growth of these relations was carried by four key countries in Latin America, and by the diversification of trade and business relations towards manufactures and services, it did not explain the more fundamental reasons why trade and business relations increased. Identifying those reasons is important because it facilitates the discovery of the foundations for further growth and diversification, and the formulation of relevant government initiatives that may facilitate this process. That is the purpose of this chapter.

Section two will argue that several preconditions for an intensification of Australia's business relations with Latin America have been established. These are the result of the difficult but fundamental processes of trade liberalisation, market deregulation and structural reform in both Australia and key Latin American countries since the 1980s. The shared experience of these economic and trade policy reforms has greatly expanded the range of interests that Australia and the countries of Latin America have come to share in the international trade policy agenda. This also enhances the scope for closer trade and business relations.

Section three of this chapter will examine the scope for realising the promise that has long been considered to exist in building a closer trade and business partnership between Australia and Latin American countries. It will probe the increased scope that exists for pursuing shared trade policy objectives in

---

1   As in chapter five, Latin America is broadly defined to comprise South America and Central America, including the Caribbean, although further discussion will focus on Australia's main business partners in Latin America.

the World Trade Organisation (WTO), as well as the opportunities for closer cooperation through new and important regional, plurilateral and bilateral economic and trade initiatives.

New partners in globalisation: Shared experiences in structural reform and trade liberalisation

Despite the remaining differences in the business environments of Australia and the countries of Latin America, the trade and business relations between Australia and Latin America have grown, as chapter 5 established. A major underlying reason for this development is the fact that Australia and key Latin American countries shared experiences in structural reform and trade liberalisation that created new business opportunities across the Pacific. To appreciate the importance of these developments it is relevant to sketch the situation that existed 25 to 30 years ago, and then trace the changes that have occurred since. In doing so, this section will set the scene for the discussion in section three of the opportunities that exist to enhance trade and business relations between Australia and Latin America.

Prior to the 1980s, Australia and Latin America regarded each other primarily as trade competitors rather than trade partners. There were a number of reasons for this. Perhaps the most important was that Australia and key Latin American countries such as Brazil, Argentina, Chile and Colombia were competitive exporters of the same temperate and subtropical agricultural products—such as beef, grains, sugar, fruit and fruit products—and minerals—especially iron ore in the case of Brazil—to northern hemisphere markets in Europe, North America and North Asia. Nevertheless, as exporters of agricultural products there was at the same time a shared interest in defending their agricultural trade against the protectionist agricultural policies of the European Community (EC) and the United States as exporting members of international commodity agreements and through the dispute settlement provisions of the General Agreement on Trade and Tariffs (GATT).[2] However, the scope for this shared interest to foster closer cooperation on broader trade policy issues was muted by the primacy that Latin American countries gave to developing their international trade policy stances through the United Nations Conference on Trade and Development (UNCTAD) during the 1960s and 1970s. This limited the opportunities for effective coalition building in the pursuit of shared trade objectives in GATT trade negotiations, which tended to be dominated by the industrialised countries.

---

2   Don Kenyon and David Lee, *The Struggle for Trade Liberalisation in Agriculture*, 2006, pp. 25–7; 45–9.

Both Australia and Latin American countries also followed essentially inward-looking industry and trade policies. Industry policies pursued import substitution, high tariffs and non-tariff trade barriers to manufactured imports, managed exchange rates and foreign exchange controls, and a relatively high level of government involvement and management of the economy. Such policy stances also hindered the scope for broader trade and business links across the Pacific that could have been a basis upon which to dilute competitive relations concerning agricultural exports. In addition, it meant that Australia and Latin American countries found each other on opposite sides of the divide between less-developed and developed countries characteristic of international trade discussions and negotiations, especially in successive GATT rounds of negotiations on trade liberalisation, as well as in UNCTAD.

Another dividing factor was that Australia and the countries of Latin America pursued different priorities regarding regional economic integration. For both Australia and Latin America during the 1970s and 1980s the priorities were north–south, rather than east–west. In the case of Australia, besides maintaining its relations with the United States, the trade policy priorities were oriented towards fostering relations with newly emerging markets in East Asia, particularly Japan, South Korea, the ASEAN countries, and more recently China. Such efforts were focused on Australia's exports of the commodities produced by Australia's agricultural and mining industries. In the case of Latin American countries, considerable attention was given during the 1960s and 1970s to fostering regional economic integration. In fact, regional integration efforts during this period were driven by the aim of creating a more effective developing country counterweight to the dominance of the United States in western hemisphere trade. But the inward-looking trade and industry policies of Latin American countries made effective cooperation to that end difficult.

By the early 1980s, the successive shocks caused by oil price hikes, long periods of stagflation in the mature industrial economies of Europe and North America, and the emergence of an industrially more competitive Japan—followed soon after by South Korea; Taiwan; Singapore and Hong Kong; key ASEAN countries; and China—were creating a new situation that called on countries to consider ways to increase their global competitiveness. Tariff protection and economic systems with a high degree of government intervention were giving way to more open trade policies, deregulated industries and floating exchange rates. Australia and Latin American countries were caught up in this wave of renewed globalisation.

In Australia, a period of recession, rising unemployment and soaring current account deficits during the late 1970s and early 1980s ushered in a period of fundamental change in economic and trade policy from 1982. It saw the deregulation of currency and exchange controls and the floating of the Australian dollar, the dismantling of the protective system of high tariffs on manufactured products, deregulation and privatisation of many previously government-controlled and owned industries, followed by regulatory reforms of the financial sector and the lifting of restrictions on foreign investment.[3] In all, by the early 1990s Australia had developed an integrated and internationally competitive financial sector, as well as a significantly reduced role for government in the management of the economy. And during the 1990s, the different sectors of the Australian economy became increasingly open and internationally competitive.

Similar changes took hold in key Latin American countries, albeit that the process of economic reform was in some countries interrupted by major financial crises that resulted in two steps forward, one step back. In Mexico, the external debt crisis of 1982 gave rise to a program of wide-ranging economic reforms. Mexico joined GATT in 1986, which marked the start of a process of reducing tariff protection as well as introducing programs of privatisation and regulatory reform. Further financial crises in 1990 and 1994 halted the process temporarily, but the entry into force of the North American Free Trade Agreement (NAFTA) with Canada and the United States in 1994, in particular provided new momentum for trade liberalisation in Mexico and the country's integration into global markets.

In the case of Brazil, the process of integration into global markets started in earnest in 1994, after several years of high to hyperinflation. In that year, the implementation of the *Plan Real* stabilised the currency exchange rate relative to the US dollar in order to address the debilitating problem of inflation. This was supported by a vigorous program of privatisation and deregulation that during the rest of the 1990s opened up the economy to market-based principles. The changes were not without difficulties, particularly in terms of the threat of inflation and currency convertibility. Nevertheless, prudent economic management secured economic stability and significant economic growth followed, to the extent that the currency appreciated during much of the 2000s and remained relatively stable after the Global Financial Crisis of 2008.

In the early 1990s, Argentina took similar measures to Brazil in order to resolve the problem of debilitating high inflation. It too suffered the consequences of heavy reliance on government management of the economy. In 1991 the peso was pegged to the US dollar, while the government imposed drastic discipline on public expenditure. As in Brazil and Mexico, processes of privatisation and deregulation, as well as reducing barriers to foreign trade and investment, allowed economic recovery and growth. But the process was interrupted in 2002, when it proved impossible to sustain pegging its currency to the US

---

3   Kenyon and Lee 2006, *op. cit.*, note 2, pp. 52–3.

dollar. Further policy action, such as abandoning full convertibility with the US dollar, stabilised the currency a year later and sustained a new process of recovery and growth.

In the case of Chile, economic reforms had already begun in the mid-1970s, when the government opted to lift barriers to trade and investment and embark on a process of privatisation and financial market deregulation. These were the foundations for significant economic growth during the 1980s and 1990s, which was sustained by Chile's increasing engagement in global markets. Chile's foreign trade has expanded rapidly following the global deregulation of trade barriers since the late 1980s. Table 6.1 shows that Chile is now one of the Latin American countries with the lowest trade tariffs.

Table 6.1 Tariffs in Australia and Latin American countries, 2011

	Simple average, %	Duty free	Duties higher than 15%	Duties higher than 3x average	Number of distinct non-ad valorem duty rates
		% shares of HS 6-digit sub-headings			
Australia	2.8	48.8	0.1	4.1	17
Argentina	13.6	5.1	37.2	0	14
Bolivia	11.2	6.4	19.5	5.5	6
Brazil	13.7	5.3	37.1	0	19
Chile	6.0	0.3	0	0	4
Colombia	8.4	2.2	2.0	0.8	13
Costa Rica	5.4	52.3	1.1	1.1	19
Equador	10.1	44.7	27.1	0.7	18
Guatemala	5.5	51.1	0.9	0.9	11
Mexico	8.3	47.8	13.8	7.4	86
Paraguay	10.2	13.9	31.3	0	24
Peru	3.7	53.2	0	12.4	3
Uruguay	10.5	15.1	35.1	0.4	19
Venezuela	12.5	0.6	28.1	0.2	9

Note: Most favoured nation status applied in all cases. HS is the Harmonised System to classify commodity trade.

Source: WTO, 2012, pp. 2–6.

These four Latin American countries embarked on processes of deregulation, privatisation and liberalisation of trade and investment policies for their own reasons and with their own institutional legacies. A closer look reveals significant differences between each of them, as well as with other Latin

American countries.[4] Hence, their experiences cannot be readily extrapolated to other countries in the region. In several cases, such as Venezuela and Ecuador, countries did not experience such changes, while in others, such as Colombia and Peru, similar changes occurred much more recently. Nevertheless, sketching the developments in these key countries helps to explain why they dominate the business relations of Latin America with Australia. The main conclusion that can be drawn from these sketches is that since the 1970s these four countries and Australia have undergone similar processes of economic change that have resulted in their increasing engagement with global markets. At the same time, it should be noted that global trade of goods and services, as well as investment flows, increased rapidly during the 1990s and 2000s, to a much greater degree than had ever occurred before.[5] This growth was sustained by global adherence to trade liberalisation following the end of communism in Eastern Europe around 1990, the successful conclusion of the GATT Uruguay Round (1986–93), and continued efforts to reduce trade barriers multilaterally, particularly for services, under the mandate of the WTO. Consequently, during the last 20 to 25 years these countries enhanced their ability to participate in international trade and business, and consequently benefit from it.

A major spur to these fundamental reforms in both Australia and Latin America was the realisation that in a global economy increasingly dominated by large multinational corporations—and in which trade in services across borders was becoming increasingly important—policies of import substitution supported by high levels of protection had run their course. While in earlier decades such policies had sustained economic growth, structural change and growing employment opportunities in industrial sectors, by the early 1980s it became increasingly clear that the resolution of global economic stagnation required a change of tack.

The reform programs also came at a fortuitous time for both the global economy and the future of business relations across the Pacific. The GATT Uruguay Round of multilateral trade negotiations had been languishing since its launch in the midst of the global economic crisis of the mid-1980s. The rollout of domestic economic reform and trade liberalisation programs across the industrialised and less-developed world through the 1980s enabled the Uruguay Round to be successfully concluded in 1993. This delivered several outcomes that fostered global trade, including ground-breaking agreements on agriculture and textiles; significant further reductions in industrial tariffs around the world; the creation

---

4   Nevertheless, these policy changes affected Latin America to a significant extent and were hailed as Latin America's 'New Economic Model', which fostered FDI inflows during the 1990s: see e.g., Michael Mortimore, 'Corporate Strategies for FDI in the Context of Latin America's New Economic Model', *World Development*, 2000, 28, pp. 1611–26.

5   WTO, *International Trade Statistics 2009*, Geneva: World Trade Organization, 2009, p. 173; UNCTAD, *World Investment Report 2009*, New York: United Nations Conference on Trade and Development, 2009, p. 4.

of a new set of trade rules for the liberalisation of trade in services; and new agreements to enforce intellectual property rights, to strengthen the GATT/WTO dispute settlement system, and to limit the use of subsidies and to impose greater discipline on technical barriers to trade, including standards and sanitary and phytosanitary restrictions.

The successful conclusion of the Uruguay Round negotiations was also of particular importance in giving new impetus to the future prospects for the trade and business relationship between Australia and Latin America. A major trade and political problem that the GATT negotiations had to confront was the challenge to the major trade interests of both Australia and Latin American countries posed by the agricultural policies of the then European Community (EC), the United States, Japan and South Korea. The export subsidy war on agriculture between the EC and the United States had brought world agricultural trade to a crisis point by the beginning of the Uruguay Round in 1986. Australia took the initiative to bring 14 developed and developing countries together in a coalition to fight this major trade bloc. Five Latin American countries—Argentina, Brazil, Chile, Colombia and Uruguay—became members of this Cairns Group (CG) of agricultural exporting countries.[6] The success of the CG in the negotiations in helping to bring the export subsidy war on agriculture to an end demonstrated that developed and less-developed countries could work closely together to achieve common trade policy objectives. The confidence established during these negotiations dispelled much of the earlier reticence towards working together that had previously been a feature of relations between Australia and Latin American countries, at least at an intergovernmental level. The shared experience of the CG in the Uruguay Round did much to breathe new life into the trade and business relationship between Australia and Latin America.

Hence, by the mid-1990s, the prospects for future partnership between Australia and Latin America had been transformed. The old competitive default setting over agriculture was largely a thing of the past. The divide between developed and less-developed countries was no longer a barrier to closer trade cooperation, both in WTO and in bilateral trade relations. As a consequence, the promise of closer trade and business relations which had proved elusive in the past showed better prospects of being fulfilled. In addition, the shared experience of implementing economic and trade reform policies put Australia and key Latin American countries on more comparable paths of economic and trade openness, which created new opportunities for closer business relations across the Pacific.

---

6   During the Uruguay Round negotiations 14 countries constituted the CG: Argentina, Australia, Brazil, Canada, Chile, Colombia, Fiji, Hungary, Indonesia, Malaysia, New Zealand, Philippines, Thailand and Uruguay. After the end of the Uruguay Round, Fiji and Hungary left the CG, but five additional Latin American countries—Bolivia, Costa Rica, Guatemala, Paraguay and Peru—plus Pakistan and South Africa have subsequently joined, bringing current membership to 19 countries.

As chapter 5 has already noted, a combination of factors contributed to a new foundation for the expansion of business relations between Australia and Latin America: the experience of the Uruguay Round; the ongoing processes of liberalisation and deregulation; the increasing participation in global markets; and the ongoing processes of growth and structural change in Australia and the four key countries in Latin America. It had put them through comparable challenges and experiences, and contributed to the development of more open, increasingly advanced and internationally competitive economies. This was particularly the case in regard to the conversion of non-tariff trade barriers on agriculture into tariffs, and the reduction of tariff protection, which forced companies in these countries to restructure in response to the pressures of international markets. It obliged industries in these countries to readjust according to the comparative advantage of their economies.

Increasing investment opportunities combined with reduced barriers to investment fostered this process; it is one of the reasons why Australia-based mining companies such as BHP Billiton and Rio Tinto increased their engagement in operations in Latin America, and why Brazilian company Vale established coal mining operations in Australia. In addition, following privatisation and increased liquidity, there is increased Australian investment in infrastructure such as roads, airports and ports, telecommunications services, as well as real estate in Latin America, and vice versa. Likewise, new opportunities have opened up in tourism, education, and professional services such as engineering, architecture and accounting.

As noted above, this process of growing business relations between Australia and Latin America took place in a context of growing global markets. Consequently, the magnitude of change in the business relations between Australia and Latin America is easily overlooked in this international context. Even though primary commodities are still important in the trade relationship, as noted in chapter 5, a significant change has been the diversification of trade relations to encompass a greater range of manufactured products and services. For example, the role of computer peripherals and combustion engines in Mexico's exports to Australia in recent years is directly related to Mexico's engagement in NAFTA with Canada and the United States, and its process of structural change; NAFTA encouraged American and Canadian firms to establish manufacturing assembly facilities in Mexico for export purposes.

While the processes of economic change have increased the competitiveness of Australia and the four Latin American countries discussed in this section, it should be noted that a range of issues remain, particularly for the Latin American countries. They range from the issues that shape the business environment in these countries—as discussed in chapter 5—to broader issues such as labour market rigidities and the significant and tenacious problem of income inequality and poverty. In addition, processes of deregulation are still incomplete in several sectors of Latin American economies, particularly financial services. Such resulting regulatory divergences continue to impose significant impediments to goods and services trade across the Pacific. Arguably, these issues are more or less important depending on the particular country concerned. For example, Chile's business environment is more comparable with Australia's than that of other countries, as chapter 5 established.

In this context, disappointment has been expressed in Latin American countries in recent years with how slowly the benefits of economic reform are emerging. A comparison is sometimes made with the stellar growth performance in East Asian economies following the economic reforms implemented there in the 1970s and 1980s. Some have concluded that Latin American countries' failure to deliver similar economic results is due to the inadequacies or inappropriateness of 'neoliberal' economic policies to Latin America.[7] Walton examined two alternative concepts of 'neo-liberalism': a narrow interpretation that refers to a limited shift towards greater reliance on market forces; and a broad interpretation involving a 'wholesale change in the relationship between the state and society with a more vigorous embrace of the market being part of a generalised withdrawal of state provisioning and action'.[8] He concluded that the reform programs pursued in Latin American countries accord more with the first interpretation. They comprise fiscal and monetary reforms and trade liberalisation at a macroeconomic level, as well as privatisation, financial sector deepening, capital market opening, tax reform and property rights reform. Walton also concluded that these reforms continue to retain a significant role for governments in social provisioning, and that they have generally been positive for economic development. The extent to which this mix of reform policies has failed to yield the full anticipated benefits in terms of greater prosperity for the peoples of Latin American countries is due more to the incomplete implementation of the reform programs in particular countries than to their inadequacies or shortcomings.

Towards a new partnership: Multilateral, regional and bilateral

The shared experiences of the past decades of economic reform and trade liberalisation programs have put Australia and key Latin American countries

---

7 Kurt Weyland, 'Assessing Latin American Neoliberalism: Introduction to A Debate', *Latin American Research Review*, 2004, 39 (3), pp. 143–9; Eric Hershberg and Fred Rosen, (eds), *Latin America after Neoliberalism: Turning the Tide in the 21st Century?* New York: The New Press, 2006.

8 Walton, Michael, 'Neoliberalism in Latin America: Good Bad or Incomplete?', *Latin American Research Review*, 2004, 39 (3), pp.165–83.

on a comparable path of development that is characterised by greater openness. Nevertheless, the continued diversity of business environments in Latin America, as well as between Australia and Latin American countries, makes it necessary for these countries to pursue a range of different, but interrelated multilateral, plurilateral and bilateral options in an effort to broaden and deepen their trade and business relationships. This section will offer reflections on the opportunities that exist to that effect.

Table 6.2 Membership of international organisations and regional trade agreements relevant to Australia–Latin America trade and business relations, February 2013

	International			Regional				
	WTO	UNCTAD	APEC	LAIA	Mercosur	CACM	CAFTA	NAFTA
Australia	√	√	√					
USA	√	√	√				√	√
Argentina	√	√		√	√			
Bolivia	√	√		√	√			
Brazil	√	√		√	√			
Chile	√	√	√	√				
Colombia	√	√		√				
Costa Rica	√	√				√	√	
Cuba	√	√		√				
Dominican Rep.	√	√					√	
Ecuador	√	√		√				
El Salvador	√	√				√	√	
Guatemala	√	√				√	√	
Honduras	√	√				√	√	
Mexico	√	√	√	√				√
Nicaragua	√	√				√	√	
Paraguay	√	√		√	√			
Peru	√	√	√	√				
Uruguay	√	√		√	√			
Venezuela	√	√		√				

Notes: WTO = World Trade Organization; UNCTAD = United Nations Conference for Trade and Development; APEC = Asia–Pacific Economic Cooperation; LAIA = Latin American Integration Association; Mercosur = Mercado Común del Sur [Southern Common Market]; CACM = Central American Common Market, CAFTA = Central American Free Trade Agreement, NAFTA = North American Free Trade Agreement.

Sources: WTO, RTA Data Base, http://rtais.wto.org; UNCTAD, http://www.unctad.org.

Table 6.2 shows that Australia and all the key countries of Latin America share only two forums that could be the basis for multi-country discussions on common interests in advancing trade and business relations: the World Trade Organization (WTO) and the United Nations Conference on Trade and Development (UNCTAD). UNCTAD is effectively a forum that allows less-developed countries to draw attention to their concerns about international trade and investment issues, and to develop solutions in cooperation with developed countries. It is not a forum in which multi-country coalitions can generate leverage in order to advance the agenda of trade liberalisation. Nor does UNCTAD provide a forum for trade negotiations or constitute a body of trade rules in the way that the WTO does. Table 6.2 also shows that several Latin American countries also participate in regional trade agreements, also including the United States. However, the non-participation of Australia makes it difficult for them to be seen as vehicles to advance common interests. In effect, that leaves the WTO as the major international forum in which Australia and countries of Latin America can cooperate for the purpose of forging ties that may benefit mutual interests in trade liberalisation.

Multilateral partnerships

From the high tide of deregulation and globalisation of the mid-1990s, public expectations of the WTO in more recent years appear to have receded, especially as a result of the difficulties of bringing the 11-year-old WTO Doha Development Agenda trade negotiations to a successful conclusion. However, such judgements underestimate the capacity of the WTO to continue to deliver real benefits for trade liberalisation and trade cooperation, and to maintain an open world trading system from which all member countries benefit. The role of the WTO as a forum for periodic trade liberalisation negotiations receives the most public attention. But the GATT/WTO system also constitutes a body of international trade law that applies to its 159 members. This covers trade in goods and services, as well as intellectual property rights. It also includes a dispute settlement system which has amply demonstrated its capacity to ensure adherence by member countries to the trade rules.

Beginning with an initial membership of 23 mainly industrialised countries in 1947, GATT focused during its first 30 years on negotiating reductions in import tariffs that affected manufactured goods. Its membership continued to grow, encompassing 123 less-developed and developed countries by 1986 at the beginning of the Uruguay Round negotiations. From the Tokyo Round of negotiations (1973–79), GATT increasingly began to bring non-tariff trade barriers into its negotiating agendas. The Uruguay Round extended the trade rules to services and intellectual property issues and, as section two indicated, achieved an agreement which finally brought agriculture and textiles more fully under the trade-liberalising GATT rules. It also created a new dispute settlement system, which significantly strengthened the capacity of WTO members to ensure that the trade rules on both goods and services were respected. The key element of the new dispute settlement system is the 'reverse consensus' rule, under which judgements against a member found to be in breach of the trade rules can only be rejected by consensus among member countries. Previously, reports had to be adopted by consensus, enabling a defendant in a GATT rules case effectively to veto judgements being made against it. The Uruguay Round also achieved another breakthrough important for boosting the credibility of the WTO system in that it effectively ended the north/south or developed/less-developed international divide, which had previously limited the active participation in periodic trade liberalisation negotiations to a relatively small number of industrialised countries.

In the more open, less autarchic, increasingly globalising environment of the late 1980s, the major less-developed countries, including all Latin American countries, participated very actively in the Uruguay Round. It is perhaps appropriate to note at this point that Mexico only acceded to the GATT on the eve of the Uruguay Round and thereafter participated enthusiastically throughout the eight years of negotiations. Not only did these negotiations see the full participation of less-developed countries for the first time, but the Uruguay Round ushered in another new phenomenon; that of developed and less-developed countries working actively together in pragmatic coalitions to achieve outcomes on a subject-by-subject or issue-by-issue basis. The standout example in the Uruguay Round was the Cairns Group, discussed in section two. But the Cairns Group was not the only instance of north/south coalitions that drove the agenda of negotiations during the Uruguay Round. Prior even to the launch of the negotiations in 1986, the 'Group of 48' developed and less-developed countries co-convened by the Swiss and Colombian ambassadors in Geneva and also including Chile, Mexico and Uruguay from Latin America, was influential in achieving a mandate for the negotiations of sufficiently broad scope to ensure that the trade negotiating priorities of both developed and developing countries were adequately covered.[9]

Thus the Uruguay Round firmly established the practice of developed and less-developed countries working together in pragmatic coalitions to realise shared trade liberalisation objectives. This practice has been developed further during the Doha Development Agenda negotiations. Moreover, since the beginning of the Uruguay round, a further 36 countries have joined the WTO, including China and Russia, so that the organisation today is more than ever a genuine multilateral trade organisation that brings together both developed and less-developed countries in the pursuit of continuing trade liberalisation. Agriculture is again

---

9   Preeg, Ernest H., *Traders in a Brave New World: The Uruguay Round and the Future of the International Trading System*, Chicago: The University of Chicago Press, 1995, pp. 3–6; 58–62.

the most high profile example of north/south coalition-building in the Doha negotiations. Consequently, the Cairns Group continues to play an active role and five additional Latin American countries—Bolivia, Costa Rica, Guatemala, Paraguay and Peru—have joined. Brazil also brought together the 'Group of 20' less-developed countries to work on agriculture in the Doha negotiations. These coalitions impact on the configuration of small groups playing a key role in reaching compromises on agriculture and more broadly across the negotiations. The geometry has varied, for example, from FIPs (Five Interested Parties: US, EU, Brazil, India and Australia), G6 (FIPs plus Japan), G4 (US, EU, Brazil, India), G5 (US, EU, Brazil, India and China) and most recently G7 (G5 plus Japan and Australia) and G11 (G7 plus Argentina and Canada, as well as South Africa and Mauritius for the African, Caribbean and Pacific group of countries).

The unilateral trade liberalisation programs undertaken by Latin American countries since the 1980s also resulted in the circumstance of a number of these countries now having interests in other elements of the Doha negotiating agenda that are more in line with the interests of developed countries such as Australia than with other less-developed countries. The negotiations on issues such as industrial tariff liberalisation, services and WTO rules are prime examples. There are several areas of negotiations on rules and services issues where Australia has been working in coalition groupings with some combination of either Argentina, Brazil, Mexico or Chile, such as fisheries subsidies, the 'Colorado group' on trade facilitation issues, the mutual recognition of professional qualifications for architects and engineers, computer related services, logistics and maritime transport.[10] Since the creation of the 'Really Good Friends of Services' group of countries in 2005, six Latin American countries—Chile, Colombia, Costa Rica, Mexico, Panama and Peru—have participated in plurilateral negotiations along with Australia, the United States, the European Union and others, to reach a plurilateral agreement on services trade liberalisation following the impasse facing the Doha negotiations. Australia and Latin American countries have also shared interests in specific dispute settlement cases in which they work together in the WTO. Such cases provide significant opportunities to develop trade policy and business links further. Prominent examples in recent years have been the 'Byrd Amendment' case (2001) brought by Australia, Brazil, Chile, and others including the European Union against an item of US anti-dumping legislation, and the 'Sugar Export Subsidy' case against the European Union that was brought to the WTO jointly by Australia, Brazil and Thailand.[11] Both of these joint actions went through the entire WTO dispute settlement procedure: panel investigation; the appeals process; and arbitration. The WTO

---

10   Diego-Fernández, Mateo, 'Trade Negotiations Make Strange Bedfellows', *World Trade Review*, 2008, 7, pp. 423–53, 450.
11   *Ibid.*, p. 442.

dispute settlement system is not only an effective mechanism with which to enforce adherence to the trade rules: through its judgements, the system also makes significant contributions to trade liberalisation.

A third way in which the WTO contributes to trade liberalisation is through the accession negotiating process. All countries that accede to the WTO—and the GATT prior to 1 January 1995—are required to negotiate the terms of their accession. These terms aim to reflect not only the collectivity of commitments made by existing WTO members up to the most recently concluded trade negotiating round; they also frequently seek to extract concessions that go beyond existing multilateral commitments, thereby foreshadowing trade liberalising objectives of future rounds of negotiations. Thus, for accessions that followed the establishment of the WTO in 1994—such as in the cases of China and the Customs Territory of Taiwan—WTO members have sought and secured 'WTO plus' trade liberalisation commitments from the newly acceding countries. In this way, the WTO accession process also contributes to trade liberalisation.

For all these reasons, the WTO provides a valuable forum for trade policy cooperation between Australia and Latin American countries that could foster trade and business links across the Pacific. Joint action in pursuing shared trade liberalisation objectives in multilateral rounds such as the Uruguay Round in the past and the current Doha Development Agenda bring Australian and Latin American trade policy objectives closer together. They can be especially effective in dealing with international trade problems such as agricultural and other subsidies that can only be successfully negotiated multilaterally. Joint action in dispute settlement cases and accession negotiations dealing with shared trade problems strengthens habits of working together and at the same time increases understandings across the Pacific. Finally, the more Australia and Latin American countries work together in the WTO, the more likely they are to find common cause in developing a future post-Doha agenda for the WTO. This may be especially relevant with regard to dealing with the 'behind the border' barriers to trade such as product standards and domestic services regulations, which are becoming increasingly important as major impediments to trade and investment flows around the globe.

Plurilateral partnerships

The economic and trade liberalisation programs implemented by Latin American countries from the 1980s were followed by the rapid conclusion of regional and extra-regional agreements with major trading partners of the northern hemisphere, with Mexico and Chile leading the way. Shortly following its accession to GATT in 1986 and participation in the Uruguay Round negotiations, Mexico concluded the NAFTA with the United States and Canada (1994). This was followed by the Mexico–EU agreement (2000) and the Mexico–EFTA agreement (2001). Chile concluded agreements with the EU (2002), the United States (2004) and EFTA (2004). Chile in particular has continued an active pursuit of Free Trade Agreements (FTAs) with a wide range of countries: it now has FTAs with no less than 54 trading partners, including Australia (2009). Similarly, FTAs now cover over 90 per cent of Mexico's total trade.[12]

These agreements are for the most part 'new generation' FTAs in the sense that they aim to be 'WTO plus', not only in terms of satisfying the tariff liberalisation requirements of GATT article XXIV on free trade areas and customs unions, but in going beyond the Uruguay Round commitments in the new WTO areas of services trade liberalisation and intellectual property protection. They also achieve new, more liberal commitments in domestic regulatory policies that impact on trade and investment flows, such as product standards, domestic services regulations, public procurement policies, investment restrictions, and protection and business visas.

This is not the place for a detailed analysis of the extent to which these 'new generation' FTAs entered into by Mexico and Chile and other Latin American countries are indeed 'WTO plus' or, possibly in some respects, 'WTO minus' in their detailed provisions. Marconini analysed this issue for services, while Sauvé examined it for investment.[13] Suffice to say that the existence of these agreements that have been entered into by Latin American countries since the establishment of the WTO in 1994 bear witness to their readiness to extend beyond tariffs liberalisation in agreements that aim to open markets. The scope of these agreements is recognition also that in continuing down this broadly based path of opening markets, future outcomes may best be pursued by negotiating directly on the domestic regulations that hinder trade and investment flows, rather than continuing to focus on border measures such as 'market access' and 'national treatment' commitments in the case of services under the General Agreement on Trade in Services (GATS).[14]

A recent plurilateral development that may further strengthen Australia's business relations with the Latin American region is the process by which the G20 group now operates. The group was established in 1999 in the wake of the 1997 Asian crisis, with the aim of stabilising global financial markets. Its role was heightened during the recent Global Financial Crisis.[15] This process grew

---

12   JEG, *Australia–Mexico Joint Experts Group on Strengthening Bilateral Economic Relations: Joint Report*, 2009, p. 31.

13   Mario Marconini, 'Services in Regional Agreements between Latin American and Developed Countries', *CEPAL Serie Commercio Internacional No.71.* (ECLAC), 2006; Pierre Sauvé, 'Trade and Investment Rules: Latin American Perspectives', *CEPAL Serie Comercio Internacional No.66.* (ECLAC), 2006.

14   Marconini, *op. cit.*, note 13.

15   The G20 members are Argentina, Australia, Brazil, Canada, China, France, Germany, India, Indonesia, Italy, Japan, Mexico, Russia, Saudi Arabia, South Africa, South Korea, Turkey, the United Kingdom and the United States, as well as the European Union.

out of a realisation that other existing arrangements for international financial management and economic cooperation were not sufficiently representative of the countries that were required to find solutions to the crisis. As a result, the G20 summits have recently emerged as the principal forum for global economic cooperation, and may continue in this role in the future. Current G20 members account for more than 85 per cent of global GDP and 80 per cent of global trade. Australia and three major Latin American countries—Argentina, Brazil and Mexico—are members.

At their meetings in Washington in 2008, and London and Pittsburgh in 2009, G20 leaders pledged, inter alia, to develop programs for strong, sustainable, balanced growth subject to peer review; to refrain from protectionist trade measures; and to seek an ambitious as well as balanced conclusion to the Doha negotiations. Successive G20 summits in June 2010 in Toronto and Seoul in November 2010 placed increasing emphasis on core strategies for recovery from the global financial crisis, reform of the international financial regulatory system, and reform of the IMF. The G20's focus on crisis and recovery has been successful in the sense that trade protection or capital controls have hardly been used to respond to the crisis. But with the 2008 crisis and its aftermath fading, the group has become increasingly engaged with relatively marginal issues during its recent summits in Cannes in November 2011 and Los Cabos in June 2012. Nevertheless, the G20 dialogue will provide useful opportunities for exchanges between Australia and the three Latin American members of the G20, on sustainable economic growth and financial stability objectives in an open trade environment, that are also likely to strengthen trade and business links across the Pacific.

The Asia–Pacific Economic Cooperation (APEC) forum is another trans-Pacific plurilateral grouping that can make a significant contribution to building closer trade and investment links with Latin America, despite the non-membership of economic heavyweights Argentina and Brazil. As Table 2 shows, along with Australia, Chile, Mexico and Peru are members.[16] APEC is more specifically focused on trade integration than the G20, but it is well placed to contribute to supporting and delivering on the broader agenda of the G20, involving trade and economic growth. Having already made a significant contribution over the past two decades to the liberalisation of physical trade barriers in the APEC region—and more globally through APEC's influence on multilateral negotiations—APEC members are now increasingly focused on reducing

---

16   APEC's 21 members are Australia, Brunei, Canada, Chile, China, Hong Kong, Indonesia, Japan, South Korea, Malaysia, Mexico, New Zealand, PNG, Peru, The Philippines, Russia, Singapore, Taiwan, Thailand, the United States and Vietnam.

regulatory barriers to trade, especially in relation to competition policy, customs procedures, the mutual recognition of standards, and reducing trade barriers imposed by domestic regulations on services.

In the longer term the Australian government is interested in the development of an overarching 'Free Trade Area of the Asia–Pacific' (FTAAP). This could include all APEC-member economies and is therefore likely to require a lengthy period of preparatory work. While the FTAAP initiative had some resonance in APEC-member countries Chile, Mexico and Peru, particularly in the business world, it remains to be seen whether the governments of these countries will be interested in participating in such an overarching FTA. However, the current APEC focus and work program on regulatory trade reform will of itself continue to make a valuable contribution to strengthening business links between Australia and the Latin American members of APEC.

Finally, plans have been underway since 2008 for a Trans Pacific Partnership Agreement (TPP) that originally brought together Australia, Brunei, Chile, New Zealand, Singapore, Peru, Vietnam and the United States. Subsequently, Canada, Mexico, Malaysia and Vietnam have joined the group, and most recently— March 2013—Japan expressed willingness to join. TPP is another important initiative strengthening links across the Pacific.[17] Participants are expected to aim for a 'WTO plus' plurilateral agreement that increases economic integration in the Asia–Pacific region, especially as membership is expected to increase over time. At the first round of negotiations in Melbourne in March 2010, the then Australian Minister of Trade said that the TPP agreement 'represents a pathway towards achieving APEC's long-term goal of a Free Trade Area of the Asia–Pacific'.[18] Hence, the TPP could be a step towards multilateralising or at least regionalising existing FTAs between TPP partners, although at the second round of negotiations in San Francisco in June 2010 it was argued that existing FTAs would remain alongside the TPP, and TPP discussions are still in train.

Bilateral partnerships

An issue that has only been hinted at above, but that still has a significant impact on Australia's business relations with Latin America is that of the discriminatory impact of bilateral FTAs on trading partners that are not parties to bilateral preferential agreements. Australia and the countries of Latin America are to a greater or lesser extent engaged in bilateral and plurilateral preferential trade agreements with different combinations of countries. While such agreements in

---

17   DFAT, *Annual Report 2008/09*, Canberra: Department of Foreign Affairs and Trade, 2009, p. 102.
18   Simon Crean, 'Trade at the Centre of the Global Recovery', Speech to the Foreign Correspondents' Association, Sydney, 16 February 2010; 'Pushing Forward with the Korean FTA and the Trans-Pacific Partnership', Media Release, Department of Foreign Affairs and Trade, Canberra, 15 March 2010.

principle foster trade relations for the countries involved, in several ways they also discriminate against countries that are not parties to a particular agreement. For example, Mexico's engagement in NAFTA and other preferential trade agreements cover over 90 per cent of its trade.[19] By favouring trade with the United States and Canada in particular, such agreements implicitly discriminate against Australia and other countries.

This issue makes Australia's bilateral relationship with Mexico more complex than with other Latin American partners. Chapter 5 has shown that after Brazil, *Mexico* is Australia's largest market in Latin America. Mexico's focus on extracting maximum benefits from NAFTA and its growing concern with competition from China in the US market, complicate its relations with other trading partners, including Australia. Nonetheless, the bilateral relationship is a positive one and trade continues to grow. A 'Joint Expert Group' (JEG) established by the governments of Australia and Mexico under the Australia–Mexico Trade and Investment Agreement (1994) carried out an exhaustive study into strengthening the bilateral economic relationship.[20] The report identified scope for 'increased economic cooperation' and 'an enhanced trade policy dialogue' through the Joint Trade and Investment Commission established by the 1994 agreement.[21] A bilateral 'Plan of Action' was concluded in 2011.

Australia's major trade and business interests in Mexico are centred on exports of mining commodities and investment in mining ventures, as well as agriculture and agribusiness services. Australia has an interest in eliminating Mexico's discriminatory import tariffs against, for instance, Australian beef. Mexico's major trade interests in Australia are in attracting more FDI in the mining sector from the major international mining conglomerates such as BHP Billiton and Rio Tinto, and in obtaining relief from Australia's phytosanitary barriers against Mexico's horticultural exports. The bilateral trade and business relationship continues to be hampered by a mutual lack of awareness of trade and investment potential, poor air and sea transport links, as well as a variety of regulatory problems, including customs' procedures, standards, services regulations and public procurement policies. Table 6.3 shows that Australia and Mexico have several operative trade-related bilateral agreements, and in recent years a growing number of relevant MoUs have been added, which might be taken to enhance the trade and business relationship. For example, the renegotiation of the Memorandum of Understanding (MoU) on Mining and the conclusion of a new MoU on Agriculture in 2010, opened a dialogue on reducing regulatory barriers to cross-border trade, including in services in the form of the mutual recognition of professional qualifications. It also opened

---

19   JEG, *op. cit.*, note 13.
20   *Ibid.*
21   JEG, *op. cit.*, note 12, p. 47.

a dialogue on options for regulatory cooperation more generally, which may encompass customs' procedures, public procurement policies and standards, including on agriculture.

Ever since it embarked seriously on economic restructuring and trade liberalisation, Chile has continued down the path of trade openness and regulatory reform. While having a smaller population than Australia's other trading partners in the region, the country now has an economy that—after two decades of solid economic and trade reform—is the most open in Latin America. Chile is a founding member of the Cairns Group and, despite its extensive network of FTAs, is a strong supporter of the WTO. It is also a long-standing and active participant in APEC and, like Mexico, a partner with Australia in the TPP negotiations. As with Mexico, Chile is focused mainly on the US market, which takes around 25 per cent of Chile's exports and provides around 15 per cent of Chile's imports.[22] A significant number of Australian companies have been attracted by the openness of the Chilean market, and have chosen it as a base for their Latin American operations (see chapter 5). In addition, amongst others, BHP Billiton has significant mining investment in Chile—Escondida and Spence copper mines; clothing firm Rip Curl has a licensee that makes and sells its products in Chile; while its competitor Billabong has its own subsidiary venture GSM Chile for that purpose.

The further development of Australia's trade and business relationship with Chile over the immediate period ahead will be largely determined by the FTA (ACI–FTA), which entered into force in 2009. It may also depend on how the TPP negotiations unfold, as they could provide a first step towards multilateralising the commitments already contained in the FTAs that individual TPP-partner countries have with the United States and with each other. The ACI–FTA appears to be consistent with the GATT article XXIV requirement that 'substantially all of the trade' is liberalised and with respect to the commitments on services trade liberalisation, investment and public procurement provisions, it would appear to be a 'WTO plus' agreement. An Australia–Chile air services agreement has been in operation since 2001. There are additional areas where Australia and Chile might build on the provisions of the FTA to develop trade, investment and business relations in the period ahead. This could include action to go beyond the WTO Agreement on Technical Barriers to Trade in pursuing agreements for the mutual recognition of standards. In addition, it could include early action to give effect to the provisions in the FTA to pursue mutual recognition agreements on professional qualifications such as for engineers and architects. Consideration could also be given to developing an 'early warning' system of consultations on regulatory changes that in future could impinge on trade and investment flows between Chile and Australia.

---

22   EIU, *Country Profile* (Argentina, Australia, Brazil, Chile, Mexico), London: The Economist Intelligence Unit (annual), 2007–12: 2008, p. 36.

Table 6.3: Business-related bilateral agreements between Australia and Latin American countries

	Argentina	Brazil	Chile	Mexico	Colombia	Peru	Uruguay
Free trade agreement	-	-	2009	-	-	-	-
Air services agreement	1992	2010	2001	2011	-	2013*	2012
Investment protection agreement	1997	-	1999	2007	-	1997	2002
Double taxation agreement	2000	-	2010	2004	-	-	-
Trade and investment agreement	-	-	-	1997	-	-	-
MoU on trade and investment	-	-	-	-	2009	-	2010
MoU on education and training	2001	2005	2004	2008	2002	2006	-
MoU on work and holiday visas	2011	-	2005	-	-	-	2012
MoU on scientific and technological cooperation	2003	2001	-	2004	-	-	-
MoU on sanitary matters	-	1998	-	-	-	-	-
MoU on development of rail infrastructure	2010	-	-	-	-	-	-
MoU on energy cooperation	-	-	-	2005	-	-	-
MoU on mining cooperation	-	-	2006	2010	-	-	-
MoU on agriculture cooperation	-	-	2009	2010	-	-	-

Notes: * = expected. Years indicate when the agreement came into force, or when a memorandum was signed.

Sources: United Nations Treaty Series http://treaties.un.org; DFAT Annual Reports and Treaty Database http://www.info.dfat.gov.au/Info/Treaties/treaties.nsf/; Department of Infrastructure (Australia) http://www.infrastructure.gov.au/aviation/international/agreements.aspx; Treasury Department (Australia) http://www.treasury.gov.au/Policy-Topics/Taxation/Aus-Tax-Treaties; Sistema de Información sobre Comercio Exterior (SICE, Organization of American States) http://www.sice.oas.org.

As chapter 5 has shown, Brazil is the largest economy in Latin America. It is also Australia's largest trading partner in Latin America, with continuing scope for a very significant increase in two-way trade. Mutual flows of FDI are growing, as are Australia's imports of manufactured products from Brazil, e.g., civil aircraft. The scope for developing trade and business relationships is enhanced by similarities in the domestic economic and export profile of the two countries. Resources, agriculture and services occupy comparable importance in the GDP and exports of both Brazil and Australia. In contrast, Brazil maintains a more important manufacturing sector. Like Australia, Brazil has a broadly based export profile with North Asia, especially China, which is now playing an increasingly important role compared to Brazil's traditional export markets in North America and Europe. This comparable profile of trading interests opens up significant opportunities for increased trade and investment in mining, mining technology and agribusiness, as well as professional, business, consultancy and financial services.

Unlike Mexico, access to the Brazilian market is not compromised by the existence of preferential FTAs with the large industrial powers of the northern hemisphere. However, Brazil is a member of the Mercosur customs union, along with Argentina, Paraguay and Uruguay, which was established in 1991. Mercosur has created a common external customs tariff—with some remaining exceptions. In tariff terms, Mercosur therefore needs to be dealt with as a single entity across the four countries. The customs union has not attempted to deal with non-tariff barriers to trade.

The major obstacle to growing Australia's trade and business relationship with Brazil is that there are many 'behind the border' non-tariff barriers and domestic regulations that impact on trade. These include investment restrictions, competition policy issues, tax measures, and issues related to public procurement and product standards. Hence, Brazil's transition to a fully open trading system is still a work in progress. Table 6.3 shows that Australia concluded an air services agreement with Brazil in 2010. An agreement for science and technology cooperation is being negotiated and there may be scope for the negotiation of a 'Trade and Investment Facilitation Agreement'. Beyond this, Australia reached an intergovernmental agreement in 2008 to establish a 'Plan of Action to Achieve an Enhanced Partnership'. Moreover, a Mercosur–CER dialogue was established in 1996 to strengthen cooperation on issues of global trade. It has not met since 2004 and does not appear to have been very effective in advancing the bilateral trade relationship, as exchanges so far appear to have been focused mainly on multilateral trade issues. Nevertheless, there may be scope to reinvigorate this dialogue.

A significant way forward in fostering bilateral trade and business relations between Australia and Brazil would appear to be a focused dialogue on regulatory obstacles to increasing trade and investment. Perhaps this could be achieved through both the 'Enhanced Partnership' action plan and a revitalised Mercosur–CER dialogue that would focus more on the bilateral flows of trade and investments between the two trade groupings. A revitalised Mercosur–CER dialogue could have the advantage of Australia and New Zealand engaging Brazil at the sub-WTO level in dealing with international trade issues. In particular, enhancing and deepening the Mercosur–CER dialogue might offer a fruitful avenue for encouraging the Latin American partner countries to address 'behind the border' regulatory impediments to trade on a Mercosur–CER-wide level. Finally, as is the case with Mexico, development of the business relationship between Australia and Brazil is hampered on both sides by lack of awareness of the available opportunities. Maintaining high-level political contacts and involvement from senior ministers from both Australia and Brazil could therefore be useful in giving impetus to the relationship.

Argentina, the fourth major market for Australia in Latin America, would be included in any revitalised Mercosur–CER dialogue. Argentina is in many respects Australia's longest-standing economic partner in Latin America. Their shared interests as important exporters of meat and grains to the world market have thrown them together over many years in bilateral, plurilateral and multilateral efforts to defend their interests. By so doing they have pitted their efficient producers and exporters of agricultural products against the protectionist agricultural policies of the major northern hemisphere producers, exporters and importers of agricultural products. These shared interests have forged close economic and trade bonds between Australia and Argentina over many years. Argentina was also a founding member of the CG in 1986 and a very active participant through the Uruguay Round. Table 3 shows that Australia and Argentina have concluded several bilateral agreements that support bilateral business relations. Along with Brazil and Mexico, Australia and Argentina share membership of the G20 leaders' process, as noted above. Australia and Argentina also have common trade and investment interests in mining and mining technology and services. A major obstacle to the bilateral relationship was Argentina's fragile economic recovery from the major setback it suffered during the financial crisis of 2002–03. For example, its balance of payments problems required import restrictions through licensing, which depressed Australia's exports to Argentina until about 2008. But the continued depreciation of the Argentinian peso relative to the US dollar by 60 per cent since 2008 increased Australian imports from Argentina significantly, but limited the growth of Australia's exports to Argentina.

Two other Latin American countries with capacity to become more important trading partners for Australia are Colombia and Peru. Both appear to be following Chile's path of economic reform and trade openness. Australia has concluded a memorandum of understanding with Colombia aimed at strengthening trade and investment links. Australia's mining interests in Peru are growing and an Australia–Peru air services agreement is currently under negotiation. Colombia is also interested in becoming a member of APEC. It is increasingly interested in engaging more with the Western Pacific—as is Colombia—and is a partner with Australia and others in the TPP negotiations. All of this creates foundations for further dialogue that may foster Australia's trade and business relations with both countries.

Conclusion

Chapter 5 noted that the scope for closer trade and business relations between Australia and Latin America slowly materialised during the past 20–30 years. The complementarity that has always been a major driver of trade expansion and close business links between Australia and the East Asian region has hitherto not extended across the Pacific to the countries of Latin America. Until quite recently—up to the early 1980s—both Australia and key Latin American countries such as Brazil, Argentina, Uruguay and Chile, thought of each other primarily as competitive exporters of agricultural products and mineral resources to the industrialised markets of the northern hemisphere, rather than as close trade and investment partners. Also, until the early 1980s, Australia and the countries of Latin America ran import substitution policies in their manufacturing sectors with high industrial tariffs, which did not encourage trade across the Pacific in non-agricultural products. Much has changed since then.

The global economic challenges of the late 1970s and early 1980s resulted in significant reassessments—both in Australia and in Latin American countries such as Mexico, Brazil, Argentina and Chile—of the way their economies were organised and the nature of their engagement with the global economic and trading environment. From the mid-1980s, programs of domestic economic reform and trade liberalisation were instituted. Trade restrictions were progressively dismantled and high industrial tariffs reduced. New competitive industries in services were created and manufacturing made more efficient. As a result, the economies of Australia and key Latin American countries became more open to international competition and trade. These important changes placed Australia, Brazil, Mexico, Argentina and Chile on comparable paths of economic and trade openness, creating new opportunities for increased trade and investment flows across the Pacific. As chapter 5 has shown, trade has increased and diversified, particularly in Australian exports of services, especially education services to Latin America and in Latin American exports of manufactured products to Australia.

Chapter 5 analysed a number of reasons why the prospects for increased trade and business relations between Australia and Latin America over the past two decades may have been so slow to materialise. Despite the economic and trade openness resulting from reforms of the 1980s and 1990s, significant differences in business environments remain. Progress in the economic reform programs of some key Latin American countries such as Brazil, Mexico and Argentina has been interrupted by periodic financial crises such as the Asian financial crisis of the mid-1990s, and, in Argentina's case, by the more recent financial crisis of 2002–03. As a consequence, reform processes in many major Latin American economies, particularly in relation to domestic regulatory policies that impact on trade and investment, still have a way to go. Differences in per capita GDP, continuing market rigidities, income inequalities and—in some cases—international payment restrictions, are factors that sustain a significant 'economic distance' between Australia and its major Latin American partners. Latin American countries generally still have less favourable rankings than Australia in international risk, opacity, economic transparency and 'ease of doing business' indexes that reflect perceptions in the business world of the continent. Sustained efforts will be needed to address these hurdles, which in part relate to the incompleteness of economic reform and trade liberalisation programs in a number of Latin American countries. The NAFTA, which binds Mexico in an economic and trade sense very closely to the United States, is another factor limiting the scope for development of the trade and business relationship between Australia and Mexico. The incompleteness of Latin American economic and trade reform programs, remaining 'economic differences' and differing foreign trade priorities have left a legacy of lack of awareness of the expanding opportunities across the Pacific between Australia and Latin America.

Nevertheless, trade and business relations between Australia and Latin America are on the move. An especially interesting factor is the growth in operations of large multinational mining companies such as BHP, Rio Tinto, Vale and Xtrata on both sides of the Pacific. A number of other Australian mining companies and mining technology and services companies are also showing increasing interest in Latin America. Interest at an intergovernmental level on both sides of the Pacific in fostering closer trade relations is also growing through, for example, the intergovernmental Joint Expert Group between Australia and Mexico, and scope for closer dialogue on bilateral trade issues with Brazil and Argentina at the Mercosur level. The ACI–FTA between Australia and Chile, which entered into force in 2009, provides strong evidence of commitment on both sides to deepening the trade/economic relationship beyond tariffs liberalisation to domestic regulatory cooperation.

Beyond these bilateral efforts, a number of plurilateral opportunities for deepening trade and business relations across the Pacific also exist. The TPP negotiations, which formally began in Melbourne in March 2010, could bring

Chile, Mexico, and Peru together with Australia, Brunei, Canada, Malaysia, New Zealand, Singapore, Vietnam and the United States to comprise what could be a new generation 'WTO plus' regional free trade agreement. In addition, the APEC and G20 summit processes will increasingly provide opportunities for closer dialogue between Australia and the Latin American countries that are members of these forums on structural reforms which, over time, could further strengthen trade and business links across the Pacific. Finally, the WTO provides a unique opportunity for cooperation in the pursuit of shared multilateral trade liberalisation goals. Close Australian–Latin American cooperation in the WTO began with the Cairns Group in the Uruguay Round of trade negotiations (1986–93) and has continued in the Doha Development Round, not only on agriculture, but also on a number of other services, trade, and GATT rules negotiations issues. Into the future, the WTO provides an opportunity for Australia and Latin American countries to work closely together on common interests relating to WTO accession negotiations, dispute settlement cases; and in helping to set the agenda for future trade negotiating rounds. In all, these developments may enhance the opportunities and incentives for the further growth of Australia's trade and business relations with Latin America in the coming years.

References

Serials

EIU, *Country Profile* (Argentina, Australia, Brazil, Chile, Mexico), London: The Economist Intelligence Unit (annual), 2007–12.

EIU, *Country Report* (Argentina, Australia, Brazil, Chile, Mexico), London: The Economist Intelligence Unit (monthly), 2008–12.

Other

Crean, Simon, 'Trade at the Centre of the Global Recovery', Speech to the Foreign Correspondents' Association, Sydney, 16 February 2010.

Crean, Simon, 'Pushing Forward with the Korean FTA and the Trans-Pacific Partnership', Media Release, Department of Foreign Affairs and Trade, Canberra, 15 March 2010.

DFAT, *Annual Report 2008/09*, Canberra: Department of Foreign Affairs and Trade, 2009.

Diego-Fernández, Mateo, 'Trade Negotiations Make Strange Bedfellows', *World Trade Review*, 2008, 7, pp. 423–53.

Hanrahan, Charles E. and Randy Schnepf, *WTO Doha Round: The Agricultural Negotiations*, Washington DC: Congressional Research Service for Congress, 2006.

Hershberg, Eric and Fred Rosen, (eds), *Latin America after Neoliberalism: Turning the Tide in the 21st Century?* New York: The New Press, 2006.

JEG, *Australia–Mexico Joint Experts Group on Strengthening Bilateral Economic Relations: Joint Report*, Canberra/Mexico City: Department of Foreign Affairs and Trade/Ministry of the Economy, 2009.

Kenyon, Don and David Lee, *The Struggle for Trade Liberalisation in Agriculture: Australia and the Cairns Group in the Uruguay Round*, Canberra: Department of Foreign Affairs and Trade, 2006.

Marconini, Mario, 'Services in Regional Agreements between Latin American and Developed Countries', *CEPAL Serie Comercio Internacional No. 71*. Santiago (Chile): UN Economic Commission for Latin America and the Caribbean (ECLAC), 2006.

Mortimore, Michael, 'Corporate Strategies for FDI in the Context of Latin America's New Economic Model', *World Development*, 2000, 28, pp. 1611-26.

Preeg, Ernest H., *Traders in a Brave New World: The Uruguay Round and the Future of the International Trading System*, Chicago: The University of Chicago Press, 1995.

Sauvé, Pierre, 'Trade and Investment Rules: Latin American Perspectives', *CEPAL Serie Comercio Internacional No. 66*. Santiago (Chile): UN Economic Commission for Latin America and the Caribbean (ECLAC), 2006.

UNCTAD, *World Investment Report 2009*, New York: United Nations Conference on Trade and Development, 2009.

Walton, Michael, 'Neoliberalism in Latin America: Good Bad or Incomplete?', *Latin American Research Review*, 2004, 39 (3), pp. 165–83.

Weyland, Kurt, 'Assessing Latin American Neoliberalism: Introduction to A Debate', *Latin American Research Review*, 2004, 39 (3), pp. 143-9.

WTO, *International Trade Statistics 2009*, Geneva: World Trade Organization, 2009.

WTO, *World Tariff Profiles 2012*, Geneva: World Trade Organization, 2012.

7. Latinos in Australia

Victor Del Río

Introduction

This chapter takes us into the past, present and future of Latin Americans living in Australia. It represents the first comprehensive quantitative study of the integration of Latinos into their adopted motherland. The only precedent is the study carried out by the Spanish-born Rafaela López in 2002 on the contributions of Spanish and Latin American people in Victoria.[1]

It provides ample evidence that historically Latino communities have been part of the fabric of Australia, albeit in small numbers. It confirms also the communities' struggle to insert themselves into Australian society and their success in achieving it.

It finds that the Latino integration process in the past 40 years operated at two speeds. The first wave of Latino immigrants who arrived before the mid-1990s integrated rather slowly. They had to negotiate a new language and fight for the recognition of their members' work experience and studies obtained abroad. They had to follow an integration path that began in factories performing manual labour and which allowed them to begin climbing the economic and social ladder.

The second Latino migrant wave, which began in 1998, is integrating faster than the first. Language skills and recognition of qualifications are no longer barriers, either because the first wave of Latinos smoothed the path for recognition of overseas qualifications or because the most recent arrivals possessed qualifications gained as international students, most at Australian institutions. Yet these second-wave migrants had to overcome other obstacles. The new and highly qualified Latino communities have to reassert their credentials in the local employment market; they also need to develop social support networks that help to ease their political, economic, and social integration into Australia.

---

1   Rafaela López, *Orígenes. Influencia y contribución de origen español y latino Americano en Victoria, 1901–2001* (*The presence and contribution of Victorians of Spanish and Latin American origins, 1901–2001*). Australia: CELAS, the Spanish Latin American Welfare Centre, 2002. For short entries on Latin Americans in Australia, also see James Jupp (ed.), *The Australian People: An Encyclopedia of the Nation, Its People and Their Origins*, Cambridge University Press, Second edition, Cambridge, 2001. For Argentinians, p. 170; Brazilians, p. 187; Chileans, p. 195; Colombians, p. 226; Ecuadorians, p. 273; Peruvians, p. 619; Salvadorans, p. 642; Uruguayans, p. 719; Latin Americans in general, p. 552.

Latino communities: Definitions and categories

For the purpose of this chapter the concept of Latino includes anyone from the Spanish and Portuguese-speaking peoples from Latin America living in Australia.[2] Out of this group we selected the ten most significant Latino communities in Australia based on population—as per the 2011 Census—on which to conduct detailed analysis. Both terms—Latino and Latin-American—are used interchangeably,[3] and they are applicable to both plural and singular usage. Whenever possible, information from the Spanish community is also included.[4]

It is clear from statistical analysis that we have two identifiable categories of Latino communities. The first is formed by Latinos who settled in Australia in the 1970s and the 1980s and migrated mainly under the Special Humanitarian Program and/or Family Reunion Programs from: Argentina, Uruguay, Chile, El Salvador, Guatemala, Honduras and Nicaragua.

The second group arrived in Australia in the 1990s and at the turn of the 21st century and migrated following the opportunities opened by Australia to international students. They largely hail from Brazil, Colombia, Mexico, Venezuela, Peru and Ecuador. Researchers such as Angel Calderón identify the immigration period from 1990 to 2000 as a distinctive wave that was 'dominated by family reunion and waning conflict'.[5]

Both groups exhibit distinctive characteristics and contribute differently to Australia. For instance, Uruguayans have participated strongly in Australia's political life and in the employment market. Most of the members of the new migration wave, including from Brazil, Colombia, Venezuela and Mexico, have impressive credentials.

---

2   Although geography plays an important role, it is not always something that determines the main characteristic of our target group. Language is important, too, as there are several countries in Latin America which have English and French as their official language. For this reason a restricted definition of Latin America is used here: mention of Latin America indicates countries where either Spanish or Portuguese are spoken as the official language. After applying this filter, 20 countries were left in the target research list, excluding the Falkland/Malvinas Islands.

3   In a strict sense 'Latino' is not the perfect term, as in Romance languages it also includes French. But it is a widely accepted concept in the United States and less controversial than others such as Hispano-American, Ibero-American, etc., which have historical connotations linked to the Spanish conquest.

4   As language is one of the core filtering characteristics in this research, people from Spain could not be set aside without losing conceptual consistency. Latin American countries are intrinsically linked to Spain by history, which is therefore an important selective characteristic to take into consideration. Spanish people have also played an important role in the Latin American settlement process in Australia, both politically and academically. For instance, the first political links between Latin American communities and Australia emerged from the Spanish community—see detailed discussion in the section related to political participation. Academically, the first comprehensive analysis of the Spanish-speaking people in Victoria was produced by the Spanish-born Rafaela López.

5   Angel Calderón, 'Latin America tertiary education as an emerging system—Australia's future market', paper delivered at Melbourne–Latin America Dialogue, The University of Melbourne, August 2012.

This chapter focuses on the first generation of Latinos in Australia, as the information from the 2011 Census is not specific enough to conduct a detailed analysis of the second generation. Future writers may take this gap as an opportunity to research further into the second generation's integration process and its contribution to Australia.

Latino history in Australia

The first recorded 'Latino' in Australia

There is both direct and indirect evidence of five Chileans arriving in Australia in 1837. The most prominent of these, Ramón Freire,[6] played a key role in Chile's history. Freire arrived in Sydney on 3 July 1837, after being ousted from his position as President of Chile and exiled by a military coup. He was also the patriarch of a dynasty of future presidents, with his direct descendant, Eduardo Frei Montalva, assuming the role from 1964–70, and Montalva's eldest son, Eduardo Frei Ruiz-Tagle, reviving the dynasty by becoming president during the term 1994–2000. Ramón Freire's high public status allows us to track his activities during his stay of more than a year in Australia.

Perhaps the most interesting anecdote of Freire's time in Australia was chronicled in *The Sydney Herald*—where his name was printed as Fryre— which described him defending the Colony's reputation. This public defence is remarkable because it is the first of its kind to be mentioned in the *Hansard* of the Legislative Council. The Colonial Secretary had instigated an enquiry to challenge the findings of a Committee of the House of Commons regarding the 'lack of moral standing' of the colony. These allegations 'had created a feeling in the mind of the English public that was prejudicial to the colony'.[7] During a Legislative Council Meeting on 6 July 1838, the Colonial Secretary was recorded as stating that:

> he had heard many who came to the colony for the first time say that they were surprised it was so well, and he particularly asked General Fryre, the President of Chili [sic], and he said that before he came here he had no expectations of finding the country in so forward a state, in fact as much safety here as in any country he had visited. If the country was immoral he thought he could turn round to the people of England

---

6   *Sydney Herald,* 'Shipping Intelligence. Arrival', 3 July 1837, p. 2.
7   *Sydney Herald,* 'Legislative Council', Friday 6 July 1838, pp. 2–3.

and Ireland who send all their criminals to this colony, and they say they wonder that there were thieves here; who send out thousands of street walkers to this colony...[8]

Freire was not to be the last high-profile Chilean living in Australia. In 1975, Verónica Michelle Bachelet Jeria, daughter of Air Force Brigadier General, Alberto Bachelet Martínez, who opposed the dictator Augusto Pinochet, lived in exile in Sydney for six months. Bachelet was herself destined to become the first woman to secure the presidency of Chile, in 2006. On 7 May 2013 both the Socialist Party and the Party for Democracy in Chile again named Bachelet as their representative in the opposition primaries to obtain their nomination as presidential candidate; Bachelet returned to the presidency in March 2014.

The historical perspective

According to the 1891 Colonial Census, in the late 1800s there were people from at least 14 Latin American countries living in Australia (see Table 7.1). The same source indicates that there were fewer than 500 people of Latin American extraction living in the Colonies, excluding the state of South Australia, which did not have disaggregated figures. In any case Latin Americans in South Australia could not have reached more than 50 people. This represented just 0.02 per cent of the population of the Australian colonies. Brazil had the highest presence in Australia, representing 31.5 per cent of the Latin American population, followed by Chile (20 per cent), Mexico (ten per cent), and Argentina (eight per cent).

The Latin American arrivals of the 19th century coincided with the gold rush of the 1850s, which supports the view that most Latinos were associated with this massive mining activity. However, the newspapers of the time make it clear that there were other commercial motives. For instance, a relatively high number of advertisements appeared in *The Sydney Herald* and *The Argus* (Melbourne) from 1838 to 1916 relating to the Mexican product—'Mexican Walnut Oil'. The oil was popular in Australia for people who wanted to dye their grey hair.[9] So while the key attraction may well have been gold, there may have been other commercial magnets accounting for this small but early migration to Australia.

---

8   *Ibid.*
9   *Argus*, 'Classified Advertising', Melbourne, Vic.: 1848–1956, 21 August 1916, p. 1.

Table 7.1: Colonial Censuses 1891

Country	Victoria	NSW	QLD	WA	Tas	Total
Argentine	11	14	6	2	2	35
Brazil	52	45	11	28	2	138
Chili	11	53	18	5		87
Mexico	10	16	14	5		45
Panama			1			1
Paraguay			1			1
Peru	8	11	5	2		26
Santa Cruz (Bolivia)			1			1
Hayti or Santo Domingo	2	3				5
Nicaragua	1					1
New Granada	1					1
Feudador (Ecuador)	1	1				2
Uraguay (Uruguay)	1	4		1		6
Colombia		1				1
South America (no country stated)	41	56	38	9	3	147
Total	139	204	95	52	4	438

Note: The South Australia Colonial Census does not have disaggregated figures for America.

Source: HCCD Historical Census and Colonial Data Archives.

The 1970s immigration wave

Before the 1970s there were so few Latin Americans that the 1961 census did not individually register any community from this region. But significant migration came in the 1970s when policy changes made by Gough Whitlam's Labor government became the engine behind the big Latin American immigration wave which surged from 1973 to the early 90s.

The following statistical figures give us an idea of the speed and size of this migration movement. It took 25 years (1901–1966) for the Latin American population to quadruple in numbers from a low base of 770 to 3119 people. In contrast, in just five years (1971–1976), there was a growth rate of 215 per cent, when the Latino population grew to 11,335 people. From 1976 to 1981 it once again almost trebled, lifting the population to 32,339. This figure represented 0.29 per cent of the total population in Australia in 1981. This population growth of Latin Americans in Australia has not been seen since.

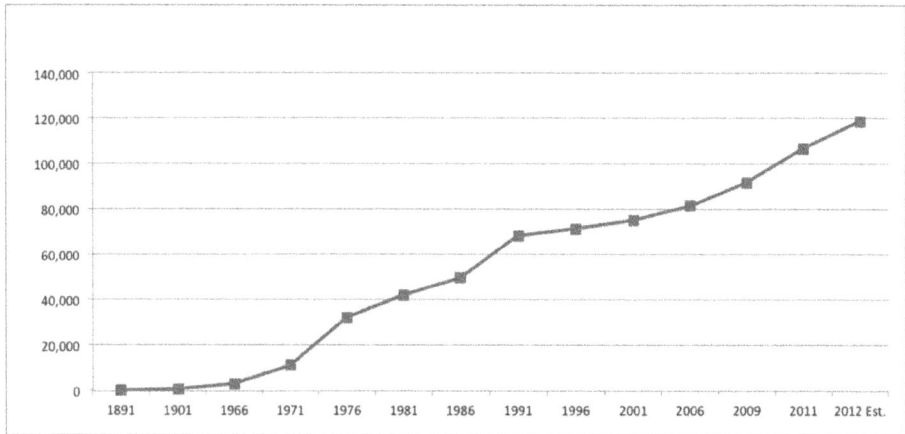

Figure 7.1: Latin Americans in Australia from 1891 to December 2012

Source: 3105.0.65.001 Australian Historical Population Statistics, 2008, Released at 11.30am (Canberra time) 5 August 2008.

The 1972 abolition of the White Australia Policy (known as 1901 *Immigration Restriction Act*)—the main aim of which was to maintain Australia's Anglo-Celtic culture and ethnic background unchanged—was the first fundamental step towards opening the door to Latin American countries and people from elsewhere. However, it wasn't until 1973 that it really took effect when Minister for Immigration, Al Grassby, delivered the 'Family of the Nation' speech in which he introduced two new terms: 'multiculturalism' and 'social justice', and linked them. The nail in the coffin for the old White Australia policy was the passing of the 1975 *Racial Discrimination Act*, making any form of racially based selection criteria illegal. A policy of multiculturalism started to flourish across the public policy spectrum. In an historic moment, in 1973, a bipartisan parliament agreed to accept people from Chile as refugees. This bipartisan immigration program for Chile marked:

> a break from previous refugee programs that tended to support refugees who were fleeing Communist governments. Between 1974 and 1981, about 6000 Chileans were taken in and (many more) thereafter until the ending of military rule in 1990.[10]

This planned humanitarian program, introduced in 1977 and 1978, replaced the ad-hoc approach that allowed a post-Second World War immigration boom.[11] Since then, the program's focus has changed each year in response to the global need for resettlement.

---

10 Barry York, 'Australia and Refugees, 1901–2002: An Annotated Chronology Based on Official Sources', *Social Policy Group*, Department of Immigration and Ethnic Affairs, Review 1990, Canberra, 1990.

11 Department of Immigration and Citizenship (Economic Analysis Unit, Chief Economist), 'Population flows Immigration aspects 2009–2010 edition', Australian Government, Canberra, 2010, pp. 3, 69.

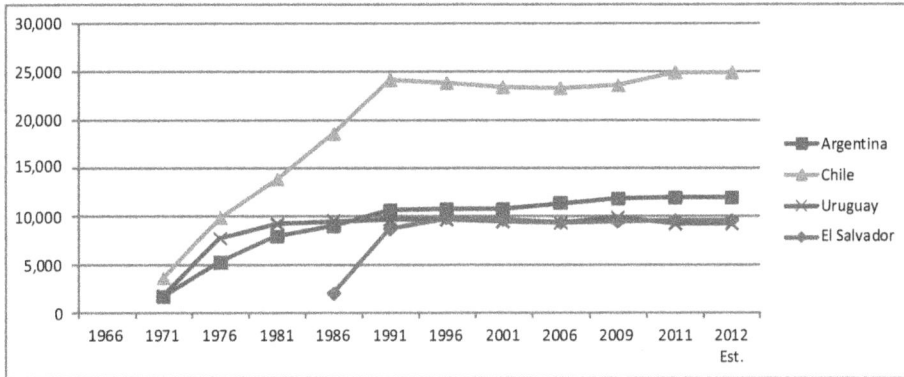

Figure 7.2: Top four Latin American people in Australia under the Special Humanitarian Program (SHP)

Sources: Infosheets by country, Museum of Immigration Victoria and the Department of Immigration and Border Protection: Migration and settlement research and statistical information 1966-2012.

As part of this new approach, people from other Latin American countries like Argentina and Uruguay were officially included in the list of those permitted to apply for refugee status.

In 1978, the new categories of skilled migration and family reunion also opened a new avenue to expand the number of Latinos in Australia.

However, not all Latino groups warmly embraced these new immigration opportunities. Australia took only a small number of Cubans (40) as most Cubans leaving Cuba wanted to settle in the US.[12] In fact the number of Cubans in Australia has remained very small, with only 635 Cubans identified in the Census of 2011.

Malcolm Fraser's Liberal government extended more immigration opportunities to Latin Americans in 1981 and 1982 with a review of its refugee policy. This review resulted 'in the termination of the White Russian program and the extension of the Latin American program'[13] and, in 1982, to a substantial number of people from El Salvador and, to a lesser extent, other Central America countries (Guatemala, Nicaragua and Honduras) being accepted into Australia under the refugees and Special Humanitarian Program (SHP).[14]

Again reviewing the immigration program in 1983 the Hawke Labor government endorsed the refugee policy but 'diversifie[d] the intake to reflect the global

---

12   UNHCR, *The State of the World's Refugees, 1997–1998*, Oxford University Press, 1997, p. 48.

13   Department of Immigration and Ethnic Affairs, *Review '81*, Canberra, 1981, pp. 6, 56.

14   Department of Immigration and Ethnic Affairs, *Review '82*, Canberra, 1982, pp. 56, 57.

dimensions of refugee problems'. [15] The result was a greater focus on Central and South America than earlier. This move is clearly reflected in the arrivals statistics. In 1985, there was a significant increase in resettlement of people from South and Central America (1717), half of whom were Salvadorans. [16]

An earthquake in Chile in March 1985 prompted Australia to hasten the processing time for family visas from the affected country. The flow of refugees from Latin America remained quite steady for the following two years. In 1985, there was yet another boost when Labor Treasurer, Paul Keating, announced an increase in the Family Reunion Program. [17]

However, the Humanitarian and Special Humanitarian Program (SHP), like any other massive program of this nature, was open to abuse. When I was working for the Spanish Latin American Welfare Centre (CELAS) in 1986, I became aware of a number of people related to the Salvadorian death squads arriving in Australia under the program. In 1986, Rafaela López, the President of CELAS, wrote a letter to the Department of Immigration and Ethnic Affairs complaining about the alleged violations of the spirit of this program. CELAS demanded an enquiry. However the Department did not respond. These abuse allegations were given further weight by the SBS Television program, *Vox Populi,* which interviewed five alleged Salvadorian victims.

Another direct example of irregularities came from Professor Desmond Cahill who wrote an obituary for Father Bruno Moretti in which he mentioned that '[Father Moretti] also came in contact with a man who claimed he had been the one who had killed Archbishop Oscar Romero in El Salvador in 1980 and came to Australia on false papers'. [18]

Sister Beatry Santos, who researched the Salvadorian community in Australia, also noted that the community was 'paralysed by fear', as the people whom she met and interviewed claimed that very dangerous individuals belonging to the guerrilla and the death squads were living in Australia. She argued that the fragmented Salvadorian community habit of maintaining a low political and social profile in Australia could well be the result of this fear and trauma. I have learnt through unofficial channels that the Department of Immigration and Ethnic Affairs had, indeed, launched an internal investigation. Unfortunately, there are no public records of the investigation's findings.

Another case, this time related to Uruguay, was documented by the ABC filmmaker, Ian Walker, who investigated the arrival of at least one infamous

---

15   Department of Immigration and Ethnic Affairs, *Review '83*, Canberra, 1983, pp. 1, 27, 31.
16   Department of Immigration and Ethnic Affairs, *Review '85*, Canberra, 1985, pp. 68–9.
17   *Ibid.*, p. 135.
18   *The Age*, Obituaries 'Priest at home with Melbourne's migrants', 13 January 2005, p. 7.

Uruguayan torturer to Australia. According to Mr Walker, the torturer's arrival was the product of negotiations between intelligence services: 'The CIA, ASIO and a large American multinational all conspired to have him resettled in Australia'.[19] Notwithstanding these examples the vast majority of people under these programs were legitimate.

The participation rate of Latin Americans in the humanitarian programs (mainly from Chile and El Salvador) remained very strong until 1990, even when other world events looked likely to affect the Latin American intake. On 27 June 1989, the government granted Chinese nationals who were in Australia at the time of the Beijing Tiananmen Square incident temporary residence for four years under a special category of permit. There were about 20,000 people in this category in Australia in 1990. However, in 1991 people from Latin American countries were still representing 20 per cent of the Australian refugee and SHP intake program.

The big shift downward came in 1992, when the Labor Minister for Immigration, Gerry Hand, in announcing the Refugee, Humanitarian and Special Assistance migration categories for the next financial year, indicated that 'numbers admitted under the Central American and Indo-Chinese programs will be smaller than in recent years reflecting declining resettlement needs'.[20] This marked the beginning of the end of the migration intake under the Humanitarian and Special Humanitarian programs. By 1996 the Latin American migration under the Humanitarian and Special Humanitarian Programs had effectively closed for El Salvadorians. However the government accepted a small number of Colombians (13) in 2001–02, under these programs.

The new Howard Liberal government in 1996 changed the immigration policy as soon as it took power. In October of that year, Minister Ruddock criticised the Opposition for creating a migration program when it was in office that was 'out of balance and rapidly losing public confidence'.[21] According to the Minister, family migration had grown significantly at the expense of the skilled intake, and he intended to restore the balance. He accordingly increased the Skilled Migration Program (SMP) and decreased the Family Reunion quotas. The new migrant Latin American numbers coming under the Family Reunion Program quickly diminished.

---

19   ABC Radio National, 'Tortured Questions', *Background Briefing*, 26 May 1996.
20   Minister for Immigration, Local Government and Ethnic Affairs, *Media Release*, MPS 41/92, 24 July 1992.
21   Minister for Immigration and Multicultural Affairs, Media Release, MPS27/96, 3 July 1996 and MPS70/96, 30 October 1996.

Table 7.2: South America, Central America and the Caribbean refugee and SHP programs

FY	Colombia	El Salvador	Other	Total
91/92	-	916	36	952
92/93	-	288	9	297
93/94	-	132	17	149
94/95	-	154	24	178
95/96	-	137	41	178
96/97	-	77	-	77
97/98	-	49	1	50
98/99	-	7	17	24
99/00	-	9	10	19
00/01	-	5	9	14
01/02	13	-	13	26

Source: Infosheets by Country, Museum of Immigration Victoria and the Department of Immigration and Border Protection: http://www.immi.gov.au/media/fact-sheets/#stats.

For instance, in 2002–03, 64 per cent of Latin Americans migrated to Australia under the Family Reunion category and 27 per cent did so under the SMP. By 2008–09 the Family Reunion Program representation had fallen to 44 per cent and the skilled migration representation had increased to 53 per cent. In particular, people migrated under the newly created category of Independent Migration using the Visa Sub-class 885 and Visa Sub-class 886. These two visas were created by the Howard government to attract international students living in Australia who had obtained an Australian certificate as a result of at least two years of study. From 2002–03 to 2010–11 the number of Latin Americans settling in Australia every year under the Independent category grew by 300 per cent, from 249 to 1013 people. These visas became the means by which many Latin American immigrants have been able to settle permanently in Australia. In particular, these visas benefited Latinos from Brazil, Colombia and Venezuela, and swelled the numbers in Australian Latino communities by 40 per cent from 2009 to December 2012.

The Latin American population in 2012

In December 2012, there was a Latin American first generation population of 105,886 people—this figure excludes Spain—living as residents or citizens in Australia.

This represented 0.49 per cent of the total population of Australia (21,507,715)—substantial compared to the 0.04 per cent registered in 1891.[22]

According to the 2011 Census, the ten largest national groupings of Latin American peoples in order of population size in Australia are those from: Chile, Brazil, Argentina, Colombia, Uruguay, El Salvador, Peru, Venezuela, Mexico and Ecuador. The Department of Immigration figures from 2011 to December 2012 indicate that Colombia and Argentina have already shifted places.

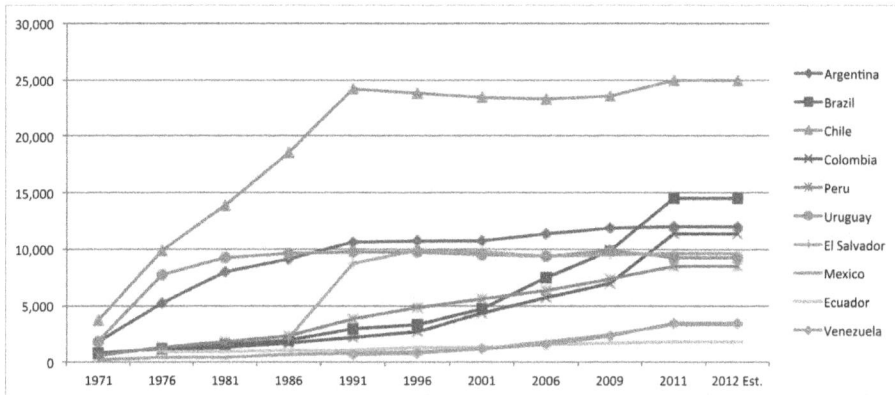

Figure 7.3: Top ten Latin Americans in Australia by country of origin from 1971 to December 2012

Source: ABS Census 2011 plus the Department of Immigration net additions from 2011 to December 2012.

Latino age profile

The age profile of the Latino Community confirms the demographic differences between old and new Latino settlers.

Uruguayans have an older population, with 42 per cent at 60 years of age and over, and only two per cent under the age of 19. Conversely, Venezuela has 13 per cent under 19 years of age and only three per cent who are 60 years of age and over. Brazilians comprise an overwhelmingly young community, with 76 per cent under 39 years of age, compared with 54 per cent for the entire Australian population.

---

22   These figures are based on the 2011 Census as well as on Department of Immigration and Citizenship statistical information concerning new permanent arrivals and departures (net additions) and do not discount people who died from 1 July 2011 to 30 December 2012, as this information was not available by country of birth.

It is interesting to note that although we classify Ecuador as a member of the new immigration wave, its community is relatively older than the others, as 25 per cent of its members are 60 years of age and over. This represents five per cent more than the Australian average of 20 per cent.

The new Latino communities' relatively youthful age profile indicates that the best contribution they can make to Australian society is yet to occur.

Table 7.3: Latin American people by country of origin and age group

Age	0-19 years	20-39 years	40-49 years	60 years and over
Australia	26%	28%	27%	20%
Argentina	5%	29%	39%	27%
Brazil	8%	68%	20%	5%
Chile	4%	27%	40%	28%
Colombia	9%	64%	21%	6%
Ecuador	8%	32%	35%	25%
El Salvador	3%	44%	39%	15%
Mexico	12%	61%	20%	6%
Peru	7%	42%	35%	16%
Uruguay	2%	15%	42%	42%
Venezuela	13%	57%	27%	3%
Spain	5%	17%	35%	43%

Source: ABS Census 2011, ABS. Information extracted by the author using Table Builder Basic & Pro, 8-21 May 2013.

The future—migration trends

The composition of the community has changed dramatically in the last ten years and will continue to do so. Current migration trends will be affected by changes in the skilled and business migration visas, which have been taking place since 2009. These changes and their impact on migration have yet to be fully measured, but if we consider the intake from 2009 onwards, Brazilians, Colombians, Mexicans and Venezuelans have benefited most.

On current trends, first generation Brazilians will occupy the top rung in the Latino ladder in Australia by 2015. Brazil was number four in skilled migration sourced from the student population in Australia, and fifth in business migration, according to the Department of Immigration's 2011–12 immigration ranking by country (highest-ranking source countries for different types of visas). Colombia was second.

In the same period Colombia occupied the 14th place of all countries from where immigrants came to settle in Australia, sourced from the international student population. Among the Latin American sources, Colombia has already taken the third place from Argentina and may overtake Chile by 2020, leaving the Chileans ranked third. Venezuela and Peru follow very closely.

The ranks of Latin American communities will also be increased annually by a floating population of students, temporary workers, and family visits. These new permanent and temporary Latin American communities will shape the attitudes, political and cultural manifestations of the whole Latino community in Australia in a rather different way than in earlier generations. It is expected that the new migration wave will exploit its qualifications and English proficiency to enhance the commercial and economic relationship between Australia and Latin America. We have seen signs of these changes with the opening of new high-quality Mexican and Argentinean restaurants in Australia since 2010 owned by first generation Mexicans and Argentineans.

Family migration and particularly people who came to study in Australia for postgraduate degrees are filling the void left by the exclusion of Latin American countries from Australian refugee and special humanitarian programs. This new Latin American wave will make its own mark on the future history of Australia.

Integrating into the new motherland

The goal for governments is that migrants adjust rapidly to their adopted country. The OECD highlights the importance of this process:

> ...the active participation of immigrants and their children in the labour market and, more generally, in public life is vital for ensuring social cohesion in the host country and migrants' ability to function as autonomous and productive citizens, and also for facilitating the acceptance of immigrants by the host-country population.[23]

The OECD *Indicators of Immigrant Integration 2012 Report* defines and benchmarks a number of indicators to measure the outcomes for immigrants and their children. The 2011 Census allowed us to extract the relevant information to produce and compare, whenever possible, the immigrant outcomes in Australia with the indicators contained in the OECD Report and the pertinent Australian average rate.

This following section analyses civic engagement—represented by citizenship, political participation[24] and volunteer participation indicators—economic participation—labour force representation, unemployment, levels of income, occupation, and

---

23   OECD (Organisation for Economic Co-operation and Development), *Settling In: OECD Indicators of Immigrant Integration 2012 Report*, p. 5.
24   Karina Anthony, 'The Political Representation of Ethnic and Racial Minorities', Briefing Paper 3/06, *NSW Parliamentary Library Research Service*, 2006.

employment by industry indicators—education participation—levels of education and English proficiency indicators—and social participation—need of assistance indicator—in order to measure and judge the level of Latino integration in Australia.

Future studies may analyse other indicators and up-to-date information that would improve our current picture of the quality of the settlement process for Latin American people in Australia: this would permit more accurate international comparisons.

Civic engagement: Rates of citizenship

The OECD states that civic engagement or 'taking an active part in society' is probably one of the best indicators of integration. It demonstrates the extent to which an immigrant has settled in a community and broadened involvement beyond material necessity.[25] The OECD also notes that a reliable indicator of civic engagement is the rate of citizenship. The report 'Settlement Outcomes of New Arrivals' concurs with this, saying that 'the obtaining or intention to obtain citizenship can be an indicator of connectedness for new migrants'.[26]

Invalidation of citizenship of the applicants' country of origin is regarded as increasing the commitment of migrants to a new country. Citizenship of the new country is also regarded as a particularly accurate indicator of community and national commitment because of the stringent legal requisites enforced by the host country that the new migrants are required to overcome. In the case of Australia, the *Citizenship Act* 2007 calls for a minimum of four years of residency including a period of 12 months as a permanent resident immediately before making an application, and a limited number of absences from Australia of no more than 12 months in total in the four years prior to application, with not more than 90 days in the 12 months immediately prior to application.

The 2011 Census shows adjusted citizenship figures by reducing the number of people who arrived after 2009 and who, for statutory requirements, were ineligible to apply for citizenship—this re-calculated rate is also known an 'adjusted naturalisation rate'. Based on this indicator we can determine that both the old and new Latino communities are well integrated into Australian society compared with the national average of 85 per cent adoption of citizenship for all migrant communities in Australia.

Moreover, the citizenship figures for Latino communities in Australia are far above the latest OECD figures from 2005–06, in which the average citizenship rate for migrant communities was 48 per cent.

---

25 OECD, *Settling In, op. cit.*, note 23, p. 133.
26 Department of Immigration and Citizenship, *Settlement Outcomes of New Arrivals: Report of Findings*, Policy Innovation, Research and Evaluation Unit, Department of Immigration and Citizenship, April 2011.

The Salvadorian communities have a citizenship rate of almost 98 per cent, 13 per cent above the national average. The Argentineans and Uruguayan communities are just above the national average with 88 per cent, while Chile has almost 84 per cent. In the case of Venezuela, dual citizenship is recognised for people of less than 25 years of age only. Despite this barrier, an impressive 88 per cent of Venezuelans acquired Australian citizenship. The rest of the new Latino communities possess consistent citizenship rates, with their time living in Australia just below or above the national average of 85 per cent.

Table 7.4: Latin American people by country of birth and citizenship

Country of birth	Adjusted naturalisation rate 15 years and over						
	Australian	Not Australian	Not eligible yet	Not Australian/ eligible	Total Australian plus eligible residents	% over eligible residents	Ranking
Australia						85%	
Argentina	9,906	1,577	236	1,341	11,247	88.1%	3
Brazil	4,724	8,832	5,734	3,098	7,822	60.4%	10
Chile	18,883	5,144	1,449	3,695	22,578	83.6%	4
Colombia	4,424	6,167	5,203	964	5,388	82.1%	8
Ecuador	1,263	378	158	220	1,483	85.2%	5
El Salvador	8,972	435	234	201	9,173	97.8%	1
Mexico	1,192	1,722	1,139	583	1,775	67.2%	9
Peru	5,560	2,380	1,460	920	6,480	85.8%	6
Uruguay	8,483	536	631	1,167	9,650	87.9%	2
Venezuela	1,371	1,659	1,469	190	1,561	87.8%	7
Total	64,778	28,830	17,713	12,379	77,157	84.0%	

Note: The figure of not eligible yet was estimated as we did not have the information by age.

Sources: ABS Census 2011, ABS Information extracted by the author using Table Builder Basic & Pro, 8-21 May 2013.

Although the Brazilian and Mexican communities are part of the new arrivals category, both exhibit low citizenship rates of 60 and 67 per cent respectively, even though there are no barriers to dual nationality. Since 9 June 1994, dual citizenship has been allowed under Brazilian law. In Mexico dual nationality has been recognised since 1998.[27] The low citizenship rate of both countries must therefore be caused by other unknown factors. In relation to the OECD average

---

27 Nationality Act, ('New Law published in the Official Journal of the Federation on January 23, 1998'), Ley de Nacionalidad Cámara de Diputados del H. Congreso de la Unión, Secretaría General, Secretaría de Servicios Parlamentarios, Dirección General de Bibliotecas, 20 March 1998.

of 48 per cent citizenship rate, the Brazilian and Mexican communities have nonetheless performed well. It is clear that neither loss of country-of-origin citizenship nor the arduous requirements to obtain Australian citizenship are significant deterrents to the strong drive for both the old and new waves of Latino migrants to integrate into Australian society.

With an overall citizenship average of 82 per cent, Latino communities now regard Australia as their home, and arguably have developed a sense of connectedness and permanency with the rest of the community.

Civic engagement: Volunteer work

The 2012 OECD Report, *Settling In*, includes volunteer work as another important indicator of civic engagement:

> Dimensions to gauge the extent to which migrants feel involved in society include involvement in broad voluntary societal activities, which might include membership and participation in associations, volunteer work, and, if by choice, enrolment in trade unions or political parties. Political participation is one dimension of implication in society.[28]

The *World Giving Index 2011*,[29] which includes volunteer work, rated Latin American countries well down in rankings for philanthropic contributions. Australia is number three in the ranking and the closest Latin American country is Chile, at 43. The Australian figures from the 2011 Census indicate that all the Latino communities except Mexico rate below the national average of 19 per cent in volunteer work. The Venezuelan community follows with 16 per cent.

Given that Mexicans have one of the lowest rates of citizenship but the highest rate of volunteer work, there is a contradiction between the first civic engagement indicator—the rate of citizenship—and the second—volunteer work. This contradiction warrants further study.

According to the Census 2011, Uruguay possessed the lowest volunteer work rate, with 11 per cent. In the *Giving Index* Uruguay rated 124th. Colombia, Ecuador and Peru were close on Uruguay's heels with 12 per cent.

There is some evidence to suggest that the low participation of some Latino populations may be explained by cultural factors. According to sources such as the *Giving Index*, it is uncommon by international standards for Latinos to volunteer in their countries of origin.

---

28   OECD, *Settling In, op. cit.*, note 23, p. 133.
29   Charities Aid Foundation (CAF), *World Giving Index 2011: A Global View of Giving Trends*, pp. 44–5.

Table 7.5: Latin American people by country of birth and volunteer work

	Not a Volunteer	Volunteer	Total	%
Australia	12,851,394	3,090,876	15,942,270	19%
Argentina	9,528	1,615	11,143	14%
Brazil	11,448	1,951	13,399	15%
Chile	20,452	2,760	23,212	12%
Colombia	9,228	1,225	10,453	12%
Ecuador	1,385	206	1,591	13%
Peru	6,766	966	7,732	12%
Uruguay	7,641	954	8,595	11%
Venezuela	2,512	495	3,007	16%
El Salvador	7,923	1,176	9,099	13%
Mexico	2,330	557	2,887	19%
Total	79,213	11,905	91,118	13%
Spain	10,482	1,301	11,783	11%

Note: The figure of not eligible yet was estimated as we did not have the information by age.

Sources: ABS Census 2011, ABS Information extracted by the author using Table Builder Basic & Pro, from the 8th to the 21st of May 2013.

Civic engagement: Political participation

The OECD points to the inclusion of participation in voting in political elections, union and political party memberships and participation in the political system as indicators of integration. For instance, the OECD Report concluded that: 'In most countries, immigrants report a lower participation rate in the most recent election than their native-born counterparts'.[30]

This indicator could not be analysed with the same level of statistical detail as others, since the relevant information is not available. In order to evaluate this indicator, relevant studies such as ethnic participation in Australian parliaments was analysed and qualitative information obtained through face-to-face interviews with community leaders who have played critical political and advocacy roles: these included Australia's first Latino MP Telmo Languiller; political adviser Cesar Piperno; activist Angel Calderón; ACTU executive Jorge Nava; electoral advisor Carlos Baldovino; Labor Party candidate Eric Dale; and researchers Beatriz Santos and Rafaela López.

---

30   OECD, *Settling In, op. cit.*, note 23, p. 138.

Successful migrant political participation

In Australia there is strong evidence of success in first and second generations of Greek and Italian communities in voting popular representatives into the federal and state parliaments and local union movements. The Greek community produced Federal MPs Maria Vamvakinou, Steve Georganas, Petro Georgiou, and Victorian MPs Theo Theophanous, John Pandazopoulos and Nick Kotsiras, among others. From an Italian background were NSW MP Franca Arena (1981–99), Governor of Victoria James Gobbo, and the Member for Makin (SA) Tony Zappia.

However, Latin American political representation has been non-existent at the federal level and very slight, at best, at the state and local council and political party and trade union levels. Victoria has had by far the most Latin American political representation of any state or territory; it is the only state with a member of parliament with Latin American ancestry, Telmo Languiller (Uruguayan), elected in 1999. There have been other popularly elected Latinos, for instance Andrés Puig (Uruguayan), who was Major of the Brimbank Council in 2002; Jenny Barbosa (Uruguayan), who was a former Council member for Brimbank; and Cesar Piperno (Uruguayan), President of the Multicultural Affairs and Population Policy Committee of the Labor Party. South Australia follows with Jorge Navas (Colombian), who has been the Secretary for the Health Services Union since 1987. Navas became a member of the executive committee of the ACTU. At the Federal level a further two Uruguayans have held positions of influence: Carlos Baldovino was the electoral officer of the former Prime Minister Julia Gillard,[31] and the deceased Fernando Moya worked in the electorate of Holt for Anthony Byrnes, former Parliamentary Secretary for Trade and Parliamentary Secretary to the Prime Minister.

Carlos Baldovino arrived in Australia in December 1977 as a political refugee. Uruguay gave Carlos a painful introduction to life within a dictatorship. In his country of origin he was captured, imprisoned and tortured for five months by the military regime. Carlos joined the Labor Party in 1993. He was raised in a politically charged environment by his father Elvio Baldovino, who maintained a strong commitment to the Labor Party. From 1993 Carlos occupied several administrative positions in the Labor Party, including state and national conference delegate and member of the public office selection committee. He tried to win an Upper House seat in Victoria, failing by just .098 per cent, 1,402 votes short of the 140,000 required to succeed.[32] Carlos became an electoral officer for Julia Gillard when she was elected to Federal Parliament in 1998.

---

31   Carlos Baldovino, interview, 9 December 2010.
32   Victorian Electoral Commission, 'State Election 1999: Eumemmerring Province'.

Eric Dale was born in Chile in 1947, and arrived in Australia in 1964. In 1975 he joined the Labor Party as a member of the Ferntree Gully branch. Dale was motivated to join the party by his outrage at the dismissal of the Whitlam government. He has occupied a number of Labor administrative positions, from branch secretary to branch treasurer. Dale co-ordinated the Eastern Suburbs campaign of the Victorian Labor Party that resulted in the electoral victory of the Cain government in 1982. In 1985 and 1988 Dale was himself the ALP candidate for Burwood. He endured an uphill electoral battle and came close to winning the seat held by Jeff Kennett, the Leader of the Liberal Party, since 1976. In 1985 Dale was 1,500 votes short of winning the seat and changing the political history of Victoria. From 1982 to 1989 he worked as adviser to Jim Simmonds, Minister of Employment and Training and later Minister of Local Government. From 1989 to 1992 Dale worked as electoral officer for George Crawford, member for Jika-Jika. He performed the same role for Jean McLean, member for Melbourne West from 1992 to 1996. From 1999 to 2001 Dale worked for Andrew Theophanous as chief of staff. Dale ceased being active within the Labor Party after 2001.

In 1999 Rubén Alex Sánchez tried unsuccessfully to win the seat of Camden in NSW for Labor, losing to Liberal Liz Kernohan.[33] Mario John Fonseca ran for a seat in the NSW parliament in 2003, representing the Green Party, but secured only 5.6 per cent of the votes.[34]

Why Victoria?

Most members of the ten largest Latin communities in Australia live in NSW, with their second choice of residence being Victoria—except Brazilians, whose second preference is Queensland; and the community from El Salvador, which prefers Victoria, with Queensland as the second choice. So it may appear unusual that much of the political engagement by the Latino population in Australia has been in Victoria.

In 2005 more than 20 per cent[35] of Victorian parliamentarians were either born overseas or had parents who were. NSW followed with 14 per cent: migrant representation in the Victorian parliament has been very strong, with greater successful political involvement of the Latin American community in Victoria than in any other state in Australia. The total representation of ethnic parliamentarians at the national level was only 12 per cent. This percentage was, however, a significant improvement on the seven per cent reported for non-English speaking countries by the Department of Immigration and Citizenship

33   New South Wales Election Results 1856–2007 (as at 5 July 2007), 'NSW Elections: Camden – 1999'.
34   New South Wales Election Results 1856–2007 (as at 5 July 2007), 'NSW Elections: Smithfield – 2003'.
35   Anthony, Karina, 'The Political Representation of Ethnic and Racial Minorities', 2006.

in 1989.[36] Before September 1999 not one parliamentarian was Latino. The Uruguayan-born Telmo Languiller changed this by winning the lower house seat of Sunshine in Victoria—currently Derrimut—in 1999.

Table 7.6: Latin Americans place of residency

Country	First settling's choice	Second settling's choice	Third settling's choice
Argentina	NSW	Vic	Qld
Brazil	NSW	Qld	Vic
Chile	NSW	Vic	Qld
Colombia	NSW	Vic	Qld
El Salvador	Vic	Qld	NSW
Peru	NSW	Vic	Qld
Uruguay	NSW	Vic	Qld
Mexico	NSW	Vic	Qld
Venezuela	NSW	Vic	Qld
Ecuador	NSW	Qld	Vic
Spain	NSW	Vic	Qld

Source: ABS Census 2011, ABS. Information extracted by the author using Table Builder Basic & Pro, 8-21 May 2013.

Table 7.7 Ethnic membership in Australian parliaments in 2005

State/ Territory	Cth	NSW	Vic	SA	Qld	WA	NT	ACT	Tas	Total
Total house members	226	135	132	69	89	91	25	17	40	824
Total ethnic minority members	10.6%	14.0%	20.0%	11.0%	5.6%	8.8%	12.0%	17.6%	5.0%	12.0%

Source: Karina Anthony, (2006) The Political Representation of Ethnic and Racial Minorities, Briefing Paper 3/06, NSW Parliamentary Library Research Service.

Overall the total ethnic representation in parliaments was well below the 30 per cent of people who were born overseas or had parents who were not born in Australia.

---

36   Department of Immigration and Citizenship, *National Agenda for a Multicultural Australia*, http://www. immi.gov.au/media/publications/multicultural/agenda/agenda89/issues.html.

Table 7.8: Ethnic members by party 2005

State/ Territory	Cth	NSW	Vic	SA	Qld	WA	NT	ACT	Tas	Total
Total ethnic members by party	24	19	27	8	5	8	3	3	2	99
ALP / Territory Labor	38%	74%	85%	63%	89%	75%	67%	33%	50%	66%
Democrats	4%	0%	0%	0%	0%	0%	0%	0%	0%	1%
National Party	4%	16%	0%	0%	0%	0%	0%	0%	0%	4%
Country (Liberal) Party	54%	5%	15%	25%	20%	25%	33%	67%	50%	27%
Independent / Minor Party	0%	5%	0%	13%	0%	0%	0%	0%	0%	2%

Source: Karina Anthony, (2006) The Political Representation of Ethnic and Racial Minorities, Briefing Paper 3/06, NSW Parliamentary Library Research Service.

The role of the established migrant communities (Spanish and Greek)

The Spanish and Greek communities played a central role in advancing the Latin American political resettlement process within the Australian system. As the oldest Spanish-speaking community in Australia, Spaniards had settled well before the arrival of Latin Americans in the 1970s. Spaniards migrated all over the world after 1940 to escape the dictatorship of General Franco. During the 1970s they had already established links with the union movement in Australia. For instance, they initiated the workers' commissions (*comisiones obreras*) in conjunction with the Greek community and with links to the unions.[37] Both the Spanish and Greek communities shared a similar ideology and held common interests and enemies, as each had first-hand experience of the horrors of dictatorships. This common heritage encouraged a loose alliance between the Spanish and Greek communities.

The Latin Americans' lack of English skills and political and union contacts in Australia was compensated for by a strong will to advance the human rights and democratisation agendas in their own motherlands. The Spaniards and the Greeks were sympathetic to this cause and were more than willing to provide logistical support to the new Latin Americans. This support allowed them to organise and to form resistance groups in exile against dictatorships in Latin America. For instance, the Spanish community frequently lent the Spanish Club

---

37   Telmo Languiller, interview 25 April 2010.

located in Gertrude St, Fitzroy, to the new politically active groups. The Greek community did the same by lending its premises, the 'Democrat's Building' in Nicholson St, Fitzroy.[38] The alliance between Spaniards and new Latin Americans grew stronger throughout the years, due to mutual recognition of their common experience of political persecution in their home countries.

The unions' role

The new Latin Americans were also supported by the trade union movement in Australia, which sympathised with the human rights and democratisation agendas of the politically active new migrants. This support took the form of providing access to venues for meetings and to office equipment, interpreting, and printing facilities.

Incrementally the Australian union movement also became aware of the importance of attracting new arrivals to their ranks. A number of unions gathered to establish a working commission to achieve this goal. Among these were the Metalworkers' Union, the Meat Workers' Union, the Textile and Clothing Union, the Miscellaneous Union, the Liquor Trade Union, and the Health Services Union. The commission established the Trade Union Migrant Workers' Centre (TUMWC) in 1976[39] and employed María Pozos, a Spaniard, to serve as a conduit with the Spanish-speaking groups and to facilitate the new arrivals' integration into the Australian union movement.[40] María filled a crucial role which sought to redress the lack of English-language skills characteristic of new arrivals. Telmo Languiller commented: 'I had a number of meetings with her and these encounters were crucial to opening my eyes and to establishing solid relationships with the union movement'.[41] Joe Caputo, one of the people who established the TUMWC, explained the role of this organisation during an interview in February 2009:

---

38 *Ibid.*
39 The Trade Union Migrant Workers' Centre (TUMWC) was established in 1976 by a small group of unions as a result of a proposal during the second Migrant Workers' Conference in 1975. The Centre's primary aim was to strengthen the links between non-English speaking workers and their unions. Membership of the TUMWC was open to any Victorian union affiliated with the Victorian Trades Hall Council. It was funded by unions that recognised and understood the needs and problems of migrant workers, and by various state and federal government funding programs during its existence. The Centre was based at the Metal Trades Union, East Melbourne, until the TUMWC's move in the late 1980s to the Trades Hall building. The Centre's role included assisting injured workers with Workers' Compensation matters, translation and interpreting, case work and counselling. By the late 1980s the Centre had lost a component of its government funding and affiliation fees from trade unions were insufficient to maintain its previous staffing levels and programs. Despite attempts to provide a more secure financial base through the establishment of a Migrant Workers' Bureau at Trades Hall, the TUMWC closed on 23 July 1991, having insufficient funds to continue. See: Victorian Trades Hall Council. Archives at the University of Melbourne 101/27, 1976–91, 13 Arki Boxes http://www.lib.unimelb.edu.au/collections/archives/collections/.
40 Rafaela López, interview, 14 May 2010.
41 Telmo Languiller, interview, *op. cit.*, note 37.

...90 per cent of it was used for translating, interpreting for union officials; translating documents for union journals and the like. But even that was a step forward, at least there was recognition that you had people from different backgrounds and they needed to be—you know, you needed to communicate to those people in their languages.[42]

According to Languiller, the creation of the TUMWC was in recognition of the need 'to respond to non-English speaking workers' needs.'[43] Languiller remembers a number of conversations with Jim Ralston, Metal Workers' Union Secretary about the ways in which to do this. Languiller's informal links with the Union developed into a formal relationship when the TUMWC organiser, Jim O'Neill, recommended him to John Halfpenny, Victorian Secretary of the Amalgamated Metal Workers' Union, to fill a new organiser position within the TUMWC. Languiller's journey with the union movement lasted 14 years; seven years with the TUMWC and another seven with the Health Services Union. Other Latin Americans have followed this route, such as the Chilean Tony Medina, former CFMEU organiser and Victorian asbestos campaigner who died in 2008 of asbestosis at the age of 43—Medina worked with the well-known union campaigner, Bernie Banton;[44] and Colombian Jorge Navas, Secretary of the Health Services Union in South Australia since 1987.

The story of Jorge Navas is not dissimilar to that of Telmo Languiller. A chance encounter with Don Dunstan, then Premier of South Australia, opened the possibility for Jorge to remain in the country after a difficult separation from his Australian partner. Once his immigration status was resolved, Jorge began working for the Health Services Union as a cleaner, kitchen-hand and operations theatre technician. For many years after his arrival Jorge did not develop political relationships with the Australian Latin American community as he was committed first to obtaining proficiency in the English language: he regarded a close relationship with other Latin Americans as unhelpful in achieving this goal. Jorge was proactive in enrolling new members to a union which in the late 1980s was very weak. His efforts were recognised by a union secretary in 1987, who asked him to adopt this role. As a member of the union he actively participated in supporting Nicaraguan and Colombian solidarity groups and victims of HIV/AIDS. He has remained close to the human rights agenda linked to Colombia.

42   Migrant Workers' Centres in multiculturalism. Joe Caputo locates the key role of Migrant Workers' Centres in the development of multiculturalism. Created: unknown. Date Added: 18 February 2009. Source: not available. Format: mov (Quicktime); File size: 14.9 MB. Length: 05min 43sec.
43   Telmo Languiller, interview, *op. cit.*, note 37.
44   See *Bernie Banton Foundation*, http://www.berniebanton.com.au/, accessed 2 November 2013.

The path from union engagement to the Labor Party

The Labor Party also supported the human rights and democratisation agendas of new migrants, in particular those from Latin America. This support took the form of providing access to solidarity groups, office equipment, communications, printing facilities, and access to venues.

The arrival of Elvio Baldovino was a political landmark within the Latin American community. Baldovino had been a ports union leader in Uruguay. He fled Uruguay when union officials warned that the army was searching for him. In the late 1970s he organised the first Labor Party branch of the Spanish-speaking community in Kensington, with 25 members.[45] However, the success of this incipient branch was limited, due to the lack of English-language skills of the branch members. This experience was instrumental for Languiller and others in realising the need to learn the basics in organising party political branches. The 1980s and the 1990s brought a new political reality to the Latin American community in Australia. One by one the dictatorships in Central and South America fell. The fresh air of democratic change removed the drive to continue with activities related to human rights and democratisation agendas.

However, Jeffrey Kennett's election victory as Liberal Premier of Victoria in October 1992 gave new impetus for members of the Latin American community to work for the union movement. Kennett held a clear anti-union agenda, which galvanised the community to fight against his policies. The Labor Party understood the need to unite a number of non-English speaking people for this task. The Greek MP, Nicky Dollis, former Labor member of the Victorian Parliament, influenced Languiller to become more active within the Party. Languiller had long been a supporter and member of the Uruguayan Communist Party and was reluctant to redirect his political interest from Uruguay to Australia. As a young student in Uruguay he had performed communication activities for the *Movimiento de Liberación Nacional Uruguayo*, known then as *los Tupamaros*. Languiller's involvement with *los Tupamaros* included a politically motivated shooting incident in which he received leg wounds, and several close encounters with the Uruguayan secret police. These incidents eventually persuaded Languiller of the need to leave the country. He escaped to Argentina, and from there he sought asylum with his family in Australia as a political refugee. The changed political landscape in Uruguay and the conservative policies of the Kennett Government were strong incentives for Languiller to refocus his attention on Australia. There was also support from other active political voices in Victoria to allow wider participation of migrants in the political system. According to Languiller there were members of political parties and religious leaders, who had been supportive of the solidarity agenda

---

45   Cesar Piperno, interview, 16 June 2010.

pursued by the Latin American community, who encouraged him and others to become politically active. Among them were Reverend Dick Wootton, Jean McLean, Brian Howe, Don Chipp, Cyril Primmer, Andrew Theophanous, Billy Davis and Alan Missen, all of whom supported the pro-democracy movements in Latin America in the 1970s.

The ascension of Languiller in 1999 as the first Uruguayan and first Latin American member of a parliament in Australia was the culmination of this process. In 2002 Languiller was promoted as Parliamentary Secretary for Community Services. In 2006 he retained the same position but also covered the portfolio of Multicultural Affairs, and one year later moved to the human services secretariat. Languiller has been an active spokesperson; he was the first parliamentarian to deliver speeches in the Mayan and Spanish Languages,[46] and the first to cite *Don Quixote de la Mancha* in the Victorian legislative chamber.[47]

As with other ethnic groups, Latinos have been used for ghost political engagement. There have been cases of both Liberal and Labor parties stacking branches, whereby non-politically active members are signed up to swell branch numbers and to block-vote for a particular agenda. Melbourne newspaper *The Age* accused Languiller of branch stacking. However, he was exonerated after a parliamentary investigation, an internal Labor Party investigation, and a police and an Auditor General's report. Regardless of this, the electoral defeat of the Brumby Government in November 2010 removed Languiller's chance for promotion to a Ministry in the medium term. Like former Premier Brumby, Languiller moved to the back-bench. This defeat also deferred the Latin American community's short-term possibility of securing a representative in a position of senior leadership within the Australian political system.

The Communist Party of Australia

A relatively recent Latin American arrival to Australia in 1995 quickly climbed the ranks of the Communist Party of Australia. Wikipedia describes Vinicio Molina as:

> a union official with the Construction, Forestry, Mining and Energy Union, WA branch. Mr Molina arrived in Australia in 1995 from his native Guatemala, Central America. A carpenter by trade, he worked as a trade unionist and a student activist in the 80s and 90s. He was elected as the Communist Party of Australia president at a meeting of the CPA

---

46   Victorian Parliament Speech, *Hansard*, 20 March 2003.
47   Victorian Parliament Speech, *Hansard*, 14 September 2005.

Central Committee in February 2009. Mr Molina has worked tirelessly in solidarity with Latin America and he currently holds the position of president of the Australia–Cuba Friendship Society, ACFS WA branch.[48]

Although a number of solidarity groups remain in close contact, there is no evidence of any other Latin Americans being involved with the Communist Party of Australia.

Political participation: The Latino community in the 21st century

Political participation of the Latin American community in Australia in the 21st century may be substantially different to that experienced by migrants in the 1970s and the 1980s. There is strong evidence that ethnic minorities have tended historically to align with the Labor Party. In her analysis of the Political Representation of Ethnic and Racial Minorities for the NSW Parliamentary Library Research Service, Karina Anthony expanded on this issue:

> A brief examination of federal electorates reveals an apparent link between high proportions of NESB constituents, and electorates held by the ALP. After the 1998 federal election, only one of the top twenty ethnic electorates was not held by the ALP. Two-thirds of all ethnic electorates were held by that party (Zappalá: 2006). Federal electorates with high NESB populations are concentrated in Sydney and Melbourne. Of thirty-two electorates with more than 20 per cent of the population born in non-English speaking countries, sixteen are located in Sydney, fourteen in Melbourne and two in Perth. In 2001, 28 of these were held by the ALP and only four by the Liberals. According to Jupp this 'political domination' has 'lasted for many years and embraces some of the ALP's safest electorates, including those of five of the party's seven leaders over the past forty years' (Jupp: 2003).[49]

This also raises questions as to whether people migrating under different programs exhibit different voting patterns. The Latin American migration wave of the last two decades arrived under the skilled migration program, which tends to attract a different kind of migrant population than the earlier political refugees. In general terms, people under the skilled migration program

---

48   See: 'Vinicio Molina', *Wikipedia*, http://en.wikipedia.org/wiki/Vinicio_Molina.
49   Anthony, *op. cit.*, note 24. For Zappalá and Jupp (cited by Anthony), see: Gianni Zappalá, 'The Political Representation of Ethnic Minorities: Moving Beyond the Mirror' in Marian Sawer and Gianni Zappalá (eds), *Speaking for the People: Representation in Australian Politics*, 2001, p. 156; James Jupp, *How Well Does Australian Democracy Serve Immigrant Australians?* Report No 1 for the Democratic Audit of Australia, Centre for Immigration and Multicultural Studies, The Australian National University, Canberra, 2003, n. 6, pp. 30–31.

moving to Australia are seeking better economic opportunities. Given their different ideologies and motivations to emigrate in comparison with the pre-1990s Latin American population, it is arguable that the new arrivals may tend to be more politically aligned to the Liberal rather than the Labor Party. Ada and Bernard Finifter found that 'new political learning is generally dependent upon previously established political attitudes. Nevertheless, migrants' political adaptation is also affected by the political context of the new residence'.[50] At best, the likelihood exists that a split now separates generations of Latin American migrants as followers of Liberal and Labor parties.

This snapshot of civic engagement reveals the variety of ways in which Latinos have been integrated into Australia society. While Latino migrants demonstrate above-average citizenship rates, they continue to display low levels of political participation nationally. To understand more fully the extent to which Latinos are integrated in Australian society we need to consider other indicators.

Education participation: English-language skills

A number of studies have concluded that immigrants fare worse in the labour market when their language skills are poor. Migrants tend to receive income below the earnings of comparable native-born workers. While researching the Spanish-speaking community in the USA in 2007, Chiswick and Miller explained that '[migrants' economic] disadvantages arise because of the less-than-perfect international transferability of immigrants' human capital, their lack of knowledge of the institutions of the US labor market, and perhaps through discrimination'.[51] Language is seen as one of the most important factors in the process of integration.

According to census figures, language is no longer an integration barrier for Latino communities in Australia. At least 80 per cent of the Latino community speak English either very well or satisfactorily. In the case of Mexico, 70 per cent of the census respondents declared that they have a very good command of English. It is interesting to note that despite above-average employment and income rates, only 47 per cent of Uruguayans speak English very well; Colombians also have the same low percentage of English-language facility.

---

50   Ada W. Finifter, and Bernard M. Finifter, 'Party Identification and Political Adaptation of American Migrants in Australia', *Journal of Politics*, Vol. 51 1989, (3), pp. 599–630.
51   Barry R. Chiswick, and Paul W. Miller, 'Modeling Immigrants' Language Skills', in B. R. Chiswick (ed.) *Immigration (Research in Labor Economics)*, Volume 27, 2007, pp. 75–128.

Table 7.9: Latin American people by country of birth/level of English-language proficiency

Level of English proficiency		El Salvador	Mexico	Argentina	Brazil	Chile	Colombia	Ecuador	Uruguay	Peru	Venezuela	Total
Absolute	Very well	4,723	1,872	5,959	7,335	10,358	4,643	806	3,637	3,705	1,799	45,036
	Well	2,547	668	2,743	3,617	7,440	4,076	482	2,629	2,587	944	27,791
	Not well	1,231	114	806	979	2,890	999	157	1,237	812	158	9,396
	Not at all	223	34	111	124	415	127	10	162	158	20	1,388
	Total	8,724	2,688	9,619	12,055	21,103	9,845	1,455	7,665	7,262	2,921	83,611
Relative	Very well	54%	70%	62%	61%	49%	47%	55%	47%	51%	62%	54%
	Well	29%	25%	29%	30%	35%	41%	33%	34%	36%	32%	33%
	Not well	14%	4%	8%	8%	14%	10%	11%	16%	11%	5%	11%
	Not at all	3%	1%	1%	1%	2%	1%	1%	2%	2%	1%	2%

Note: We exclude non-stated and non-applicable figures.

Source: ABS Census 2011, ABS. Information extracted using by the author using Table Builder Basic & Pro, 8-21 May 2013.

Educational participation: Level of qualifications

The OECD Report indicates that both the level of qualifications and the place where these qualifications were obtained are good indicators of integration. However, statistics relating to the Latino community in Australia cannot be compared to OECD figures because the contexts are substantially different. In most OECD countries migrants obtain their qualifications abroad. However, the first wave of Latinos has resided in Australia for more than 25 years, and during this time have either revalidated their qualifications or started anew. And having been drawn from the international student pool, the second wave of Latino migrants also have at least two years of studies in Australia as a minimum requirement to apply for residency. Australia has a strong share of the Latin American internationally mobile student market, which according to Calderón was:

> [two] per cent in 2009 (compared to 1.5 per cent in 2001). For Australia, the total value of trade in educational services with Latin American countries totalled A\$886 million in 2010, compared with A\$147 million in 2001. The Latin American student market represents five per cent of Australia's educational services exports.[52]

The comparison here is between the Latino communities and the national average, although simply comparing the education processes between the first and second wave Latino immigrants offers useful results. The qualifications of the first wave were hard-won and occurred over many years. Except for Salvadorians, which are lower, in 2011 the postgraduate rates of these Latino communities were equal to or better than the Australian national postgraduate average of three per cent. The Mexican postgraduate rate was 18 per cent, more than four times the Australian national average, and Venezuelans—13 per cent—and Colombians—12 per cent—more than three times.

In 2011, 23 per cent of Australians held a Bachelors degree or above, but migrants from Venezuela, Colombia, Peru, Brazil and Mexico had more than twice this percentage: the new Latino settlers are more qualified in the tertiary education sector not only over their Latino counterparts but also in relation to the rest of Australia. This gives the new Latino migrant wave a distinct educational advantage and as a consequence the prospect of a much faster pace of integration.

---

52 Angel Calderón, *Latin American Perspectives and Drivers for Tertiary Education Development: A PEST Analysis*, The Observatory on Borderless Higher Education, London, September 2012.

Table 7.10: Latin American people by country of birth and qualifications

	Skill level 1 Postgraduate degree level	Skill level 1 Graduate Diploma and Graduate Certificate level	Skill level 1 Bachelor degree level	Skill level 2 Advanced Diploma and Diploma level	Certificate level	Level of education inadequately described/ not stated/not applicable	Total
Australia	631,122	297,281	2,340,510	1,393,047	3,134,912	13,710,847	21,507,719
Argentina	638	233	2,035	1,309	2,111	5,659	11,985
Brazil	1,360	380	5,185	1,413	1,136	5,036	14,510
Chile	812	337	3,483	2,803	5,682	11,819	24,936
Colombia	1,354	263	4,041	1,116	952	3,591	11,317
Ecuador	88	28	274	208	301	842	1,741
El Salvador	220	114	1,554	1,190	1,967	4,607	9,652
Mexico	581	41	1,183	240	191	1,020	3,256
Uruguay	195	106	703	874	1,981	5,381	9,240
Venezuela	453	103	1,339	275	230	1,004	3,404
Peru	578	141	2,146	1,110	1,351	3,115	8,441
Spain	655	157	1,423	904	2,455	7,461	13,055
Australia	3%	1%	11%	6%	15%	64%	100%
Argentina	5%	2%	17%	11%	18%	47%	100%
Brazil	9%	3%	36%	10%	8%	35%	100%
Chile	3%	1%	14%	11%	23%	47%	100%

	Skill level 1 Postgraduate degree level	Skill level 1 Graduate Diploma and Graduate Certificate level	Skill level 1 Bachelor degree level	Skill level 2 Advanced Diploma and Diploma level	Certificate level	Level of education inadequately described/ not stated/not applicable	Total
Colombia	12%	2%	36%	10%	8%	32%	100%
Ecuador	5%	2%	16%	12%	17%	48%	100%
El Salvador	2%	1%	16%	12%	20%	48%	100%
Mexico	18%	1%	36%	7%	6%	31%	100%
Uruguay	2%	1%	8%	9%	21%	58%	100%
Venezuela	13%	3%	39%	8%	7%	29%	100%
Peru	7%	2%	25%	13%	16%	37%	100%
Total Latinos	**8%**	**2%**	**24%**	**10%**	**14%**	**41%**	**100%**
Spain	5%	1%	11%	7%	19%	57%	100%

Source: ABS Census 2011, ABS. Information extracted using by the author using Table Builder Basic & Pro, from 8–21 May 2013.

Turning now to other education and training qualifications, in 2011, 21 per cent of Australians in the age bracket 15–64 had Advanced Diploma, Diploma and Certificate-level qualifications. Comparisons here show that the older communities from Chile and El Salvador had 34 and 32 per cent—well above the national average. The new Latino communities of Brazil and Colombia had 18 per cent, three points below the national average. Mexico and Venezuela had percentages of technical education well below the Australian average, with 15 and 13 per cent respectively.

Table 7.11: Latin American people 15-64 years by country of birth and qualifications: Bachelors degree or above vs advanced diploma or below

Country	Bachelor degree or above	Country	Advance diploma or below
Argentina	24%	Argentina	29%
Brazil	48%	Brazil	18%
Chile	19%	Chile	34%
Colombia	50%	Colombia	18%
Ecuador	22%	Ecuador	29%
El Salvador	20%	El Salvador	33%
Mexico	55%	Mexico	13%
Uruguay	11%	Uruguay	31%
Venezuela	56%	Venezuela	15%
Peru	34%	Peru	29%
Spain	17%	Spain	26%

Source: ABS Census 2011, ABS. Information extracted by the author using Table Builder Basic & Pro, 8-21 May 2013.

Based on the above it is evident that both the old and new Latino communities are highly qualified, but in different sectors—the new communities in higher education and the most settled communities in the vocational education and technical training sector. So while both migration waves are well integrated based on educational outcomes, the newer ones were able to integrate much faster.

Economic participation: Labour force representation

This indicator is defined by the International Labour Organisation (ILO) as:

> a measure of the proportion of a country's working-age population that engages actively in the labour market, either by working or looking for work; it provides an indication of the relative size of the supply of labour available to engage in the production of goods and services.

The OECD Report found that 'In 2009–10, the average employment rate among immigrants across OECD countries was 64 per cent'.[53] The Australian workforce participation rate was 65 per cent in 2011.

Older Latino communities tend to have lower participation rates than newer ones as their members have retired, are receiving medical treatment, or include long-term unemployed members who have ceased looking for employment.

All the Latino communities except Spaniards and Uruguayans have labour force participation equal to or higher than the OECD rate in 2009–10 and the Australian average rate in 2011. These two communities had very low labour force rates of 51 and 58 per cent respectively that cannot be accounted for on demographic grounds alone. Further study is required.

Table 7.12: Latin American people by labour force participation

Country	Labour force participation rate
Australia	65.0%
Argentina	68.7%
Brazil	79.0%
Chile	65.0%
Colombia	79.8%
Ecuador	67.2%
El Salvador	71.2%
Mexico	73.9%
Uruguay	73.1%
Venezuela	79.8%
Peru	71.6%
Spain	51.1%

Source: ABS Census 2011, ABS. Information extracted by the author using Table Builder Basic & Pro, 8-21 May 2013.

Of the new Latino communities, Colombia and Venezuela were at the top of the ladder in workforce participation with almost 80 per cent, followed closely

---

53   OECD, *Settling In, op. cit.*, note 23, p. 90.

by Brazil at 79 per cent. These percentages compared well with the national participation rate of 65 per cent and are consistent with the age profile of both communities. Generally the degree of workforce participation within the Latino community is consistent with the national average, thus displaying a strong level of integration.

Economic participation: Unemployment rate

Analysis of this indicator shows that there is some room for improvement in integration. The OECD Report states: 'On average, the immigrant unemployment rate is about 1.5 times higher than that of the native-born—about 12 per cent compared with 8 per cent in 2009–10. In all OECD countries, with the exception of Hungary, the unemployment rate among immigrants is higher than that among the native-born'.[54] To indicate the level of integration using this criterion a comparison is required between the national unemployment rate in Australia and the unemployment rate among Latino communities and that reported by the OECD. In 2011 the unemployment rate in Australia was 5.6 per cent, and many of the first wave of Latino immigrants are commensurate with this rate, although Uruguay has a lower level of five per cent.

The overall Latino unemployment rate average in 2011 of just over seven per cent compares well to the unemployment rate in the Latino population in 1987 of more than ten per cent. Youth unemployment at that time in some Latino communities exceeded 18 per cent.[55]

However, the new Latino settlers from Mexico, Brazil, Venezuela, Ecuador and Peru have higher unemployment rates. Mexicans in particular, despite a high level of qualifications—55 per cent Bachelors degrees or above and 18 per cent postgraduates—have an unemployment rate of 9.7 per cent, 1.7 times higher than the national average. This percentage is also higher than the 1.5 times ratio reported by the OECD for the migrant population. Venezuela experienced an 8.7 per cent unemployment rate, 1.55 times higher than the Australian average. The remaining Latino communities had unemployment rates closer to the OECD benchmark. This is a clear sign that two of the new communities, Mexicans and Venezuelans, have problems adapting to the employment market.

---

54   OECD, *Settling In, op. cit.*, note 23, p. 98.
55   Victor Del Río, *Unemployment Amongst the Spanish-Speaking Youth*, Victorian Ethnic Affairs Commission and the Spanish Latin American Welfare Centre (CELAS), Melbourne.

Table 7.13: Latin America people in Australia: Unemployment rate

Job status	Employed	Unemployed	Total	Unemployment rate
Argentina	7,406	440	7,846	5.6%
Brazil	9,994	790	10,784	7.3%
Chile	14,550	1,002	15,552	6.4%
Colombia	7,929	583	8,512	6.8%
Ecuador	1,029	79	1,108	7.1%
El Salvador	6,237	469	6,706	7.0%
Mexico	1,952	209	2,161	9.7%
Peru	5,333	454	5,787	7.8%
Uruguay	4,879	257	5,136	5.0%
Venezuela	2,215	210	2,425	8.7%
Total Latinos	**61,524**	**4,493**	**66,017**	**7.2%**
Spain	5,861	358	6,219	5.8%
Total	**67,385**	**4,851**	**72,236**	**7.0%**

Source: ABS Census 2011, ABS. Information extracted by the author using Table Builder Basic & Pro, 8-21 May 2013.

Economic participation: Income

The OECD Report states that:

> In all OECD countries for which data are available, immigrant household median income is lower than native-born income and, in half of the countries, it represents less than 80 per cent of the native-born median income. Aside from Austria, mixed household median income is comparable with that of native-born households and is even substantially higher in the case of Australia, Norway, Portugal, Switzerland, the United Kingdom and the United States.[56]

In Australia information on household income by country of birth was not available in the 2011 Census, so individual income has been used here. The census information points towards serious challenges in this integration indicator for the new Latino communities, both in obtaining employment or a source of income. The national average for people with 'nil income' was six per cent, but Mexico has 14 per cent, and Brazil and Venezuela at 12 per cent are still double the national average. However, once in the labour market, the highly qualified members of these communities ultimately tend to secure well-paid jobs. For

---

56   OECD, *Settling In, op. cit.*, note 23, p. 55.

instance, while the national average of people with weekly incomes of $2,000 dollars and more was five per cent, the Venezuelan and Mexican communities in this category had ten per cent.

Table 7.14: Latin American people in Australia: Weekly income earners 2011

Weekly earnings	Nil to $599	$600 or more
Australia	51%	41%
Argentina	46%	36%
Brazil	42%	32%
Chile	49%	39%
Colombia	48%	38%
Ecuador	48%	38%
El Salvador	47%	37%
Mexico	43%	33%
Peru	46%	36%
Uruguay	54%	44%
Venezuela	40%	30%
Total Latinos	**46%**	**36%**
Spain	53%	43%

Source: ABS Census 2011, ABS. Information extracted by the author using Table Builder Basic & Pro, 8-21 May 2013.

The weekly income bracket occupied by the largest number of Australian income earners—nine per cent of the total—is the $400 to $499 range. Colombia had the highest representation in this bracket with 14 per cent, followed by Brazil at 13 per cent. The Spanish and the Uruguayan communities were consistent with the national figure.

Table 7.15: Latin America people by country of birth and income

	Negative income	Nil Income	$1-199 ($1-10,399)	$200-299 ($10,400-15,599)	$300-399 ($15,600-20,799)	$400-499 ($20,800-31,199)	$600-799 ($31,200-41,599)	$800-999 ($41,600-51,999)	$1,000-1,249 ($52,000-64,999)	$1,250-1,499 ($65,000-77,999)	$1,500-1,999 ($78,000-103,999)	$2,000 or more ($104,000 or more)	Total
Australia	102,113	1,314,281	1,285,556	179,356	1,715,819	2,006,076	1,799,650	1,436,397	1,372,002	959,619	1,120,842	1,081,279	2,1507,719
Argentina	65	791	628	1,478	1,197	1,367	1,261	1,021	992	732	861	873	11,988
Brazil	217	1,675	641	795	1,079	1,832	1,829	1,609	1,182	738	856	930	14,509
Chile	120	1,883	1,528	3,466	2,434	2,806	2,927	2,436	2,134	1,367	1,418	953	24,938
Colombia	129	1,174	665	912	1,139	1,583	1,382	1,029	828	601	559	464	11,318
Ecuador	13	174	128	206	166	165	215	152	138	87	94	65	1,740
El Salvador	44	600	604	1,289	861	1,195	1,419	144	909	493	446	230	9,652
Mexico	34	470	203	230	187	297	306	226	234	203	262	243	3,257
Peru	85	887	551	821	766	892	944	812	690	443	483	409	8,441
Uruguay	34	471	459	1,706	1,240	1,074	984	789	732	486	476	339	9,238
Venezuela	30	419	187	192	234	321	251	256	223	222	303	355	3,404
Spain	87	864	728	2,214	1,734	1,413	999	863	856	665	708	763	13,057
By percentage													
Australia	0%	6%	6%	8%	8%	9%	8%	7%	6%	4%	5%	5%	100%
Argentina	1%	7%	5%	12%	10%	11%	11%	9%	8%	6%	7%	7%	100%
Brazil	1%	12%	4%	5%	7%	13%	13%	11%	8%	5%	6%	6%	100%
Chile	0%	8%	6%	14%	10%	11%	12%	10%	9%	5%	6%	4%	100%
Colombia	1%	10%	6%	8%	10%	14%	12%	9%	7%	5%	5%	4%	100%
Ecuador	1%	10%	7%	12%	10%	9%	12%	9%	8%	5%	5%	4%	100%
El Salvador	0%	6%	6%	13%	9%	12%	15%	12%	9%	5%	5%	2%	100%
Mexico	1%	14%	6%	7%	9%	11%	9%	7%	7%	6%	8%	7%	100%
Peru	1%	11%	7%	10%	9%	9%	11%	10%	8%	5%	6%	5%	100%
Uruguay	0%	5%	5%	18%	13%	12%	11%	9%	8%	5%	5%	4%	100%
Venezuela	1%	12%	5%	6%	7%	9%	7%	8%	7%	7%	9%	10%	100%
Spain	1%	7%	6%	17%	13%	11%	8%	7%	7%	5%	5%	6%	100%

Source: ABS Census 2011, ABS. Information extracted by the author using Table Builder Basic & Pro, 8-21 May 2013.

Economic participation: Employment/qualifications

It is generally assumed that employment is strongly correlated to the level of qualifications. If this is the case, the new Latino communities have a clear advantage over the old ones. But in relation to employment status other variables (such as length of settlement), may be as or more important than the level of qualifications. We conducted an income/qualifications cross tabulation analysis to test this assumption.

In Australia only four per cent of people with postgraduate degrees were unemployed in 2011. Two of the old Latino communities with postgraduate qualifications were just below this unemployment rate: Argentina, at three per cent, and El Salvador—2.2 per cent. El Salvador's rate is surprising as it is a group which tends to have low numbers of postgraduate qualifications, low weekly earnings and high levels of unemployment. However, it appears that the few Salvadorians at the top of the qualification ladder have managed to insert themselves successfully into the Australian employment sector. Ecuador displayed the highest employment rate among its postgraduate members. However, this figure has to be taken with caution because the absolute number of postgraduate Ecuadorians is very low, at 75.

Venezuelans also have an employment challenge among their most qualified compatriots, with an unemployment rate of more than nine per cent. The postgraduate members of the Chilean community have adapted healthily to the employment market. People from El Salvador and Argentina, with postgraduate qualifications, are inserted into the job market on a better footing than those born in Australia.

Table 7.16: Latin America people cross tabulation: Top qualifications/employment status

Qualification status	Postgraduate degree level	Postgraduate degree level	Total	Postgraduate degree level	Postgraduate degree level	Total	Unemployment rate
Employment status	Employed full time	Employed part time	employed	Unemployed full time	Unemployed part time	unemployed	
Australia	**382,086**	**106,233**	**488,318**	**14,672**	**5,681**	**20,353**	**4.0%**
Mexico	352	100	452	27	4	31	6.4%
El Salvador	136	39	175	4	0	4	2.2%
Argentina	425	118	543	14	3	17	3.0%
Brazil	782	257	1,039	43	29	72	6.5%
Chile	476	147	623	24	13	37	5.6%
Colombia	812	286	1,098	44	24	68	5.8%
Ecuador	56	9	65	10	0	10	13.3%
Peru	393	83	476	21	12	33	6.5%
Uruguay	126	24	150	7	3	10	6.3%
Venezuela	284	74	358	27	9	36	9.1%
Spain	409	105	514	20	19	39	7.1%
Total	4,251	1,242	5,493	241	116	357	6.1%

Note: In these figures we exclude away from work figures.

Source: ABS Census 2011, ABS. Information extracted by the author using Table Builder Basic & Pro, 8–21May 2013.

Economic participation: Employment by industry

The 2011 Census paints a clear picture of the industries in which most Latinos are employed. It seems that each community targets specific industries. For instance, Mexicans and Venezuelans are over-represented in the professional, scientific and technical services industries, with 16 per cent each, in relation to a national average of seven per cent.

At 14 per cent of people working in the manufacturing sector, Chileans have a much higher percentage than the national average of nine per cent. Brazil is high in the accommodation and food services industry with 16 per cent, more than double the national average of seven per cent. Mexico and Colombia with 13 per cent are also considerably higher than the national average for the hospitality industry.

Fully 21 per cent of people from El Salvador work in the health care and social assistance industries, which is nine per cent more than the national 12 per cent average. The Chilean and Peruvian communities also both register a high proportion of their workforce in these industries—17 per cent.

On the other hand, there are industries in which Latino workforce participation is minimal in relation to the rest of the Australian population. Among these are agriculture, forestry and fishing; mining; electricity, gas, water and waste services, as well as information media and telecommunications, rental, hiring and real estate services, arts and recreation services.

Table 7.17: Latin American people by country of birth and industry

	Agriculture, fisheries, forestry	Mining	Manufacturing	Electricity, gas, water and waste services	Construction	Wholesale trade	Retail trade	Accommodation and food services	Transport, postal and warehousing	Information, media and telecommunications	Financial and insurance services	Rental, hiring and real estate services
Australia	249,827	176,560	902,892	115,609	828,910	403,801	1,057,309	650,397	479,182	377,352	178,190	158,853
Argentina	47	56	821	57	615	316	515	292	393	156	324	94
Brazil	68	194	1,069	48	561	392	722	1,566	323	184	289	108
Chile	42	146	1,935	114	1,116	538	861	668	865	270	493	167
Colombia	36	94	536	62	417	254	458	1,010	234	147	257	76
Ecuador	6	6	113	6	45	28	71	62	67	26	47	10
El Salvador	29	44	758	48	312	229	426	280	327	91	236	67
Mexico	15	25	168	14	66	97	150	252	42	59	81	25
Peru	16	80	536	45	280	190	344	376	215	87	259	46
Uruguay	11	15	594	44	436	204	286	176	398	90	187	61
Venezuela	8	89	200	26	104	99	153	206	63	81	88	30
Spain	69	81	673	80	584	236	429	320	241	90	212	90
Australia	3%	2%	9%	1%	8%	4%	11%	7%	5%	4%	2%	2%
Argentina	1%	1%	11%	1%	8%	4%	7%	4%	5%	2%	4%	1%
Brazil	1%	2%	11%	0%	6%	4%	7%	16%	3%	2%	3%	1%
Chile	0%	1%	14%	1%	8%	4%	6%	5%	6%	2%	3%	1%
Colombia	0%	1%	7%	1%	5%	3%	6%	13%	3%	2%	3%	1%
Ecuador	1%	1%	11%	1%	5%	3%	7%	6%	7%	3%	5%	1%
El Salvador	0%	1%	12%	1%	5%	4%	7%	5%	5%	1%	4%	1%
Mexico	1%	1%	9%	1%	3%	5%	8%	13%	2%	3%	4%	1%
Peru	0%	2%	10%	1%	5%	4%	7%	7%	4%	2%	5%	1%
Uruguay	0%	0%	13%	1%	9%	4%	6%	4%	8%	2%	4%	1%
Venezuela	0%	4%	9%	1%	5%	5%	7%	9%	3%	4%	4%	1%
Spain	1%	1%	12%	1%	10%	4%	8%	6%	4%	2%	4%	2%

Source: ABS Census 2011, ABS. Information extracted by the author using Table Builder Basic & Pro, 8-21 May 2013.

Economic participation: Employment by occupation

As stated earlier, the Latino communities tend to concentrate in specific occupational areas. Venezuela and Mexico are more represented in the professional category and they have 38 and 36 per cent respectively in relation to the national average in this occupation category of 22 per cent. Chile is also well represented with 17 per cent in the technicians and trade workers category in relation to the 14 per cent rate nationwide. Sixteen per cent of Brazilians worked in community and personal services, as compared with ten per cent in the overall Australian population.

Uruguayans, with ten per cent, have a strong presence as machine operators and drivers, compared to seven per cent nationwide. Colombians have a substantial presence as labourers, with 25 per cent compared to nine per cent in the rest of the country's working population. Conversely, people from El Salvador, with six per cent, are under-represented as managers compared to 13 per cent Australia-wide. Mexico and Venezuela are also under-represented in the technicians and trades workers category, with eight per cent compared to 14 per cent for the rest of Australia.

This data again indicates that settlement groups tend to prefer specific occupations, possibly as a result of their networks, and again indicating a strong ability to integrate.

Table 7.18: Latin American people by country of birth and occupation

	Managers	Professionals	Technicians and trades workers	Community and personal services workers	Clerical and administrative workers	Sales workers	Machinery operators and drivers	Labourers	Total
Australia	1,293,970	2,145,441	1,425,146	971,898	1,483,559	942,140	659,550	947,607	9,978,463
Argentina	884	1,955	1,042	710	1,085	442	386	768	7,368
Brazil	996	2,424	1,051	1,571	1,084	584	344	1,771	9,899
Chile	1,228	2,736	2,405	1,814	1,972	722	1,251	2,104	14,410
Colombia	610	1,779	818	1,139	831	415	233	2,004	7,882
Ecuador	69	203	113	116	171	64	81	185	1,021
El Salvador	342	1,141	852	889	858	353	503	1,171	6,195
Mexico	256	698	163	248	270	135	35	119	1,947
Peru	409	1,218	680	702	802	277	253	889	5,275
Uruguay	504	794	743	483	779	278	495	690	4,831
Venezuela	254	836	186	242	260	145	62	199	2,204
Spain	765	1,403	942	536	840	394	304	518	5,793
Australia	13%	22%	14%	10%	15%	9%	7%	9%	100%
Argentina	12%	27%	14%	10%	15%	6%	5%	10%	100%
Brazil	10%	24%	11%	16%	11%	6%	3%	18%	100%
Chile	9%	19%	17%	13%	14%	5%	9%	15%	100%
Colombia	8%	23%	10%	14%	11%	5%	3%	25%	100%
Ecuador	7%	20%	11%	11%	17%	6%	8%	18%	100%
El Salvador	6%	18%	14%	14%	14%	6%	8%	19%	100%
Mexico	13%	36%	8%	13%	14%	7%	2%	6%	100%
Peru	8%	23%	13%	13%	15%	5%	5%	17%	100%
Uruguay	10%	16%	15%	10%	16%	6%	10%	14%	100%
Venezuela	12%	38%	8%	11%	12%	7%	3%	9%	100%
Spain	13%	24%	16%	9%	15%	7%	5%	9%	100%

Note: We exclude from this table the inadequately described column.

Source: ABS Census 2011, ABS. Information extracted by the author using Table Builder Basic & Pro, 8–21 May 2013.

Social participation: Need for assistance

The OECD does not regard the need for assistance as an indicator of social participation and therefore a factor towards integration. However, it can be argued that the 'need for assistance' imposes a great burden on society generally. The affected members would tend to focus on solving their individual problems rather than focusing outwards.

The 2011 Census offers a useful snapshot of the communities' need for assistance. Included in this category are older people, and people with disabilities or who are disabled for health reasons. In Australia, five per cent of the population comprised this category in 2011. Spain had the highest rate with ten per cent, which is double the national average, closely followed by Uruguay, with eight per cent. The new Latino communities of Mexico, Brazil, Colombia and Venezuela had the lowest need for assistance with a rate of just one per cent.

Table 7.19: Latin American people by country of birth and needs for assistance

	Has need for assistance	%	Does not have need for assistance	%	Not stated	Total
Australia	998,602	5	19,287,677	90	1,221,440	21,507,719
Argentina	577	5	11,252	94	158	11,987
Brazil	162	1	14,153	98	194	14,509
Chile	1,349	5	23,219	93	370	24,938
Colombia	158	1	11,002	97	158	11,318
Ecuador	78	4	1,635	94	27	1,740
El Salvador	495	5	9,022	93	134	9,651
Mexico	41	1	3,170	97	46	3,257
Peru	277	3	8,044	95	120	8,441
Uruguay	778	8	8,296	90	163	9,237
Venezuela	33	1	3,343	98	29	3,405
Total Latinos	3,948	4	93,136	95	1,399	98,483
Spain	1,247	10	11,563	89	245	13,055
Total	9,143	4	197,835	94	3,043	210,021

Source: ABS Census 2011, ABS. Information extracted by the author using Table Builder Basic & Pro, 8-21 May 2013.

This data is consistent with the argument that the new Latino communities have fewer barriers to integration, as their need for assistance is minimal—one per cent or less—in comparison to the national average of five per cent.

Conclusion

Analysis of relevant data reveals that Latin American communities have settled successfully in Australia compared to other OECD countries; and compared to other ethnic immigrant groups and the national Australian average.

For the more established arrivals in the Latino community, the changed political and economic circumstances in their respective countries of origin encouraged them to refocus their attention on Australia. As a result some of them have participated more actively in the political, economic and academic life of their new country. Their members shifted their position, from being outward-looking communities in the 1970s and 1980s, to becoming inward-looking from the mid-1990s onwards.

For the new Latino communities the process of settlement in Australia has been faster than that of the earlier wave, largely because they possess a sound command of English and strong qualifications on arrival, which they have expanded with local education.

Most of the indicators analysed describe a Latino community that is comfortable with itself and which has achieved a high level of integration (see Table 7.22). Out of 12 integration indicators, the Latino community rated high in five, medium in four, low in two and very low in one, namely political participation. For both the old and the new Latino migrants, integration into the economic and educational sectors of Australia is on the right track.

A sense of permanency: The old and new Latino migrants have a clear purpose and the relevant skills to settle in Australia permanently. Factors that inhibited integration in the past have been left behind, including nationalism, detachment from the new country, lack of English proficiency, low levels of education, transplantation from rural to urban regions, and full and exclusive political commitment to their own countries of origin.

A high level of language skills and qualifications acquired locally: The old and new Latino settlers have high levels of vocational and educational qualifications, most of which were acquired in Australian tertiary institutions or vocational education and training institutes; hence, their contribution to Australia has been substantial and immediate.

In the ladder of the integration process, political participation and policy-making participation are at the top. In these areas Uruguayans have excelled, but other Latino communities are lagging behind. The Latino community needs more political representatives, and increased involvement in political parties and non-governmental organisations.

Table 7.20: Summary of integration indicators

No.	Dimension	OECD indicator	Other international indicator / reference	Indicator in relation to Australia	Latino community average	Evaluation	Comment
1.	**Civic engagement**						
	Citizenship	48%	N/A	85%	84%	High integration	Comparative purpose only (Minor differences in definition)
	Volunteer work	N/A	Low volunteer participation in Latin American countries	19%	13%	Low integration	
	Political participation	N/A	Representation in Australian parliaments	12%	0.12%	Very low integration	Based on the population size, the Latino communities should have 0.49% of parliamentary representation. Equivalent to four parliamentarians.
2.	**Education**						
	English-language skills	N/A	N/A	97%	87%	High integration	
	Level of qualification						
	Bachelor degree or above	N/A	N/A	15%	34%	High integration	
	Advanced diploma or below	N/A	N/A	21%	24%	High integration	
3.	**Economic**						
	Labour force participation	64%	N/A	65%	72%	High integration	
	Unemployment rate	N/A (generally 1.5 times higher than OECD rate)	N/A	5.6%	7.2%	Medium integration	Latino unemployment rate is 1.3 times over the the Australian average.
	Income						
	Nil - $599 per week	N/A		51%	46%	Medium integration	
	$600 or more per week	N/A (but generally is 80% of the native born median income)	N/A	41%	36%	Medium integration	It is 8% below the OECD median income expectation of 80% if earnings.
	Economic / Education						
	Unemployment for people with postgraduate qualifications	N/A (generally 1.5 times higher than OECD rate)	N/A	4%	6.5%	Low integration	Latino unemployment rate is 1.3 times over the the Australian average.
4.	**Social**						
	Needs for assistance	N/A	N/A	5%	4%	Medium integration	Less need for support.

Source: ABS Census 2011, ABS. Information extracted by the author using Table Builder Basic & Pro, 8-21 May 2013.

The lack of networks and targeted employment programs by government or business initiatives may also be a factor slowing the speed with which new waves of Latinos are joining the labour market.

The section below identifies a number of opportunities that would reduce the political and economic integration gaps in the quest to hasten the integration process, so that Latino communities can fully contribute their skills and experience to help build a stronger Australia.

Opportunities

There is a clear opportunity to increase engagement in political, economic and academic matters, policy implementation and institutional and capacity building, in order to reposition and integrate Latinos into Australian society in areas such as:

Developing strategic partnerships between Australia and the Latino community: There is a wealth of experience and human and intellectual capital among the Latino communities. This wealth of knowledge and experience could be used by government and the private sector in Australia to enhance the economic and social relationships with the wider Spanish-speaking world.

Policy-making: The Latino communities can play a vital role in the formulation and implementation of policies and the development of strategic papers aimed at improving the political, economic and educational relationships with Latin America. For instance, Uruguayan-born Telmo Languiller and Argentine-born Alexis Esposto were two of the main drivers behind the strategy paper 'Latin America in Victoria: a vision for growing trade, investment and cultural links', launched in October 2010.[57] More can be done.

Institutional and capacity building: In Australia we have a number of institutions which are actively engaged with Latin America, for example the Council on Australia Latin America Relations (COALAR), and Austrade. There is a clear opportunity to strengthen these organisations by:

1. including representatives of the Latino communities;

2. replicating these organisations at state level, in particular in those states where most of the Latino communities are located (NSW, Victoria and Queensland);

3. linking representatives of the Latino communities with academic and research institutions.

---

57 Minister for Industry and Trade, 'Victoria to tap into Latin American Opportunities', Australia–Latin America Business Council (ALABC), 1 November 2010.

Institutional services delivery: There are opportunities to increase the participation of the Latino community in the delivery of key services. For example, during the Royal Melbourne Institute of Technology (RMIT) First Ibero-American Network Event held on 9 May 2013, Roger Frankel, the Honorary Consul of Brazil in Victoria—and former Australian Ambassador to Venezuela, Colombia, Ecuador and the Dominican Republic—suggested scrapping the English-language skills requirement for receiving an Australian student visa. This novel idea could provide new impetus to the educational sector by increasing demand for the provision of English-language courses and the delivery of training in languages other than English in Australia. It could also promote the learning of second languages in the country. The Latino communities could play a strategic role in such an educational enterprise.

The strategic need to speed our mutual understanding: The speed of settlement of Latinos into Australia can also be assisted by increasing the knowledge and understanding of Latin Americans about Australia, and of Australians about Latin America. For instance, Australia has strategic interest in its relationship with the United States. The influence of the Spanish-speaking communities in that country is growing rapidly, and may have an impact on future government priorities. Australia has the opportunity to develop its understanding of the Latin American people by looking at the aspirations and motivations of the Latino communities in Australia: it is a local window of opportunity.

There are other things that could improve this understanding. Even now, in the 21st century, Latin American-born immigrants have to fill an out-dated immigration form that geographically defines South America as any country south of the US border—although this error is understood by the immigration authorities, they are reluctant to correct it for economic and statistical reasons. The Australian Bureau of Statistics (ABS) classifies Mexico as part of Central America instead of North America. There is also a measure of diplomatic insensitivity: for instance, the ABS identifies the controversial islands off the coast of Argentina as the 'Falklands Islands' instead of 'Las Malvinas'. Given that the UN considers the sovereignty of the islands an unresolved issue and demands dialogue between the UK and Argentina to resolve this dispute, Australia should take the diplomatic stance of referring to these islands as the Falklands/Malvinas Islands.

Promoting the teaching of the Spanish and Portuguese languages: Teaching of these languages would encourage mutual understanding, and increase economic and educational exchanges. The Latino community is qualified to support this endeavour.

Development of local networks: As the above analysis shows, the key to making sure there is faster integration into Australian society is to develop networks and increase the understanding of Latin America by Australian-born people. For instance:

Business networks: by establishing Australia–Latino networks through national and country-specific Chambers of Commerce such as the Australian Latin American Business Council (ALABC) and the Mexican–Australian Chamber of Commerce. These chambers allow cross-fertilisation between Australian-born and Latino people. For instance, the current President of the Mexican–Australian Chamber of Commerce is Victor Perton, a former Australian parliamentarian and Victorian Commissioner to the Americas. A person like Victor brings a wealth of knowledge and strong local networks to the Mexican business world in Australia.

Academic networks: It is paramount to support research networks such as the Association of Iberian and Latin American Studies of Australasia (AILASA), the Institute of Latin American Studies (ILAS) at La Trobe University, the Australian National Centre for Latin American Studies (ANCLAS) at The Australian National University, the Sydney University Research Community for Latin America (SURCLA), and the recently formed Ibero-American Network at the Royal Melbourne Institute of Technology (RMIT), among others.

Promoting regional and country to country workshops, such as the University of Melbourne's Australia–Latin American Dialogue that took place in August 2012 and the Bi-National Workshop Australia—Argentina that took place from 8–10 May 2013 in Bahia Blanca and brought together Australian representatives from the universities of New England, Melbourne, La Trobe, Swinburne, Sydney, and the CSIRO, and Argentinean universities such as Quilmes, Nacional del Sur and Bahia Blanca.

Women's Networks, such as the *Colectivo Mujer* in Sydney, a group of Latinas who strongly identify with Latin American cultures as well as contribute to feminism in their community and Australia generally.

Researcher to researcher networks: Researchers in Australia have developed their own field-specific networks. It is important to learn about these enterprises and, whenever possible, build upon them. A good example is the Chilean-born Professor Rodrigo Marino (Melbourne University) and the Argentine-born Alex Esposto, who are building strong research networks between the University of Melbourne, Swinburne Institute of Technology and Chilean and Argentinean educational institutions.

Student networks: One of the strongest student networks in Australia is the one developed by Zoe Dauth at Melbourne University. It offers an effective model for future inter-university student networks. Students' participation in university affairs is a recognised stepping-stone in the path towards political participation.

Social media networks: Linkedin and Facebook and specific interest blogs could assist to connect both the early and new Latino settlers in order to further their chances of gaining employment. This is already occurring in the case of *Mexbourne*, a Yahoo group created by Mexican IT Engineer Pedro Chan; and by MexVic, the Mexican community association in Victoria.

These networks alert their members to new employment opportunities. Even informal groupings, such as the one I belong to—'El Sindicato': formed by people from seven different nationalities and who have met every week for the last 25 years—can provide invaluable support for research activities.

Developing professional profiles: Many migrants have occupied high professional and executive positions in their own countries of origin. It would be in the interest of the wider Australian community to collect information concerning the working experience gained by Latinos while living in their own countries of origin. This information will help identify more precise ways to capitalise on this expertise from a policy-making and implementation perspective.

Establishing links with employment organisations: On the one hand, there is a clear need in Australia for highly qualified people, as demonstrated by the 83,840 people working with temporary 457 visas as at 31 December 2012. None of the top 15 countries sourcing the 457 Visa are from Latin American countries. Out of the 33,720 holders of 457 visas in 2011–12, 83 per cent were classified as having Skill 1 and 2 levels. Interestingly enough, the skill levels required by Australian employers match those from the Latino community. There is an opportunity to explore further the extent to which some of the 1,636 unemployed Latinos with skill level 1—post-graduate qualifications and Bachelors degrees—could fill part of this employment gap, thereby reducing the number of workers having to be sourced from elsewhere.

Self employment: It would be desirable to have assistance programs linking new migrants in general, and the Latino community in particular, to micro-financing and self-employment opportunities. The profile of the new Latino communities indicates a strong inclination to start self-employment businesses. Therefore, there is an opportunity to create information channels to facilitate the creation of businesses and access to capital. For example, there are successful stories of microfinance programs initiated by NAB and Westpac, which are targeting this new wave of business immigrants. The government could improve access to world's best practice self-employment programs such as the New Enterprise Incentive Scheme (NEIS), which assists unemployed people. It is pertinent to note that the current President of NEIS is Ariel Moses, who was born in Chile.

Mentoring economic and political participation: The old Latino communities could play a mentoring role for the new ones. The oldest settlers, represented by Uruguay and Spain, have already adjusted. Uruguay, in particular, can be singled out as the Latino community which has integrated most fully. The unemployment rate of members of this community is lower than their Latino counterparts and that of the rest of the country, and they earn the highest weekly income average. It also has strong political engagement.

Although members of the new communities also hold the advantage of being better qualified to fill highly skilled jobs, they lack cultural and political skills to participate actively in the Australian political system; in this regard there would be value in connecting the established Latino community with emerging immigrant groups.

English proficiency: The new and younger Latino communities represented by Brazil, Colombia, Venezuela, Peru and Mexico with high levels of English proficiency could become 'language and cultural' ambassadors between Australian and Latin American businesses and, one day, expand the offer of educational services in Australia by providing courses in the Spanish and Portuguese languages.

These communities are growing most quickly, and at current trends will be paramount on the Latino population ladder, sooner rather than later.

Conclusion

This analysis provides the evidence to affirm that both the first- and second-wave Latino communities are generally well integrated into Australian society but still have more to offer. They each have advantages and disadvantages that can be worked with to build stronger communities, which contribute more fully to the wider Australian society. The first-wave communities are savvy, with strong networks, and the second-wave communities are smart, with strong qualifications. Working together and with the right government policies these groups can help to develop a stronger Australia internally, but also to develop stronger external ties with the growing economic powerhouses of the Latin American region.

This is a side of the multicultural agenda that has not been fully explored. All the pieces of the puzzle are now on the table: it is time to bring them together so that Latinos can contribute to Australia's bigger picture.

References

ABC Radio National, 'Tortured Questions', *Background Briefing*, 26 May 1996, http://www.abc.net.au/rn/.

backgroundbriefing/stories/1996/10766.htm, accessed 14 October 2011.

Age, 'Priest at home with Melbourne's migrants', *The Age*, Obituaries, 13 January, 2005, First Edition, Business Section Page 7. [no locatable reference].

Anthony, Karina, 'The Political Representation of Ethnic and Racial Minorities', Briefing Paper 3/06, *NSW Parliamentary Library Research Service*, 2006.

Argus, 'Classified Advertising', Melbourne, Victoria: 1848–1956, 21 August 1916, p. 1, http://nla.gov.au/nla.news-article1591391, accessed 27 September 2011.

Baldovino, Carlos, interview, 9 December 2010.

Bernie Banton Foundation, http://www.berniebanton.com.au/, accessed 2 November 2013.

Calderón, Angel, 'Latin America tertiary education as an emerging system—Australia's future market', paper delivered at Melbourne–Latin America Dialogue, The University of Melbourne, August 2012.

————, *Latin American Perspectives and Drivers for Tertiary Education Development: A PEST Analysis*, The Observatory on Borderless Higher Education, London, 2012.

Charities Aid Foundation (CAF), *World Giving Index 2011: A Global View of Giving Trends*, https://www.cafonline.org/pdf/world_giving_index_2011_191211.pdf, accessed 2 November 2013.

Chiswick, Barry R., and Paul W. Miller, 'Modeling Immigrants' Language Skills', in Barry R. Chiswick (ed.) *Immigration (Research in Labor Economics)*, Volume 27, 2007, pp. 75–128. DOI: 10.1016/S0147-9121(07)00003-9.

Del Río, Victor, *Unemployment Amongst the Spanish-Speaking Youth*, Victorian Ethnic Affairs Commission and the Spanish Latin American Welfare Centre (CELAS), Melbourne, 1987.

Department of Immigration and Citizenship (Economic Analysis Unit, Chief Economist), 'Population flows Immigration aspects 2009–2010 edition', Australian Government, Canberra, 2010.

Department of Immigration and Citizenship, *National Agenda for a Multicultural Australia*, http://www.immi.gov.au/media/publications/multicultural/agenda/agenda89/issues.html. [This is not accessible online.]

Department of Immigration and Citizenship, *Settlement Outcomes of New Arrivals: Report of Findings*, Policy Innovation, Research and Evaluation Unit, Department of Immigration and Citizenship, April 2011, http://www.immi.gov.au/media/publications/research/_pdf/settlement-outcomes-new-arrivals.pdf, accessed 2 November 2013.

Department of Immigration and Ethnic Affairs, 'Review '81, Canberra', Parliament of Australia, Parliament Library, 1981, accessed 16 June 2010.

——————, 'Review '82, Canberra', Parliament of Australia, Parliament Library, 1982, accessed 16 June 2010.

——————, 'Review '83, Canberra', Parliament of Australia, Parliament Library, 1983, accessed 16 June 2010.

——————, 'Review '85, Canberra', Parliament of Australia, Parliament Library, 1985, accessed 16 June 2010.

Finifter, Ada W., and Bernard M., Finifter, 'Party Identification and Political Adaptation of American Migrants in Australia', *Journal of Politics*, Vol. 51, 1989, (3), pp. 599–630.

Jupp, James (ed.), *The Australian People: An Encyclopedia of the Nation, Its People and Their Origins*, Cambridge University Press, 2nd edn, Cambridge, 2001.

——————, *How Well Does Australian Democracy Serve Immigrant Australians?* Report No 1 for the Democratic Audit of Australia, Centre for Immigration and Multicultural Studies, The Australian National University, Canberra, 2003.

Languiller, Telmo, interview, 25 April 2010.

López, Rafaela, interview, 14 May 2010.

López, Rafaela, *Orígenes. Influencia y contribución de origen español y latino Americano en Victoria, 1901–2001* (*The presence and contribution of Victorians of Spanish and Latin American origins, 1901–2001*). Australia: CELAS, The Spanish Latin American Welfare Centre, 2002. ISBN: 0-9579773-0-1.

Migrant Workers' Centres in multiculturalism, 18 February 2009. Source: not available. Format: mov (Quicktime); File size: 14.9 MB. Length: 05min 43sec. [Not locatable with this reference.]

Minister for Immigration and Multicultural Affairs, *Media Release*, MPS27/96, 3 July 1996, http://www.aph.gov.au/library/pubs/online/refugees, accessed 16 October 2011.

Minister for Immigration and Multicultural Affairs, *Media Release*, MPS70/96, 30 October 1996, http://www.aph.gov.au/library/pubs/online/refugees, accessed 16 October 2011.

Minister for Immigration, Local Government and Ethnic Affairs, *Media Release*, MPS 41/92, 24 July 1992, http://www.aph.gov.au/library/pubs/online/ refugees, accessed 16 October 2011.

Minister for Industry and Trade, 'Victoria to tap into Latin American Opportunities', Australia–Latin America Business Council (ALABC), 1 November 2010, http://www.alabc.com.au/News/tabid/1965/ID/516/ Victoria-to-tap-into-Latin-American-Opportunities.aspx, accessed 2 November 2013.

Nationality Act, ('New Law published in the Official Journal of the Federation on January 23, 1998'), Ley de Nacionalidad Cámara de Diputados del H. Congreso de la Unión, Secretaría General, Secretaría de Servicios Parlamentarios, Dirección General de Bibliotecas, 20 March 1998. http:// www.yucatan.gob.mx/gobierno/orden_juridico/Federal/Leyes/nr215rf1. pdf, accessed 2 November 2013.

New South Wales Election Results 1856–2007 (as at 5 July 2007), 'NSW Elections: Camden – 1999', http://www.parliament.nsw.gov.au/resources/ nswelectionsanalysis/1999/Camden.htm, accessed 2 November 2013.

New South Wales Election Results 1856–2007 (as at 5 July 2007), 'NSW Elections: Smithfield – 2003', http://www.parliament.nsw.gov.au/resources/ nswelectionsanalysis/2003/Smithfield.htm, accessed 2 November 2013.

OECD (Organisation for Economic Co-operation and Development), *Settling In: OECD Indicators of Immigrant Integration 2012 Report*, OECD Publishing. http://dx.doi.org/10.1787/9789264171534-en, accessed 2 November 2013.

Piperno, Cesar, interview, 16 June 2010.

Sydney Herald, (NSW: 1831—1842) Article, 'Legislative Council', Friday 6 July 1838, pp. 2–3, *Trove: digitised newspapers and more*, http://trove.nla.gov.au/ newspaper/... ["Fryre"], accessed 15 October 2011.

Sydney Herald, (NSW: 1831—1842) Article, 'Shipping Intelligence. Arrival', 3 July 1837, p. 2, *Trove: digitised newspapers and more,* http://trove.nla.gov.au/ndp/del/article... ["Fryre"], accessed 15 October 2011.

UNHCR (United Nations High Commissioner for Refugees), *The State of the World's Refugees, 1997–1998*, Oxford University Press, 1997, accessed 16 June 2003 Parliament of Australia, Parliament Library.

Victorian Electoral Commission, 'State Election 1999: Eumemmerring Province', https://www.vec.vic.gov.au/.

Results/state1999resultEumemmerringProvince.html, accessed 2 November 2013.

Victorian Parliament Speech, *Hansard,* 20 March 2003.

Victorian Parliament Speech, *Hansard*, 14 September 2005.

Victorian Trades Hall Council. Archives at the University of Melbourne, 101/27, 1976–91, 13 Arki Boxes www.lib.unimelb.edu.au/collections/archives/collections/, accessed 2 November 2013.

'Vinicio Molina', *Wikipedia*, http://en.wikipedia.org/wiki/Vinicio_Molina, accessed 2 November 2013.

York, Barry, 'Australia and Refugees, 1901–2002: An Annotated Chronology Based on Official Sources', *Social Policy Group*, Department of Immigration and Ethnic Affairs, Review 1990, Canberra, 1990, accessed 16 June 2003, Parliament of Australia, Parliament Library.

Zappalá, Gianni, 'The Political Representation of Ethnic Minorities: Moving Beyond the Mirror', in Marian Sawer and Gianni Zappalá (eds), *Speaking for the People: Representation in Australian Politics*, Melbourne University Press, 2001.

8. Print and Electronic Media

John Sinclair

Introduction

This chapter provides an overview of the contrasting structure of the media industries in Australia and Latin America, and outlines some of the technological and corporate trends associated with globalisation. In Australia, there is a small commercial market of print and electronic media for people of Latin American origin, but this has inherent limitations, the advantages endowed by a common language, on one hand, being offset by the internal diversity of national and other kinds of difference on the other. In such circumstances, government plays a benign and supportive role as both a broadcaster and an advertiser. There is also a grass-roots community sector. By contrast, the media in Latin America have developed on a mass commercial basis, and have had to continually negotiate their relative independence from governments always anxious to circumscribe media influence.

Thus, compared to Latin American countries, the media environment in Australia is quite distinctive, particularly as regards the electronic media. Ever since the days of radio, Latin American broadcasting developed for the most part on the commercial model first established in the United States; that is, where broadcasters seek to attract audiences which advertisers will pay to gain access to, either by sponsoring programs or buying time spots. Commercial broadcasting was also established in Australia, but given the nation's British colonial origins, this occurred in conjunction with public broadcasting institutions largely based on the British Broadcasting Corporation (BBC) model, with an Australian Broadcasting Corporation (ABC) responsible for fostering national culture at 'arm's length' from government.

In the more recent decades during which Latin American immigrants have been arriving in Australia, the Special Broadcasting Service (SBS) has been institutionalised by government to meet the needs of a multicultural society, with a vibrant community television and radio sector growing alongside which gives linguistic and ethnic minorities direct access to the airwaves. This chapter will first present a broad comparison of the structure of the commercial media industries in Australia and Latin America, and note some global trends. An outline and analysis of the limitations of the commercial market for print and electronic media for people of Latin American origin in Australia then follows, and finally, the whole range of media available to these people will be described and discussed.

The commercial media industries in Australia and Latin America

There are certain similarities to be found in comparing the commercial media industries in Australia and Latin America. A common factor is that the print and electronic media have been allowed to become concentrated in their ownership, mainly under the control of a few oligarchical families. In Australia, around two-thirds of the daily press is published by News Corporation, the publishing division of the global Murdoch-owned Twenty-first Century Fox Group.[1] Although international private equity capital investment has become significant in recent years, the traditional media scenario in Australia is very much the legacy of generations of Murdochs, other major families being the Packers and the Fairfaxes. To mention the most significant Latin American cases, in Brazil the two major media groups, Globo and Abril, are run today by scions of the Marinho and Civita families respectively—the grandsons of the founders—while similarly, media development in Mexico has been driven by Televisa, with successive heads of the Azcárraga family at the helm. On both sides of the Pacific, these are companies which are accustomed to dominance over their traditional print and broadcast media markets, relatively unperturbed by domestic competitors or threatened by government regulation.

However, the simultaneous intensification of globalisation and the advent of new forms of media communication in the last two decades have challenged the complacent arrangements of the preceding 'golden age' of mass media. Beginning in the 1980s, the advent of television channels distributed over international satellite-to-cable services set the stage for a new global order. Just as international news services from CNN and the BBC then became ubiquitous in the English-speaking world, so were Latin American domestic television markets opened up to CNN en Español from the US, and TVE Internacional from Spain. Several other US-based and some European channels followed, although with the next technological stage of direct-to-home satellite services, the leading entrepreneurs in Brazil and Mexico were successful in establishing partnerships with the US-based owner, DirecTV. For their part, other major

---

1   David McKnight, *Rupert Murdoch: An Investigation of Political Power*, 2012, p. 7; Nick Tabakoff, 'Historic shift for News as it returns to publishing roots', *The Australian*, 5 December 2012, p. 19.

global media corporations such as News and Time Warner have long recognised the dominance which the Globo and Televisa groups enjoy in their home markets, and have at certain stages been in joint ventures with them.[2]

In the era of media convergence, the internet must also be taken into account, not only for the ready access to information which it gives, and its unprecedented capacity for social networking, but also as a means of delivering the traditional media of print, radio and television. Internet television has become one of the drivers for the rapid growth in broadband take-up occurring in Latin America. The region is estimated to be home to just over ten per cent of the world's internet users. Brazil has by far the largest number, followed by Mexico, Argentina, Colombia, Venezuela and Chile. Although this is very roughly in line with the relative size of these countries' populations, the percentage of penetration varies considerably: in Argentina, 67 per cent of the population has internet access, compared to 39 per cent in Brazil and 37 per cent in Mexico. The regional average is 40 per cent.[3]

The internet service provision business has become wholly 'Latinised', notably through initiatives taken by formerly state-owned telecommunications entities. In spite of efforts by AOL (America On Line) and other US-based ISPs (internet service providers) to corner the Latin American market in the early days of commercial internet development, it has been the Brazilian-based UOL (Universo Online) which dominates that market, while in Mexico, it is Telmex. UOL is majority-owned by the newspaper group Folha de São Paulo.[4] UOL's comprehensive portal attracts 70 per cent of Brazilian users,[5] the remainder being shared between Globo's internet arm, and Vivo, a brand of Telefónica. In Mexico, the former state-owned telecommunications provider Telmex is now owned by the fabled entrepreneur Carlos Slim, whose Infinitum service dominates the market.[6]

Telefónica is also present in Mexico, but although it is considerably outflanked there, as in Brazil, it is a significant regional player, offering its combined ISP/portal access in 17 Latin American countries, as well as in the United States, and its home base of Spain. Once Spain's state-owned telecommunications company, Telefónica is now one of the world's largest telecommunications conglomerates, with multiple interests in Latin America, and perhaps the most striking example of the influx of Spanish investment to the region over recent decades. Notwithstanding the relatively marginal position of Telefónica's ISP companies in Brazil and Mexico, it

---

2   John Sinclair, *Latin American Television: A Global View*, 1999; News Corporation, DIRECTV Group and News Corporation Announce Reorganization and Consolidation of Satellite TV Platforms in Latin America, 2004.
3   Internet World Stats, 'Latin American Internet Usage Statistics 2011'.
4   Business News Americas, 'Folha merges with UOL to form Folha-UOL'.
5   Sobre UOL, 'UOL, the best internet content'.
6   Paul Budde Communications Pty Ltd, 'Latin American Broadband and Internet Market'.

is prominent in the next largest markets. In Argentina, where it is now branded as Speedy, it shares the market behind Telecom Argentina's Arnet, and Fibertel, the ISP division of Grupo Clarín, which publishes the region's most widely read newspaper and owns several major broadcasting and other media properties. Telefónica leads the market in Colombia, in collaboration with government, while in Chile all of Telefónica's operations have been consolidated under the name which formerly identified its mobile division, Movistar.[7]

People of Latin American origin in Australia as a media market

Whereas the media markets of Latin American countries are huge and thoroughly commercialised, and dominated by major corporate players at global, regional and national levels, people of Latin American origin in Australia constitute a niche market which has inherent commercial limitations, and which relies for its existence on the direct involvement of individuals and their communities, as well as on the indirect support of government. The term 'people of Latin American origin' is the appropriate term to use here, since the media market seeks to include not only the 86,156 Australian residents who declared in the 2006 Census that they were born in South America, Central America or the Caribbean, but the further 93,795 who said they were of such ancestry. This adds up to 179,951, less than one per cent of the Australian population. Note that the corresponding information for the 2011 Census is not available at time of writing, although it has counted 111,400 people who speak Spanish at home, 22 per cent of whom were born in Australia.[8] Thus, the first limitation is the size of the market, but the difficulties are more complex than that, in that the market is significantly divided by language, national identity and ideological orientation.

By far the greatest majority of people of Latin American origin in Australia have Spanish as their mother tongue, the significant exception being the Portuguese-speaking population of Brazilian origin, which requires a separate analysis. Just as native-born Australians enjoy the privilege of having a world language as their mother tongue, so do Latin Americans with Spanish, but this common language conceals underlying differences not only between national groups, but within them. It is important to appreciate that, just as Australians or North Americans are not English, even if that is what we call the language we speak, Latin Americans speak Spanish but distinguish themselves not only from Spaniards, but from

---

7   *Ibid.*; 'Redusers, Relevamos los Proveedores de Internet de Argentina'; Telefónica, 'About Telefónica Latinamérica'.

8   Australian Bureau of Statistics, '20680–Country of Birth of Person (minor groups) by Sex—Australia 2006'; '20680–Ancestry (full classification list) by Sex—Australia 2006'; 'Reflecting a Nation: Stories from the 2011 Census, 2012–2013'.

each others' nationalities. As well, in the same way as English in England differs from its Australian, North American and other variants, just so does Spanish in Spain differ from the 'Spanishes' of Latin America.

This 'pluricentric' character of Spanish[9] has both advantages and disadvantages from the point of view of media market formation. As minority media, Spanish-language media are able to address a wider range of nationalities than many other minority language media in Australia: Spanish is the official language of 19 countries in Latin America, including those from which most Latin American immigrants have come to Australia—Chile, El Salvador, Argentina and Uruguay. Yet even after more than two decades in which migration from Latin America had totally eclipsed that from Spain, Australia's oldest Spanish-language newspaper, *El Español en Australia*, dating from 1965, was still giving preference to stories from Spain, as the title implies, rather than catering to those from the new source countries.[10]

To take a related example; unlike speakers of, say, Croatian, Spanish speakers form a large enough audience for SBS to be able to provide a television news service in Spanish every day of the week, just as it does for several other of the larger minority language groups in Australia. However, that service comes from RTVE (Radio Televisión Española), the national broadcaster of Spain, except on Sundays, when news from Chile's state broadcaster, Televisión Nacional de Chile is broadcast as 'Latin American News'. Spanish speakers are thus at an advantage over speakers of most national languages, in that, regardless of their country of origin, they can be aggregated into an audience for news in Spanish, but at a disadvantage in the sense that, unless they are Spanish or Chilean, the news that they get is not from their particular country of origin nor in their own vernacular. Similarly, the much smaller audience of Brazilians is provided with a news service in Portuguese, but it comes from RTP (Rádio e Televisão de Portugal), Portugal's national broadcaster.

Whether for commercial or public service purposes, the traditional media for minorities have the problem of achieving and maintaining critical mass, the level at which readership or audience size becomes commercially viable or can justify public expenditure.[11] In this regard, the owners of such media have a vested interest in emphasising commonality at the expense of difference, and this encourages the practice of 'aggregation',[12] that is, minimising the linguistic, national, ideological and other divisions within the target community, or communities, and accentuating what they have in common. Even in the United

---

9   Michael Clyne and Sandra Kipp, *Pluricentric Languages in an Immigrant Context: Spanish, Arabic and Chinese*, 1999.

10   María-Teresa Herrera-Keightley, 'The Spanish Language Ethnic Press in Australia', 1989, pp. 93–107.

11   John Sinclair and Stuart Cunningham, 'Diasporas and the Media', 2001, pp. 1–34.

12   Guilherme D. Pires and John Stanton, *Ethnic Marketing: Accepting the Challenge of Cultural Diversity*, 2005.

States, where the self-identifying census category of 'Hispanic' or 'Latino' has come to constitute over 16 per cent of that country's total population of 308.7 million, that is, more than 50.5 million Hispanics in over 308 million people,[13] language is used as a basis of commonality amongst peoples of diverse ethnic or national origins. Spanish-speaking minorities in the US are in a unique position in that they are served by two national television networks as well as abundant local press and radio media. The critical mass of the audiences so formed is great enough to merit the production of both programming and advertising specifically for them. Yet even so, there is an aggregation process at work which emphasises the unity wrought by the speaking of Spanish at the expense of actual diversity, in which people identify themselves as Mexican–American, Cuban–American, or even just American.[14]

From the point of view of commercialising a minority audience, it can be readily understood how the traditional print and broadcasting business model requires the aggregation of a critical mass of people whose attention is attracted by the provision of certain information and entertainment, so that the readership or audience so formed can then be sold to whichever advertisers want to gain access to them. Classically, this has been the basis on which the mainstream commercial press has developed, but minority newspapers, particularly in languages other than English, are restricted in the size and range of advertisers that they are able to attract. Most large mainstream advertisers tend to feel uncertain about the value of targeting minorities. Often there is a perception that minorities, particularly recently arrived immigrants and refugees, have too little purchasing power to be worth the trouble, while with long-established groups, the advertisers' perception is that they will have assimilated and do not require any special targeting. There is also the crucial issue of the lack of measurement: as for other minority newspapers in Australia, there are no audited circulation figures for the Spanish-language press, nor do they have the resources to do readership research, so larger advertisers prefer to use the measured, mainstream media.[15]

Yet this being said, the resistance or perhaps indifference which large advertisers show towards minority marketing should not be exaggerated, since there are certain major corporations that do take it seriously, particularly in the form of what is called 'co-operative advertising'. This is when a large global or national advertiser collaborates in advertising with a retailer of its products or services. An unpublished content analysis of advertising in Australian Spanish-language newspapers yields the examples of ads for Toyota and Ford local car dealerships,

13   US Census Bureau, 'The Hispanic Population of the United States'.
14   Arlene Dávila, *Latinos Inc.: The Marketing and Making of a People*, 2001.
15   Alvin M. Chan, 'Tapping the multicultural market in Australia', 2006, pp. 238–52; Sophia Russell 'Waking up to Multicultural Marketing', *B&T*, 27 April 2007, p. 8.

alongside local travel agencies promoting LAN (Línea Aérea Nacional), Chile's national airline, and Western Union, the US-based international commercial services corporation. Travel agencies were in fact the most frequently occurring type of advertiser across the four papers in the study, typical of the small scale and community-specific character of most of the other kinds of advertiser, some of them not even commercial: social clubs, sports associations and community broadcasters. Along with migration and other legal services, and specialised food outlets, these are mostly advertisers in and of the community which they seek to reach.[16]

However, to look more generally at marketing to minorities in Australia, the role of government deserves special note. The federal government has fostered minority marketing, both as an advocate and as an advertiser. Past pursuit of multiculturalism and productive diversity policies has required close involvement in 'multicultural marketing' by government, including subsidies in the form of a fixed allocation of its print media budget to the 'ethnic' press.[17] Apart from both federal and state government departments advertising their services and pursuing particular campaigns from time to time, government-owned entities, such as the health insurance company Medibank Private, are prominent amongst advertisers in the minority media.[18] An informed contemporary source within the industry estimates that 48 per cent of print advertising is from government.

There is a sense in which government has sought to prime the pump for other large advertisers, in a situation which might otherwise amount to what economists call 'market failure'. Similarly, some state governments have been consistent promoters of minority marketing: New South Wales, the most populous state, still conducts the Australian Multicultural Marketing Awards it implemented in 1991.[19] Thus, in Australia, government is one of the major forces pushing minority marketing and media, putting itself in the company, and as clients of, such like-minded private sector interests as the Australian multicultural divisions of global marketing communications groups: Etcom, connected via national parent company STW to WPP globally, and the McCann Worldgroup-linked Multicultural Marketing and Management.

The situation with the electronic media is more complex, not only as it concerns the mix of public, private and community involvement, but in regard to transformations underway in the underlying commercial business model itself. While historically this model has functioned well for majority audiences in the

---

16   Leticia Worley, 'Cultural Diversity in Print Advertisements: Spanish-language Newspapers', Unpublished research paper, Victoria University, Melbourne, 2005.
17   Corrine Condie, *Multicultural Marketing,* Canberra, Department of Immigration and Multicultural Affairs, 1997.
18   Russell, Sophia, 'Waking Up', 2007, p. 8.
19   Ian F. Wilkinson and Constant Cheng, 'Multicultural Marketing in Australia: Synergy in Diversity', *Journal of International Marketing,* 7: 3, 1999, pp. 106–25.

golden age of mass media alluded to earlier, the advent of subscription-based or 'pay-TV' made possible by satellite and cable delivery has given rise to an alternative model in which the media owner can derive revenue merely from providing the service to subscribers, either with no advertising at all, or with advertising in an attenuated form. While such a model still needs a minimum number of subscribers to be viable, it does not necessarily require the physical concentration of those subscribers in the same geographical area, thus transcending the earthbound limitations of free-to-air broadcasting.

In fact, such 'post-broadcasting' distribution technologies as satellite-to-cable and direct-to-home or DBS (direct broadcast satellite) television, now being followed by nascent internet television delivery systems such as IPTV (internet protocol television) made possible by the spread of digital broadband, are particularly well-suited to providing services to widely dispersed subscribers with specialised demands, and minority language speakers are an excellent case in point. For several years now, individuals have been able to mount a satellite dish on the roof and pick up programming from their home country, however isolated they might be. More recently, companies have arisen to provide more user-friendly packages or 'bouquets' of international channels on a subscription basis. This is the phenomenon of 'global narrowcasting': services for self-selecting, widely distributed audiences, of which the diaspora of linguistic and/or ethnic minorities is a prime example.

An extensive mapping study of satellite television flows around the world in the 2000s observes that although national markets continue to be the main target for the bulk of transmissions, an impressive array of international services flows across national borders, and not only in major world languages like Spanish, but minority languages such as Basque. The US case is most extreme: 'In the best of cases nine out of every 10 people in the United States who speak a language other than English at home have the possibility of gaining access to satellite television broadcasts in their family language'.[20] However, the Australian experience has been that satellite services are not commercially viable, given the small size of most linguistic minority audiences. On the other hand, specialised services are becoming available over the internet, in addition to other kinds of online information and entertainment.

Finally, to understand the media environment in Australia for people of Latin American origin, or indeed of whatever source, the role of the public and community media sectors must be taken into account. As noted at the outset, SBS is a public broadcasting institution which provides national 'ethnic' radio and 'multicultural' television free-to-air broadcasting services, as well as online

---

20 Josu Amezaga Albizu, 'Geolinguistic Regions and Diasporas in the Age of Satellite Television', *International Communication Gazette*, 69:3, 2007, pp. 239–61, p. 254.

access. The two radio networks (AM and FM) are defined as 'ethnic' in that they provide programs in a host of community languages, while the two television channels are 'multicultural' in the sense that most programs are in English, but the wide breadth of non-English entertainment—although not news—programs are subtitled in English. SBS is partly funded from the federal government budget, but also by advertising as on the commercial channels. It has its own board and professional management, at arm's length from both government and the communities it serves.[21]

Augmenting SBS's role, there is also a significant community broadcasting sector which gives non-English-speaking groups direct access to the airwaves. A notable example is 3ZZZ, a radio station which broadcasts on FM throughout Melbourne, but is accessible nationally over the internet. It is mainly funded by listener subscriptions, but does have sponsorship, as distinct from commercial advertising. It is owned and managed by a non-profit community organisation, and run by volunteers who present programs in many languages.[22] As well, Australian cities have several local community radio stations, some of which have programs mounted by non-English-speaking groups. Regarding television, there are community stations licenced in the major cities which have programs by and for various non-English-speaking community groups.[23]

The media environment for people of Latin American origin in Australia

At this point, we can now turn to review the whole range of media offerings for Latin Americans in Australia. We should begin with the distinct case of Portuguese-speaking Brazil, given that it is Latin America's largest nation in terms of its economy, its territory and its population. However, people of Brazilian origin form one of the smallest, albeit fastest-growing Latin American communities in Australia. The 2006 Census counted 6,647 residents born in Brazil, with a further 7,491 of that ancestry.[24] As with Latin Americans in general, the majority, by far in this case, lived in Sydney. Given the absence of critical mass, there are no Brazilian newspapers, but the Brazilian communities in Sydney[25] and Melbourne[26] do have websites which feature newsletters as

21   Ien Ang, Gay Hawkins and Lamia Dabboussy, *The SBS Story*, Sydney, University of New South Wales Press, 2008.
22   3ZZZ, Melbourne Ethnic Community Radio.
23   Department of Broadband, Communications and the Digital Economy, 'Community Television'.
24   Australian Bureau of Statistics, '20680–Country of Birth of Person (full classification list) by Sex—Australia 2006'; '20680–Country of Birth of Person (minor groups) by Sex—Australia 2006'.
25   BRACCA,' Brazilian Community Council of Australia'.
26   ABRISA, 'Brazilian Association for Social Development and Integration in Australia'.

well as guides to services and events; community announcements about film screenings, language classes and the like; very modest local classified advertising; and links to Brazilian newspapers and other information sources. A particularly interesting link is to 'Brazilians in the world', which is a site maintained by the Brazilian Ministry of Foreign Affairs for the benefit of the worldwide diaspora of Brazilians.[27] As for electronic media, SBS provides a radio program in Portuguese, as well as the television news service aired weekly on SBS One and daily on SBS Two.

In spite of the theoretical advantages of the technology, specialised television subscription services, not only for Spanish and Portuguese speakers but most linguistic minorities in Australia, have had a history of failure. Two such services arose during the 2000s, but both had disappeared by 2012. Firstly, in 2004, Sydney-based United Broadcasting International Pty Ltd, trading as UBI World TV, emerged from the ashes of Television and Radio Broadcast Services (TARBS), a similar but unsuccessful prior business. Over digital satellite, it offered Spanish speakers international services from Chile (both Chilevisión and Canal 13), Argentina (Telefé), Colombia (RCN), Mexico (Galavisión) and Spain (TVE), along with special interest Latin film, music and *telenovela* channels. Portuguese speakers could subscribe to a package of *telenovelas* on TV Globo from Brazil, in addition to one public and one private channel from Portugal. The other service was SelecTV, owned by Bruce Gordon's WIN Corporation, the major regional media and telecommunications company. It offered a more limited range: TV Chile, the international channel of the national broadcaster, Televisión Nacional de Chile; Latele Novela, a packaged *telenovela* channel; EuroNews; Fashion TV; and also TVE.

In 2011, SelecTV went into voluntary administration, never having made a profit. They had 45,000 subscribers (across all languages), but argued that they needed 80,000. Within 18 months, UBI collapsed, having 55,000 subscribers at that time, and $25 million in debt.[28] Even when augmented by advertising revenue, it would appear that such pay-TV services lack the critical mass to be commercially viable.

Spanish speakers still have access to televisual news and entertainment on the public and community channels, but on a limited schedule, rather than as a continuously available service. Mention has already been made of SBS's news services from the national broadcasters of Spain and Chile, and the limits of their appeal. SBS also shows films, on an irregular basis, from Spain and Latin

---

27   Brasileiros no mundo, 'Ministério das Relações Exteriores', Brasil.
28   Media Spy, 'Time called on WIN's pay TV company'; Perthnow, 'Australia's foreign TV service goes belly up'.

America, but like the news, the selection of films reflects their availability on the international market rather than the composition of the national origins of the potential audience.

In community television, Antena Hispana, a not-for-profit production company with volunteer personnel, has been producing programs for the Channel 31 community television channel in Melbourne since 1996, when its Spanish-language program 'Entre Todos' first appeared. From 2004 until 2010, it also produced 'Fusión Latina', in English, which was shown interstate on the community stations TVS in Sydney, QCTV in Brisbane, C31 in Adelaide, and, as of 2010, on WTV in Perth. These programs covered community events and issues, and 'Hispanic culture's food, music, dance and language'.[29]

With regard to radio, there are also public and community programs available. SBS Radio broadcasts one or two hours of programming in Spanish every day, which is also available nationally, whether on AM or FM, digital, online or podcast. The aforementioned 3ZZZ has at least one program in Spanish each day throughout the week, accessible nationally. In Melbourne, one of Australia's first community radio stations, 3CR, has a number of Spanish-language or bilingual programs during the week over AM and online, mainly progressive news and current affairs from Latin America, such as 'Voice of Chile',[30] while Brisbane's ethnic community station 4EB FM has separate Spanish, Portuguese and Latin American programs each week.[31] The exception to this predominantly public and community scene is a privately owned, continuous, commercial Spanish-language service, Radio Austral. Beginning in 1992 and broadcast out of Sydney, where it is available on FM, and accessible elsewhere over the internet, Radio Austral offers news, current affairs, sport and music, supported by advertising.[32]

Turning now to print, there is only one newspaper published more than once a week, *The Spanish Herald*, which comes out each Tuesday and Thursday, with a print run of 1,400. It reaches into all states and territories, although most of its circulation is in New South Wales. It is notable that all of the Spanish-language press is based in Sydney, consistent with the distribution of people of Latin American origin, though *El Español en Australia*, with a print run of 1,200, is more evenly distributed in sales nationally. Others, with less than 1,200, are *Extra Informativo* and *Noticias y Deportes*.[33]

Note that most of these circulation figures have not varied much in the last ten years, during which there has been a worldwide downward trend in newspaper

29 Antena Hispana.
30 3CR, 'About 3CR'.
31 4EB FM, 'About Radio 4EB'.
32 Radio Austral, 'Radio Austral Spanish Radio Network'.
33 Unpublished research by Robert Austin, provided in personal communication from Nelson Cabrera, Director of *El Semanario en Español*, 10 April 2013; Worley, 'Cultural Diversity', n.p.

readership that these papers are unlikely to have escaped. The papers survive not so much on circulation as advertising, particularly from government, which is in effect a public subsidy. Furthermore, there is a tendency for newspaper readers to be concentrated amongst the older members of the population. By contrast, as Professor Alfredo Martínez Exposito observes, 'Younger generation Latinos are using the internet like everyone else, that is, in forms which challenge traditional audience modes—peer to peer, blogs, social websites and so on have largely replaced the newspaper and the news bulletin for young people'.[34]

The trend to online communication is apparent with the magazine *Viva*. From 2000 to 2010, it came out as a print publication every two months, claiming a circulation of 7,000. It is now online as a monthly. Unlike the newspapers, *Viva* is in English, and oriented very much towards participants in a Sydney-based crossover youth culture, with its coverage of Latin music, dance and nightlife. In effect, it is 'the only Australian lifestyle magazine about the Latin world'.[35] Similar magazines that were available in print format only, notably *Coqueta* and *Latin Time*, are now defunct.

Indeed, the internet is by far the most vibrant medium in the Spanish-language mediascape in Australia, with both not-for-profit and commercial dimensions, but it is subject to instability. The website of the Melbourne-based Chilean community organisation, Fonda la Clínica, formerly provided a good example of grass-roots use of the internet, with extensive community news and useful links in Spanish, but, at the time of writing, had not been updated since September 2012.[36] Another non-commercial site, that once allowed Spanish speakers to watch or download video podcasts on current affairs, politics, medicine, education and the like, now has its domain name up for sale.[37] On the other hand, enterprising individuals have initiated online news and information sites. A Sydney-based journalist from Uruguay provides a professional internet news service in Spanish, plus quality features and a community directory, claiming a notional but highly unlikely estimated universe of 90,000 Latin American families in Australia. Again, a Catalan journalist in Melbourne maintains Spanish Australia, more of a cultural and lifestyle site, of interest to a hip Spanish, Latin American and English-speaking audience.[38] However, the continuity of these sites depends absolutely on what the individuals sustaining them do with their lives: for example, *El Diario Australiano*, a serious news and feature article service in Spanish, ceased when the Venezuelan journalist running it moved overseas.

34   Alfredo Martínez Exposito, Professor of Spanish, University of Melbourne, Personal email communication, 5 March 2010.
35   Viva, 'Viva Magazine'.
36   Fonda la Clinica.
37   Huge Domains.
38   Latinhub.

Much less transitory has been an online newspaper, *El Semanario en Español*. Established in 2007 and now received by 5,200 subscribers, nationally and internationally, this electronic weekly has achieved a circulation which compares more than favourably with the printed press, as detailed earlier.[39] A rather different kind of internet venture is *Latino America Viva*. This describes itself, inaccurately, as 'the only Latin daily online news in Australia'. In fact, it is more of a content aggregation site, run by a marketing consulting company, offering magazine-style content with links to local and Latin American news sites, and carrying display and classified advertising, as well as sponsorships.[40]

To conclude, we have seen that, whereas the mainstream both in Australia and in the major countries of Latin America is dominated by large private media corporations, Australia is distinct because of the role assigned to public broadcasting in particular. The public broadcasting institution SBS is prominent in the provision of services for people of Latin American and other non-English-speaking immigrant origin in Australia, while government more generally gives strong support to the community's own media via its high level of advertising. Looking beyond this subvention by government, community television and radio and even some online services are well-named, both in the sense that they rely on the good will and voluntarism of individuals in the community, and that they are capable of reflecting the ethno-national composition of the Spanish-speaking community in a way that public broadcasting does not. The commercial side of Spanish-language media in Australia is largely restricted to the press. While the titles are well established, the organisational basis is more small-scale entrepreneurial than corporate, and the advertising revenue is to a large degree limited: reliant on government, a finite revenue source.

All this being the case, and given the inherent limitations which have been discussed, it is hard to see much scope in the immediate future for further development of the Spanish-language media market in Australia. The dependence of the press on government advertising, the demise of the specialised television subscription services, and the marginal and fugitive nature of other media offerings outside SBS all make clear the commercial limitations of a small market, particularly for traditional print and broadcast media. On the other hand, the discernible shift to the provision of news and entertainment services over the internet, along with the emergent technology of online television, points the way to a future mediascape in which local, grass-roots ventures can co-exist with access to more transnational fare.

---

39   Nelson Cabrera, Director of *El Semanario en Español*, Personal communication by email, 10 April 2013.
40   Latino America Viva.

References

3CR, 'About 3CR', http://www.3cr.org.au/about_3CR, accessed 4 April 2013.

3ZZZ, Melbourne Ethnic Community Radio, http://www.3zzz.com.au/, accessed 4 April 2013.

4EB FM, 'About Radio 4EB', http://www.4eb.org.au/?q=node/6, accessed 5 April 2013.

ABRISA, 'Brazilian Association for Social Development and Integration in Australia', http://www.abrisa.org.au/en/index.htm, accessed 4 April 2013.

Albizu, Josu Amezaga, 'Geolinguistic Regions and Diasporas in the Age of Satellite Television', *International Communication Gazette*, 69: 3, 2007, pp. 239–61.

Ang, Ien, Gay Hawkins and Lamia Dabboussy, *The SBS Story*, Sydney, University of New South Wales Press, 2008.

Antena Hispana, http://latinoamericainaustralia.blogspot.com.au/2013/03/antena-hispana-fiesta.html, accessed 4 April 2013.

Austin, Robert, (unpublished research) provided in personal communication from Nelson Cabrera, Director of *El Semanario en Español*, 10 April 2013.

Australian Bureau of Statistics, '20680–Country of Birth of Person (full classification list) by Sex—Australia 2006', http://www.censusdata.abs.gov.au, accessed 12 April 2013.

————. '20680–Country of Birth of Person (minor groups) by Sex—Australia 2006', http://www.censusdata.abs.gov.au, accessed 12 April 2013.

————. 'Reflecting a Nation: Stories from the 2011 Census, 2012–2013', http://www.abs.gov.au/ausstats/abs@.nsf/Lookup/2071.0main+featur es902012-2013, accessed 26 April, 2013.

BRACCA, 'Brazilian Community Council of Australia', http://bracca.org/2012/, accessed 4 April 2013.

Brasileiros no mundo, 'Ministério das Relações Exteriores', Brasil, http://www.brasileirosnomundo.itamaraty.gov.br/, accessed 4 April 2013.

Business News Americas, 'Folha merges with UOL to form Folha-UOL', http://www.bnamericas.com/news/telecommunications/Folha_merges_with_UOL_to_form_Folha-UOL, accessed 27 March 2013.

Cabrera, Nelson, Director of *El Semanario en Español*, Personal communication by email, 10 April 2013.

Chan, Alvin M. 'Tapping the multicultural market in Australia', in C. P. Rao (ed.), *Marketing and Multicultural Diversity*, Aldershot, Ashgate, 2006, pp. 238–52.

Clyne, Michael and Sandra Kipp, *Pluricentric Languages in an Immigrant Context: Spanish, Arabic and Chinese*, Berlin and New York: Mouton de Gruyter, 1999.

Condie, Corrine, *Multicultural Marketing*, Canberra, Department of Immigration and Multicultural Affairs, 1997.

Dávila, Arlene, *Latinos Inc.: The Marketing and Making of a People*, Berkeley, University of California Press, 2001.

Department of Broadband, Communications and the Digital Economy, 'Community Television', http://www.dbcde.gov.au/television/community_television, accessed 4 April 2013.

Exposito, Alfredo Martínez, Professor of Spanish, University of Melbourne, Personal email communication, 5 March 2010.

Fonda la Clínica, http://www.fondalaclinica.com.au/, accessed 9 April 2013.

Herrera-Keightley, María-Teresa, 'The Spanish Language Ethnic Press in Australia', in Abe W. Ata and Colin Ryan (eds), *The Ethnic Press in Australia*, Melbourne, Academia Press and Footprint Publications,1989, pp. 93–107.

Huge Domains, http://www.holahispanos.com/, accessed 9 April 2013.

Internet World Stats, 'Latin American Internet Usage Statistics 2011', http://www.internetworldstats.com/stats10.htm, accessed 27 March 2013.

Latinhub, http://www.latinhub.com.au/; Spanish Australia, http://www.spanishaustralia.org, accessed 9 April 2013.

Latino America Viva, http://www.latinoamericaviva.com.au/, accessed 9 April 2013.

McKnight, David, *Rupert Murdoch: An Investigation of Political Power*, Crow's Nest NSW, Allen & Unwin, 2012.

Media Spy, 'Time called on WIN's pay TV company', http://www.mediaspy.org/2011/02/04/time-called-on-wins-pay-tv-company/, accessed 13 October 2013.

News Corporation, 'DIRECTV Group and News Corporation Announce Reorganization and Consolidation of Satellite TV Platforms in Latin America', 2004, http://www.newscorp.com/news/news_221.html, accessed 27 March 2013.

Paul Budde Communications Pty Ltd, 'Latin American Broadband and Internet Market', http://www.marketresearch.com/product/display.asp?productid=2392719, 21 July 2009, accessed 29 March 2013.

Perthnow, 'Australia's foreign TV service goes belly up', http://www.perthnow.com.au/business/australias-foreign-tv-service-goes-belly-up/story-e6frg2rc-1226405967387, accessed 5 April 2013.

Pires, Guilherme D. and John Stanton, *Ethnic Marketing: Accepting the Challenge of Cultural Diversity*, London: Thomson, 2005.

Radio Austral, 'Radio Austral Spanish Radio Network', http://radioaustral.com.au/about/, accessed 5 April 2013.

'Redusers, Relevamos los Proveedores de Internet de Argentina', http://www.redusers.com/noticias/relevamiento-de-los-proveedores-de-internet-en-argentina/, accessed 4 April 2013.

Russell, Sophia, 'Waking up to Multicultural Marketing', *B&T*, 27 April 2007, p. 8.

Sinclair, John and Stuart Cunningham, 'Diasporas and the Media', in Cunningham, Stuart, and John Sinclair (eds), *Floating lives: The Media and Asian Diasporas*, Lanham, Rowman & Littlefield, 2001, pp. 1–34.

Sinclair, John, *Latin American Television: A Global View*, Oxford and New York: Oxford University Press, 1999;

Sobre UOL, 'UOL, the best internet content', http://sobreuol.noticias.uol.com.br/index_en.jhtm, accessed 27 March 2013.

Tabakoff, Nick, 'Historic shift for News as it returns to publishing roots', *The Australian*, 5 December 2012, p. 19.

Telefónica, 'About Telefónica Latinamérica', http://www.telefonica.com/en/latam/html/ about_telefonica_latin_america/home.shtmla, accessed 4 April, 2013.

US Census Bureau, 'The Hispanic Population of the United States', http://www.census.gov/population/hispanic/data/2011.html, accessed 4 April 2013.

Viva, 'Viva Magazine', http://www.vivamagazine.com.au/joomlasite, accessed 9 April 2013.

Wilkinson, Ian F. and Constant Cheng, 'Multicultural Marketing in Australia: Synergy in Diversity', *Journal of International Marketing*, 7: 3, 1999, pp. 106–25.

Worley, Leticia, 'Cultural Diversity in Print Advertisements: Spanish-language Newspapers', Unpublished research paper, Victoria University, Melbourne, 2005.

9. Culture as a Key to Connections: Using culture to promote Australia's strategic relationship with Latin America

Ralph Newmark

Introduction: A new lateral approach

In the second decade of the 21st century, globalisation and the digital revolution have made culture, in all its manifestations, a powerful vehicle for building global relationships and creating business. It was once said, in international relations, that culture follows commerce; however, this chapter sees culture as commerce itself and as a means of leading to greater commercial relations via knowledge transfer. It sees culture as a broad reciprocal phenomenon. While on the one hand, the flow of Australian cultural products into Latin America serves to enhance our profile in the region and also provides access for our artists to one of the largest markets in the world, on the other hand, the flow of Latin American culture into Australia has many significant benefits. Indeed, in terms of advancing Australia's strategic relationship with Latin America, the role of culture—especially popular music, dance and food—can be seen both as a means of developing a sadly lacking awareness and understanding of the region in this country and as a means of expanding existing—and developing new—commercial activities for Australians in Australia via the popularity and proliferation of Latin American culture. All these connections will generate economic benefits for Australia and Latin America.

However, a relationship cannot flourish in ignorance and apathy. This chapter seeks to make recommendations that will make the cultural context of Australia-Latin American relations more productive. It is time to implement a lateral approach; to use a multi-faceted strategy in which culture can play a vital role. The chapter argues that while continuing calls for government to make Latin America a higher priority in terms of policy initiatives, the recent burgeoning popularity of Latin American culture in Australia should be harnessed and promoted as a means of increasing Australia's familiarity with and knowledge of Latin America and thus our connections to the region. This organic shift in consciousness and understanding will in turn help to create the conditions in which the potential of Latin America as a region for advancing Australian interests will permeate government, business, the education sector and the general community. Latin American culture can therefore be used in Australia to stimulate benefits for Australians, both domestically and in Latin America. In short, the link between culture and the overall strategic relationship with the region is that greater cognisance will lead to greater engagement on all levels.

Despite heroic efforts and achievements in the past by people such as Justin Macdonnell and organisations including the Australia Latin American Foundation (ALAF), a fragmented, piecemeal approach has been the hallmark of culture's role in Australia's relationship with Latin America. Accomplishments are manifest, but relatively modest: Australia needs to use the extraordinary domestic explosion of interest in Latin American culture to its best advantage.

Advancing strategic links must be seen as a multi-pronged integrated strategy, with each sector considered in this book doing what it does best. The role of culture is primarily to create appreciation and understanding, but it can also be profitable in itself. From a macro perspective, the promotion of Latin American culture in Australia as part of a total strategy makes sense. Linked together with all the other components analysed within this volume—such as trade, investment, and the education sector—we can promote and advance a reciprocal strategic relationship. If culture can put Latin America on the radar in Australia and vice versa, then all sorts of mutual benefits will flow. Some people may see this use of culture as somewhat nebulous, but it could be argued that this is the key role of culture in any broad strategic plan: its ability to create a knowledge platform from which to develop trade relationships.

This lateral approach also comprises boundless economic opportunities for people in Australia to gain from the popularity of domestic Latin American culture. In purely economic terms, Latin American culture in this country is becoming an important area of commercial activity for Australian business, via sales of recorded and now online music, as well through the proliferation of entertainment venues, dance schools and concert tours. In addition, there has been an explosion of interest in the region's cuisine.

Each part of this chapter will provide an assessment of the present situation in historical perspective, identify the major stakeholders, and also suggest future strategies in order to enhance our relationship with Latin America using culture as one key to connections and commerce. Part 1 examines Australia's cultural presence in Latin America, while Part 2 analyses Latin American culture in Australia. Finally a number of general recommendations are set out for future directions.

Part 1: Australia's cultural presence in Latin America

The present situation

Latin America and Australia have traditionally shared a relationship characterised by ignorance and apathy. This is surprising given that both share many historical characteristics, such as conquest and settlement by Europeans. Perhaps the fact that for many years we have been competitors in terms of export commodities has inhibited the development of trade linkages. Nevertheless, in recent times economic connections have steadily increased through investment, trade educational exports, and cultural exchanges.

Beginning in the 1980s, culture became a factor in this relationship through the pioneering work of Justin Macdonnell, who undertook a number of studies for the Australia Council on the development of a cultural tours program for Australian artists. In his report of May 1991, Macdonnell argued that 'a potential new market clearly existed in Latin America for shrewdly chosen Australian [cultural] product'.[1]

In 1992, Macdonnell's submission to the Senate hearing on Australian–Latin American relations recommended: 'There needs to be a recognition that without a change in the present low priority in our cultural relationship with at least the five 'priority' nations of Mexico, Argentina, Venezuela, Chile and Brazil, Australia runs the risk of failing to build bridges for the future'.[2]

Soon after, a group of Australians and Latin Americans resident in Australia led by Mario Estrella and Macdonnell established the Australia Latin America Foundation (ALAF) in order 'to promote better cultural relations between Australia and the countries of Latin America'.[3] Starting in the early 1990s, the ALAF successfully implemented many cultural exchanges with Latin America. The foundation's website clearly details its record of achievements, commencing in 1992 when the ALAF was launched:

> for the five hundredth anniversary of the first encounter between the peoples of Europe and the peoples of America (the Columbus Quincentenary). This was marked by a major Australian presence in the Caracas International Theatre Festival and the IberoAmerican Theatre

---

1 Senate Standing Committee on Foreign Affairs, Australia and Latin America: 'The Report of the Senate Standing Committee on Foreign Affairs, Defence and Trade, Companion Volume 6', 1992, p. 2063.
2 *Ibid*, p. 2012.
3 Australia Latin America Foundation, 'Columbus Quincentenary', http://alafoundation.com/, accessed 20 May 2013.

Festival of Bogotá in March of that year. This included Circus Oz, the Sydney Dance Company, Theatre of Image, Stretch Mk 1, playwrights Richard Whaley and Alma de Groen, arts critics Leonard Radic and Martin Portus. That, in turn, was complemented by a major Latin American presence at the Melbourne International Arts Festival in October that year, involving the National Ballet of Cuba, Jaime Torres y su Gente, Daniel Binnelli Quintet, and NucleoDanza. This was the first time that such a focus on the other region's culture had occurred in either place. All were curated by the Foundation.[4]

Since then the ALAF has worked with a range of public and private organisations as well as individuals 'to promote and manage Australian artists and ensembles to tour on a select and strategic basis in Latin America', and 'has worked with or co-presented Latin American artists with the Adelaide, Melbourne and Sydney Festivals', and lately at the 2012 Brisbane Festival.[5]

Recent developments and current projects involving the ALAF include: liaising with Latin American embassies in Canberra; key foundation associate Frank Madrid's appearance at the Latin Alternative Music Conference in New York; a Music Road Show in Argentina; arranging in Argentina, Colombia and Mexico for co-productions with Australian performing arts institutions and artists over the next three years; and organising residencies for Australian artists in Mexico City and Guadalajara. One can only applaud the efforts of the ALAF: its work provides a vehicle for promoting the presence of Australian artists in Latin America and this is an important contribution.

On the level of government involvement in cultural policy, a decade after the Senate report on Latin America, COALAR commissioned Justin Macdonnell from the ALAF in 2002 to write a report that 'considered how to improve coordination of Australian cultural activities in the region'.[6] Significantly, the 2002 Macdonnell report entitled *Australia's Cultural Presence in Latin America* called for cultural policy that employed 'a whole of government approach to maximise both input and outcome' and went on to emphasise that:

> partnerships within government and between tiers of government will be crucial; that partnerships with those private interests in the cultural and business sectors which have a stake in region, whether based in Australia or in Latin America, should be reinforced where they exist and promoted where they do not.[7]

---

4 *Ibid.*
5 *Ibid*; see also 'ALAF Projects', http://alafoundation.com/projects.htm, accessed 20 May 2013.
6 Justin Macdonnell, *Australia's Cultural Presence in Latin America: Programs and Prospects,* Prepared for COALAR, by ALAF Limited, February 2003, p. 3.
7 *Ibid.*

In April 2009, The Australia Council launched a new market development strategy in Latin America concentrating on Brazil and Mexico:

[The Australian Export Strategy for Latin America]...promotes and profiles emerging and established Australian contemporary artists and companies from the small to medium sector in South America, with a specific focus on Mexico and Brazil. Mexico and Brazil are key cultural centres attracting buyers, artists and tastemakers throughout the world. Both have considerable cultural history and significant contemporary practice as well as sizeable Indigenous communities, making them a good fit for contemporary Australian work.[8]

The identification of Indigenous connections here is of great importance. Both Australia and Latin America have traditionally been guilty of tragically hypocritical approaches to their original inhabitants. On the one hand, there are mutual histories of dispossession, cultural destruction and racism. Yet when it comes to the construction and marketing of identifiable national symbols and cultural products by some commercial organisations, the use of stereotyped images of Indigenous peoples and indeed animals has been clearly exploitative. Let us hope that all future collaborations will be directed and conducted by the Indigenous peoples themselves on their terms.

Another opportunity for Australia to make an impact in Latin America is at the Sixth World Summit on Arts and Culture in January 2014, conducted by the Chilean National Council for Culture and the Arts. Australia held the Fifth World Summit, co-hosted by the Australia Council for the Arts and the International Federation of Arts Councils and Culture Agencies (IFACCA), in Melbourne during October 2011 and it attracted 501 delegates from 72 countries. According to the Australia Council:

The theme of the Summit, Creative Intersections, was explored by over 80 speakers who provoked wide-ranging debate around the role of innovative government policy in facilitating intersections between the arts and other sectors for the benefit of the broader community, including health and well-being, education, environmental action, business, international aid, social inclusion and digital technologies.[9]

This Australian–Latin American 'Pacific Rim' continuity between the two Summits provides an ideal opportunity to enhance dialogue on cultural collaboration.

---

8   Australia Council, 'Targeted strategies for key international markets', *Australia Council Media Release*, 8 April 2009.
9   Australia Council, 'Let the Proceedings Begin: The Fifth World Summit on Arts and Culture Kicks Off Today in Melbourne', http://www.australiacouncil.gov.au/news/items/news, accessed 20 May 2013.

In 2010, the Victorian state government published a vision statement for the enhancement of that state's relationship with Latin America. The 29-page document included trade, investment and culture and acknowledged that culture through music, the visual arts and theatrical projects had a significant role to play in establishing connections. According to the report, 'a number of projects are being pursued by Victorian arts and cultural organisations in 2010–2013:

- Museum Victoria pursued the opportunity to host a touring exhibition from Mexico on Aztec culture in 2010–11.

- Latin America featured in a new forward plan around international touring being developed by the Melbourne Symphony Orchestra. The Melbourne Symphony Orchestra actively pursued Latin American touring opportunities including a visit to Chile.

- The Australian Centre for Contemporary Art extended its international tour of a prestigious Patricia Piccinini sculpture exhibition (Singapore, India and Japan) including Mexico in 2010–11.

- Multicultural Arts Victoria was invited by the Chilean Bicentenary Commission to send a culturally diverse music ensemble, Melbourne Ska, to perform in three locations in northern Chile in 2010.'[10]

These Victorian initiatives are excellent examples of what can be achieved at the state level and it can only be hoped that future state governments continue to implement this agenda.

Nevertheless, since the 1990s the most notable example of an Australian cultural presence in Latin America has been at Colombia's *Festival Iberoamericano de Teatro de Bogotá*. This prestigious festival has drawn Australian performers since 1992, and the list of participants is impressive. According to Colombian educator Jorge Leiva, while Australia's presence is much appreciated, a better identification of Australian acts, especially in the realm of street theatre, would serve to create a wider knowledge of Australia's contribution to the festival.[11]

Individual artists with a love of Latin American culture have also played a role in promoting Australia in Latin America. An important example is Melbourne jazz guitarist Doug de Vries, who along with singer Diana Clarke are Australia's foremost exponents of Brazilian music. De Vries and Clarke have visited Brazil many times and De Vries comments that:

10   Department of Innovation, Industry and Regional Development (DIIRD), Victoria, *Latin America and Victoria: A vision for growing trade, investment and cultural links*, Melbourne, State Government of Victoria, 2010, p. 15.
11   Newmark, Interview with Jorge Leiva, 8 October 2010.

Many Brazilians I've encountered in Rio, São Paulo, Salvador, Recife and other cities have a fascination for Australia and are quick to point out the similarities, such as our beaches, rainforests, deserts and climate. They also comment on the relative youthfulness of our colonial histories and how we share a relaxed lifestyle…. they are often surprised and delighted when they learn of my knowledge and expertise in samba, choro and bossa nova, and are enthusiastic about how this musical dialogue has developed.[12]

At the micro level, these artistic encounters are encouraging and very helpful.

Mention must also be made here of a number of Australian rock bands that have great popularity in Latin America. These include AC/DC, INXS and, in the past, Men at Work, as well as bands that fall within the surfie sub-culture. Although internationally fans are aware that certain groups happen to be Australian, the problem is that our contemporary musical culture is derived from Anglo and US genres, so, in comparison to Latin American music, most of our music lacks a clear identity overseas.

Finally, there is sport. While both Australia and Latin America share a passion for sport, the main spectator sports only overlap to a limited extent. Australia's presence at the last two soccer World Cup finals in 2006 and 2010 certainly created interest in Latin America, as did the Socceroos' epic but failed attempts to qualify in 1994 against Argentina, and in 2002 against Uruguay. As Brazil is about to host the two biggest sporting events in the world—World Cup 2014 and the Olympic Games 2016—it is hoped that Australia's presence at both events will create an impact.

These two major events have also created linkages via sport on other levels. Australia's very successful staging of the Olympic games in 2000 has led to a demand for our expertise in the areas of sports administration and sports facilities. A considerable number of Australian companies and sports organisations have been active in Brazil in the lead-up to the momentous sporting occasions scheduled for the Brazilians in 2014 and 2016.[13]

Nevertheless, our love of cricket and the four-way split in football codes means that niche sports are the key to future connections. Surfing and tennis stand out as vehicles for promoting Australia's presence in Latin America. Brazil and

---

12 Newmark, Interview with Doug de Vries, 18 January 2011.
13 See ABCC—Australia Brazil Chamber of Commerce, 'Feed Back on FIFA World Cup 2014 and Rio Olympics 2016 Business Mission', http://www.australiabrazil.com.au/index.php?option=com_content&task=view&id=274, accessed 26 May 2013; Austrade, '2014 Brazil FIFA World Cup and 2016 Rio Olympic Games—For Australian exporters', http://www.austrade.gov.au/Export/Export-Markets/Countries/Brazil/Industries/2014-Brazil-FIFA-World-Cup-and-2016-Rio-Olympic-Games, accessed 26 May 2013; ICN—Industry Capability Network, 'Victorian Industry prepare for Rio Olympic Games following success in London', http://www.icnvic.org.au, accessed 27 May 2013.

Peru are great surfing nations and our champions are important icons in those countries. Also the Australian Open, as one of the international Grand Slams, attracts many great Latin American players, especially from Argentina and Chile.

Future strategies

In order to promote the cultural presence of Australia in Latin America, two further strategies in addition to those already discussed ought to be implemented.

First, Australia should take advantage of the historical links between our continents to promote our profile in the region. Many important political, artistic and scientific figures visited and worked in both areas during the 18th and 19th centuries and have left wonderful historical legacies. People such as Charles Darwin, Charles Joseph La Trobe—who spent time in Mexico during 1834—and Australia's third Prime Minister, Chris Watson—who was born in Valparaiso, Chile—come to mind. Indeed, Watson was the world's first elected head of a national government to come from the labour movement, in this case the ALP. Brazil's 2010 'Connections' exposition held in Canberra, Sydney and Melbourne was a good example of the use of history to forge bonds and build profiles. This exhibition highlighted the geological, biological, and artistic links between the two nations. Another fruitful project using history could be developed with Paraguay that considers William Lane's utopian experiment of the 1890s. Cultural attachés at Australian embassies in Latin America should be encouraged to explore these historical connections and develop exhibitions in consultation with historians.

As a second additional strategy, there should be a strict policy of clearly identifying Australian performers in Latin America. This is especially crucial in the genres of street theatre and outdoor concerts. As most Australian performing artists address universal themes and rightly eschew clichéd cultural stereotypes, accompanying promotional content would help to ensure that mass audiences linked these performances to Australia.

Each of the initiatives discussed in this section has served to promote the presence of quality Australian performers in Latin America and are of great merit. They should not only continue, but be expanded. They serve to raise Australia's profile as a diverse, sophisticated, and developed nation in the eyes of Latin American audiences. While most of them target niche demographics, taken together they can reach a range of people from influential elites, in the case of concert hall performances, to sections of the general public during street theatre. The flow of Australian cultural products into Latin America serves to enhance our profile in the region and also provides access for our artists to one of the largest markets in the world. Nevertheless, as we shall see in Part 2, it may well be on the home front that culture can make the most dynamic contribution to this strategic relationship.

Part 2: Latin American culture in Australia

The popularity of Latin American popular culture in Australia has undergone steady growth since the 1980s and is presently experiencing a significant boom. Prior to the 1980s, interest in Latin American culture was generally confined to a small group of academics and activists. But from the late 1970s, inner-suburban gentrification was linked to the rise of a young, educated and sophisticated urban demographic. This group developed a distinct appetite for cultural exotica and as a consequence the market expanded for 'Third World' food, music and culture in general.

In terms of food, this market was catered for by the wave of immigration that flowed into Australia after the abolition of the White Australia Policy. However, for other forms of culture such as music and dance, the market for exotica took another course. As immigration from Latin America to Australia had not been similar to the levels experienced from Asia, our experience of the region has been characterised by a distinct lack of knowledge. Paradoxically, this situation has served to fuel the perception of the exotic for anything deriving from Latin America. When added to the inherent sensory and sensual appeal of Latin America's hybrid culture, consisting of Indigenous, Iberian, and African elements, the exotic appeal of the region's culture has had particular resonance with the predominantly inner-suburban, educated and middle-class audience. In this period—the 1980s to the mid-1990s—genres such as salsa and tango rapidly gained popularity. In terms of immigration, one must add that while the numbers of Latin Americans coming to Australia has been relatively small, migrants from Chile, El Salvador, Argentina, Uruguay and more recently Colombia and Brazil have played a key role in forming musical groups that service the public's appetite for Latin music.

Since the mid-1990s another factor has served to expand the appeal of Latin American culture in Australia: the explosion of a visible and assertive Latino culture in the United States. The globalised US-driven music industry now serves to spread interest in Latin music and this has captured a new Australian audience, both younger and more diverse, that regularly listens and dances to contemporary genres of Latin American music. These range from modern techno-salsa and merengue to Latin hip-hop and reggaeton. The music emanates from countries such as Colombia, Peru, Argentina, Mexico and Brazil, and not just the United States. There is also a strong demand for music from Cuba.[14]

The present situation

Recorded music

In recent years the recorded music industry has been undergoing a revolution in delivery formats. Digital media such as MP3/MP4 formats and, increasingly, online streaming are rapidly replacing physical formats such as CDs, and 'while revenue levels are adjusting to the change due to cheaper prices and piracy, the market for music will continue to grow in the long term'.[15] According to the Australian Bureau of Statistics (ABS) figures, the wholesale value of recorded music sales in Australia for the year ending 31 December 2012 totalled $398.1 million. These figures come during a period of dramatic transition in delivery systems. In 2007 digital sales accounted for $39.9 million in sales value. By 2012 this number had risen to $184.3 million.[16]

In global terms, during 2009 'Digital music sales, which include song downloads, mobile music, online subscriptions and streaming via advertising-supported services [such as YouTube] grew by 24 per cent globally to $US3.78 billion.'[17] By 2012 that figure reached US$5.6 billion. Leading providers of digital music include iTunes, Amazon.com, and bigpondmusic.com, while delivery systems include mobile phones, iPods, digital music systems, and of course all forms of computers. In general terms, whether physical or online, music is big business.

Based on the figures for 2012, in Australia retail sales of World Music are estimated at around five per cent of total sales, equivalent to around $20m in value, of which approximately 70 per cent, or more than $14m in value, is Latin American music. In short, music from the region is overwhelmingly the most popular form of World Music and importantly, while beginning from a low base compared to other genres, the potential for growth is considerable.[18] While one could argue that the majority of profit from the sale of digital music in Australia does not accumulate here, in terms of the range and accessibility of Latin music now available in Australia, the digital revolution has been a boon for the growth of our interest in Latin American music.

---

14 For an analysis of the history and appeal of Latin American music in Melbourne see Neil Orchard, 'Oz Salsa: A True Multicultural Dip?', unpublished Honours Thesis, La Trobe University History/Anthropology Programs, 2008.

15 Australian Recording Industry Association (ARIA), *Annual Report 2008*.

16 Australian Recording Industry Association (ARIA), *Annual Report 2012*.

17 ABC News, 22 April 2009.

18 Interview with JB HiFi sales staff, Camberwell, Victoria Music Department, May 2013.

Concert tours

Linked to the growing popularity of Latin American culture is a proliferation of concert tours undertaken by individual artists, bands, and increasingly by showcase productions that present aspects of musical culture from the region. Tours by Latin American musical groups go back to the 1970s, when Chilean Nueva Canción ensembles including Inti-Illimani and Quilapayún drew a predominantly politically motivated audience. By the 1990s the worldwide phenomenon of the Buena Vista Social Club led to a succession of popular tours that showcased Cuban music and in many ways served as a massive stimulus to the popularity of Latin American music in Australia. Further, between 2009 and 2013 numerous shows dealing with Brazilian and Cuban musical culture toured Australia.

Venues: Live music and clubs

In Melbourne and Sydney and other capital cities there is now an abundance of venues that present Latin American music every week. The audiences for these clubs are drawn from a demographic range, but the vast majority are people from non-Latin American backgrounds, confirming the argument that Latin music clearly moves beyond its ethnic base. Local musicians, many of who are migrants from Latin America, service Australia's music and dance venues, but, increasingly, recorded Latin music provided by DJs is used in clubs. While this is bad news for live music entertainers in the capital cities, it is at least a relatively cheap means of spreading the experience and consumption of Latin American culture.

Festivals

There is a significant number of Latin American cultural community festivals held each year in Australia. While the various multicultural communities from Latin America and Iberia usually organise these events, the attendance at the major festivals derives overwhelmingly from the general public. Once again the inherent exotica and sensuality of Latin American culture serves to draw a broad range of patrons to these festivals. At the events most of the traders are involved in domestic commercial activities that relate to Latin American culture, ranging from music sellers to restaurant owners, and have stalls showcasing their products. In Melbourne, the annual Hispanic-Latin American Festival held in Johnson St, Fitzroy has become a major attraction, while the Chilean Festival held each year at Sandown Park draws significant crowds. The South American Festival at the Bondi Pavilion features Sydney's large Brazilian community and both the Darling Harbour Fiesta—Latin Dance and Music Festival and the Sydney Salsa Congress are also indicative of the Latin American cultural boom in Australia.

The other type of festival attracting the general public to Latin American culture is the state arts festival, of which there are several examples. While presenting a diversity of artistic activities, these have tended in recent years to include performance groups from Latin America. These appearances often link with national concert tours already mentioned. In 2012 the Melbourne International Arts Festival, the Sydney Festival, the Adelaide Festival of the Arts, the Brisbane Festival, and the Perth International Arts Festival all featured artists from Latin America.

Online information services

Perhaps the most important means of disseminating information regarding Latin American culture in Australia is the emergence, in Melbourne and Sydney, of websites that provide extensive news of events and especially music and dance venues and schools. These online services have become the main conduits for publicising events and are favoured by contemporary aficionados. The main websites are in Melbourne, *Latin Lover* and *Latinhub*; and in Sydney, *Viva Magazine* and *spanishaustralia*.[19]

Dance

One of the most popular manifestations of Latin American culture in Australia has been dance. Thousands of people regularly frequent dance schools to learn various forms of Latin dancing such as tango and salsa as well as the Brazilian martial arts/dance form capoeira.

An additional dimension to dance has been the emergence in Australia of Latin American-related exercise classes. The Zumba dance fitness phenomenon was created by dancer and choreographer Alberto ('Beto') Pérez in Colombia during the 1990s, but is now based in Florida. It provides a frenetic workout to the rhythms of predominantly Latin American-based musical forms such as cumbia, salsa, merengue, mambo, cha-cha, reggaeton, samba and tango. In Australia there appear to be over 1,000 different classes available to people who are drawn to this potent mix of sensual Latin American culture and the developed world's obsession with weight loss and fitness.[20]

Food and drink

The engagement of Australians with Latin American cuisine is certainly one area of cultural appreciation that should be part of a greater cultural knowledge strategy. Australia has for some time embraced the Cal-Tex-Mex Americanised versions of Mexican food, but the magnificent complexity and diversity of Mexico's cuisine has had little exposure in this country. One recent development with potential for

---

19 See *Latin Lover*, http://www.latinlover.com.au/, accessed 27 May 2013; *Latinhub*, http://www.latinhub.com.au/latin-culture, accessed 27 May 2013; *Spanishaustralia*, http://www.spanishaustralia.org/arts, accessed 27 May 2013; *Viva Magazine* http://www.vivamagazine.com.au/, accessed 27 May 2013.
20 See *Zumba Fitness*, http://search.zumba.com/classes/internationalresults.

disseminating a broader appreciation of Latin American food is Melbourne food expert Stephanie Alexander's keen interest in the region. On a trip to Mexico she linked her home town with a dish that no Australian diner would have enjoyed at a local Mexican chain restaurant; she recounted asking a market vendor in Mexico 'how to prepare the *nopales*—after all, I walk past stands of prickly pear along the banks of the Yarra River and might give it a go sometime'.[21]

The present trajectory of Mexican cuisine in Australia has been polarised. At the top end of the market, the present fad for up-market 'Modern-Mex' cuisine has led to the proliferation of very popular and expensive restaurants that serve creative versions of Mexican classics. At the other end of the spectrum, the so-called 'Taco Truck' phenomenon has brought late-night mobile Mexican food to the streets with locations announced through social media.

The cuisine of Brazil is yet another genre which is underdeveloped in Australia. In this country Brazilian restaurants have chosen to concentrate predominantly on the southern Brazilian tradition of Churrascarias. The extraordinary food of Bahia, which includes an array of African flavours, would be an exciting addition to the culinary landscape of Australia. SBS should be encouraged to produce a television series that concentrates on Latin American food in all its diversity.

As for beverages, Mexican beer and spirits are well established here and probably increase familiarity with Latin America—hopefully beyond stereotypical images. One area that could be promoted is the world of Cuban cocktails based on rum produced in Cuba. The Mojito, Daiquiri, and Cuba Libre are well suited to the Australian climate and are becoming very popular.

Film

Film is yet another cultural medium that can be used for promoting familiarity and knowledge of Latin America. In Melbourne, for over a decade, the Filmoteca group has led the way in bringing Latin American films to the Australian public. Also there are a number of annual film festivals that concentrate on films from the region. Indeed, there has been a virtual explosion in the popularity of Latin American cinema in Australia, with the Melbourne and Sydney Latin American Film Festivals as outstanding examples and the La Mirada Film Festival also providing 'A showcase of contemporary and timeless film classics from Spain and Latin America'.[22]

---

21   Stephanie Alexander, 'Colours you can taste', *The Age* (*Epicure*), 13 October 2009.
22   See *La Mirada Film Festival 2012*, http://www.lamirada.org.au/.

Education

Education is an invisible Australian export: the country provides educational services to Latin America by attracting fee-paying students from the region. However, the teaching of university-level subjects in Australia involving Latin American history, politics and culture also has a role to play in enhancing our nation's knowledge of the region. In particular, Victoria's La Trobe University has pioneered the use of popular culture as a means of teaching Latin American history. Indeed, in 1976 La Trobe's Institute of Latin American Studies (ILAS) became Australia's first academic centre dedicated to the study of Latin America, and since then has been involved in teaching and conducting research on the region. Over the past 17 years, ILAS's summer and winter Intensive Schools have specialised in using popular culture as a vehicle to bring knowledge of Latin America to both students and the general public in Victoria.[23]

Over the years universities in other states began to offer subjects that dealt with the region, many of which had some cultural components, especially University of New South Wales and Flinders University of South Australia. In recent times, University of Technology, Sydney, University of Queensland, Sydney University, University of Western Sydney, The Australian National University, Melbourne University and Monash University have all begun to focus on Iberian and Latin American areas of study.

The founding of the Association of Iberian and Latin American Studies of Australasia (AILASA) in 1993 was an important milestone, as its agenda was to:

• promote research into and the teaching of Iberian and Latin American Studies in Australasia;

• promote the professional development of its members;

• promote public recognition of and interest in the Iberian Peninsula and Latin America;

• stimulate and encourage interchange between Australasia and the Iberian Peninsula and Latin America; and

• coordinate and rationalise available resources among member institutions through the interchange of students, teachers and resources.[24]

But overall, while there has been a very welcome increase in the proliferation of subjects dealing with language and literature, there needs to be increased support for teaching and research in disciplines such as Latin American History, Politics, Cultural Studies, Sociology and Economics.

---

23   The Institute of Latin American Studies (ILAS), La Trobe University, Faculty of Humanities and Social Sciences, School Humanities: Latin American Studies Program: see http://www.latrobe.edu.au/ilas/.
24   Association of Iberian and Latin American Studies of Australasia (AILASA), See: http://www.ailasa.org/.

A promising initiative in the area of educational exchange has been the *Mi amigo internacional* (My international friend) project run by Melbourne-based Colombian educator Jorge Leiva's *peopleartpeople* organisation. This program seeks to provide 'A creative journey in which young people in Australia explore and exchange with a friend in Colombia their sense of identity, family and world through visual arts shared through the web'.[25] This pilot project linked year nine and year ten art students from the Margaret Lyttle Memorial School in Preshil, Australia, with Colombian students as part of the Art and Youth for Peace Social Project from the Academia de Artes Guerrero. The program covered 20 one-hundred-minute sessions and the students from each country created:

> artworks that addressed topics such as: Me, My family and home, My school, You and me, Our world, My country, My city, etc. Images of the artworks were exchanged via a website and discussed in class. According to Leiva, the pilot produced impressive results.[26]

Projects such as this are invaluable in creating awareness in the next generation of the world beyond Australia: the innovative use of contemporary technology via the internet is to be applauded. In the context of Australia and Latin America we see here the use of a cultural medium as a means of enhancing connections, recognition and understanding.

Future strategies

In order to consolidate the presence of Latin American culture in Australia a number of strategies should be implemented. The recent explosion in the popularity of Latin American culture should be encouraged, harnessed and used as a means of increasing Australia's consciousness and knowledge of the region by promoting and funding public festivals and events involving Latin American music, dance and food. Furthermore, support should be provided through COALAR for increasing the development of educational resources in Australia aimed at teaching courses that deal with Latin American culture and Latin American Studies in general, as well as the Spanish and Portuguese languages. In addition, the implementation of programs such as *Mi amigo internacional* (My international friend) should be encouraged in order to benefit a wide range of schools. Bringing cultural exchange to the level of secondary education will create a platform of knowledge that will produce benefits for Australia and Latin America.

---

25   See http://www.peopleartpeople.com/education.html.
26   Jorge Leiva, 'Mi amigo internacional [My international friend] project', http://www.peopleartpeople.com/education.html.

Summary of recommendations and future directions

Cultural policy should play a role in a multi-pronged integrated strategy designed to advance Australia's strategic relationship with Latin America, both here and in Latin America. This cohesive approach should involve all the sectors covered in this volume and could well be coordinated by an organisation such as COALAR. The particular role of cultural relations is both educational and commercial and must harness the recent explosion of popularity of Latin American culture in Australia. The crucial linkage is culture's power as both a means of increasing Australia's connection to the region and providing profitable goods and services within the domestic market, especially those markets involving Latin American music, dance and food.

In terms of Australia's cultural presence in Latin America, the guidelines outlined in Justin Macdonnell's, *Australia's Cultural Presence in Latin America: Programs and Prospects,* should continue to be followed, in conjunction with the Australia Council (OZARTS) and the Australia Latin America Foundation (ALAF). In addition, during performances in Latin America, Australian artists should be more clearly identified, and in both Australia and Latin America exhibitions should be mounted which emphasise the historical links between the regions.

Support should be given through COALAR for increasing the development of educational resources in Australia aimed at teaching courses that deal with Latin American culture and languages as well as Latin American Studies in general. Ultimately, in terms of advancing Australia's strategic relationship with Latin America, the role of culture—especially popular music, dance and food—should be seen as a powerful means of developing awareness and understanding of the Latin American region in this country; more crucially, it should be recognised as a means of expanding existing, and developing new commercial activities for Australians. We must harness the boom. In the end, all of these connections will generate economic benefits for both Australia and Latin America.

References

Published and unpublished sources

ABCC—Australia Brazil Chamber of Commerce, 'Feed Back on FIFA World Cup 2014 and Rio Olympics 2016 Business Mission', http://www.australiabrazil.com.au/index.php?option=com_content&task=view&id=274, accessed 26 May 2013.

Alexander, Stephanie, 'Colours you can taste', *The Age* (*Epicure*), 13 October 2009.

Austrade, '2014 Brazil FIFA World Cup and 2016 Rio Olympic Games—For Australian exporters', http://www.austrade.gov.au/Export/Export-Markets/Countries/Brazil/Industries/2014-Brazil-FIFA-World-Cup-and-2016-Rio-Olympic-Games, accessed 26 May 2013.

Australia Council, 'Targeted strategies for key international markets', *Australia Council Media Release*, 8 April 2009 and http://www.australiacouncil.gov.au/news/items/news, accessed 20 May 2013.

————, 'Let the Proceedings Begin: The 5th World Summit on Arts and Culture Kicks Off Today in Melbourne', http://www.australiacouncil.gov.au/news/items/2011/let_the_proceedings_begin_the_5th_world_summit_on_arts_and_culture_kicks_off_today_in_melbourne, accessed 20 May 2013.

Australian Recording Industry Association (ARIA) *Report* 2008; http://www.aria.com.au/pages/statistics.htm, accessed 25 July 2011.

————, 'Wholesale Figures', http://www.aria.com.au/documents/2012wholesalefigures.pdf, accessed 15 May 2013.

Bendrups, Dan, 'Melbourne's Latin American Music Scene', *Perfect Beat,* vol. 5, no. 2, 2001, pp. 19–29. Department of Foreign Affairs and Trade, Australia, Committee on Australia–Latin America Relations (COALAR), *Annual Reports, 2002–2003 to 2008–2009.*

Department of Innovation, Industry and Regional Development (DIIRD), Victoria, *Latin America and Victoria: A vision for growing trade, investment and cultural links*, Melbourne, State Government of Victoria, 2010.

ICN—Industry Capability Network, 'Victorian Industry prepare for Rio Olympic Games following success in London', http://www.icnvic.org.au, accessed 27 May 2013.

Leiva, Jorge, 'International Creative Partnerships for Cultural Education and Promotion: The Case Between Colombia and Australia', unpublished Master of Teaching thesis, Melbourne Graduate School of Education, The University of Melbourne, 2010, p. 64.

Leiva, Jorge, 'Mi amigo internacional (My international friend) project', http://www.peopleartpeople. com/education.html, accessed 27 May 2013.

Macdonnell, Justin, *Australia's Cultural Presence in Latin America: Programs and Prospects,* Prepared for COALAR, by ALAF Limited, February 2003.

Orchard, Neil, 'Oz Salsa: A True Multicultural Dip?', unpublished Honours Thesis, La Trobe University History/Anthropology Programs, 2008.

Senate Standing Committee on Foreign Affairs, Australia and Latin America, 'The Report of the Senate Standing Committee on Foreign Affairs, Defence and Trade, 1992', and companion volumes 1–6.

Interviews and correspondence:

Correspondence with ABC, January–April 2010.

Correspondence with SBS, January–May 2010.

Interview with JB HiFi Music Department, Camberwell, Victoria, 27 January 2013.

Interview with Jorge Leiva, 8 October 2010.

Interview with Doug de Vries, 18 January 2011.

Interview with Justin Macdonnell, 10 June 2010.

Interview with Max Vella, owner: *Night Cat Night Club,* 17 October 2010.

Key websites:

Australian Latin America Foundation, http://alafoundation.com/

AILASA—Association of Iberian and Latin American Studies of Australasia, http://www.ailasa.org/

ANCLAS—Australian National Centre for Latin American Studies, http://anclas.anu.edu.au/

Filmateca, http://www.melbournefilmoteca.org/

ILAS—Institute of Latin American Studies at La Trobe University, http://www.latrobe.edu.au/ilas/

La Mirada Film Festival 2012, http://www.lamirada.org.au/

Latin Lover, http://www.latinlover.com.au/

Latinhub, http://www.latinhub.com.au/latin-culture

Peopleartpeople, http://www.peopleartpeople.com/education.html

Spanishaustralia, http://www.spanishaustralia.org/arts

Viva Magazine, http://www.vivamagazine.com.au/

10. Doing Business in Latin America the Australian Way: Debunking myths about cross-cultural sensitivities

Bob Hodge

Introduction

Australians wanting to do business in the countries of Latin America need to understand the people they are doing business with. That means knowing more about these countries, past and present. The present book aims to provide some of that necessary knowledge. It also means as Australians we take a good hard look at ourselves: how we present ourselves and how we are likely to be interpreted by people from these countries, for both good and ill. These are considerations that the business community needs to take on board. This chapter will argue the necessity for greater cultural sensitivity, not less. Cultural sensitivity along these lines is good business and good policy.

Yet to foster more of the right kind of cultural sensitivity, we need to clear away some potent myths about cultural sensitivity that hinder better practices in understanding and relating to Latin American people as partners, competitors, customers, workmates and friends. This chapter takes on this complex double challenge: to debunk some of the myths but to do so constructively, with positive advice so that Australians will feel more confident to manage a wide range of relationships.

The chapter is written for three kinds of stakeholder. The government is already involved in promoting links with Latin America, especially through Austrade and through its support for the Council on Australia Latin America Relations (COALAR). Governments are naturally most interested in the macro-level: in relations between nations. This chapter will argue that important as they are, governmental relations are not the only drivers of the complex and growing network of relations between Australia and Latin America: social, cultural and business relations constitute the indispensable basis. The real drivers of change are individuals, engaged in business or wanting to extend their understanding of the world as Australians or Latin Americans.

On not being ashamed of being Australian

The Australian Government sees a need to be involved in the task of creating better strategies and more favourable attitudes on the part of Australians towards the outside world, including Latin America. This is one of its functions in the new global environment in which businesses operate. Austrade has taken on board a special responsibility to promote this line of activities through its publications, in print and online. There is a wealth of documents now available online that offers crash courses in the new knowledge and approaches that are needed.[1] Business people can and should use these as the first point of contact.

However, there is a common strand in these documents that may be counter-productive. I illustrate with a document first released in 2006, entitled *Doing business in the United States*.[2] This text was criticised immediately on its release by popular journalist Frank Walker:

> Don't make a joke if you want to sell anything to the Septics. Drop the Aussie self-deprecating humour and slip immediately into the 30-second hard fast sales pitch. Whoop and holler a lot. Give high fives just for pressing the lift—sorry, elevator—button.

> If you want to do business with the Americans don't be a laconic, likeable and languid larrikin such as the archetypal Aussie Paul Hogan.

> That's the message from Austrade, the government agency helping Australian companies flog goods overseas...[3]

Walker is not trying to be fair to Austrade, but this is a useful way into many key issues around the image of Australia, at home and abroad. His reaction is not what the Australian government wanted, but it is what many ordinary Australians actually think. When government and people diverge, it is unwise for business to trust only government.

The first point to focus on is what is summarised as the Austrade message: do not be a larrikin. Walker quotes David Howe, then senior trade commissioner in New York, in observing that Australian business employees should 'check their (Aussie) sense of humour at the door'.[4] Austrade here is talking about how to succeed in the United States, not in Latin America, but the text is nonetheless equally relevant to the Latin American context. Austrade transmits a general

---

1 Austrade (Australian Trade Commission), http://www.austrade.gov.org.au.
2 Austrade (Australian Trade Commission) *United States of America: Doing business*, 2013: http://www.austrade.gov.au/Export/Export-Markets/Countries/United-States-of-America/Doing-business#. UlohDBCBHIE.
3 Frank Walker, 'Septics Are No Can Of Laughs', *Sun Herald*, 8 October 2006, p. 31.
4 *Ibid.*

message that to be a 'typical Aussie' is a disadvantage. If it is a disadvantage in the United States, an Anglo-speaking culture like Australia, will it not be even more of a disadvantage in Latin America, with its Spanish or Portuguese-speaking cultures? Is being visibly Australian our source of shame, something to conceal at all costs? And if being Australian is such a mark of shame, how then do we market ourselves?

Walker offers this caricature of US business styles as our new model. Austrade's advice was not as simplistic as Walker implies. Yet on this occasion it does over-value the US style of doing business. Is this the best style even for Aussies in the USA? Walker doubts it. Might it be even less appropriate in Latin America?

The US style is a potent global brand: even in the wake of the global financial crisis the United States is the dominant economic force in all the Latin American nations with which Australia currently conducts most business: Brazil, Mexico, Chile, Argentina, Peru. However, paradoxically this dominance is a good reason for us *not* to check our Australianness at the door and disguise ourselves as wannabe Yanks. Latin American nations have a long tradition of hostility to the perceived US arrogance. Brand differentiation from the United States may be better. That way we will also do what we do best: be Australian.

The Austrade advice seems to present us with a dilemma: be an Australian and be a loser, or renounce your identity in the name of profit. But this dilemma may be just the product of a limited concept of identity. The term derives from the Latin *idem*, 'the same', cognate with 'identical'. The term 'identity' has broadened to indicate those aspects which make a group unique, while the meaning of *idem* as 'the same' persists, depending on which connections we wish to emphasise.

Australian identity can be what some of us have in common with some Australians, and not others. This may easily be what we have in common with other non-Australians also: Australian soccer fans have a common identity with Brazilians or Argentinians, perhaps more than with many Australian rugby fans. Identity is what we have significantly in common, which creates connections. In a global world where connection is a primary rule to survive and thrive, Australian identities need to emphasise the characteristics we possess that help us to connect, not those that place us in a box.

Do we need a national brand?

In August 2009 the then government announced a plan to develop a national brand image. In February 2010 Malcolm Long, communications consultant and member of the Australian Communications and Media Association, floated a discussion paper to promote the idea. Under the heading *Rebranding*

Australia, he argued that the task is long overdue to initiate a project that will 'effectively position and brand Australia in the global market place'. His core premise was that:

> For a country to make its mark in the information-rich, competitive, borderless world we now inhabit requires strategic positioning and consistent and coherent branding. This is a requirement for whole nations as much as it is for industries and products. These days a nation's branding—its personality—must be distinctive, to rise above the new global digital din.

Long's paper provoked 132 replies, only two of which were positive. The first posting, by 'Fed up', was typical:

> Australia is a continent—rich in diversity and multi-dimensional in the extreme. What's the slogan for the US, UK or France? Would it help them to have one? In fact do 'grown up' countries want or need them?

> Have a brand strategy by all means. Let it help shape the story we want to tell across tourism, business, culture, etc. But let's not delude ourselves that a slogan, logo or campaign holds the answer.

The overwhelming trend in these responses shows a similar quality to Walker's response to Austrade. There is majority resistance from ordinary Australians to be described under a single slogan, whatever its content. They do not recognise the truth in their experience of any one label. If those it is meant to describe reject it, how will it work for a moment in the world outside?

Long assumes that everyone benefits equally from such a branding exercise, which he sees as a special adaptation to the new conditions of a borderless global world. But in the borderless world he talks about, why or how is a nation still a useful brand, and to whom? Some have criticised the idea of container nationalism, the way of thinking about world affairs as if each nation effectively acts as a container of its national essence, homogeneous within fixed borders.[5] Container nationalism is not a useful way of thinking about the complex flows across boundaries which characterise the world of global business today.

Faced with this potential contradiction, Australian business people looking to Latin America can reasonably be sceptical of the aims and assumptions of a government project of nation-branding, and instead ask: What version of the nation would help me, in concrete ways, in my plans, and how would it help?

---

5   Andrew Wimmer and Nina Glick Schiller, 'Methodological nationalism and beyond', *Global Networks* 2: 4, 2002, pp. 301–34.

And looking outside Australia to the many nations to be found in the broad region of Latin America: What images emanating from those sources will help me to conduct good business?

By asking these questions, about both Australia and Latin American nations, Australian business people can secure both economic and personal benefits. They can develop a dual perspective, from outside and from inside, of their own culture and another culture. At the same time they can realise the important truth that provides a guiding thread through the multiplicity of versions of cultural difference: Australians and Latin Americans alike want to learn things about the other on which to base actions and decisions.

Even if they risk being blacklisted by Austrade, they do not—to rely on a useful Australian term—want bullshit.

In May 2010, Brand Australia was launched, with the slogan *Australia Unlimited,* a four-year campaign costing $A20 million. The research it commissioned and assembled is a useful starting point for informed reflection. The data draws on substantial numbers of international informants, and all say much the same thing. Australia is perceived as 'a vibrant, friendly and welcoming nation, with values of positivity, energy and practical solutions'.[6] These are the qualities projected by Paul Hogan in his *Crocodile Dundee* movies, popular in the United States and Latin America: the Lara Bingle and Baz Lurhmann-themed campaigns have come and gone. Hogan's campaign to promote Australian tourism remains the benchmark.

In contrast, it is hard to see what the vacuous slogan 'Australia unlimited' could mean to anyone, in Australia much less Latin America, or how it expresses the qualities the research identified. To translate this slogan into behaviours, how would you walk into a room of potential Latin American partners and act 'unlimited' (*ilimitado/a/s* in Spanish and Portuguese)? Wave your arms wildly? Speak loudly? Promise too much? It sounds uncomfortably like the caricature Yank mocked by Walker. The phrase translates badly. This is not because something that makes good sense to English-speaking Australians somehow does not translate to speakers of Spanish or Portuguese. On the contrary, the phrase is bullshit, to use the good Aussie phrase. Trying to translate it only exposes the fact.

The responses to Long's discussion paper reinforce the conclusions of Brand Australia's international studies. The Australia that Long and the Brand Australia campaign ignore is a complex, diverse mix of qualities, some old, some new. The

---

6   Australia Unlimited, 'Research: TNS Research for Building Brand Australia'.

package as it has evolved is valued in similar ways by Australians as by the rest of the world. It is a useful starting point for reflections on what we are like, as Australians exploring a new world that includes Latin America.

What is the real larrikin?

With three colleagues I wrote a book trying to find out what a larrikin is today.[7] This was based on a three-year project funded by the Australian Research Council, designed to determine whether this concept was still relevant for the world of business today, and, if so, how? We were interested in how these qualities work on the global scene, specifically in the new conceptual territory between Australia, Brazil and Mexico in which flows are beginning to take place. We asked whether the term is an anachronism, a distraction from new identities Australians need to adapt for the 21st century. Instead we found that in this new environment the larrikin tradition has already morphed into productive new forms.

Some of the results of our research are relevant to the paradox of identities this chapter began with. We found that many Australians in different kinds of organisation think that there is a distinctive, valuable way of doing things which they see as Australian. We also found that many Australians repudiate these qualities. The opposing positions in the debate between journalist Frank Walker and David Howe, trade commissioner in New York, concerning identification with an image of Australian identity and repudiation of it, are repeated at every level of Australian society. Australians are united by this division, not by denying one or other half of it.

That means that the brand that David Howe supports would be repudiated by Frank Walker, and vice versa. This may seem like a contradiction, which would be a nightmare for a marketing campaign. However, the opposite can also be true. Instead of trying to market one or other quality, a good campaign needs to market the contradiction: Australians are informal *and* effective.

I illustrate the contradiction through two representative quotations from our set of interviews of Australians, Mexicans and Brazilians, including Mexican and Brazilian Australians. Robert was an Australian middle manager, originally from Britain, offering his ideas on what a larrikin or Australian way of doing things is:

7   Bob Hodge, Gabriela Coronado, Fernanda Duarte and Greg Teal, *Chaos Theory and the Larrikin Principle*, Stockholm: Liber, 2010.

It's irreverence or seemingly irreverence for people in authority: a readiness to break rules rather than accept them rigidly. That this is the way things should be done. The larrikin will look and say 'Oh yeah, there's a better way of doing it. We won't do it that way because we can do it better.'

Liana, a Brazilian Australian executive in a small enterprise had a different take:

[Australians] accept that they have to follow the rules and the normal bureaucratic process. On the other hand, it is interesting to observe that in Australia—I saw the statistics—for example, if in Brazil it takes a year to start a company, in Australia it takes a day. It is a country where bureaucracy has been eliminated. Just compare that in Brazil we come and say 'Ah, this document needs three stamps, etcetera'. Here it is much more simple: if someone signed it you believe.

Each interviewee appears to be describing a different Australia with opposite qualities to the other. Yet they both like it. Their judgements are comparative. Robert does not mention Britain, but that is his point of reference. Liana mentions Brazil, and it is probably the reference point for both of her judgements, even though she is not asked to make comparisons.

Neither of these people feels unable to understand the Australian system. Both have lived in Australia for many years, and both have reached reasonably senior positions, though both also know what life is like at lower levels. Far from being disabled by her Brazilian background, Liana is more able to cut through the myth of Australian irreverence for authority. Yet she also sees a contradiction, which she includes in her view, even though she cannot explain it: the easiness of bureaucratic processes in Australia compared to Brazil. She understands and admires the advantages of the Australian way, in contrast to the Brazilian nightmare.

Robert likewise is insightful, distinguishing between the appearance ('seemingly') and the reality of larrikin attitudes to authority. The example he gives is not negative, destructive rebellion but an independent, genuine commitment to the goals of the organisation and the demands of the particular task. His picture is not the same as Liana's, but it connects with it. Combining them with many other versions from our interviews, we obtained a version of the larrikin which positions its contradictions in relation to different areas of national experience. British Robert reacts positively to the quality, as does Brazilian Liana. What holds the opposites together is stated by Liana ('you believe'), and implied by Robert: it is trust.

Both Liana and Robert use national categories to think with, to organise their generalisations about working life in Australia and other parts of the globe.

For each, Australianness is a flexible category, not a one-size-fits all concept. In Liana's case, as was typical of our Latin American interviewees, the national category, here Brazilianness, was not a container category—comprising all the diversity of her country into a single word—but a connecting category. She compares a patch of life in Brazil with a related patch of life in Australia.

One lesson from this small sample is that Australianness can matter and make sense, to Australians and Latin Americans alike, even if it is not a single, coherent category as presented in a brand-marketing campaign. On the contrary, Australians and Latin Americans will develop their own generalisations about the other from intelligent observations of actual behaviours.

Australian managers do not fit a larrikin stereotype, but this set of qualities and orientations flavour how they tend to run businesses: 'Australian managers are more humanistic, shrewder, less pompous and more subtle than their performance-obsessed American counter-parts, and are happy to play down performance if it threatens their quality of life'.[8]

These qualities may sometimes be responsible for lower rankings of Australian managers in international comparisons.[9] This outcome confirms David Howe's concern that Australian qualities may not impress US managers, especially on first meeting. Paradoxically it also gives reasons to agree with Frank Walker that even in the United States these qualities may be valuable. In Latin America, the Australian way, with integrity above all as a defining quality, is likely to impart a competitive advantage.

'Cultural sensitivity' and the American way

Modern global corporations are aware they need to be sensitive about the cultures of different peoples they conduct business with. 'Cross-cultural training' and 'cross-cultural management' are part of the tool-kit of Australian business people today. In this chapter I applaud this awareness. A book such as the present one is an ideal occasion to contribute to this worthy goal in the Latin American region. Yet there are some significant problems with the predominant form of theory and beliefs among those who shape attitudes and agendas in this area. These agendas need to be addressed to allow cross-cultural management and other cross-cultural interactions to work better.

Part of the problem I suggest is the excessive influence of the US style of management in Australia, as in business education in Latin America. This style

---

8   Spillane, Robert, in Paul Davidson and Ricky Griffin, (eds), *Management: An Australian perspective*, 3rd edn, Brisbane: John Wiley & Sons, 2005.
9   K. Marshall, 'Local bosses best at human touch', *Australian Financial Review*, 28 November 1997, p. 59.

dominates our university courses in management. These are fed by textbooks published in the United States, shaped by US experiences, attitudes and preconceptions. Yet as indicated earlier, Australia is not the United States. We can have a competitive advantage by doing things differently, in an Australian way that is more responsive to currents and tendencies in Latin America. Our managers are currently trained to see the rest of the globe through US eyes. We need to turn this gaze around, and look critically at how US eyes look at the world, and how that world looks back.

To illustrate what is being taught in our business schools, as in business schools in the United States, I quote from Helen Deresky, whose books on International Management are used in most Australian universities.[10]

Deresky emphasises the importance of cultural sensitivity, a main theme of her work on international management. She begins with a satisfactory definition: 'Cultural sensitivity, or cultural empathy, is an awareness and an honest caring about another individual's culture'.[11]

But this quality is rare in US businesses, she says. American managers' knowledge of other cultures lags behind their understanding of other organisational processes. Deresky cites studies that show that up to 40 per cent of US expatriate managers leave early because of poor performance, and half of the rest are only 'marginally effective'. That is, only 30 per cent are above a 'marginal' level. Deresky promises to turn this around through the influence of her book. But it might be more constructive to ask why this training is as defective as the figures indicate, rather than placing ourselves in the unsafe hands of the American Way.

A key problem of the American Way can be seen in Deresky's endorsement of the idea that American managers understand all competing organisational processes: that their only blind spot is their lack of knowledge of other cultures. What if the real blind spot is the belief, which she shares, that the American Way is consonant with the One True Way? She does not appreciate the problems that may stem from US managers' confidence in the superiority of their methods. She does not see this as arrogance, or note its effects. As I have said, this is a key difference between Australian and US styles of management and conducting business. This difference will not be cured by adding superficial US-style cultural sensitivity to basic US-style models of managerial and business behaviour.

---

10   See B. Hodge et al., op. cit., note 7; Helen Deresky, International Management: Management across Borders and Cultures, Pearson/Prentice Hall, 2005.
11   Deresky, op.cit. note 10, p. 83.

One example can illustrate the inadequacies of Deresky's advice for greater cultural sensitivity. She classifies all Latin American people under the heading 'polychronic', from Greek, 'of many times':

> Polychronic people—Latin Americans, Arabs, and those from other collectivist cultures—may focus on several things at once, be highly distractible, and change plans often.[12]

We note here that a theory of cultural sensitivities and awareness of difference assumes no differences between people from different Latin American nations, or between Latin Americans, Arabs and others not specified here. Only one cultural difference matters, between Us (Anglo-Americans) and Them.

'They' are made to seem 'distractible', unable to cope with or keep to their plans. Not like Us, who are rock-solid, focused on only one thing at a time. But if They are misrepresented, so are We. In modern business practices, no-one has the luxury of being monochronic. 'We' all have to be multi-tasked, multi-skilled, mobile in time and space. Being polychronic and flexible is a virtue in the new global work environment.

Deresky's fatal flaw, typical of US writers on cross-cultural management, is her use of the ideas of 'culture' and 'cultural sensitivity' to blind herself to power and its role in the long history that leads to the unequal present. Culture has been misused in business circles to misunderstand important issues that need to be seen in the first instance as political. Cultural sensitivity needs to begin with a short history lesson.

The term 'culture' derives from Latin *colo*, meaning to plough, and hence to work, to improve by work, to live in a place and to worship its gods. These four meanings still underlie the set of meanings of 'culture/a' in English, Spanish and Portuguese. In this area Australians and Latin Americans share more or less the same word. But all these meanings are distorted by the operation of another word possessing the same root. Latin *colonia* was a soft way to refer to a process whereby Greeks and Romans made incursions into another peoples' territory and took over the land, exploited it and lived there as if it were their own. 'Colonial' has the same basic function for each of these societies: Greek and Roman in the past; Spanish, Portuguese and English in the 16th century; the United States today.

The wars of independence in Latin America used the rhetoric of revolution, influenced by the ideology of the revolutions that were being played out in Europe, triggered by the French Revolution. Yet the real winners of these wars

---

12   *Ibid*. p. 136.

of independence were local power elites. They created highly unequal social structures which reproduced themselves for the next 200 years, still major forces in the Latin American present.

Before the Latin American revolutions and inspiring them was the American War of Independence, the radical break with the British imperial power which gave the United States its foundational charter. Yet this position embodied a contradiction which continues to the present. This is crystallised in the Monroe Doctrine, first enunciated in 1823 by US President Monroe. Monroe's liberatory message to European powers warned them against further colonisation in the Americas. By 1845 this had morphed into the doctrine of Manifest Destiny, the idea that the United States retained the right to dominate the Americas. This double message—the United States as champion of freedom and as colonial power—still creates tension and ambivalence in Latin America today.

In the early 19th century Australia was too insecure a colony to seek independence. In 1901 it achieved partial autonomy with Federation. Over the rest of the 20th century it crept towards greater autonomy, but the 1999 Referendum on whether to become a Republic was defeated. I have always found this fact difficult to explain to Latin American friends, who are bewildered. How could a modern nation like Australia still technically be a colony of a European power in the 21st century, complete with a Queen?

Brazilian theorist Darcy Ribeiro argued that Latin American nations were formed by the mixture of civilising processes, European and indigenous, producing the inequalities that mark these nations today.[13] Mexican anthropologist Guillermo Bonfil Batalla adapted Ribeiro's model to Mexico, which 500 years after the conquest he saw still divided between the Spanish-based society and a 'civilization denied', which he named 'México Profundo': deep Mexico.[14] His 'deep Mexico' is formed by interactions in which a dominant culture both suppresses and feeds off an indigenous culture. This deep culture has evolved over 500 years, he says, adapting to the dominant culture, absorbing and reframing some of its attributes. Hodge and Mishra[15] saw a similar model in Australia marking the ambivalent relationship of its Anglo–Celtic majority to Aboriginal culture and to the fact of the dispossession of Aboriginal people.

The Ribeiro–Bonfil Batalla model applies to the whole of Latin America. It also applies, with differences of history and context, to both Australia and the United States. All were created on a similar foundation. Acts of invasion and dispossession created initial disparity, maintained by sharp divisions. In all

13   Darcy Ribeiro, *Las Américas y la civilización*, Buenos Aires: Centro Editor de América Latina, 1969.
14   Bonfil Batalla, Guillermo. *México profundo: Una civilización negada*, CONACULTA, Editora Grijalbo: México, 1987.
15   Bob Hodge and Vijay Mishra, *Darkside of the Dream*, Sydney: Allen and Unwin, 1991.

these nations, indigenous people were dispossessed to differing degrees, but never eliminated. In the case of Brazil and the United States, slaves became a more prominent part of the landscape. But these and many other differences make better sense by putting them in a common frame.

Many Australians feel uncomfortable about seeing their history in this way. In academia it was debated in what was called 'the History Wars'.[16] Those outside academia may have been puzzled what the point of the battle was, because everyone agreed on the main point. Australia was founded as a result of dispossession of its Aboriginal people, as happened in the whole of the Americas, North and South. Australia has its own 'Australia profunda' to echo 'México profundo', 'Brasil profundo', 'América Latina profunda'.

If we accept this, then we can have better, more honest conversations with Latin Americans. In the process we may learn more about Australia, as well as about Latin America.

The Aussie way as transnational good

I have argued that the Aussie way of doing things can be more valued and valuable for Australians in Latin America than many believe. This is because it is less unique than is usually presented or is understood by most Australians. It allows us to connect better, and connections are the new rules of the global game.

The Larrikin Principle can be seen in this respect as a series of solutions to more general problems of power and authority. Such problems have not disappeared, in Australia or the rest of the world. Nor have the solutions become irrelevant: scepticism about authority, flexibility and creativity, openness, loyalty, trust.

There are good reasons for the deep affinities that can be felt between the Australian way and attitudes and values in Latin American nations, in addition to the common colonial origins and histories. In the first place, there are common elements in earlier forms of all these traditions. The larrikin tradition had origins in Irish Catholicism, and later influxes of migrants from Catholic countries like Italy added to the strength of Catholicism, which is now Australia's largest religion by number of adherents.

Behind Catholicism lay earlier non-Christian traditions, which blended with indigenous traditions to form the wonderful syncretic religious forms that are so attractive in Latin America. These drew on and carried indigenous elements across Latin America, and also African elements, especially in Brazil, the United

---

16   Stuart MacIntyre and Anna Clark. *The History Wars*, Melbourne: Melbourne University Press, 2003.

States and the Caribbean. These forms of culture are attractive to Australian tourists, extending their identity in unconscious ways. The larrikin tradition itself has roots in European folk traditions. 'Trickster' figures like the traditional larrikin are found in very ancient forms in Africa, Asia and the Americas as well as Europe and Aboriginal Australia. This aspect of Australian identity is fed by pre-modern global roots as well as post-modern needs.

A culture is also a set of ways of solving problems. Latin American countries are all still constrained by patterns of authority that have been around so long that they appear to be part of the identity itself. Liana identified stultifying bureaucracy as the Brazil she would not miss. Other Latin American nations have similar problems.

In this situation, Brazilians have developed a set of strategies called the *jeitinho*.[17] The term derives from *jeito*, a way (of doing things), plus *inho*, meaning a short cut; cutting through bureaucratic tangles, in the diminutive form, which imparts a familiar, affectionate flavour to the word. Mexican Spanish has a similar diminutive in *–ito*. So *favor*, bending the rules, becomes *favorcito*. Mexicans have other words for related practices: e.g., *palanca*, literally a lever, is something that gives an advantage.

Informal Australian English has similar form and content. Adding *–ie* makes rule-bending seem harmless. Australian workers who take a day off for personal reasons but claim sick leave call it a 'sickie'. Bending rules to benefit someone you know is called 'mates' rates'.

Brazilian sociologist Roberto DaMatta connected the *jeitinho* to what he saw as the dysfunctional nature of Brazilian society:

> It is alarming to see that daily legislation in Brazil is a regulation of the 'can't do'.... It is precisely because of this that we discovered and perfected the *jeitinho*, a style of social navigation that is read between the lines of these peremptory and authoritarian 'can't do's'.[18]

DaMatta reads this quality not as a consistent attribute marking a stable identity, but the opposite. His Brazil today is full of contradictions. It is internationally famous as a symbol of exuberance, beauty and joy, yet the disparity in income of the wealthiest 20 per cent and the poorest 20 per cent makes it among the ten most unequal nations in income distribution in the world. He eloquently captures some of its contradictions:

---

17 Fernanda Duarte, 'Exploring the interpersonal transaction of the Brazilian jeitinho in bureaucratic contexts', *Organisation* 13/4, 2006, pp. 509–27.

18 Roberto DaMatta, *O que faz o Brasil, Brasil?*, Rio de Janeiro: Editora Rocco, 1984, p. 98.

In Brazil we have carnivals and hierarchies, equalities and aristocracies, and cordial meetings full of smiles giving away the very next moment to the terrible antipathy and violence of 'Do you know who you're talking to?' We also have the samba, cachaca [sugar-cane brandy], the futebol [soccer], but this all occurs in the midst of what came to be called a 'relative democracy' and a 'Brazilian-style capitalism', a system in which only the workers run the risks and from which they draw no profits.[19]

In this kind of situation, figures emerge whose role is to fix the problems of a broken society. For instance, *despachantes* (from *despachar* to finish or resolve a problem) are people who work as trouble-shooters in Brazilian society. They are a Brazilian version of the larrikin principle, shaped by the specific forms of dysfunctionality in Brazil. Mexico has an analogous role, commonly called *coyotes*. As the term implies, *coyotes* are dangerous tricksters, not to be trusted.

Despachantes are paid for tasks such as queuing for people in public service institutions, and sorting out bureaucratic problems related to processes such as driving licences, electoral documents and identity cards. They constitute one of many cybernetic loops whose role is to correct the huge inefficiencies of Brazilian bureaucracy. Carlo a *despachante* gives this portrait of the role: 'You must be patient; you must listen to people's stories first. Things will happen at the right time, and you must have patience to listen'. Carlo clearly does not have the opportunity to practise his samba steps or take a swig of *cachacha* while he listens carefully and waits patiently. He has absorbed the contradictions of society into contradictions in his own being, at whatever pain and cost. Clearly he does not do this because as a Brazilian he likes to, but because he has to.

Carlo is not a larrikin, but his conditions are eminently understandable to Australian readers. Business people can imagine what it would be like to walk in his shoes. From the other side, Carlo could immediately understand and respect the different conditions that Australians work under, as Liana did. Brazilian conditions and strategies go hand in hand, as do Australian ones. Cross-cultural understanding in this case, as in others, does not require socialisation from birth into the mysteries of playing *futebol* for a Brazilian or downing large amounts of beer in a single draught, as legendary Aussie Bob Hawke reputedly did. The conditions are different, but those differences can be understood, and the aspirations are the same. It is a good enough basis for Australians to understand Latin America, and to be accepted in return.

---

19   Roberto DaMatta, *Carnivals, Rogues and Heroes,* London: University of Notre Dame Press, 1991.

The shadow of corruption

This chapter argues that there is much in common across the ocean which separates Australia from Latin America. Respect and appreciation are keys to mutual understanding. Yet there is also a dark side of Latin American life which must be acknowledged and dealt with, for it will not go away. Corruption is like the elephant in the room: so big that everyone knows it is there, but too problematic to talk about.

That may seem a surprising statement. Corruption is often talked about as a problem for businesses carrying out country risk assessments. There is an international monitoring agency, Transparency International, which assigns an annual index to each country.[20] That is true. Yet this section will suggest that the corruption talked about and measured is a substitute to distract from addressing the real thing. There is serious corruption at government levels in Latin American states, but diplomatic sensitivity means that it cannot be talked about. Agencies like Austrade cannot report at length on these issues because that would breach diplomatic protocols.

'Corruption' is a loaded word with many meanings, but at its heart is the idea of a system-wide breakdown in processes that sustain that system. As a metaphor, corruption is like the spot on an apple which expands to cause the whole apple to rot. Or to use another strong metaphor, corruption is like the way a fish rots from the head. Individual acts of theft or fraud do not of themselves constitute corruption, unless they affect governance itself.

Corruption in this sense applies to the ruling regime in Colombia, where the US-sponsored war against drugs is implicated in a state infiltrated by drug interests. In Mexico, three of the past five presidents were elected under widespread suspicions of electoral fraud. These frauds cannot be proven because systems to check against them are compromised. That is a sign of even deeper corruption than the alleged frauds.

For Australian business people this creates a dilemma. What are they to do with such knowledge as they have about corruption? About most aspects of a country, the more you know the better, but not in this case. Australian citizens in a foreign jurisdiction would be unwise to become involved, or open any cans of worms. For government officials even less is possible. Given that all these nations are classified as friendly states, issues of high-level corruption and complicity in corruption simply cannot be raised in public.

---

20 Transparency International: the global coalition against corruption, *Corruption Perceptions Index 2012*, http://www.transparency.org/cpi2012/results.

Here it is useful to distinguish between governments and nations. Even in a democracy like Australia, the government in power is elected by a small majority. Its members claim to speak on behalf of a nation of people, nearly half of whom did not vote for them. In the debate about Australia's national brand, problems arose from the fact that the state controls the branding of a nation, many of whose members strongly disagree with the state's definitions of them. The same is true in Latin America. These nations are their people, not their governments. Governments cannot be ignored, and systems of governance affect the life of everyone in the nation, including foreign business people from Australia. Yet the distinction between state and people shows a way between rejecting deep corruption and understanding ordinary citizens.

In practice, corruption is commonly dealt with in relation to Latin America by redefining it, so that the 'corruption' that is denounced and campaigned against is something other than the serious corruption that is the real problem. As a striking instance of this process at work, Gabriela Coronado reported on a sign she noticed in 2008 in Polanco, a wealthy district in Mexico City.[21] The sign depicted a large image of a bottle of *Coca Cola*. At the top was the phrase, in colloquial Spanish *Pa'l chesco*, literally '[money] for a cool drink', but metaphorically a request for a tip. Below was the following: 'We are thirsty for honesty: 'No to corruption. United for Honesty.'

This was part of a campaign by a local business association, supposedly against corruption. But corruption here is symbolised by the custom of workers asking for a tip. Big business presents itself as thirsty for honesty, not for a coke. But one presumes that they will drink imported whisky without a problem, along with the soda of their honesty. For them, corruption is what others do, not their own practices. Campaigning against the corruption of others—especially those who cannot defend themselves—is a desirable form of attacking corruption for those who are corrupt. Anti-corruption campaigns like this help to increase corruption.

The target of this campaign is the informal systems that have developed in Latin American countries, as if these were the problem rather than a solution to the often-dire situation of many citizens. It is true that the informal economy is burgeoning in Mexico and other Latin American countries, as a product of government measures often driven by neoliberal policies. It is also true that the total system, consisting of the formal and informal economies, is often incoherent and dysfunctional. But the solution is not to remove the informal system, without which the society and economy would collapse. Alternative forms of payment, often barely enough to survive on, are not the problem. Blaming them prevents a proper understanding of the problem.

---

21 Gabriela Coronado, 'Discourses of Anti-corruption in Mexico: Culture of Corruption or Corruption of Culture?' *Portal: Journal of Multidisciplinary International Studies*, 5(1), January 2008, pp. 1–23.

The 'Australian way' of doing things as advocated by the Larrikin Principle gives greater value to informal practices, to doing what has to be done in order to get by. The relaxed Australian way of adapting rules where they do not apply is the commonsense response to so-called 'anti-corruption' campaigns like this one.

The same reasoning applies to the way corruption is officially described and measured by international agencies as guidance for business people, Australians and others. The defining marker of corruption is the presence of bribes: payments outside a regular schedule of costs. No one likes paying any more than a listed cost, and the need to pay bribes is irritating and inconvenient, for Australians as for Latin Americans. However, in many cases these extra costs can be regarded as an incentive for functionaries who are not paid enough to survive on their normal salaries.

Business the US way is also run by financial incentives: performance bonuses for top executives and sales staff, free gifts with commodities, etc. This may not always lead to efficiencies in US and Australian business practices. It may sometimes produce serious corruption, as in the case of Enron's bonus system.[22] This is not called 'bribery', much less 'corruption', because it is accepted business practice. Yet the principle is the same. Tips in restaurants are not called bribes, either, yet they too are similar in principle. In each case, extra money ensures that an under-resourced system limps along in a better way than if those incentive payments were not in place.

This double standard provides a flawed basis for international systems of surveillance. As mentioned earlier, the international body, Transparency International, purports to monitor levels of corruption in countries through the propensity to take bribes, which it uses as its main proxy for estimating levels of corruption. In the 2012 index, New Zealand came equal first, and Australia a very respectable seventh out of more than 150 nations. The United States squeezed into the top 20 at 19. Of Latin American nations, Chile came a respectable 20th, but Brazil was at 69, Peru at 83, Argentina at 102, and Mexico equal at 105 with Bolivia.[23]

Does that mean what it seems to? As argued above, bribes at this low level are poor indicators of serious corruption. Another problem with this measuring instrument is that it only measures reports of those who paid bribes. These are ordinary victims of corruption rather than perpetrators. It relies on their honesty in making the reports. It does not ask the seriously corrupt to indicate how corrupt they are, because the seriously corrupt do not fill in questionnaires, and sensible social scientists do not ask them to. As a result the figures country-by-

---

22   Bethany McLean and Peter Elkind, *The Smartest Guys in the Room*, Harmondsworth: Penguin, 2003.
23   Transparency International, *Corruption Perceptions Index, op. cit.* note 20.

country make the problem seem to arise from the large number of victims who have paid the bribes, as though this is somehow their fault, as if the problem would go away if these ordinary Mexicans, Brazilians or Argentinians did not gratuitously hand over this money.

Yet considered carefully, the broad tendencies indicated by these figures do say something. Aussies and Kiwis do have a reputation for not being corrupt, for being good citizens—and it is a precious asset. Americans are less trusted, and corruption is indeed endemic in Latin American countries.

There are four main lessons for Australians doing business in Latin America.

1. Make a large distinction between what is called 'grand corruption' and 'small corruption'. Grand corruption is immoral, unethical and usually criminal. There is no need for 'cultural sensitivity' over grand corruption. It is denounced by all Latin American governments, whatever complicity they may have in practice. It is rejected by most Latin American citizens, good people who are victims of these practices.

2. Do not trust campaigns against corruption, national or international. Their basis is so flawed that they are worse than useless, since they foster the belief that they provide some guidance to complex issues.

3. Do not use the powerful, vague, emotive word 'corruption' for the range of informal systems found in Latin American life. Call the practices by their specific names. Avoid those that you can and wish to, especially if they are currently illegal in some way, as some—but not all—bribes are. But do not see yourself or those you do business with as corrupt if these become the terms in which you do business. Do not feel shame or guilt, and do not blame these individuals. Save the label corrupt for the small minority of wealthy and powerful citizens of Latin America and other states—including the United States and Australia—who engage in seriously corrupt behaviour.

4. Do not be corrupt yourself. Treat your integrity as a more vital part of your Aussie identity than putting another shrimp on the barbie, or calling everyone 'mate'.

Conclusion

This chapter has argued that cultural sensitivity is sometimes a counter-productive way of achieving goals which are themselves admirable: of improving understanding between individuals, businesses and nations, in this case Australia and Latin America. By emphasising difference under the name of culture, it makes the differences seem absolute and hard to understand or negotiate. That is unhelpful if the aim is to increase the wish to understand others. Nor does it describe the situation adequately. Australians have many differences between them, which are part of the fabric of life which we deal with every day. People of Latin America similarly possess many differences. To emphasise what they have in common as completely different to what Australians have in common is to miss all the many ways in which Australian characteristics are recognisable and valued in Latin America, and vice versa. By imagining Latin Americans as unimaginably different from us we cannot hope to understand them. The cultural sensitivity paradigm replaces the realities of Australia and Latin America with fantasies about both. That is not a good basis for forming any kind of relationship, in business or in other spheres of life.

There are three applications of these principles for different stakeholders:

1. Australians, in government and business alike, should accept Australian values that have emerged over time as a complex reality and asset to build on. These should provide the basis for business and government strategies alike.

2. Points in common in the history, politics and culture between Australia and Latin America need to be followed up, as networks of understanding, in order to frame a better understanding of points of difference. Anything that seems familiar probably is.

3. The understanding of the many things that it means to be Australian can be increased by attempting to understand and interact with Latin Americans. Go there, as tourists, as business people, as ambassadors, and interact with those at home as the diverse people they really are. That is how better understanding grows.

References

Austrade (Australian Trade Commission), *United States of America: Doing business*, http://www.austrade.gov.au/Export/Export-Markets/Countries/United-States-of-America/Doing-business#.UlohDBCBHIE, accessed 13 October 2013.

Australia Unlimited, 'Research: TNS Research for Building Brand Australia', http://www.australiaunlimited.com/page/brand-australia/media-tool-kit/research, accessed 11 October 2013.

Bonfil Batalla, Guillermo. *México profundo: Una civilización negada*, CONACULTA, Editora Grijalbo: México, 1987.

Coronado, Gabriela. 'Discourses of Anti-corruption in Mexico: Culture of Corruption or Corruption of Culture?' *Portal:Journal of Multidisciplinary International Studies*, 5(1), January 2008: 1–23, http://epress.lib.uts.edu.au/journals/index.php/portal/article/view/479/581, accessed 13 October 2013.

DaMatta, Roberto. *O que faz o Brasil, Brasil?*, Rio de Janeiro: Editora Rocco, 1984.

——————, *Carnivals, Rogues and Heroes*, London: University of Notre Dame Press, 1991.

Davidson, Paul and Ricky Griffin, *Management: an Australasian Perspective*, Melbourne: Sage, 2003.

Deresky, Helen. *International Management: Management across Borders and Cultures*, Pearson/Prentice Hall, 2005.

Duarte, Fernanda. 'Exploring the interpersonal transaction of the Brazilian *jeitinho* in bureaucratic contexts', *Organisation* 13/4 (2006): 509–27.

Hodge, Bob and Vijay Mishra, *Darkside of the Dream*, Sydney: Allen and Unwin, 1991.

Hodge, Bob, Gabriela Coronado, Fernanda Duarte and Greg Teal, *Chaos Theory and the Larrikin Principle*, Stockholm: Liber, 2010.

Marshall, K. 'Local bosses best at human touch', *Australian Financial Review*, 28 November 1997, p. 59.

MacIntyre, Stuart and Anna Clark. *The History Wars,* Melbourne: Melbourne University Press, 2003.

McLean, Bethany, and Peter Elkind, *The Smartest Guys in the Room*, Harmondsworth: Penguin, 2003.

Ribeiro, Darcy, *Las Américas y la civilización*, Buenos Aires: Centro Editor de América Latina, 1969.

Spillane, Robert, in Paul Davidson and Ricky Griffin, (eds), *Management: An Australian perspective*, 3rd edn, Brisbane: John Wiley & Sons, 2005.

Transparency International: the global coalition against corruption, *Corruption Perceptions Index 2012*, http://www.transparency.org/cpi2012/results, accessed 13 October 2013.

Walker, Frank, 'Septics Are No Can Of Laughs', *Sun Herald*, 8 October 2006, p. 31, http://www.septics.com.au/septics-articles/2006/10/8/septics-are-no-can-of-laughs/, accessed 13 October 2013.

Wimmer, Andrew and Nina Glick Schiller, 'Methodological nationalism and beyond', *Global Networks* 2/4, 2002, pp. 301–34.

www.ingramcontent.com/pod-product-compliance
Lightning Source LLC
Chambersburg PA
CBHW041119280326
41928CB00061B/3382